WORLDLY
GOODS

Also by JAMES GOLLIN

PAY NOW, DIE LATER

WORLDLY GOODS

The wealth and power of
the American Catholic Church,
the Vatican,
and the men who control the money

by

JAMES GOLLIN

Random House  New York

262.02

For JANE
with love

CONTENTS

ACKNOWLEDGMENTS

Scores of different people have given me help and encouragement at various stages of this project. First of all, my special thanks must go to the members of a small group who are my allies in the creation and production of the entire book. Thus, as well as supplying the initial impetus, Robin Jones has all along wielded the sharpest but gentlest of editorial pencils. Lynn Nesbit, my agent, has demonstrated patience and interest perhaps a million times greater than duty ever calls for. At Random House, Jim Silberman has turned a blind eye to deadlines and an indulgent ear to problems. Alice Mayhew, assigned by Random House as my official editor, has been much more than that. She has been my instructor in Catholic doctrine, my commentator on church politics, my sponsor in official and quasi-official church circles, my multi-volume reference encyclopedia and my friend. Over many a disputatious evening, moreover, Miss Mayhew's brother, Leonard Mayhew, has earned a post I'm sure he detests, that of resident theologian and final arbiter on matters of nomenclature.

Almost as vital was the aid a second, somewhat larger group contributed. Two members of this group, Msgr. George G. Higgins and Rev. Francis X. Murphy, C.SS.R., are priests. In the Introduction, I explain the importance of their contribution. There, also, I mention the generosity of Bill Pepper, who at the time of my visit to Rome was head of the Rome bureau of *Newsweek*. Through Bill and through Jack Kroll, a *Newsweek* senior editor and a friend of long standing, I met Ken Woodward, editor of *Newsweek*'s religion department in New York. Ken's help and that of Mimi Sheils, Ken's research associate, have been valuable beyond measure. I'm grateful also to Robert G. Hoyt, editor of the *National Catholic Reporter*, and to James Andrews, formerly news editor of this Catholic publication, for encouragement and for a voluminous file of original information about church finance. Lillian R. Block, head of the remarkable Religious News Service of the National Conference of Christians and Jews, permitted me the use of the RNS morgue as a research file. Ed Rice, former editor and publisher of *Jubilee* magazine, turned over to me another file of data, this one on lay Catholic organizations. Jack Bickett, editorial writer for the *Oklahoma Courier* (one of the liveliest of diocesan newspapers), supplied financial and other information about the Diocese of Oklahoma City-Tulsa. Jerry Goodman, editor of *Institutional Investor* (and the "Adam Smith" who wrote *The Money Game*), made a number of thoughtful suggestions and kindly offered me room in the columns of his excellent magazine. John Leo, formerly with *The New York Times* and always one of this country's best religious-news reporters, furnished a number of interesting items. John O'Connor, another outstanding journalist of religion, allowed me to read the manuscript of his flavorful book, *The People Versus Rome*. Mary Perkins Ryan took time out of a crowded schedule to lend encouragement to this project.

To turn from the world of journalism to that of business, the list of those who have lent me their expertise and their valuable time is too long even to begin to set forth here. But some names I must mention. First among them is that of Dan W. Lufkin. As one of the founders of Donaldson, Lufkin & Jenrette, Inc., Dan has been an ideal—and a very patient—consultant on matters of investment. As a member of Cardinal Cooke's Committee on Education of the Archdiocese of New York, Dan (a non-Catholic) first described to me the activities of this key study group. He then made it possible for me to meet other members of the committee and, ultimately, to gain the cooperation of archdiocesan officials in my own study. In addition, Dan Lufkin's personal encouragement and support of the project have been infinitely reassuring. Through Dan, I met T. Murray McDonnell, chairman of the Committee on Education, whose counsel on diocesan fiscal procedures was most useful and whose interest in the education issue alerted me to its importance. Paul McDonald, another committee member and a specialist in the investment needs of the Catholic religious orders, discussed with me the attitudes toward investment he found characteristic of church officials. Thomas O. Jones, a computer scientist and systems engineer, commented on the data-processing project he designed for the study of parochial schools in New York. He also described his experiences in the financing of parochial schools in Philadelphia and made available to me a draft of his article, "The Crisis in Parochial Education."

On the links between the church and commercial banks, I've benefited from discussions with Thomas H. Petschek.

Tom, another old friend, is a vice president of the Manufacturers Hanover Trust Company and head of the bank's office in Frankfurt, West Germany. Minos Zombankakis, formerly Manufacturers Hanover Trust representative in Rome and now in charge of the same bank's merchant-banking affiliate in London, did his delightful best to explain Vatican banking to me without revealing any secrets of the trade.

On questions of insurance, Brian Black of the Insurance Company of North America was most helpful. I've also discussed insurance matters with Christopher M. Waldorf, whose New York firm handles insurance for many Catholic institutions and religious orders (including the Jesuits), and with my friend Walter Samples, Vice President of administration for the American Insurance Association.

A lively lecture on the general subject of church real estate holdings was the result of a meeting with Charles J. Dunn, head of the firm which handles realty transactions for the Archdiocese of Los Angeles. For comment on problems of property construction, valuation and resale, I'm indebted to Robert F. Borg of New York. Jerrold Morgulas was the source of much information about the legal aspects of institutional property ownership.

On the problems and the opportunities of fund-raising for Catholic causes, Leo J. Laughlin of Community Counselling Service, Inc. was most helpful. Jan Krukowski, head of the New York office of the Barton-Gillet Company (creators and designers of fund-raising materials), added valuable comment.

Within the official church itself, the following members of the Catholic hierarchy extended to me their direct co-operation and that of their subordinates. *Archbishops:* Cardinal Terence J. Cooke (New York), Cardinal Lawrence Shehan (Baltimore). *Bishops:* Walter W. Curtis (Bridgeport), Ernest J. Primeau (Manchester), Fulton J. Sheen

(Rochester), Robert E. Tracy (Baton Rouge). *Religious superiors:* Anita Caspary (former Superior of the California Institute of the Sisters of the Most Holy and Immaculate Heart of the Blessed Virgin Mary), Sister Jogues Egan (former Provincial, New York Province of the Religious of the Sacred Heart of Mary), Very Reverend William Ferree (Provincial, Cincinnati Province of the Society of Mary), Very Reverend Robert A. Mitchell (Provincial, New York Province of the Society of Jesus). Each of these officials welcomed me into the administrative offices of his own organization and encouraged me to work closely with the men in charge of finance and administration. In other cases, informal contact with chancery and other officials brought me such specific information as diocesan financial reports and complete balance sheets. These locations include the archdioceses of Boston, Miami, Newark, Omaha and St. Louis and the dioceses of Buffalo, Cleveland, El Paso, Joliet, Oklahoma City, Spokane and Trenton. Similar contacts have brought in official reports on the Dominican Sisters of the Congregation of Siena and the Sisters of Charity of Halifax.

In the given Catholic jurisdictions and institutions, many more church officials have assisted me. In particular, I wish to thank: Msgr. Joseph P. Murphy (New York), Msgr. Porter J. White (Baltimore), Msgr. James F. Devine (Bridgeport), Msgr. Albert W. Olkovikas (Manchester), Rev. Joseph W. Dailey (Rochester), Msgr. Paul J. Gauci and Rev. Donald Songy (Baton Rouge). These were (most still are) the senior financial officials of the Catholic sees I visited. To their names I must add those of Rev. Eugene J. Quigley, S.J., Brother William A. Bruggeman, S.M., and Rev. Paul C. Reinert, S.J. The first two are the treasurers of the New York Province of the Society of Jesus and the Cincinnati Province of the Society of Mary, respectively. Father Reinert is president of Saint Louis University. All three have taught me much about the finances of the Catholic religious orders. Rev. Boniface L. Wittenbrink, O.M.I. (Oblates of Mary Immaculate), former secretary of the Conference of Major Superiors of Men in Washington, D.C., helped to arrange meetings with these and other officials of religious orders.

Additional help came from lay administrators in Catholic dioceses and organizations. For loans of reference materials and for keen insight into church management policies, I'm especially grateful to Patrick O'Maera, head of the Schools Study Group of the Archdiocese of New York. Others whose kindnesses have been notable include John Sharkey (also of New York), John Shaw (Oklahoma City-Tulsa), John J. Kennedy (Baton Rouge), J. Early Hardesty (Baltimore) and Irene Greene (Bridgeport). Robert E. Rambusch, a leader in the American Catholic liturgical reform movement and an outstanding designer of church interiors, shared with me his immense knowledge of the church-supply business.

On various aspects of life within the Catholic Church, interviews with Msgr. James R. Searson, Msgr. Charles O. Rice, Rev. Thomas Green, Rev. George G. Hagmaier, C.S.P. (Paulist Fathers) and Rev. William Clancy proved enlightening. For a discussion of the significance of the vow of poverty, I'm grateful to Rev. William R. Walsh, S.J.

In Rome, Msgr. Andrea Deskur, Under-Secretary of the Pontifical Institute for Social Communication, discussed with me the various organs of Vatican finance and the shifting fiscal needs of the papacy.

If I were to expand this list to include everyone, Catholic and non-Catholic, religious and lay, who has helped me with this book, my acknowledgments would continue indefinitely. Personal friends have contributed their comments. Total strangers, overhearing a conversation or curious about a book I was carrying, have raised questions. Business ac-

quaintances have encouraged my inquiries. To these anonymous assistants as well as to those named here, I express my
thanks. To everyone who helped, let me say simply that
much of the credit but none of the blame for what I've
written belongs to you.

For my two sons, Timothy and Douglas, this book has
been a demanding (and surely an unwanted) step brother.
Their interest, their forbearance and their understanding
over so many years seem to me to deserve this special
acknowledgment.

J.G.

Worldly Goods is a book about the wealth of the Roman Catholic Church; or, to be more exact, about the financial and administrative workings of this oldest and strangest of Western institutions. The origin of the book I can pinpoint to the day and hour. Indeed, almost to the minute. But the idea behind this book is less easy to nail down. Nor was the idea exclusively my own property. In truth, this book was engendered by the casual curiosity of one of my friends, and in a special way given shape by the equally casual credulity of another. So as a matter of simple justice to both of them, and because the story of a book's beginnings sometimes does cast light on the book itself, I feel I should give an account here of what happened at the very start.

On August 15, 1966, I was lunching with Robin Jones,

the first of the two friends just mentioned. Earlier that year, in the spring, I had finished writing and he had painstakingly edited my first book. It was to be published in the fall, and our luncheon—so we both thought—would be one of those relaxed author-editor sessions which both parties can only really enjoy after the final work on a book has been done. Then, over coffee, Robin neatly slipped the serpent into the garden. It seems he'd read a news story that morning. "The Union Minière du Haut-Katanga," he said, "has just lost a zinc mine to the Congolese rebels." I must have grunted my lack of sympathy over this blow to a very rich, very exploitative Belgian company. "But what's interesting about it," Robin went on, "is that the Union Minière had a partner, the Vatican. How can the Vatican own eighteen per cent of a zinc mine?"

Without being at all sure how, I found myself explaining that a church, like a university, a hospital or any other endowed organization, must on occasion have surplus funds to invest. So probably a banker or a broker for the Union Minière had contacted a banker or a broker who represented the Vatican and they had worked out a deal together. It was as simple as that.

After I finished, there was a long silence. Then Robin said, "You know, I think you've just stumbled over your next book."

To this notion, my first reaction was (to put it mildly) highly skeptical. Right away, I could foresee three major problems: 1) as a non-Catholic, I knew about the Roman Catholic Church only what most non-Catholics know, which is almost nothing; 2) I had no reason to believe that those who did know about the church and its finances would ever disclose to me, an outsider and a writer, information which I did know the church has always kept utterly secret; 3) even if I could familiarize myself with the structure of the church, and then somehow gain access to its hidden financial dealings, most people feel strongly indeed about the church, its wealth and its activities. Whatever I discovered, how could I convince readers—who would of course be non-Catholics as well as Catholics—that I was telling the truth?

"Think about it," Robin said. But the advice was unnecessary, because I already was thinking about it. Furiously. To counterbalance the problems, I was thinking I could detect certain positive elements. For one thing, a decade's worth of business experience did give me some sense of how the church, or any huge enterprise, had to be organized and managed. For another, having just written at length about one vast financial institution, the American life-insurance industry, I felt that what I'd learned might in some ways be applicable to this other institution. For still another, being an outsider might not be a liability. It might even give me some advantages. As an outsider, I could ask the naïve questions and record the guarded or deceitful answers, all without fear of reprisal. I could claim to possess a sense of fairness that might convince the insiders to speak freely. And as for my own feelings about the church, I could say as truthfully as anyone that I had no axe to grind.

But most important of all, I was experiencing those metaphoric flashing lights and clicking circuits which writers do feel—which most people feel—when they get hold of a compelling project. Apart from the sheer challenge, I could see that a book about the wealth of the Catholic Church and about the issues surrounding this wealth might be useful to many readers. In general, we all know much less than we should know about institutional wealth. About its special place in our society, its power and the limits of its power. In this sense, a book about the church, especially about the American church, would be a study in contemporary economic and social values. Furthermore, a book in which facts, figures and personal testimony would for the first time document the true extent of Catholic ecclesiastical wealth and power should be more than useful. It might be explosive. And it would be unique. To write the book, I'd have to learn secrets which no other writer had ever learned before.

To sum it all up, the Vatican's zinc mine had done its work. Despite my reservations, I was hooked. Before we got up from the luncheon table, I had committed myself (and in his editorial capacity, Robin Jones also) to this book.

The one other episode which seems to me to have shaped what I've written occurred several months later, after I'd already done some of the preliminary planning and research. This time, the occasion was a dinner engagement. My wife and I had persuaded another couple, a lawyer and his wife who were friends of long standing, to make the journey into New York from suburban New Jersey for an evening. As I recall, we were lingering over our first course when I mentioned that I'd signed a contract to write a book about the finances of the church. Ben (for reasons that will be obvious, I won't use his last name) leaned forward in his chair. Lowering his voice dramatically, he said, "I've got a great piece of information for you. Somebody very high up in the chancery [the administrative office] of the Newark diocese told me. I can't give you his name, because it was confidential. But *he* said"—here Ben paused for maximum effect—"that the church owns all of the stock in a company that makes birth control pills!"

Now, Ben is no mere layman. He's a graduate of an Ivy League college who ranked spectacularly high in his class at Harvard Law School. He spent several years in Washington, D.C. as an attorney for the United States Treasury Department. At thirty-six, he was made a senior partner in his law firm. Above all, Ben's mind works exactly as you'd expect a first-rate legal mind to work. He's a precise, meticulous and hardheaded thinker, a tough opponent in an argument.

Therefore, even as I went through the motions of deflating the "information" he had passed on,* I found myself thinking about this book. It seemed to me that if someone as sophisticated as Ben would swallow such absurdities, then there was indeed a need for a study that would substitute fact for myth, explanation for fantasy, about the finances of the Catholic Church. At that point, I made up my own mind to base this book only on the kinds of evidence which even a lawyer like Ben would be willing to accept. On such undramatic but revealing material as financial reports, accountants' statements, realty appraisals, management studies and other official documents. On interviews not only with the bankers, brokers and others who do business with—and for —the church but also with the priests in actual charge of the financial mechanisms by which the church operates. In short, I determined to rely not on hearsay or on rumor but on fact. Where the facts spoke for themselves (whether well or ill of the church), I'd let them do so. Where there was to be conjecture, I'd label it as such. But my conjectures, too, would be grounded in facts that others could check and verify.

In the opening chapter, I outline briefly where this pursuit of the facts will take readers of the book itself: from the neighborhood parish church all the way to Rome. In the Acknowledgments, I have listed the names of those,

* This tired story, as I already knew, had been circulating in the press since 1956. Despite official denials, it still occasionally crops up. As I pointed out to Ben, hundreds of church organizations do own stocks. Among the shares held, some were undoubtedly those of pharmaceutical companies making The Pill. While this is no doubt an inconsistency, other, similar anomalies were endemic in investing. For instance, life-insurance companies which preach thrift are major lenders to finance companies offering high-cost cash to consumer borrowers. As for the fiction that the church owned *all* the stock, this is utterly inconsistent with the realities of church investing.

inside the professional church and outside, who have led me to the facts, who have answered my inquiries and who have explained what I was so often slow to understand. There, too, I pay to those men and women some measure of the tribute I feel they deserve.

As I look back over the four and a half years during which this book was written, other incidents return to mind. Some were discouraging. For instance, I recall an interview in March, 1967, with Msgr. Thomas P. McGovern, Director of the Bureau of Information of the Archdiocese of New York. To set me at ease in his paneled, carpeted office, Msgr. McGovern chatted with me about his last summer's vacation cruise on a friend's forty-four-foot yacht. Then, when I asked him if he could help with the book, he commented bluntly, "Your background doesn't seem to me to qualify you for writing about the finances of the church. I'd have greater hopes for accuracy and scholarship if such a book were written by a religious [i.e., a priest, brother or nun] who also taught economics." To this, I could only answer that Msgr. McGovern might well be right. Yet curiously enough, no such perfectly qualified candidate had ever presented himself (or herself). In the absence of the perfect party, it had fallen to me to ask for his aid. He still refused it. Fortunately for me and for the book, Msgr. McGovern's superiors in the Archdiocese of New York have turned out to be less dubious about my qualifications. I can only hope now that the result will prove not too distressing to this genial priest.

I also remember an interview two years later (January 3, 1969) with Bishop John J. Wright of Pittsburgh. When I asked Bishop Wright if he'd make available for this study the financial data of his Pittsburgh diocese, he looked at me sharply and said, "How do I know you're not just another one of those guys who wants to kick the Pope in the head?" I replied that as far as I could see, a book about the finances of the church had little in common with a physical assault on Pope Paul VI. He suggested that I try him again in a few weeks. When I did see him three weeks later, at a luncheon in New York on January 23, he assured me that his office would be in touch with me. Once again, it was fortunate for my book that not every churchman in Pittsburgh is so forgetful. Bishop Wright is now a cardinal in Rome. If this book should reach him there (as it probably will), I trust that he, too, will find his apprehensions groundless.

Inevitably, I've had some bizarre encounters as well. For instance, in 1968 I was contacted by one New York priest with strange tales to tell of his persecution by superiors in the hierarchy. As a favor, he promised to set up a meeting for me with his friend and protector Cardinal Egidio Vagnozzi, who is a key figure in the Vatican's financial administration. Swearing to keep his promise (and asking at one point if I could pay half of his air fare), he departed for Rome. On the evening of October 15, 1968, a cable arrived from Vatican City. It read: "Telephoning next week." I've never heard from him since.

On March 13, 1970, there began another singular episode. I received a late-afternoon telephone call from someone who identified himself as Albert R. Kraus, the editor of the Sunday financial section of *The New York Times*. He had heard, he said, from a stringer in Kansas City that I was writing a book about the finances of the church. *The Times* wanted to do a feature story on the book. Could he set up an appointment? Pleased but just a bit mystified (who in Kansas City could have known Albert R. Kraus?), I agreed to see him on the following Monday. Splendid; would I mind answering just a few questions over the telephone? When I asked him what he wanted to know, my caller rattled off a series of queries about the investments held by the Archdiocese of New York. Although he sounded professional enough, something about his manner made me suspicious. So I put him off, called *The Times* and learned from the real Albert R. Kraus that the caller, whoever he was, wasn't the Sunday financial editor of that estimable newspaper. Later, the same caller called again, asking for a change in the time of our appointment. I made the tactical mistake of questioning his credentials too closely. His replies were glibly convincing, but evidently I scared him off. At least, he never did show up for his "interview."

But in contrast to the occasional run-in with a suspicious, a defensive or a disturbed mentality, I can recall scores of extraordinary kindnesses. Of these, none ever could surpass the princely generosity of Curtis Bill Pepper to a puzzled writer just starting his book. We met (May, 1967) in Rome, where Bill Pepper was then the bureau chief of *Newsweek* magazine. As a reporter and as a personality, Bill had, as he still has, access to all of Rome (indeed, to all of Europe). And his contacts within the Vatican are superb. If I had been in Bill Pepper's place, I wonder how free with information I would have been had a competitor appeared on my beat. Yet for this competitor, Bill opened his personal files, made a dozen telephone calls and countless suggestions and introduced me to the special universe of Vatican journalism. For all of this, and for his personal hospitality and his professional encouragement, I'm profoundly grateful.

Through Bill Pepper, I met still another professional who took both this book and its author under his wing. During his varied career, Rev. Francis X. Murphy, C.SS.R. (the initials identify a member of the Redemptorist order) has been a parish priest in the Bronx, a military chaplain in France, Germany and Korea and the resident chaplain of the United States Naval Academy. Father Murphy's official specialty at present is patristic moral theology. On this subject, he lectures regularly at the Alphonsian Academy, a graduate-level institute for priests in Rome. And he has written a number of essays and books on the teachings and moral traditions of the fathers of the church.

But to categorize Father Murphy as a teacher and a scholar is like saying that St. Paul sometimes wrote letters or that Peter the Hermit was a hermit. In ways far too numerous to catalogue here, but in particular via his journalism, Father Murphy is one of the great advocates of openness, responsiveness and love in the Catholic Church. He himself firmly denies that he's anything other than an ordinary priest. He denies, for example, being part of the team which (under the pseudonym of "Xavier Rynne") writes *The New Yorker*'s "Letters From Vatican City" about the events and the politics of the contemporary church. Certainly, I must respect Father Murphy's sense of journalistic privacy. But like many others, I've been the beneficiary of his extraordinary intellect. Ever since we first met, also in Rome, Father Murphy has been a source of shrewd advice and a reviver of flagging energy. For his professional help, he knows he has my gratitude. For his friendship, I'm much more than grateful.

Another priest who has helped immeasurably is Msgr. George G. Higgins. His career, too, is far more varied than any brief sketch of mine could reveal. Professionally, George Higgins is one of the best-known labor consultants in the United States, in constant demand as a counselor and arbitrator. Officially, Msgr. Higgins is head of the Division for Urban Life, which in turn is part of the Social Action Department of the United States Catholic Conference. Personally, he's quiet, thoughtful and utterly fearless in defense of a good cause. The decision of Msgr. Higgins to offer me assistance turned my hunt for information into a planned, manageable quartering of the ground. His lucidity as an instructor in the administrative niceties of the church saved me months of time and years of bafflement. Through his efforts, I was introduced to those priests in various sectors of the church who alone could supply the facts and figures I needed. It's therefore no exaggeration to say that without the aid of Msgr. Higgins, this book could not have been written.

Here, let me make certain key points about the book itself.

First of all, despite the cooperation I've received from church authorities, *Worldly Goods* is entirely my own book. This means several things. One of the most important is that its perspectives, biases and judgments are mine alone. Thus, except for the routine purpose of verifying quotations, I've neither requested nor permitted any official of any branch of the Catholic Church to read my manuscript. Nor has any other partisan outsider inspected what I've written. This policy may possibly have cost me some valuable aid, but I know of no other way for a writer to preserve his editorial independence. Readers of the book itself will see quickly, I'm sure, that I've given the church no guarantees of gentle treatment. But readers cannot see, and hence must be told, that no such guarantees were ever asked. In fact, of the scores of Catholic bishops, chancellors, pastors, religious superiors, lay consultants and other officials interviewed for this book, not one has attempted to falsify a fact, minimize a problem or persuade me or pressure me into a conclusion favorable to the church. As I've already indicated, there have been those who, like Bishop Wright, were personally evasive. Others, for reasons sometimes plausible and sometimes unconvincing, have entirely refused to cooperate with me. But these have been the exceptions. Most of those whom I've contacted have spoken freely and frankly indeed. Many have greeted with relish the prospect of helping to end the long silence about church wealth and the needless mystery surrounding it.

To stress that the book is my own handiwork is *ipso facto* to acknowledge its limitations. For me, the most frustrating aspect of this entire project is that, with time and space limited, I've had to brush in only lightly (or else omit) so many intriguing matters. At one extreme, I've been forced to eliminate whole fistfuls of the tiny but telling facts which place larger issues in precise focus. For instance, what better indication is there of the growth of Catholic ecclesiastical wealth in this country than a sketch of church finance in 1849? The year of the California Gold Rush was also the year when a group of New York Catholic laymen, acting as trustees, purchased from the city for exactly $5,550 (plus $51.53 in interest and another $83.32 in fees) the parcel of land on which Saint Patrick's Cathedral now stands, a parcel currently worth $20 million. What could tell readers more about the internationalism of the church than the fact that a Jewish furrier in New York City, who steadfastly refuses to let me mention his name, is the official supplier of ermine for the ceremonial robes of the popes in Rome? What says more about the cost of high status in the Catholic hierarchy than the prices a new cardinal must pay for the hats he wears? (The red beaver hat he needs for formal occasions will set him back about $50. A black hat with a gold band for semi-formal wear sells for $40. For everyday use, he can buy for only $15 another black hat with the proper gold trim. His *galero*, the hat a cardinal receives at his elevation ceremony and later displays in a glass case at his official residence, the pope presents to him as a gift.)

To me, and surely to others as well, details like these are fascinating and revealing. But every detail does absorb a certain amount of space. And too much detail turns a book into a miscellany of unconnected facts and anecdotes. Because of the problem of length, and because I'm unwilling to blur the major issues, I've regretfully consigned to the files much material which, however entertaining, is not entirely relevant.

Even more reluctantly, I've accepted that if this book is to be of reasonable length, it cannot cover certain important sectors of the Catholic ecclesiastical economy. For instance, an entire industry has grown up around the liturgical (i.e., the ritual and ceremonial) requirements of Catholic worship. The vestment-makers, the suppliers of candles, the sellers of altar vessels and the architects and designers of churches constitute a specialized business. As I've discovered, this has its own customs and even its own small business district (on and near Barclay Street in lower Manhattan). The men who run the Catholic church-supply houses, most of which are small family-owned firms, speak a vivid language of their own. In good times their industry sells about $20 million worth of liturgical merchandise and furnishings a year. What they say about the trade today, paints a vivid picture of change within the church. But much as I'd enjoy sharing with readers the shop-talk and the shrewd insights of these merchants, there's simply no room in this book for their story.

Nor is there room for an even bigger story about the most important mirror of change in the church, the Catholic press. Ever since 1821, when Bishop John England founded the *United States Catholic Miscellany*, Catholic publications have proliferated in America. According to the 1970 *National Catholic Almanac*, 89 of the 160 Catholic archdioceses and dioceses publish their own weekly newspapers, while 35 make official use of one of the five national Catholic weeklies. Twelve foreign-language papers bring the total number up to 136, with a combined circulation of 6,312,226. Add to these figures the total of 290 Catholic magazines appearing regularly, and the quantitative dimensions of the Catholic press in this country are large indeed. And although editorial quality is often piously insipid, a surprising number of these publications are exceptions to the rule.

In theory, the economics of the Catholic diocesan press are straightforward. In the typical diocese, every Catholic family must subscribe to the newspaper. It's the responsibility of the parish pastors to collect from their parishioners the subscription fees. Whether or not they actually do so, the pastors must turn over to the bishop each year a total sum for the cost of all subscriptions in their parishes. Supposedly, the income from subscriptions covers the fixed expenses of the publication: its payroll, its printing and other production costs and the cost of its distribution. The additional revenue from the sale of advertising space is thus a source of profit. Sometimes the bishop himself pockets the gains, but more often these are ploughed back into the publication.

Today, however, this theory no longer works. Financially, the trade press of Catholicism is in serious trouble. Rising costs on the one hand and static revenues on the other have trapped diocesan and other Catholic periodicals in an economic cul-de sac. Furthermore, the old-fashioned coverage of Altar Guild meetings and high school sports appeals to fewer and fewer readers. Like today's Catholic audiences, today's Catholic writers and editors want more controversy in their journals than some bishops are prepared to tolerate. The unresolved question of how free a Catholic press can be or should be is thus a source of increasing tension between church officials and the once-docile chroniclers of church news.

In gathering financial material, I've met many members of this special segment of the press. From those who cover the unfolding story of the church I've received indispensable aid. Because their problems are in essence the problems of every journalist (myself included), I find their job interesting and its pitfalls and possibilities intriguing. And because the current money difficulties of the Catholic press do reflect the difficulties of the church at large, I'd like to be able to include this story, too, in *Worldly Goods*. But to squeeze into too little space a subject that demands full-scale treatment (indeed, a book of its own) would simultaneously do injustice to Catholic journalism and violence to the form of this book.

Finally, for a writer the limitations of time and space always merge into one compelling limitation, a deadline. By the time this book is published, some of the problems discussed in its pages may be solved. But to wish for more space and more time in which to contain this huge, complex subject is both futile and unnecessary. As another writer, Martin P. Mayer, once said of an equally taxing subject—schools—"there comes a time when a man who writes for a living must sit down and write his book." Then, too, in any institution, the economic machinery at its core almost by definition will be the slowest of all of its parts to change. For this reason, the truth today about the finances of the Catholic Church will also, I'm sure, be the truth tomorrow.

Implicit in all the chapters that lie ahead is an editorial attitude that should be brought into focus at the start. In one respect at least the Catholic Church (along with every other religious establishment) does resemble the proverbial seamless garment. There is no ready way to determine where, in its fabric, matters of money leave off and matters of spiritual import begin. So necessarily in this book, issues of Catholic belief, church doctrine, liturgical practice and even theology are sometimes interwoven with issues of economics and finance. No one, I'm sure, will mistake the result for a treatise on the spiritual mission of the church. But neither is my concentration on the economy of the church a denial of the reality of this mission. Today especially, only a very shallow commentator would see in Catholicism a secular enterprise and nothing more.

The reason, of course, is that after decades and even centuries of somnolence, change has at last burst upon the church. In the words of Frederick Franck, a non-Catholic layman who has fallen in love with the idea of a renewed church, the image of the old church is crumbling.

It is crumbling because within the Church itself a mutation of consciousness seems to be taking place which is rapidly undermining those aspects of the Church which are now felt by increasing numbers of people as incompatible with her spiritual mission. This new consciousness has resulted in a rapid evolution of insubordination that is changing the Church from the bottom up . . . The picture is disintegrating also because of the papacy of Angelo Roncalli, John XXIII.

Franck calls his book *The Exploding Church*. For a more recent journalistic survey of the issues—from birth control and divorce through priestly celibacy and papal authority— that are shattering the old absolutist image, *Time* magazine had a simpler title, "Rebellion in the Catholic Church."

Certainly, the church has not been the same since 1959, when John XXIII, "Good Pope John" to millions of his admirers, announced to the late Cardinal Giuseppe Tardini his intention of summoning into council the Catholic bishops of the world. To the astonishment of every onlooker (and the audience proved to be vast), the Second Vatican Council (1962-65) completely altered the course of the institutional church. With the quiet backing of the Pope, the 2,600 Catholic bishops struggled for control of the proceedings against a small group of traditionalist Vatican cardinals and their associates. Neither side won an outright victory. But on such crucial topics as liturgical renewal, ecumenism (the attitude of the church toward other churches), the role of the laity and the scope of their own episcopal authority, the bishops succeeded in opening the church to new ideas and to a collegial (rather than a monarchical) concept of

Catholic ecclesiastical government. Not even the death of Pope John in June, 1963, entirely halted the process of *aggiornamento*, or renewal. Indeed, during the remainder of Vatican II and afterward, John's successor, Paul VI, has made abundantly clear that the administrative reform of the church, if not its theological reform, is to continue. Although his quiet reshuffling of the ranks of Vatican officialdom makes little news today, the present Pope is determined to set his house in something approaching modern order.

But neither John nor Paul, or the hierarchy under their dominion, ever bargained on the real consequences of Vatican II; or anticipated its electrifying effect on the lower-echelon clergy and the laity. And so, instead of gaining glad cooperation in the housecleaning of their establishment, the princes of the church have found themselves awash in a wave of revolt against everything indicative of authoritarianism in the establishment itself. Predictably, in this country as elsewhere, many senior members of the hierarchy are outraged. And inevitably, they are reacting exactly as are the heads of the other institutions—from the universities of the world all the way to the F.B.I.—whose rule is challenged. Thus Cardinal James F. McIntyre, former Archbishop of Los Angeles, is said to have remarked grimly in 1966, "None of the proposals of the Second Vatican Council will be promulgated in my archdiocese during my lifetime." To other equally conservative Catholics, the moves of more moderate bishops to expedite the changes voted by the Council seem downright heretical. But many priests, nuns and laymen view these same moves as belated and defensive, and to more than a few Catholics they appear bleakly reactionary.

So foreshortened an account of the Council and its reverberations through the whole church does scant justice to what has been called "the most important religious event of the century." My only reason for inserting this sketchy account here is simply to make another critical editorial point. If the inseparability of the economic and the eternal poses problems for a writer about the wealth of the church, today's momentous changes in the church open an abyss beneath his feet.

Perhaps the best way to stress this point and its meaning properly is to tell a story. At one stage of my research, I was invited to the annual convention of the National Liturgical Conference, an organization of priests, nuns and lay specialists pressing for innovation and renewal in Catholic liturgy for the needs of contemporary worship. The convention was held in Washington, D.C., and from the earnestness and enthusiasm of its 4,500 delegates any outsider could have learned much about the changing church in America. As people do at any convention, groups of liturgists gathered in hotel rooms to sip highballs, compare notes and exchange gossip. In somebody's suite, I was asking a series of questions about the minutiae of church structure when another member of our group, a young and sensitive ex-priest, broke in. He insisted that I was taking "much too juridical and formalistic a view" of the church. I should realize, he went on, that the old static structure, the outworn Roman thing, wasn't the church at all. Soon, in fact, it would be swept away entirely. In its stead, there would be a pilgrim church, a dynamic community of souls sharing a common search for a living Christ.

This belief in a new kind of church moved me profoundly, and still does. If indeed my view of the church is too formalistic, he is one of many who has tried to change it. But delving into the economics of the church has led me to wonder whether or not "the outworn Roman thing" really is dying. First of all, I think it's a mistake to underestimate the vitality and dedication of the leaders of the old kind of church. As embattled as they now are in the effort to control the revolution they helped to foment in Rome, the bishops and their lieutenants are determined not to perish in the rear guard. Of those I've met, very many understand the need to change things, to construct a church more flexible and responsive to twentieth-century needs. Only a few seem to me to feel complacently that theirs is the best of all possible ecclesiastical worlds; and fewer still are what Pope John called "prophets of doom," resigned to a gloomy future for the institutional church.

Secondly, even a fluid, free-form church will need an economy. Every act of religion, ancient or modern, ceremonious or spontaneous, makes use of the things of this world; and, regrettable though the fact may be, the things of this world cost money. Because a pilgrim church, like a Church Militant, marches on its stomach, someone will always have to worry about the state of the exchequer. The question is: Who? And how?

So in exploring the economics of Catholicism, we do need to be alert to change and to the economic consequences of change. Over and over again, we will be reminded that yesterday's triumph of ecclesiastical architecture may be today's ruined chapel, an expensive piece of useless real estate. But such awareness is a far cry from either anticipating or willing the demise of the church.

WORLDLY
GOODS

CHAPTER ONE

The Economic Realm of the Church

No spectacle in the world occasions more sheer splendor than does a pontifical High Mass at the basilica of Saint Peter's in Rome. According to James Lees-Milne:

> The high altar . . . is covered with embroidered frontals. Seven candlesticks, a crucifix the work of Benvenuto Cellini and silver statuettes of Saints Peter and Paul are placed upon them. The pontifical throne is set in the apse in front of Bernini's *cattedra* against hangings of crimson velvet . . . Near the altar is a smaller throne of crimson and gold, without a canopy, where the Pope will sit during the singing of Terce. It is set on a scarlet dais raised upon steps covered with an emerald green carpet.

The same description goes on to follow the course of the great four-hour ceremony, from the processional to the

3

point when the Cardinal Archpriest of Saint Peter's presents to the Pope a purse containing 25 *julii* (late Roman coins each worth about $1.60), "the usual stipend for a Mass well sung."

Even in glittering Saint Peter's, so elaborate a celebration of the central liturgical act of Catholicism is rare today. Nevertheless, its magnificence is surely one appropriate symbol of the subject of this book: the temporal wealth of the Roman Catholic Church. In due course, the quest for facts about this supposedly limitless wealth does indeed lead to Rome; past the bronze doors of Saint Peter's and into the special world of the Holy See. For the Vatican is not only the repository of some of the most precious physical treasures of the church, but also the administrative and financial world headquarters of Catholicism. As fabulous as these treasures may be, the financial decision-makers within the Vatican can draw on resources far greater. All of the golden thrones and bejeweled tiaras of the popes are worth only a tiny fraction of the less visible wealth that flows into and out of the coffers of the Vatican each year.

But by no means does the story of church wealth either begin or end at the Pope's front door. In its turn, the wealth of the Vatican is far outweighed by the value of church property around the world, property over which Rome exercises little or no control. To learn something of how this farthest-flung and most complex of institutions gathers, handles and dispenses its riches, and to understand what money and property mean to the church today, we must begin elsewhere. Before we begin, moreover, we need to know the ground rules that will govern the inquiry.

To any investigator, even a brief glance at the vital statistics of Catholicism must be sobering. At present (1971) the Roman Catholic Church can lay claim to the spiritual loyalties of some 614 million people around the world. The temporal universe of the Church is divided into nearly 200,000 parishes, grouped into 1,695 dioceses and 463 archdioceses. To serve the faithful, the church calls on 279,985 priests of the parish or diocese. About half as many priests (147,208) are members of religious orders, and Catholic seminaries hold more than 79,000 candidates for the priesthood. Within the church, women religious outnumber men by two to one. More than 1 million nuns (or, in the unedifying official terminology, "women religious") perform the teaching, healing and other tasks allotted to them.

In terms of such totals, no secular corporation even comes close to matching the church. For instance, General Motors, considered the largest private employer in the world, lists 695,796 on its various payrolls, less than half the number of the Roman Catholic clergymen, nuns and brothers. Only when we turn to the mightiest bureaucracies of all, the governments of the major nations, do we find the church outmanned. To cite the most convenient example, the US government currently employs 2.7 million people, half again as many as are found in the professional ranks of the church.

If the church numbers its servants in the millions, the separate entities to which they belong can be counted in the tens of thousands. Thus, the *Annuario Pontificio*, the official yearbook of the church, devotes more than 100 pages of very fine print to the mere listing of the *istituti religiosi e secolari maschili* (in free translation, the "male religious orders and lay religious societies"). Another 100 pages of this fat red-bound volume are required for the alphabetical list of the orders of nuns. To consider organizations of a different kind, in the United States alone the church operates 1,959 high schools and nearly 10,000 grade schools. It runs 283 colleges and universities. It maintains 871 hospitals and 220 schools of nursing. Every one of these institutions, of course, is a separate enterprise, with its own staff, its own rules, its own physical plant and its own financial superstructure.

Given statistics of these magnitudes, one conclusion is surely self-evident. No single book, however encyclopedic in scope, could possibly contain all the facts or encompass the entire story of the wealth of the church. Nor, certainly, does this book pretend to the whole truth about so immense a subject. Rather, the chapters that follow focus on specific domains of the wide realm of the church, and on selected—if crucial—aspects of church financial affairs. In a word, the book is neither a statistical compendium nor a treatise, but a financial profile.

Much of the book deals with the Catholic Church in the United States, with its particular pattern of parish, diocese and archdiocese, with its educational and other establishments and with its monetary arrangements. Apart from sheer convenience, the main reason for concentrating on the church in this country is a simple one. Nowhere else on earth is the Catholic Church as wealthy and as flourishing as it is here. And nowhere else are the issues surrounding the material status of this and other spiritual institutions more sharply drawn or more controversial.

Eight years ago, Rev. C. Richard Ginder of Pittsburgh wrote in *Our Sunday Visitor*, a mass-circulation Catholic weekly:

> The Catholic Church must be the biggest corporation in the United States. We have a branch office in almost every neighborhood. Our assets and real estate holdings must exceed those of Standard Oil, A.T.&T. and U.S. Steel combined. And our roster of dues-paying members must be second only to the tax rolls of the United States Government.

As a matter of fact, Father Ginder erred in several significant details. In 1960, the combined assets of Standard Oil,

A.T.&T. and U.S. Steel totaled $37,429,569,000, a figure considerably higher than the total assets of the Catholic Church in the United States. As for the church's "roster of dues-paying members," it's worth noting that in 1960 the U.S. Catholic population of 40.2 million was easily out-ranked by at least one private company's list of customers, that of the 45 million Americans who paid premiums to The Metropolitan Life Insurance Company of New York.

Nevertheless, Father Ginder's point was—and still is— provocative. Viewed as a single monolithic establishment, the Catholic Church in this country does seem a formidably large financial enterprise. Its collective assets in the U.S. range from its 175 cathedrals to commercial real estate in prime locations across the country. It owns stock in hun-dreds of blue-chip corporations. The "ordinary income" of its 18,244 parishes (the income derived only from seat offerings, regular weekly or monthly collections and offer-tories at Masses) can be estimated at close to $2 billion a year.

Facts like these about the economic life of the church prompt some obvious questions. For example:

How much is the church in this country really worth?
Who handles the financial affairs of the church?
How does its financial machinery work?

But while the questions may be obvious, the answers are— or at least have long been—shrouded in mystery. Certainly the age-old reluctance of the church to divulge information about its holdings is still a serious barrier to accurate finan-cial analysis. Later in this book, we'll consider in detail the multiple causes and the disturbing consequences of this leg-endary reticence. For the moment, we can accept with re-lief the fact that not all Catholic prelates take the position on financial disclosures voiced, according to *The New York Times* (March 10, 1967), by one high Vatican official. When asked to comment on a relatively straight-forward aspect of church investment practice, this unnamed spokesman replied, "Why should we? We have neither stockholders like a corporation, nor voters and tax-payers like a government."

The first half of this wry response is more to the immediate point. For, *pace* Father Ginder, not even in a metaphoric sense is the Catholic Church one giant corporation. Indeed, in terms of its temporalities, the *unam sanctam ecclesiam* much more closely resembles the conglomerate: a group of companies in different industries wired loosely together by an expansion-minded but permissive top management. Or, in another light, the church looks something like a cartel: a set of competing enterprises allied together to maintain control of one industry.

Such analogies are naturally tempting, and at various stages of our explorations they may well prove useful. But they too are far from being final definitions of the temporal order of the church. As we'll come to realize, in long perspective the church is closer still to being an actual economy, complete with "have" and "have-not" sectors, foreign exchange transactions, balance-of-payment problems and other benchmarks of modern economic systems.

But for the moment, the vital thing to keep in mind about this quasi-economy is its extreme decentralization. This, far more than the tradition of secrecy, makes questions about church finance difficult even to phrase intelligently, let alone to answer. Indeed, of all the surprising truths that shape this book, the truth most contrary to legend and logic alike is that there exists no great Catholic clearing house—in Rome or elsewhere—where all the facts are known, all the figures added up and all the orders issued.

An organization chart of the church in the U.S. would show this country as divided into twenty-nine "ecclesiastical provinces," each containing one archdiocese and a group of seemingly subordinate "suffragan sees." At the head of the chart, there would be room for the National Conference of Catholic Bishops and its many ancillary organizations, and for the office of His Excellency, the Most Reverend Luigi Raimondi, the current Apostolic Delegate to the United States. But despite appearances, not all authority flows from the top to the bottom of this neat pyramid. Thus, the real control of most of the temporal holdings of the church here is vested in what *Fortune* magazine calls "the formidable body" of archbishops and bishops who rule over the dioceses of the United States. Economically speaking, moreover, each bishop is a law unto himself. Within his own diocese, the bishop (and the clerical administrators and lay advisers he appoints or inherits) makes the important financial decisions. In so doing, he rarely seeks counsel from his brother bishops and never expects guidance from Rome. As Bishop Ernest J. Primeau of Manchester, New Hampshire, remarked in our conversation on the subject, "I haven't any idea of what's going on financially in the state next door. And when we're all together, we almost never talk money."

Obviously, then, for information about church wealth and its management, we must consult the bishops themselves, and their aides in chancery offices across the country. We need to learn whether or not bishops are shrewd, innovative managers of what Catholic canon law calls their temporalities. We need to know how the books are kept and the banks satisfied; how real property is bought, sold and traded; how investment funds are handled. We need to discover how dioceses buy their insurance and arrange their credit; and how the church can sometimes act as its own banker. Above all, we must find out how key officials of the church think and feel about money—and what they know about money—so that we can measure their ideas and their performance against the economic realities confronting the church today.

Much of what we must investigate is to be found at the diocesan level. But real insight into the economy of the church begins with the micro-economy of the parish. For here, where clergy and laity come together, the money of the church is raised. Here also, much of this money is spent. In a reasonably prosperous parish, roughly 70 per cent of all the money collected (and 95 per cent of the ordinary income defined earlier) goes to cover the expenses and maintain the surplus of the parish itself. And while the financial authority of a pastor, or parish priest, is by no means as absolute as is that of a bishop, in most dioceses pastors exercise a startling freedom of choice in money matters.

What sort of economic man is a parish priest? This question opens up still other realms of inquiry. Non-Catholics in particular will want to know something about the priest's daily economic life: about how—and how much —he's paid; about the supposedly lucrative extras he receives; about his general style and standard of living. Catholics are much more likely to realize that strict rules, some of them centuries old, govern the priest in his dealings with money. But they may not be aware of how these rules can be made to accommodate life in our secular money society. For instance, today's priests are being encouraged to carry credit cards, to open charge accounts and to borrow money for personal needs.

As interesting and far more important is the question of how the pastor gathers and dispenses the money of the parish. Even though fund-raising may be a familiar story to every churchgoer, Catholic fund-raising does hold a special interest. Surely the envelope system of soliciting contributions (now a computerized operation in more than one diocese) deserves more than a glance. So also do various other methods, some ingenious, some repellent, but all devised to keep parishes in the black. Not least among them is bingo, the lowly game which has developed a strange folklore and a stranger following; and which can provoke real mental anguish in the pastor who resorts to it.

Most important of all, Catholic parents will know—achingly—the price they must pay to be certain their religion accompanies and shapes the education their children receive. But other readers may not know that the parochial school with its relentlessly increasing cost already absorbs most of the income of even the affluent parish, and demands far more money than poorer parishes can ever raise. According to Catholic educators, parochial schooling costs Catholic Americans $3 billion a year. And although the demand for this schooling is intense, educators and parents alike are alarmed over the inadequacy of the budget. Indeed, some specialists are saying that the financial crisis of Catholic education could bankrupt the entire church.

Whether or not they are right, no issue in the entire domain of church economics is more complex or more sensitive. And in the wider arena of American political and social striving, none has more explosive implications. Because the future of Catholic education does matter profoundly to every American, we must devote a chapter of this book to the educators, their problems and their critics.

The school aside, the Catholic pastor must also contend with a host of other financial questions. As the "line executive" of the church, he is expected to solve problems of administration, purchasing, construction and maintenance, personnel and accounting that would tax the abilities of a Harvard MBA. In the day-to-day job of running his parish, he may or may not delegate authority to his curate (assistant priest), if one is assigned to him. He may or may not make use of "expert" advice either from lay parishioners or from his local chancery office. And he may or may not be an effective guardian of the temporalities under his control. To find out about the skills and attitudes of priests in money management, not only must we ask the priests themselves, but we must also probe in such seemingly remote areas as the education of seminarians and the personnel practices of the bishops. Throughout, we especially need to ponder the significance of the one comment that recurs like a chorus in discussions of this topic: "Priests aren't financial men."

Diocesan and parochial economic practices are, of course, only one part of the story. Of the nearly 60,000 priests in the country, nearly 40 per cent (21,141) are what the church calls "religious" priests. (In a characteristically puzzling twist of official nomenclature, the church designates as "secular" priests those who work in parishes or for dioceses. Those who belong to religious orders in general are known as "religious" priests. Religious priests who have taken the solemn vows of such orders as the Franciscans, the Dominicans and the Benedictines are called "regular" priests, taking their title from the Latin *regulum*, which means "rule".) As we have noted earlier, the economic world of the religious orders is a world of its own.

Even to those who should know better, the names of the religious orders apparently evoke medieval images of cowled monastics leading cloistered lives and yet somehow controlling vast wealth. Thus, writing in *Playboy* magazine (April, 1967), the late James A. Pike, former Episcopal Bishop of California and once an examining attorney for the Securities and Exchange Commission, bolstered his appeal to "Tax the Churches" with a set of startling financial statistics about the Society of Jesus. This largest of Catholic priestly orders, he asserted, owns 51 per cent of the Bank of America (the California banking empire ranked largest in the country, with assets of over $21 billion).

The Jesuits also own the majority stock in both Phillips Petroleum and Creole Petroleum Company . . . The Society of Jesus is also a heavy investor in Republic Steel, National Steel and our four largest aircraft companies: Boeing, Lockheed, Curtis-Wright and Douglas. From these and other holdings, the Jesuits realize a yearly income of at least $250,000,000 . . .

A number of commentators have since pointed out that Bishop Pike's article was literally a tissue of errors. A Jesuit educator with a deficit quipped to me that "unfortunately" the Bank of America is not in the hands of the Society of Jesus, but rather in those of some 200,000 stockholders and their directors. Neither Phillips Petroleum nor Creole Petroleum (95 per cent of which is owned by Standard Oil of New Jersey) has ever been a Jesuit property. And so on. Indeed, Bishop Pike apologized for the inclusion of these figures—supplied, he explained, by *Playboy*'s "research department"—in his essay.

But the fact remains that Catholic religious orders do own and operate temporal resources quite independently of the diocesan hierarchy. Their wealth, moreover, is apt to be conspicuous wealth, in the form of the bricks and mortar of universities, schools, hospitals, retreat houses and other institutions. Especially because the orders do play so visible a role as the educators, healers and missionaries of Catholicism, the logic of studying their financial and administrative techniques is self-evident. And because so much of Catholic education pivots on the relationship between the religious orders (in particular, the teaching nuns) and diocesan authorities, we should analyze in detail this delicate balance of power.

Parish, diocese, archdiocese, motherhouse (the ecclesiastical term for the headquarters of a religious order, whether male or female): in just these expected places, the basic truths of church organization and finance are to be found. But the economy of the church has other intriguing facets as well. Never obvious, and sometimes even secret, is the participation of laymen—prominent lawyers, bankers, insurance men, stockbrokers, accountants, contractors, consultants—in the management of church affairs. The extent and the significance of such top-level involvement has long been the subject of fascinated conjecture. No other human enterprise, so the legend goes, receives from its adherents the favored treatment that the Catholic laity gives the Catholic Church. From the Vatican on down, financiers and specialists in all walks of economic life wait in the shadows for the summons of the hierarchy, ready with inside market information and crafty investment counsel. This they supply for the greater glory of God and the lasting (and tax-free) profit of the church. Their supposed reward: satisfaction plus, possibly, the medal or sash betokening membership in one of the orders of the papal nobility.

Strip away the overtones of mystery and conspiracy and the legend bears only the faintest resemblance to reality. The reality, however, pulsates with a vigorous life of its own. As initial proof, take the prosperous Irish Catholic layman who begged me, "Please don't use my name. I don't want to be tagged as a professional Catholic." Assured that his anonymity was safe, he went on to describe, guardedly but with gusto, some of the transactions that have helped him to build a tidy fortune as chief real estate man for a sizable archdiocese. Certainly, the deals he closes for his good friend the Archbishop are colorful enough by themselves to warrant a closer look. ("I'm the man who put St. Anne's Maternity Home into gas stations.") But also, despite his disclaimer and his genuine distaste for the role, this particular gentleman is indeed a professional Catholic.

As such, he belongs to a special breed. Like others who

do business on a large scale with, and for, the church, he's a trustee of more than one local Catholic institution. He's a notable fund-raiser as well as being a notably generous contributor to Catholic charitable causes. For that matter, he's a papal knight. But far from being the confidential servant of Rome, he is instead a ranking member of a singularly American aristocracy, the mission of which is to keep the church of this country stable, solvent and successful. Without the aid of such an aristocracy, many marvels of American Catholicism simply would not exist today. Yet, for a variety of reasons, its powerful presence has proved to be a mixed blessing. Unless we penetrate its ranks, we cannot possibly measure either the strengths or the weaknesses of the Catholic enterprise in America.

In a large, luxurious home at 3339 Massachusetts Avenue, in Northwest Washington, D.C., are the offices of the Apostolic Delegate to the United States. The Delegation itself is the official link between the hierarchy in this country and the Papal Secretariat of State in Rome. Like any job of liaison between a home office and an important but distant territory, the job of the Delegate is a sensitive one. In fact, when Cardinal Egidio Vagnozzi was serving as Apostolic Delegate, the late Cardinal Spellman once denounced him to Pope Pius XII as a "meddler" and a "spy for the Curia." It's easy to understand why an American prelate might be irate enough to make such charges. Among his other duties, the Apostolic Delegate must: 1) deal with the complaints of diocesan priests against their bishops; and 2) report to the Pope on the qualifications of candidates for bishoprics. Obviously, the representative of the Vatican must learn to tread lightly. Even though his head is not at stake, his ecclesiastical preferment certainly is. Conversely, however, the Apostolic Delegate to this country can always take comfort from one thought. Satisfactory performance of his delicate tasks is almost guaranteed to lead him upward, to still higher rank in the Vatican diplomatic corps and to the scarlet hat of a cardinal.

The atmosphere of the Apostolic Delegation, with its code room, its triple vault and its diplomatic pouches, makes it a good starting point for the final stage of our quest, the obligatory journey to Rome. But we should anticipate the needs of the voyage. Because the Vatican, and in particular the administrative and financial heart of the Vatican, is not to be taken by storm, some advance preparation now will serve us in good stead later.

In the 1971 edition of the *Annuario Pontificio*, the Vatican yearbook mentioned earlier, pages 1449-50 contain a description of one of the many bureaus of the Holy See. The official name of the bureau in question is the *Prefettura degli Affari Economici della Santa Sede* (literally the Prefecture for the Economic Affairs of the Holy See). Its office is just across the square from Saint Peter's itself, in a modern Roman office building. Its president is a cardinal. And in more ways than one, the formal description of its functions is very revealing. The new Prefecture is supposed to:

> 1) receive an account of the patrimony and economy of the Holy See and a statement of receipts and expenses, as well as a balance-sheet and statement of anticipated and incurred expenses presented by [each of] the administrators of the goods pertaining to the Holy See, even if [such administrators] are partially or entirely autonomous; not excluding the Commissions and Pontifical Administrations either within or outside Vatican City, but reserving the rights of the Institute for the Works of Religion.
>
> 2) examine with care the account and the valuation of the entities mentioned above, so that within a specified time the Cardinal President will be able to present a balance-sheet and statement of present and future expenses for the approval of His Holiness the Pope.

3) coordinate and control all the investments and important economic operations of the Holy See, so that each business matter will develop properly toward its own purpose.

4) examine labor projects, whether repair work or new construction, and if necessary supervise the actual work itself.

5) assess the percentages that should be turned into the General Administration of the Patrimony of the Holy See under the heading of contributions to sustain its tasks.

6) control the ledgers and the documents of justification and investigate all extraordinary expenditures: in all these matters it submits a written report to the Pope through the Cardinal President.

Let's identify some of the "entities" over which this prefecture evidently exercises some measure of financial control. For example, the papal commissions are the special groups appointed by popes to oversee such diverse matters as the revision of canon law, the progress of biblical studies and Catholic developments in Latin America. Naturally enough, each of these ecclesiastical commissions has a sizable staff and a sizable budget.

Much more significant from our economic point of view, however, is the General Administration of the Patrimony of the Holy See. This is actually the Internal Revenue Department of the Vatican. From its offices on St. Peter's Square, a mixed group of lay experts and clerical officials supervises the collections, church tax receipts, securities portfolios and other holdings of the papacy. We should also be aware that, its name to the contrary, the Institute for the Works of Religion (over which the Prefecture has *no* authority) is anything but a pious or eleemosynary organization. Rather, it's the Vatican's own private bank, founded by Pope Pius XII in 1942.

Even after we make due allowance for the turgid official prose of the *Annuario*, this extract still reads like the outline of a routine, if essential, accounting operation. In business terms, the Prefecture audits the books and assembles the financial data of the various subsidiaries of its parent organization. Like a treasurer's office, it prepares financial reports and budget analyses, and assesses future income requirements. As we sort out these undramatic functions, we're reminded that, after all, a fifteenth-century Venetian monk invented double-entry bookkeeping. Surely we shouldn't wonder that an establishment with two millennia of experience in accumulating and caring for wealth is conscious of the need for monetary planning and control.

Nevertheless, the astonishing truth is that the Prefecture for the Economic Affairs of the Holy See was established by Pope Paul VI on August 15, 1967. Until this moment in its long history, the Vatican has not only been as decentralized and economically unorganized as the rest of the church, but actually disorganized, like a business run by partners with diverging outside interests. And even now, the efforts of the Cardinal President of the Prefecture to centralize the records and accounts of the papacy are meeting sharp opposition within the Vatican. At stake are many of the present Pope's strategies for modernizing the management of the oldest corporation in the world, not to mention ultimate control over the multi-million-dollar assets of the papacy.

And so, this Prefecture is in fact an administrative battlefield. It should be—and will be—one focus of our interest when we begin to scrutinize the finances of the church in Rome. To be sure we understand the pressures behind this sedate but very serious power struggle over Vatican finance, we'll need to glance backward into the economic history of the church in Italy and elsewhere in Europe. We'll also need to plunge into the narrower realm of the Vatican itself, a jigsaw-puzzle realm that is simultaneously an Italian village and a world capital, a hive of civil servants and a great shrine. As a kind of climax to our investigations, we'll find that on the broadest scale the Pope and his circle of ministers are faced with much the same economic problems that confront the bishops and their advisers in this country. Moreover, in Rome as in Rockville Centre, the familiar answers to these problems are rapidly growing less workable. At the Vatican level as at the level of the parish, we'll see illustrated one of the central themes of this book: that, notwithstanding legends of wealth and solid realities, the Catholic Church is in dire need of economic redirection.

CHAPTER TWO

The Pastor
as Economic Innocent

The Press Club of Pittsburgh occupies the upper floors of a business edifice in the city's Golden Triangle. The club's appointments are more than comfortable, the food is excellent, the service irreproachable. I was sampling all three as the guest of a luncheon companion who is one of the most respected members of Pittsburgh's journalistic community. After lunch, this gentleman relaxed in his leather chair, flicked Dunhill pipe ashes from the lapel of his custom-fitted broadcloth suit and said to me: "Of course, I can't tell you anything about money. I don't know a damn thing about it myself." Then he cocked his head and added impishly, "Do you know something else? None of us does. Not one."

My host was a Roman Catholic priest. His official duties are important enough to have earned him the honorific title of "Monsignor." He is the pastor of a Pittsburgh parish. On his wrist is a solid gold watch. For several years, he drove not a Buick or even a Cadillac, but a Mercedes. His home has marble flooring and the walls are panelled in solid mahogany all the way up to the 15-foot ceilings. In sum, he lives like a rich man.

Much later, we'll learn that this particular priest cares little for the luxuries he enjoys. We'll satisfy ourselves that he has earned his dues, not only at the Press Club but also in a more select assembly, that of this country's front-line battlers for human rights. Here, however, our assignment is very different. In this chapter and in the ones that follow, we'll be affirming that what my priest friend says about priests and money—however unlikely the remark and odd the surroundings—is nevertheless all too true. The Catholic pastor may live well. He may behave like the bustling executive and shrewd administrator he is required to be and supposedly is. But neither his training nor his personal knowledge of money equips him for these tasks. We'll discover that, instead, the typical pastor relies on simple bookkeeping systems invented by others, on fund-raising appeals to the generosity (and sometimes the cupidity) of his parishioners, and on blind luck. So far, the systems have worked, the laity has responded and the luck has held; most parishes have more than paid their way. Despite great waste and inefficiency, thousands of parishes in this country are wealthy, and the entire church has grown wealthy along with them. But almost everywhere, the golden days of parish prosperity are drawing rapidly to a close. At the end of these chapters, we'll understand how, in the past, a Catholic parish could flourish even under ineffectual management. We must then ask whether or not the same kind of management will suffice to give the parish a future.

A brief first glance at the role of the Catholic pastor will help to define his problems. Above all else, of course, the pastor is a priest, empowered to exercise the faculties of his calling: to celebrate Mass, hear confessions, officiate at baptisms, weddings and funerals, administer the last rites to the dying, preach and teach. These are the tasks for which he was trained during eight years as a seminarian, and which he was ordained by his bishop to perform. His Latin title means shepherd. From him and through him, his parishioners expect to receive much of their spiritual nourishment.

But the pastor must do many other things as well. In addition to being the spiritual leader of his parish, he must be its temporal chieftain. In a typical parish, the pastor is certain to be: moderator of the Rosary and Altar Society, chaplain of the C.Y.O., president (or at least a board member) of the PTA, head of the Holy Name Society and so on, through a list of committees, clubs, societies and associations which even in a small parish will number in the dozens. The best comment I can make on the pastor's dizzying organizational life is to repeat the remark of a newly appointed pastor in New York City. "Don't tell anybody," he said, "but there are nights when I read *Robert's Rules of Order* instead of my breviary."

It's not surprising, then, that in a 1968 survey, pastors ranked "counselling people" first on the list of tasks which consume their time. "Directing organizations" ranked second and "financial administration" third. In last place on the list, ironically, came "liturgical functions."

For many pastors, the whirl of parish activity is only the beginning. Especially in a small or medium-sized diocese, a pastor is apt to be assigned to extra-parochial duties as well. He could thus be serving as an advocate, judge or other official on the Rota, the diocesan marriage tribunal. He might also hold a post as a diocesan consultor, or be a member of the bishop's Personnel Committee. At the same time, he could as easily be: director of the Apostleship

of Prayer; on the Bishop's Committee for Christian Home
and Family; on the Board of Diocesan Censors; a director
of the Clerical Mutual Benefit Society; a member of the
Senate of Priests; head of the Youth Council; or part of one
or two or half a dozen more of the many diocesan organizations not included in this brief roster.

In fact, a full-time pastor can even be one of the chief
administrative officers of the diocese. Take for example the
diocese of Baton Rouge (La.), in many ways a model
of sound contemporary church administration. Bishop
Robert E. Tracy's Vicar General for Financial Affairs,
Msgr. Paul J. Gauci, is also the pastor of the large parish of Sacred Heart of Jesus. "Aside from what he's done
for *us* financially," I was told by another diocesan official,
"he's put up a $250,000 rectory at Sacred Heart." In his
spare time, Msgr. Gauci likes to fly his own private
plane to Las Vegas or Los Angeles for a few days of rest.

Whether or not a pastor is given responsibilities at the
highest diocesan level, a capable man can count on plenty
of diocesan work. Then, too, almost any pastor is certain to
acquire tasks entirely apart from his more official duties.
The chances are that a pastor will, in addition to everything else, be acting as chaplain for the local fire department, or for a Catholic merchants' association. In this ecumenical era, moreover, every Catholic pastor in the land is
virtually certain of being asked regularly to serve on interfaith committees, to take part in panels and discussions and
to join ministers and rabbis in endorsing common charitable
causes. Today, even the busiest pastor thinks twice before
declining such invitations to "represent the Catholic community." But the dinners, smokers, meetings and appearances take precious time. The layman who wonders what a
pastor does with his time should spend a day or two with
an active pastor, one like the priest who muttered to me between telephone calls one morning at the rectory: "I save

souls every day between 9:15 and 9:45—unless I'm over at the school straightening something out."

His quip brings home the obvious: whatever his other duties, the pastor is always responsible for the administration of a physical plant (including, in more than half the nation's 18,000 parishes, a school and convent as well as a church and rectory) worth at least hundreds of thousands of dollars. Furthermore, he must supervise a staff which in a large parish can easily number twenty-five or thirty people. To meet these unending obligations successfully, the pastor must somehow develop and manage the resources, human and financial, of the parish community. In addition to all his other skills, in fact, he needs the skills—and something of the temperament—of the entrepreneur.

No secular corporation could possibly expect of its managers the blend of abilities or the outpouring of energy that the Catholic Church demands of its pastors. Take as evidence the envious comment of Walter H. Samples, a Catholic layman and management specialist who is administrative vice president of the American Insurance Association: "What other organization has executives on call twenty-four hours a day, seven days a week, with no family interests? What other organization pays trained managers $2,500 a year plus room and board? And wouldn't General Motors love to get a vow of obedience from every one of its employees!"

But despite the economic value of ready hearts and willing hands, it takes more than both to run a parish effectively. Before entrusting any comparable responsibility to a manager, a business organization would make very sure indeed that the man had been given the training in administration and finance he needed to do the job. If necessary, his company will send him to school to update his training. Given the complexities of parish administration, it's logical to wonder what training the church offers priests destined to become pastors. And the outsider, at least, will be startled to be told that no such formal training is ever given.

One priest who speaks with particular authority on this subject is Rev. Joseph W. Dailey. Now a pastor, he was Episcopal Vicar for Diocesan Planning in Rochester (N.Y.). Because part of Father Dailey's job was the acquisition of real estate for future diocesan use, he's comfortably knowledgeable about leasebacks, net rentals and mortgages. His expertise, however, he owes to his own efforts. As he tells the story:

"My last few weeks in the seminary, they gave us a few lessons in what we called *arithmetica sacra*, sacred arithmetic, as kind of a joke. An old retired priest came into the class and held up a fifty-dollar bill. 'Boys,' he said, 'take a good look. You won't see many of these where you're going. What you'll see is one-dollar bills. But the banks like it better if you bundle them together in fifties.' And he showed us how to put paper wrappers around the bills and how to roll up coins. That's about all I ever learned on finance as a seminarian."

Asked about formal economic training for seminarians, other senior ecclesiastical administrators shrugged aside the idea. Father Boniface L. Wittenbrink, O.M.I., is a priest who served for years as Permanent Secretary of the Conference of Major Superiors of Men's Institutes in Washington, D.C. Father Wittenbrink, whose personal notepaper is adorned with benign Snoopy cartoons, thinks that today's seminarians would reject such materialistic instruction. "They want the theology of love," he told me, "not how to balance a checkbook."

Walter W. Curtis, the energetic bishop of Bridgeport (Conn.), discounts the possibility for other reasons. "So many years pass between the time a man graduates from the seminary and the time he gets a parish that he'll have forgotten everything he was taught about money. Besides, the economy could change so much that his information would be out of date." When you realize that the newly ordained seminary graduate in the East will wait an average of thirty years before becoming a pastor—elsewhere in the U. S., bishops are beginning to appoint younger men to parishes—Bishop Curtis's reasoning makes sober executive sense.

Still, even without formal training in the seminary, the young priest presumably does have decades in which to absorb the financial and administrative techniques he'll eventually need as a pastor. During the inevitable sequence of assignments to parishes as a curate (assistant pastor), doesn't he learn from the pastors who supervise him what it means to run a parish? The answer seems to be: not very often.

In one of his wonderfully wry short stories about rectory life, "The Presence of Grace," J. F. Powers sketches the situation confronting Father Fabre, "ordained not quite a year," at Trinity. "It wasn't a well-run parish. The pastor was a hard man to interest in a problem." Powers shows us the pastor's bedroom, where

> the press of things was very great . . . statues, candlesticks, cases of sacramental wine, bales of pious literature and outdated collection envelopes, two stray pews and a prie-dieu, the implements and furniture of his calling [were intermingled].

With Father Fabre, we hear on Sunday morning

> the coin machines start up in the pastor's room, the tambourines of the separator, the castanets of the counter. The pastor was getting an early start on the day's collections. He wore a green visor in his room and worked under fluorescent tubes. Sometimes he worked a night shift. It was like a war plant, his room, except that no help was wanted.

Powers, of course, is writing fiction. Obviously, not many pastors keep the coin machines in their bedrooms, or treat the finances of the parish as if they were military secrets. On the contrary, many insist on sharing such information not only with their curates but with their parishioners as well. In hundreds of parishes, financial reports are read from the pulpit annually and published in the parish letter or newspaper. (How useful or accurate such reports really are is another story.)

Obviously, also, no assistant pastor remains completely unversed in the economics of his parish. Because he regularly celebrates Mass, the curate becomes familiar with the routines of collecting seat fees (increasingly rare) and offerings. As he visits parishioners, he's bound to learn much about the economic status of the families in the parish, givers and non-givers alike. And so on.

Nevertheless, Powers's description rings with the accent of sociological truth. While the curate won't be a complete stranger to parish money matters, he'll rarely be a full partner, either. Rather, he'll play a peripheral role in the parochial money game. The odds are high, always, that "Father"—meaning the pastor—will keep the books and control the purse strings. The reason is easy enough to understand. The system of authority in the church makes the pastor solely responsible for the financial operations of the parish. Literally as well as figuratively, it's his business. In a one-man business the boss always likes to look after money matters himself.

From what we've seen so far, the pastor brings to the managerial aspects of his job little, if any, formal training. He brings whatever management lore he has absorbed during his years of apprenticeship in the system. Also, he brings with him his own personal experience in handling money. Within what framework does the parish priest gain his experience? What does he do about money?

Members of the diocesan priesthood do not take the formal vows of poverty required of the priests in most religious orders. The fact means an enormous difference in legal and financial status. Thus, a Dominican or a Jesuit owns absolutely nothing. Legally, he possesses not even his toothbrush or the shirt on his back. Like every other item of material property he may use, these belong to his order. Nor may most priests of the religious orders acquire or keep money beyond what is needed to cover their living expenses. Outside earnings (e.g., royalties from publishers), gifts of money and inheritances must either be turned over to the order or else renounced.

By contrast, under canon law the pastor (and every diocesan clergyman right up through the Pope) is free to act privately in what the church calls the economic sphere. The diocesan priest of whatever rank can own real estate and personal property, borrow money, sell or buy, and in general behave (economically speaking) like any other citizen. He may never, of course, involve the church or church funds directly in his private dealings. But in theory at least, the diocesan priest is at liberty to do whatever he chooses with the money at his disposal.

When it comes to acquiring money, however, the diocesan priest is unlikely even to be interested, let alone expert. For one thing, his vocation is steeped in the teaching that poverty, chastity and obedience—the "evangelical counsels"—are the norms by which all priests should live. For another, the diocesan cleric knows from the start that the basic necessities of food and shelter (though not clothing) are guaranteed to him by the diocese; and that an income, however modest, will always be forthcoming. In sum, everything in the priest's background argues against an interest in accumulating money, either for its own sake or for the sake of security. Unless the life insurance agent or mutual fund salesman can convince the priest to save up for the repayment of a debt or for an eventual contribution to charity, he'll find the priest a very poor prospect.

Even priests and nuns who do take vows of poverty are occasionally surprised at how little cash a diocesan priest is allotted each year. In many dioceses, this annual salary is simply the total of the stipends parishioners give the priest for dedicating Masses to their spiritual intentions, plus the "stole fees" he receives for officiating at weddings and other sacramental occasions. The amount of the stipend is determined by the local Ordinary (the title given a bishop, archbishop or cardinal to denote his executive authority). Typically, the stipend for a scheduled Mass will be five dollars. Stole fees are set by provincial (regional) conferences of bishops. These fees vary from locale to locale, and may range between five and twenty-five dollars, depending on the service the priest renders.

In dioceses where stipends and stole fees officially support the parish priest, the pastor typically adds the money to the general collection funds of the parish. From them, he then draws the amounts he decides are adequate to cover his own cash expenses and those of his assistants. Today, this system is evidently provoking some unhappiness among curates and other junior diocesan clergymen. A 1968 opinion survey of diocesan priests below the rank of pastor shows that 85 per cent of some 3,000 respondents favored replacement of the stipend and stole-fee system by some form of regular salary arrangement. Joseph Fichter, S.J., who conducted the survey, quotes some of the juicier responses:

> An Illinois curate in his early thirties opines that "the Church that practices justice and charity should also practice just, reasonable and charitable remuneration for curates. How many pastors are there whose business acumen is limited to the counting of money they receive for the work their assistants performed?" A curate . . . who does

not get along well with his pastor says that "it seems a grave injustice that assistants have to take care of all baptisms, as well as the funerals and marriages the pastor doesn't want, and then hand over the stipends to the pastor."

"It is evident," Fichter concludes drily, "that this question is still open for much debate."

But as a matter of fact, in an increasing number of dioceses the stipend and stole-fee system is being modified, and sometimes superseded, by the introduction of salary scales. As devised by the local bishop or archbishop (who has usually sampled clerical and lay opinion on the matter), the scale indicates the approved levels of income for all priests in the diocese. Very large jurisdictions, where diocesan priests assigned to non-parish work may actually outnumber parish priests, have moved in this direction for reasons of fairness and administrative convenience. The salary scale of the Archdiocese of New York, for instance, allows pastors a base salary of $225 a month. Assistants and extra-parochial priests are entitled to $175 a month. All diocesan clergymen are permitted travel allowances of $50 a month. These basic amounts are varied for seniority: the priest with forty years of service is allotted somewhat more than the priest with thirty years; and so on.

Smaller dioceses, too, are replacing the stipend and stole-fee system of support. In 1967, Bishop Ernest J. Primeau set the salaries of pastors in his diocese of Manchester (which includes all of New Hampshire) at $350 a month. Assistants are allowed $225 a month. Here as elsewhere, the pastor is supposed to pay his own salary and those of his assistants out of the general parish revenues. Stipends and stole fees are still to be added to other collection funds, but will gradually be abolished. Priests assigned to work other than parish work are paid by the diocese directly.

In another New England diocese, the bishop has included himself in the scale at a salary of $400 a month. According to an accountant in his chancery, "His Excellency is saving most of his salary. He puts about $300 a month into a special fund of his own for charity."

To be sure, no Catholic bishop (and, as we'll see shortly, no other diocesan clergyman) must live on his salary. But the thriftiness of this particular bishop is apparently not exceptional. A sampling of parish financial reports from several dioceses suggests that priests very often draw less cash than the official salary scale allows. Where salary scales aren't used, moreover, they draw considerably less than the total of the stipends and stole fees collected. In the 153 parishes across the country I've informally surveyed for this chapter, the average amount reported to the bishop for pastors' salaries was about $2,500 for the year. Curates' salaries were lower, averaging about $1,900 a year. But in the Diocese of St. Paul-Minneapolis, the pastor of one parish drew only $1,800 himself while paying each of his assistants over $2,000. A pastor in Bishop Primeau's diocese of Manchester reported his own salary for 1967 as $1,650.

In view of amounts so modest, the whole idea of salary scales for priests might simply seem irrelevant. But in fact such scales serve several useful purposes. First of all, they mean that priests assigned to poor parishes (and many parishes are poor) can count on at least some diocesan financial support. "To expect a poor person to pay a Mass stipend is almost a sin," an inner-city curate in Pittsburgh told me. "With a salary guarantee, I can use the money of the parishioners for the needs of the parish."

Elsewhere, the salary scale eases direct dependence on a system of support which young priests in particular find distasteful. "It's degrading to live off the tips you get for saying Mass and conducting the sacraments," a young priest insisted. "The stipend may be voluntary and all that, but it's still like selling religion. Let them pay the parish and give me a salary."

Salary scales also protect those curates whose pastors find special virtue in continuous mortification of the wallet. Such hapless priests may number only a few. And yet, in a 1960 survey (this one also by Father Fichter), 22 per cent of the 2,182 diocesan priests responding reported themselves either as "always broke" or as "in debt." For nearly 1,700 respondents younger than 50 and thus likelier to be curates than pastors—the ratio was 26 per cent. Then, at least, it seems that many priests were chronically short of money. The presence of a salary scale gives a grossly underpaid curate a legal claim for relief. If his pastor won't honor the claim, the chancery office will enforce it.

Whatever portion of his salary the pastor or curate does not draw during the year remains his money, although he may leave it mingled with other parish funds in the bank. If he is transferred to another parish, or into non-parish work, he may take with him any salary money thus accumulated. Such sums are likely to be the only money that Father saves over his years of service.

To the lay outsider, the fact that parish priests can save any money at all out of their meager salaries seems like remarkable evidence of their frugality. And according to bankers and others familiar with the financial habits of priests, most do tend to be cautious about money. Take for a perfect example their use of credit cards, to millions of Americans a symbol of the urge to spend freely. James Thompson, in charge of credit-card public relations for the American Express Company, reports: "Hundreds of Catholic priests carry our card. We're not quite sure why, except that priests don't like being stranded without cash any better than you do; and I guess they have to keep financial records, too. But I've reviewed our files, and as far as we can tell without dismantling the computer, we've never yet had to chase after a priest who was a 'credit drunk.' "

Such enviable prudence aside, the ability to save money on a salary of $2,500 a year or less doesn't really mean that priests are financial miracle workers. It means something very different: that the parish priest needs only a nominal amount of cash. Except for clothing and transportation, he buys none of his essentials out of his own pocket. The expense of his food and housing is borne directly by the parish. So also, of course, are the expenses of his ministry. As for what he does buy, the cost of clothing for the priest is generally reasonable. ("But like cops and floorwalkers," a salty old pastor comments, "priests ought to buy good shoes.") His largest expenditure he makes for transportation. Many a young priest learns what little he knows about banking from the minor ordeal of financing a car.

But while the priest may be indifferent about accumulating money, and although his personal cash resources are usually minimal, only rarely does a parish priest in this country lead the life of a really poor man. On the contrary, however empty his checking account, the priest is apt to find his material cup brimful. Even if he wants to be poor, and some priests do, his search for poverty may well lead him to frustration and self-disgust in the midst of solid upper-middle-class comfort.

At the root of this seeming paradox is the peculiar status we in our money society confer on priests and other men of God. To favor the priest (and the minister and the rabbi), we cheerfully bend or break our strictest socioeconomic rules. We do so because we believe that men who devote themselves to God should receive in return at least a measure of special treatment from their fellow men. And because we naturally give what we have, we offer clergymen in general and Catholic priests in particular a life-style relentlessly prosperous and personal attentions unflinchingly deferential.

Thus, a priest dining in a restaurant is seated quickly and served with an eagerness which most of us, even if we're rich, never command. His tip may be refused, and he's told often that as a guest of the house, his check has been taken care of. If he's with lay company, Catholic or not, he almost never picks up his tab. And if he's alone, he may be invited by complete strangers to join their party.

Similarly, the priest who goes shopping can virtually count on receiving a cleric's discount of 10 per cent or more, and on red-carpet treatment as well. If he's contemplating a major purchase, a word to the right parishioner will get Father a real break on the price. Every parish of any size has its roster of loyal merchants, appliance distributors, automobile dealers and other tradesmen. If the pastor or one of his assistants wants something, these generous Catholics don't have to be asked to go easy on Father. They're delighted to have the privilege. And so, without quite knowing how, the priest finds himself driving a car just a bit grander than the model he'd decided on, but paying no more for it. Or watching his television in color rather than in black and white. Or taking his vacation in the old England, not the New.

Routinely, the priest in a well-established parish can expect to be a beneficiary of much of this good will. On a special occasion, moreover, his flock will fete him and reward him to a fare-thee-well. For instance, Rahway, New Jersey, is anything but a rich community. Its downtown areas show signs of blight, its taxes are high, its schools crowded. But when one of the priests of Rahway's largest parish (3,000 families) celebrated his twenty-fifth anniversary of service in 1968, his gifts included a new convertible, a clothing certificate, a golf cart, a set of luggage, $300 in cash and free haircutting for a year.

Not every parish will be open-handed on this scale, even on a special occasion. But still, one fact is obvious. Throughout the 18,000 Catholic parishes in the U. S., the unofficial, unrecorded inflow of donated goods and services is worth a great deal of money. Precisely because such giving is continuous and unitemized, no one knows what value it really adds to the ecclesiastical economy; and almost certainly no one can ever know.

For understandable reasons, otherwise candid priests are reluctant to talk about this particular aspect of the parish priest's relations with his parish. Sensitive Catholics, whether professional religious or members of the laity, are both embarrassed and indignant about it. This well-meant pampering of the priest, they feel, leaves the church terribly vulnerable to all those venomous old anticlerical charges of materialism and corruption. Indeed, one bishop at least has seen fit to warn his diocesan clergy against an unseemly show of prosperity. In a 1966 edict, this bishop declared bluntly:

> As priests we are invited to use carefully the money which comes into our possession for the service of the church and with proper reserve so as not to give offense or bad example to the faithful. The spiritual appreciation of our priesthood can be marred by too great a worldly display in the possession of material comforts, in frequent or expensive vacations or in the failure to exercise a generous spirit of charity in assisting those in the parish who may be in need.

In Tulsa-Oklahoma City, a young priest summed up his feelings about being cosseted by the laity with the comment: "I feel like a sacred cow. As long as I give holy milk, I can wander through the bazaar and snatch what I want. No one will rap me on the snout. You've got to realize that a priest is offered all sorts of special things, and it's terribly hard to refuse."

But despite the color TV sets, the Buicks and the golf carts, a dispassionate observer might well find the issue of priestly corruption a stale one. It's hard to believe, first of all, that the Catholic auto dealer who shaves 10 per cent off the price of Father's car really expects anything in return. If you suggested to him that by so doing he's committing an act of simony (the purchase of a spiritual benefit for a material price, strictly forbidden by canon law), he'd be either mystified or irate. If you asked him whether he might not be contributing to the corruption of Father, he'd probably heave you out of his office. He might also tell you that he offers the same discount to every clergyman, of whatever faith, who walks into his showroom.

Secondly, among its 37,000 members the diocesan clergy in this country undoubtedly numbers those more preoccupied than they should be with "the possession of material comforts." We'll encounter a few of them in the pages of this book. But at the opposite end of the scale, some parish priests are genuine ascetics who reject material comforts. And today especially, evidence is growing that thousands of Catholic priests are uneasy, not complacent, about the status and security they automatically assume when they don the cloth. If some priests still make it too easy for parishioners to be good to them, others are studying ways of disentangling themselves from such generosity.

Then, too, a key fact of priestly life, mobility, makes general pronouncements about the "corruption" of the priesthood sound more than a little naïve. Like other great corporations, the church moves its servants wherever senior management deems necessary; such mobility is apt insurance against cozy stagnation in the ranks. At the behest of his bishop, the priest living pleasantly in a prosperous suburb today may be moving tomorrow into the crumbling grandeur of a rectory in the city slums, or into a rural parish so poor that the priest must subsidize his flock, not vice versa. Like a corporate executive, the diocesan priest may spend years being switched laterally from assignment to assignment. Again like the executive, the priest will find his standard of living a flexible matter. But while the living standard of the executive will almost certainly rise steadily during his career, that of the priest is subject to no such guarantee. On the contrary, it may fluctuate sharply over the years. Even if we could assume that worldly comfort really matters to most priests, the unpredictable shifts in station which are part of the calling make it harder than it looks for any priest to settle snugly into a soft corner of the diocese.

Nevertheless, the gift-giving and the good-hearted financial support traditionally available to the priest do raise a problem. Like so much else in his background, this support insulates the priest against the daily realities and commonplace pressures of economic life. As testimony to this point, take the evocative comment of the Rev. George G. Hagmaier, C.S.P. Father Hagmaier is a Paulist priest with years of experience in the parishes run by the religious order to which he belongs.* An educational psychologist by training, Father Hagmaier was recently in charge of revising the curriculum of the Paulist seminary in New York. "The problem," says Father Hagmaier, "is that a priest never really learns the value of a dollar. On Wednesday night [by tradition, the rectory housekeeper's night off], the priest who does the shopping for dinner never gets farther than the gourmet counter. He hasn't any idea of what food costs, and what's true for food is true for everything else."

If Father Hagmaier is right—and he's vehement on this

---

* Many of the major religious orders operate parishes within a diocese; often these date back to the days when regular priests accompanied immigrants to this country and built churches where they could worship according to their native customs. Such parishes are in general subject to the rule of the local bishop.

subject—then the parish priest, far from being corrupt, is in truth an economic innocent. Or, to draw a comparison at once startling and obvious, the priest as an economic man resembles no one else in our society as closely as he does the adolescent. Thus, like a teen-ager, the priest is a participant, but never a full participant, in the economy. What money the priest has he can spend as he pleases; but, as we've seen, his discretionary income is small, more like an allowance than like the salary of an adult. True, unlike many adolescents, the priest will usually behave responsibly about money. But his opportunities for displaying fiscal skill are limited, and his economic horizons circumscribed. Indeed, in strictly financial terms, the one major difference between the diocesan priest and the American youngster in high school or college is that the latter will some day join the real economy, while the former never will.

CHAPTER THREE

Budgeting, Building and Bingo: The Parish Economy

On the basis of his background and training, a priest might well be the last man a management expert would place in charge of the economy of a parish. One such expert, Thomas O. Jones, made this point unmistakably clear to me. Jones is a systems analyst who has worked on money matters for his own pastors in various parishes and for the Archdiocese of New York. When I asked him about the problems raised by the lack of skill at the parish level, he answered with utter sincerity, "It's a good thing the priests have got God on their side."

Nevertheless, parishes do function. And pastors do manage them, because they must. How can men who are professionally untrained in finance and personally naïve about money possibly perform as financial executives?

Part of the answer is simply that, like an untrained welder or a beginning secretary, a new pastor can be given a set of systems by which to operate. If the pastor follows the systems faithfully, he's assured, then money will pose few problems and hold no mysteries. The systems, he'll find, are slow and laborious. But they work. And they can save him—most of the time—from the consequences of his own ignorance.

In actual truth, the pastor can deal with money almost by rote. For accounting and record-keeping, he uses the forms and manuals issued to him by the chancery, the administrative office of his diocese. For handling contributions, he makes use of an "envelope system" which he buys from an outside supplier. For special fund-raising efforts, he can obtain materials of all kinds from the dealers who design and produce Catholic charitable promotional campaigns.

In parish finance, there are systems for everything.

The fact itself explains how untrained but trustworthy —and trusting—men can safely be given control of million-dollar physical plants, five-figure bank accounts and complicated financial transactions. The omnipresence of systems also explains how a pastor can train himself as an administrator. For us, the details of some of these systems make good reading. From them, we can learn as much as we need to know about the economics of the parish. And the seemingly prosaic details will serve as an introduction to the pastor's actual behavior as the man in charge of bringing in money and of spending it.

Perhaps the best way to look into the heart of parish financial administration is to begin with the financial report which every pastor is required by canon law to submit to his bishop each year. The exact format of the report varies from diocese to diocese—uniformity of record-keeping is not a feature of upper-level Catholic Church administration

—but its contents are more or less standardized everywhere. On a printed form supplied by the local chancery office, the pastor is typically obliged to give: 1) a balance sheet showing parish assets and liabilities; 2) a statement of cash receipts and disbursements; 3) an appraisal of the value of all church property in the parish; and 4) explanations of any extraordinary transactions.

As prosaic as such documents are, they are nonetheless revealing. From them, we can educate ourselves in the basic truths of the economy of the church.

The Diocese of Bridgeport is representative enough to have served as model in many surveys and studies of church operations. On the income side of its official parish financial report, this diocese makes room for information about no fewer than twenty-three separate categories of income. These are divided into three classifications. The first, "Income from Ordinary Collections," includes seat fees, cash and envelope collections during Masses, special sums given during devotions, monthly or yearly envelope gifts, stole fees and miscellaneous gifts. (This last category includes such holdovers from earlier, poorer days as gifts of fuel for the church or rectory and the value of personal labor given during construction of the physical plant.)

The second classification, "Income Other Than Ordinary Collections," covers money donated by parish societies, the proceeds of cake sales, bazaars and other entertainment, poor-box donations, income from the sale of votive candles and money received for subscriptions to the *Catholic Transcript*, the diocesan newspaper. In this same classification the pastor is also to list any income from dividends or interest or from the rental of parish property. The receipts in these first two classifications are then added together and the diocesan tax (or *cathedraticum*) of 5 per cent of the total is computed.

The third classification, "Exchange Receipts," is reserved for money collected within the parish but destined either for the diocese (e.g., an assessment for diocesan high schools, a collection for the Bishop's Relief Fund) or for remoter sectors of the church economy. Here the pastor records the special sums collected for the Latin American church, for missions, for the Holy Land and for Rome (i.e., Peter's Pence).

A separate classification, "Transfers from Savings," includes not only money withdrawn from parish funds for current use but also any money borrowed by the parish during the year.

On the disbursements side of the report are listed in detail the cash expenditures for the year. These are classified under the headings of the various components of the physical plant. Thus, all priests' salaries and those of the sexton and the organist are listed as church expenses. So also are other "ordinary expenses" (outlays for vestments, sacramental wine, music books and so on) and "extraordinary expenses" (repairs, improvements and furnishings).*

Rectory expenses include food and the salaries of the housekeeper and other domestics as well as ordinary and extraordinary outlays for maintenance. School and convent expenses include salaries for religious and lay teachers and all operating expenditures. The "Exchange Receipts" mentioned above are balanced by "Exchange Expenditures," as the pastor turns over to the appropriate authorities the special collections received. Insurance costs and interest payments are duly recorded along with payroll and property

---

* This is a good time to point out that the distinction between ordinary and extraordinary expenditures, generally cut-and-dried at the parish level, is vastly more important in the upper reaches of the church. Under canon law, a priest in authority (whether he's a pastor, a bishop, a college rector or the local head of a religious order) can authorize only ordinary transactions. Extraordinary transactions must be referred upward: if necessary, to Rome. In later chapters on the diocese and on religious orders, we'll deal with the ramifications of this canonical requirement.

taxes—if any—and the *cathedraticum*. The cost to the parish of newspaper subscriptions and the miscellaneous expenditures are also listed.

At the very bottom of this page of the Bridgeport form is space for the "Total Disbursements" figure. Then comes the forthright entry, "Payments Applied to Debt." The pastor is asked for the details of parish debt repayments during the year, for the amounts of any surplus funds transferred to savings and for his cash balance at the end of the year.

The statement of assets and liabilities likewise follows a routine accounting pattern. First are listed the current assets of the parish (cash on hand and in banks, notes or other debts receivable, securities), followed by the fixed assets (land, buildings, furnishings and equipment). Any other assets are described and their value given, and a total asset value is reached. The pastor then adds up the parish liabilities, including his current bills payable and the loan and mortgage debt of the parish. If the assets add up to more than the liabilities, the difference is the current net worth of the parish.

Elsewhere on the Bridgeport form, the pastor is asked to list any property on the premises which does not belong to the parish corporation. If he's borrowing a special set of Mass vestments or renting a typewriter the insurance company will want to know. He must also supply information about safe deposit boxes in which church records, "securities, bank pass books or other valuables" are kept.

Like the Bridgeport form, the parish financial reports of other dioceses reflect the varying local concerns, and the varying degrees of expertise, of bishops and their chancery aides. Some, indeed, are much more detailed and "professional" than others. The report of the Diocese of Baton Rouge, for example, asks for all salaries by employment class (clergy, lay and religious teachers, clerical workers, janitors, etc.) and for breakdowns of such general expense categories as insurance premiums and outlay for altar supplies. Baton Rouge pastors must also submit monthly income-and-expense reports which incorporate running year-to-date figures. Even in large dioceses, such explicit reporting is the exception rather than the rule. But the accounting-minded Archdiocese of New York requires not only annual and monthly financial reports, but minutely detailed monthly analyses of all parish receipts and expenditures. In addition, New York pastors must file separate reports on school finances. This job is made no easier by the fact that the school accounting year runs from September 1 to August 31, while that of the parish coincides with the calendar year. To assist its pastors with their record-keeping, the Archdiocese distributes neatly printed procedures manuals which spell out the rules and systems with care.

Predictably, the clarity of forms also varies from diocese to diocese. Of the dozen or so I've seen, one or two are well designed and easy to follow, and most are passable. But a couple (and not necessarily the most detailed) are positively Gothic in their complexity. These make the Treasury's tax form 1040 seem like a masterpiece of clarity by comparison.

On the surface, all of these forms are matter-of-fact and businesslike. Certainly no businessman would quarrel either with the kind of information requested or, in general, with the form in which the information is supplied. Given the necessary financial records, an accountant could easily draw up a similar report in a few days for a modest-sized commercial client. The records themselves should consist of one or more journals (account books in which transactions are recorded in daily sequence) and the ledger or ledgers (the books in which all transactions are summarized and organized under specific headings, or accounts).

As we've seen, pastors aren't trained to be CPA's. Nevertheless, the new pastor soon learns that sharp pencils and a head for figures are vital equipment for his calling.

With the accounting system set by the diocese, in almost every parish the pastor simply inherits the books of his predecessor. At some stage, he'll probably ask an accountant who is also a parishioner to "spend an evening going over the books" with him. (Catholic accountants tell horror stories about what they uncover during such informal audits.) Week in and week out, however, Father himself is the one who painstakingly records—by hand—every scrap of the continuing financial history of the parish. Thus, every week he must enter against the name of each member of the parish the amount of his contribution at Mass via envelope. (He must of course check first to make sure the sums inside the envelopes match the amounts indicated on the outside.)

Another regular task of the pastor is that of accounting for each of the special collections; and of receiving and entering on the books the amounts contributed by parish societies and other groups. Part of the job, too, is writing all of the checks for parish expenditures, getting the deposits to the bank every week and balancing the checkbook every month. Over the course of the year, these and dozens of other fiscal routines add up to a staggering amount of old-fashioned bookkeeping. This the pastor must handle well enough so that, at year-end, he can promote himself to the rank of accountant for the ritual of checking his books and drawing up his financial report.

No wonder the advertising pages of diocesan directories, priests' periodicals and other professional Catholic literature are stuffed with exhortations to buy money-handling machinery and record-keeping systems. For instance: "Brandt (coin sorters) will do just about anything with mixed coins but take the collection . . . they'll even crimp the wrappers if you like." The same ad in the 1971 *Official Catholic Directory* assures Father that "thousands of Catholic churches are handling their collections with Brandt machines." Perhaps so; but thousands more are still counting their collections by hand. (This job is usually done either by a committee of ladies from the parish or by the sisters from the school, supervised by Father. The coffee and cake served afterward is duly charged against "Collection Expenses" or "Food: Rectory" in the journal.) Furthermore, despite all the marvelous collection and record systems on the ecclesiastical market (e.g., "RECORD-O-LOPES . . . self-recording Church envelopes which eliminate *weekly posting* of your offering!"), pastors everywhere still burn the midnight oil over the ledgers of the parish.

No wonder, too, that parish priests rank financial administration near the head of the list of all their labors.

In the parish as in any economic enterprise, keeping the records and adding up the results are obviously crucial functions. But the bookkeeping is only part of the pastor's total entrepreneurial task. Behind the reports, and the journals and ledgers as well, we can discern the pastor in an even more basic double role: a) as the key figure in raising the money for his operations; and b) as the executive who determines how the money is to be spent.

As a fund-raiser, the Catholic pastor owes much to the anonymous genius who invented the envelope system of soliciting money from the laity of the parish. The simple technique of asking parishioners to put their contributions into predated envelopes eases enormously the physical task of gathering money in a crowded church. For the donor, the envelope system means that his gift, at the time he gives it, is private and anonymous. During his worship, he neither shames nor is shamed by the charity of his fellow worshipers. If the pastor later publishes the list of contributors in the order of their generosity—a tactic practiced almost everywhere—the stingy of the parish may have cause to wriggle uncomfortably. But (so the theory goes) they'll also have the opportunity and the incentive to remedy their lapses from liberality.

The mechanics of the parochial envelope system are straightforward enough, although the individual pastor may develop refinements to suit his own special needs (or else succumb to the sales pitch of a favored envelope-system salesman). Once a year, every adult parishioner receives in the mail a packaged set of envelopes, each one dated for the Sundays and special days of the year ahead. The envelopes are imprinted with the name of the church, with whatever art-work the pastor deems appropriate and with a brief message to stimulate giving. Space is left for the donor to write in his name and to note or check off the amount of his contribution. The standard envelope sets used most widely also contain extra envelopes for Christmas, Easter, the Feast of the Ascension, All Souls' Day and other holy days, inserted at no extra charge. Because many churches take special as well as regular collections on almost every Sunday, most envelope-makers offer duplex envelopes. These are partitioned so that the parishioner can keep separate his offertory gift and the amount of his special contribution.

In addition to the envelopes for Sunday and holy day giving, many parishes also mail to parishioners special envelope sets for regular *monthly* contributions. All envelopes are stamped with the number assigned to the individual; these accounts are kept by number. (Only the pastor, therefore, can identify the contributor and know the amount he has given.) Every quarter, the pastor mails back to contributors statements indicating, for tax purposes, the total contributions made. In some parishes, envelopes are distributed to those children who have made their First

Communion, and their pennies, nickels and dimes dedicated to the Holy Childhood Association or some other appropriate charity. Special envelope systems have also been developed for teen-agers and for Catholic college students.

The envelope system, used universally in American Catholic parishes—and widely used in Protestant churches as well—stimulates regular, repeated giving. This in turn makes the pastor's efforts at financial planning less of an ordeal. Because most of the ordinary income of the parish is derived from envelope contributions, the pastor can safely assume a certain level of cash flow. He can then budget his fixed expenses over the entire year. And because so much financial support is systematized, the pastor can devote his personal fund-raising efforts to special projects and substantial contributors.

Its undoubted efficiency notwithstanding, the envelope system does have its flaws. Some parishioners do resent the sense of regimentation and the impersonality of this method of giving to their church. Instead of using the envelopes they receive, they drop cash into the collection plate. Or they don't contribute at all. Naturally enough, too, many Catholics are irked by the publication or posting of the contribution lists. Like many Americans, they feel that philanthropy, and especially religious philanthropy, is a private matter.

From the pastor's point of view, the advantages of the envelope system far outweigh such disadvantages. A response of 90 per cent or better to the parish envelope program—not at all unusual in Catholic parishes today—is proof enough that American Catholics are at ease with this method of financing their church. Then, too, without conscious consideration, the pastor knows that the envelope system spares him the toil of making personal solicitations. Like his parishioners, Father prefers indirect rather than overt appeals for money: he'd certainly rather be an administrator than a salesman for his religion. One pastor's remark sums it all up: "Let the Poor Clares [a mendicant order] do the begging for money. It's not my job."

But while few pastors would see the drawbacks as serious ones, the envelope system does pose problems for them as well as for a minority of their parishioners. One such problem is cost. True, in proportion to the financial return, the direct cost of distributing envelopes within a parish is relatively low. Standard sets of boxed weekly offering envelopes can be purchased for as little as 35 cents a set, a price which includes suitable imprinting ("My Weekly Sacrifice"; "This is my best for my God and my Church"). Even including postage, it costs only 60 or 65 cents for the pastor to solicit a year's worth of weekly contributions. Similarly, envelopes for "monthly mailing plans" sell for less than two cents apiece (one firm specializing in parish collection envelopes quoted me the price of $13 per thousand). Again, distributing the envelopes costs very little. And in a reasonably prosperous parish of, say, 1,000 families, envelope contributions are very likely to total $75,000 to $100,000 a year, in return for total direct expenses of about $1,500.

Indirect expenses, however, do boost these collection costs. Thus, what pastors are apt to call "successful envelope operations" presuppose a good deal of preliminary labor. To avoid wasting money by sending envelope packages to wrong addresses, the pastor must be sure that his parish address lists are up to date. Similarly, to be certain that his solicitations are reaching every Catholic in the parish, not just those who attend mass regularly, the pastor must be something of a population researcher. He is canonically required, in fact, to submit to the chancery office each year a so-called "spiritual report" embodying the results of an annual census of the parish. The census itself is usually taken by the pastor's assistants, aided by the school sisters or by lay helpers. The report lists such statistics as the total number of Catholics in the parish, the number of Catholic families, of children from infants to teen-agers, and so on. From the parish registers, the pastor adds to the report the total numbers of baptisms, marriages (including mixed marriages) and deaths during the year. He also includes information on those who convert to Catholicism and on vocations.

Thus, once a year, every pastor presumably knows exactly what he needs to know about the size and scope of his audience for fund-raising solicitations. But finding out—especially in a large parish—costs time and effort; and this indirect cost increases the cost of envelope mailings and other appeals for money. Furthermore, American Catholics, we can assume, are as mobile as all other Americans. An annual census, even if accurate, won't account either for newcomers or for those who leave during the course of a year. So apart from the added indirect cost of developing information about his market, the pastor pays a penalty for his inability to reach some of his potential contributors. Professional Catholic fund-raisers know, as pastors do not, how many prospective givers are not reached by the envelope system. In suburban areas, where mobility is high, the professionals (who refuse to be quoted directly) estimate that a pastor can miss 15 to 20 per cent of those who might give money to the church.

Still another drawback to the envelope system is the amount of time and labor required to send out the weekly and monthly envelopes, process the returns and handle the record-keeping. Here again, the real costs are indirect ones. Those pastors who can enlist volunteers to help with the clerical (but not the fiscal) aspects of the job won't even consider such indirect expenses. But volunteers aren't always easy to get and pastors themselves are short of time.

In a growing number of parishes, the pastor wants to rid himself of at least some of his clerical workload. As a result, many of the firms which supply religious envelopes are offering mailing services as well. All Father has to do is mail his list of monthly envelope contributors to the supplier. (Because the weekly offering envelopes are mailed in sets only once a year, the pastor still sends these out himself.) For a price, the envelope company prints the monthly envelopes, addresses them to the individual parishioners and drops them in the mail. The price is not cheap, but it's not prohibitive, either. The same company that quoted a price of $13 per thousand for envelopes alone charges another $26 per thousand for addressing and mailing them. The postage is extra, of course, and to save money on postage most of the envelope firms mail out three months' worth of envelopes at a time to parishioners.

In a big parish, one with, say, 4,000 adult members, perhaps half of the parishioners will be monthly givers. If the pastor uses an outside supplier to handle the mechanics of addressing and mailing, he'll pay about $1,150 a year for his monthly solicitation program. By using parish volunteers to do the same clerical work, he saves about $200 in cash per year, but gives up much more of his time.

On the basis of a similar but more detailed cost analysis, the Diocese of Baton Rouge has instructed all of its pastors to use the mailing services of one outside envelope supplier. On the diocesan-wide scale, it has paid to computerize the listing, addressing and envelope-mailing operation. In dollar terms, the ensuing quantity discounts have actually reduced costs to below what the pastors were paying individually. Furthermore, the availability of accurate lists and rapid, efficient mailing facilities has enabled—and encouraged— the chancery office of Baton Rouge to contact the diocesan laity more often. (For example, to expand the readership of the diocesan newspaper, to send out a school bulletin, to increase the response to the Bishop's Fund Drive, to release an official diocesan financial report).

Having glanced at some of the deficiencies of the parochial envelope system, we do well to remember that, according to the available figures, this method of raising money brings in close to $1.6 billion a year for the Catholic Church in America. Clearly, it's hard to quarrel with fundraising success on this scale. And yet, like much else we've seen in this chapter, the way the envelope system is operated almost everywhere does raise basic questions about the logic of money management in today's church. To ask just one obvious question here: why must the pastor, already more of a manager than his training entitles him to be, preoccupy himself with managing the details of this routine? Once again, the answer will figure in our final reckoning of the quality of parish financial management.

Part of the answer, surely, lies in the conviction of most pastors that if they don't keep close watch on the money machinery, the system will falter and the income of the parish dwindle. Thus, in words echoed in thousands of parishes throughout the land, the Most Reverend James P. Shannon, until 1969 an auxiliary bishop as well as a pastor in the Diocese of St. Paul-Minneapolis but now no longer a priest, wrote to his parishioners:

> On two Sundays in the pulpit and in two letters sent to all parishioners I have confided my concern about the fact that the regular month to month expenses of our parish are larger than the regular income of the parish at this time.
> It is imperative that we raise the amount of the regular Sunday collection. I have previously proposed that each parishioner contribute . . . 50¢ for each $1,000 of his annual salary . . . If each member of the parish would begin by increasing his Sunday contribution only by $1.00

each week, our income would at least begin to rise to meet
rising costs . . .

Bishop Shannon's former parish (St. Helena's, in Minneap-
olis) is by no means impoverished. According to the financial statement which accompanied this plea for funds, the
physical plant of the parish was worth $503,890 in 1967,
while cash and other current parish assets totaled $85,041.30.
But even though ordinary income for the year came to
more than $150,000, the pastor had had to withdraw
$103,000 from the parish savings account to cover the
cost of renovating the school.

In brief, the envelope system, and other ordinary
money-raising techniques as well, failed to bring in enough
money.

Faced with similar situations, most pastors are reluctant
to "talk money from the pulpit." Instead, they turn to
other methods of fund-raising. In a sense, Bishop Shannon's
letter testifies to his forthright professionalism in money
matters. By comparison, the methods some Catholic pastors
employ in the search for money are as amateurish as they
are disconcerting.

Many readers will be able to produce their own examples of the strange or the unorthodox in Catholic fund-
raising. One of my favorites is found far outside the borders of this country, in the Church of San Francesco in
Arezzo, Italy. On the walls of its dimly lighted choir, the
great fifteenth-century painter Piero della Francesca created the famous cycle of fresco works, *The Story of the
True Cross*. In most of the smaller European churches
which house masterpieces of art, an aged caretaker will
lead the tourist to the work and, for a few coins, run
through his lecture. In San Francesco, however, things operate differently. There, the frescos are hardly visible at all
in the gloom until the visitor locates a coin-box and drops

his 100-lire piece in the slot. This switches on the electric lights, which illuminate the walls of the choir for perhaps forty seconds. Then the lights blink out until the next 100-lire donation is made. I was told at the church that the money thus accumulated pays the light bills, helps provide for the upkeep of the frescos and yields "a couple of million lire" (about $3,000) a year for the parish besides.

In this country, a pastor is hardly likely to possess such built-in economic resources in his church. Only a few American churches attract much revenue from tourism. And even in these few, the money is apt to be spent on maintenance, with little left over. For example, Cardinal Terence J. Cooke, Archbishop of New York, estimates that Saint Patrick's Cathedral takes in $2,300 a day, but costs $2,100 a day to operate.

It's therefore startling to come across a story like the following, reported by the Religious News Service (September 16, 1968):

CATHOLIC PARISH'S 210-FOOT TOWER
BUILT TO FINANCE MISSION SHRINE

Sault Ste. Marie, Mich.—A 210-foot tower overlooking the locks on St. Mary's River between Lake Superior and Lake Huron was opened here as part of a projected "Shrine of the Missionaries."

The $670,000 structure was built by St. Mary's Church —said to be the third-oldest Roman Catholic parish in the U. S.—which hopes to attract enough visitors to it to finance an adjoining church building.

The report describes the tower:

a three-legged structure with three different observation levels . . . Eventually it is hoped to place a 61-bell carillon at the 110-foot level between the two front legs . . .
When they descend into the crypt, visitors will enter a museum and make a "Mission of Man" tour that will show the "life of Christ in the early missionaries" of the

area. Planners hope to make it "an experience of sights, sounds, color, narrative, graphics, sculpture and other evocative elements."

The tower, presumably, will be only part of a larger complex of architectural restorations and similar tourist attractions. According to the news service report, "Father Robert Monroe, pastor of St. Mary's, was concerned about the decline of his community and conceived of the tower as a project to help resuscitate the city and simultaneously give it an imposing religious center." The project was "encouraged" by Bishop Thomas L. Noa of the Diocese of Marquette (Mich.).

Father Monroe, obviously, is one pastor who thinks big. In scope, his project is remote indeed from the usual schemes devised by pastors seeking extra dollars for their parishes. The idea of erecting a $670,000 structure primarily to generate funds for additional church-building is a succeed-or-bust stroke of the imagination. Whether or not Father Monroe's tower succeeds financially—and leaving aside questions of taste—we must pay due homage to his sense of enterprise. One question, of course, does stick in the mind. If Father Monroe could raise $670,000 for this tower, why didn't he simply use the money for the mission shrine he wanted to build in the first place? The Religious News Service report contains no clue to the answer. But when pastors conceive grand plans, such questions are rarely asked at all. (The dry comment of one Catholic real estate man in New York, when I mentioned the Sault Ste. Marie tower, was: "That's an idea almost worthy of a bishop.")

Most pastors, of course, think smaller than Father Monroe does about the ways and means of raising extra dollars for the parish. Nor are their strategies, whether ambitious or modest, notable for originality. Thus, if a pastor feels that plant improvement is of pressing importance, he'll very likely do within his parish just what a bishop does at the diocesan level: organize a building fund.

In earlier days, this simply meant: 1) obtaining the permission of the bishop; 2) working out the plans and costs with architects and a trusted local contractor, invariably a Catholic; and 3) raising as much cash as possible from parishioners for the down payment. To do the last, Father might first make a formal announcement from the pulpit. He'd then pay a series of personal visits to key parishioners and announce what they were to contribute to the fund. These parishioners would be ordered to pass the word to their friends and relatives. This delegation of authority enabled the pastor to save his real persuasiveness for those "reluctant to make the full sacrifice." More important, he could concentrate on the relatively few men of means who might make substantial contributions. Once the maximum possible amount of cash had been raised, or at least pledged, the pastor could go to the local bank for the mortgage which would cover the balance of his construction costs.

While this Father-is-the-boss approach is still practiced in many parishes, times are changing and the laity is less docile. If today's pastor has a large-scale project in mind, he can first of all expect to have his request for this extraordinary expenditure given very close scrutiny by the bishop. (Indeed, as we'll see later, several diocesan administrations have declared moratoria on all new parish construction.) The architects and contractors—still almost always Catholic—are likely to be selected by the chancery, not by the pastor. Mortgage financing, too, will be arranged by the diocese. The pastor who wants smooth sailing for his project, moreover, will do well to bring in on the planning not only his bishop but at least a few of his parishioners as well. Generations of painful experience are teaching Catholics that the cost of bricks and mortar doesn't end with the down payment. Like American churchgoers of all denominations, they want to be consulted before the foundations are dug. "We have to sell them on the need, not just tell them we've decided to build," is one pastor's definition of the new style in raising funds for construction. "They don't want to be forty years paying off Father Dolan's Folly."

For most of us, the economics (and the politics) of fund-raising for an ambitious Catholic parish project will hold few mysteries. When the goal is $50,000 for a new wing on the school, the pastor's techniques differ hardly at all from those used by ministers, by rabbis or by local solicitors for such secular charities as the Red Cross and the Community Chest. The money thermometer posted in the lobby of the church, the mimeographed progress report, the appeal to status-consciousness as well as to charitable feeling—these are American, not Roman, in orientation. And if Father isn't what the paid fund-raisers call "a real pro," his amateurishness is often enough endearing, and effective as well. Of course, this effectiveness can't always be measured, for the pastor need never confess failure. According to a Catholic layman who has lived through many parish fund drives, "If we get a good start but we don't raise every dollar we set out to raise, we go ahead anyway. The down payment's a little lower and the debt's a little higher." In money terms, the parish will have to use future income to make up for the inital capital Father couldn't raise.

But especially in the urban parishes, the pastor's great days of building are over. Increasingly, instead of enlarging the holdings of the parish, he faces a less spectacular but more difficult challenge. He must somehow stretch parish income to cover the costs of all the services—religious, educational and social—which he feels his church must provide.

In one form or another, the problems raised by an insufficient income can overtake a pastor a dozen times a day.

What is he to do about new uniforms for the parish basketball team? About new desks for the sixth-grade classroom? Or about the ancient grumbling boiler in the rectory? Finding answers to such questions as these is the real art of financial administration. True, the pastor can turn over to others some of the less significant money-raising jobs. Thus, the parish Athletic Committee can be asked to provide new basketball uniforms. (To raise enough money, the committee will probably throw a smoker, with sports movies and a professional basketball star as guest speaker.) But new desks and the elderly boiler pose fiscal demands of a different sort. No committee wants to burden itself with raising money for needs so undramatic. Still, the money must be found. When ordinary parish income covers only part of the cost of running the parish, how does the pastor bridge the gap?

Naturally enough, the answer varies from parish to parish, from diocese to diocese and from region to region across the country. In smaller cities and towns and in rural areas, cake sales, bazaars and rummage sales are still the standbys of parishes caught short of operating funds. Some parishes, indeed, develop specialties of their own in the hunt for income. In his book, *Should Churches Be Taxed?*, D. B. Robertson cites a *New York Times* story (September 13, 1967) headlined: "Illinois Church Thrives on Turtle Soup Picnics." Robertson states that in the small town of Meppen, Illinois, St. Joseph's Catholic Church "builds its budget around the sale of snapping-turtle soup at an annual picnic. Members of the church (300 parishioners) prepare, cook and sell the soup, and the income has reached the figure of about $12,500 per year." In an America where quilting bees and husking contests are part of the heartland tradition, a snapping-turtle soup sale is as homey a Catholic fund-raising device as anyone could ask for.

But in a city or suburban parish, where the annual

budget might total several hundred thousand dollars, not even the tastiest turtle soup would sell well enough to balance the books. Hence, pastors have learned to rely on another tradition to help keep their parishes in the black. Particularly in the great urban dioceses of the Northeast— Boston, New York, Newark, Philadelphia—parishes have long supplemented the free-will offerings of the faithful with the revenues gained from one or another form of or- ganized gambling. So important is this extra income that a high chancery official in New York is willing to say, "If they ever outlaw [games of chance] in this archdiocese, we're dead." True, we're not meant to take his remark too literally. As we'll learn, the financial resources of the Arch- diocese of New York (and of the other major Catholic di- oceses) are proof against almost any contingency. Still, in certain areas, the wheel of fortune is an important cogwheel in the economic mechanism of the church.

Sociologically speaking, indeed, we take this fact for granted. As proof, consider an advertisement for Volkswa- gens which appeared in *Sports Illustrated* on May 26, 1969. The ad featured a photograph of a Volkswagen fastback, topped by a sign reading, "St. Mary's Bazaar. Take A Chance on a Luxurious Car! Only 25¢." Seated at a card table by the curb, a nice lady had her books of tickets ready at hand. The advertisement's message led off: "Dear Reverend, Father or Rabbi . . ." and the entire ad was a tongue-in-cheek suggestion that Volkswagens, not "Cadil- lacs, T-Birds and Continentals" are the best cars to raffle off for the church or the synagogue. The real message, of course, is aimed not at ministers, priests and rabbis but rather at us consumers. Apart from its selling purpose, however, the ad confirms that the casual wager for charity is as commonplace and acceptable as apple pie.

To almost every reader, the actual mechanics of charity gambling will similarly be as familiar as the tiny ritual of swapping a quarter for a raffle chance or a dollar for a ticket to the Firemen's Ball. Without being told, we're aware that behind every lottery or raffle or "Monte Carlo Night" there stands a committee, a sponsoring organization and a worthy cause. That local merchants have been cajoled into contributing prizes, or at least into accepting payment at wholesale rates after the ticket-selling has run its course. That as many members of the organization as possible have been drafted—under the jealous eye of a financial watchdog—to paper the neighborhood with chances. And that the lucky winner may or may not need the new car, the dishwasher or the trip for two. We know also that gambling for charity flourishes as widely among Protestants and Jews as it does among Catholics; and that secular as well as religious causes are its beneficiaries.

Precisely because such wagering is so much a part of our society, its total economic value is truly an unknown quantity. To sort out the Catholic component, moreover, is next to impossible. As in the case of the financial extras available to parish priests, the sums raised by all the car raffles and other wagering schemes sponsored by Catholic organizations can't be added up. While the net proceeds may be entered as extraordinary income in the parish ledgers, the details (the gross receipts, the administrative expenses, the cost of prizes and often the net proceeds as well) lie buried in the records of thousands of individual parishes.

In passing, we should note that if a local bishop cares to do so, he can determine how much money this homegrown gambling does raise for the parishes of his diocese. He simply analyzes the receipts recorded in the annual parish reports. But bishops are prudent men. Because this subject is a delicate one, the bishop may prefer not to know too exactly which of his parishes is raffling what. If the pastor must make use of informal gaming to keep his parish solvent, his bishop will understand. Still, for reasons which in a given diocese may be political, administrative, theological or a practical blend of all three, Catholic bishops generally steer clear of direct involvement with the gambling conducted by parish groups.

The one exception is the humble game of bingo.

This book is no place in which to cover the sociology of bingo, or to treat in detail its legal and moral status. But its background is interesting enough to warrant at least a quick look before we move on to assess its importance as a Catholic fund-raising medium. About the game itself, there's nothing very mysterious. Bingo is said to be a direct descendant of keno, which in turn was derived from lotto, a children's game played in England apparently as early as the seventeenth century. Keno, journalist Clyde Brion Davis tells us,

> was known in the New Orleans casinos in about 1840. From there keno spread up the Mississippi River and eastward, and it was well known in New York before the Civil War. Bingo is merely a slightly simplified keno, [which] . . . got its name from the French word *quine*, meaning roughly "five winning numbers."

The name "bingo" itself is probably a corruption of "beano," a rhyming term for keno as it was featured by small traveling carnivals during the late nineteenth century. With its rows of letters and columns of numbers on cards purchased by the contestant for a nickel or a dime, bingo may be the simplest of all formal games of chance. Anyone can place a marker over a number when the caller announces it; and anyone can tell at a glance when the markers cover all of the numbers in a winning row or column. As a rule, the stakes are low, and, of course, any number can play. It's thus not surprising that from the start the popularity of this game has been enormous. So widespread was its lure, in fact, that as early as 1895 commercial keno dives or "bingo parlors" were outlawed in most Eastern states. Nevertheless, local authorities have always winked at its use in fund-raising by local charitable organizations, from Elks' lodges and auxiliary fire departments to American Legion posts and churches.

While the Catholic Church in this country has made use of games of chance in its fund-raising at least since 1808,* no one knows when bingo made its first appearance in the Catholic parish hall. My own guess is that lay Catholic groups like the Knights of Columbus began the practice during the 1920's, but that parish societies and other official Catholic Church organizations took much longer to overcome their unease about a game involving money betting. This unease, moreover, still persists. In many Catholic dioceses (as in most Protestant churches), gambling for charity—especially where the winner collects cash, not prizes—is frowned upon by church officials. The Roman Catholic Archdiocese of Chicago, to name just one, forbids bingo entirely. Throughout the South, Midwest and Southwest, and indeed, wherever local anti-gambling morality is still very strong, all such gaming, including bingo, is rare. Only the most pressing financial need could induce a pastor in, say, Tulsa to countenance a bingo night in his parish. And even in such key Eastern states as New York, New Jersey, Pennsylvania, Rhode Island and Massachusetts, where bingo is either lawful or at least widely tolerated, pastors turn grudgingly to the game as an adjunct to other methods of raising money. "You see," one pastor explained to me, "bingo isn't a sign of greed. It's a confession of defeat, an admission that the parish can't keep its head above water."

New York State, where, after a bitter political battle,

* When the state of Delaware, according to historian John S. Ezell, "sanctioned St. Peter's Catholic Church, New Castle, to seek $2,000" by means of a lottery. (After seven years, Ezell adds, St. Peter's still hadn't held the drawing for prizes.)

bingo was legalized on a local-option basis in 1959, is the biggest and most important stronghold of the game. In New York, bingo is played under the control of the State Bingo Commission, a fiefdom of the Department of State. Under the scrupulously enforced state rules, only educational, charitable or religious organizations may sponsor bingo, and the regulations include such protective provisions as these:

1. The persons operating a bingo game must be a bona-fide member of the organization sponsoring the game. Professional operators (who might be crooked) are barred;
2. the organization must keep detailed records of all the financial transactions arising from the game, and make these available for audit;
3. a license (current fee, $12.50) must be secured for each separate occasion on which bingo is to be played;
4. the sponsor must pay a state tax of 3 per cent of the gross receipts.

In sum, the law is designed to make bingo accessible only to organizations well-enough established to comply with multiple legal and accounting requirements.

According to the records (which are available to any citizen willing to penetrate the usual official maze), nearly 23 million New Yorkers played bingo during the 1968-69 reporting period.* During the same period, the total amount spent by bingo-players reached a startling $111.4 million. Of this amount, $69.8 million was paid out in prizes by the 1,853 sponsoring organizations. The sponsors also paid $8.2 million worth of expenses and taxes, retaining $33.4 million as profits. As such figures indicate, bingo in New York is something of an industry.

How much of this industry is operated under Catholic

---

* Since the entire population of New York State is only about 18 million, the bingo population obviously harbors millions of repeaters.

auspices? The records reveal that approximately 40 per cent of the total dollar turnover from bingo was derived from some 750 Catholic parish groups. Other Catholic organizations sponsoring bingo (notably local chapters of the Knights of Columbus) brought Catholic participation in New York State bingo to well over 50 per cent of the total. Figures made available to me by Walter Saxton, Administrator of the State Bingo Commission, confirm that local parishes raised about $13.4 million from bingo in 1968-69, while other Catholic groups gathered roughly $3.6 million.

The Bingo Commission's reports also yield some intriguing historical statistics. Since the legalization of bingo on January 1, 1959, players have spent (the Commission shuns such words as "bet" and "wagered") more than $64 million on the game. Total net profits from bingo have reached $178.5 million. In all, Catholic organizations in New York have realized nearly $90 million from bingo over the decade ending in 1969.

Similar figures from the controlling agencies of twelve other states where bingo is legal suggest that the total annual revenue of the Catholic Church from this source is about $90 million. As we've already noted, most of this revenue is gained—and spent—in the major urban areas of the Northeast.

Impressive as they seem, these totals tell us less about bingo than we really need to know. Especially because such statistics can tempt us to exaggerate the significance of the game, we run the risk of missing the truth. So let's not forget, first of all, that, spread back over the thousands of parishes and other sponsoring units, even $90 million worth of aggregate income is no bonanza for one or another segment of the church. Secondly, let's remind ourselves that by comparison with the other income of the church, the income from bingo is a minor, if interesting, factor. Given these limiting realities, we can assess the financial impact of bingo much more accurately.

In New York State, a parish using bingo to raise money typically gains between $15,000 and $20,000 a year from its once-a-week sessions. State figures and parish financial reports together indicate that bingo profits average between 9 and 12 per cent of the total gross income of a sponsoring parish. Even in the Diocese of Brooklyn ("a hotbed of bingo," according to Bingo Commission official Hugh McGuire of New York City), revenues from the game almost never constitute as much as 15 per cent of total parish income.

A close look at other New York bingo statistics also helps clarify the role of bingo in church finance. Thus, of the 750 parishes sponsoring the game, about half are located in the general area of New York City. Most of these are parishes either of the Archdiocese of New York or of the separate Diocese of Brooklyn, which between them hold half the state's total Catholic population of 6.5 million. A number are located in the suburban Long Island diocese of Rockville Centre, adjacent to Brooklyn. Elsewhere in the state, the parishes offering bingo are mostly concentrated in or near the urban centers of Albany, Syracuse and Buffalo. In Brooklyn, nearly three-quarters of the 225 Catholic parishes feature bingo. In Manhattan and the Bronx, both part of the Archdiocese of New York, about one-half of the parishes sponsor bingo games. Elsewhere in the Archdiocese (which includes also most of New York City's suburbs other than those on Long Island) and throughout the rest of the state, the proportion is level at about one-third.

This brief venture into demography substantiates that bingo is an urban phenomenon; or, rather, that city and suburban parishes together utilize bingo much more heavily than do small-town or rural parishes. From the

examples of Manhattan, the Bronx and—especially—
Brooklyn, we might hazard that the heaviest users of bingo
are those city pastors whose parishes are losing middle-
class members, and hence revenue, to the suburbs. Certainly,
the available chancery data about the Catholic migration to
the suburbs supports this guess. In just such areas as these
three, moreover, today's Catholic pastors are the legatees of
yesterday's elaborate churches and other physical facilities.
Increasingly, too, their parishioners are drawn from New
York's Puerto Rican community and situated in black
communities. By definition, these parishes are parishes of
the poor. Faced with diminishing ordinary income and big
overhead expenses, an inner-city pastor turns to bingo (a
game appealing to the poor) as a plausible and essential
stratagem.

In particular, he turns to bingo as a means of meeting
the budget of the parochial school. But the financial
difficulties and the other imminent crises of Catholic education are another part of our story. Here we need only
mention what millions of Catholics already know or suspect. In many parishes, the fifteen or twenty thousand dollars a year the pastor can count on from bingo is the margin that makes the difference between a struggling but solvent parochial school and one that must either cut back or
else close its doors.

Perhaps the best way to sum up the significance of
bingo is to cite the comments of Walter Saxton, surely one
of the world's great experts on the topic. As Administrator
of the Bingo Commission of New York, Saxton oversees
every aspect of the Commission's legal, fiscal and administrative activities. In addition, he's a connoisseur of bingo
lore. Saxton finds the Catholic Church in New York more
than cooperative in complying with the legal regulations
surrounding bingo. Indeed, in parish accounting manuals
for the pastors of Brooklyn and New York, the meticulous

instructions for handling bingo money owe much to his personal handiwork. "We helped chanceries set up the books," Saxton says, "so we could not only account for every dollar of bingo spending by the public, but also trace the actual use of bingo profits right through the general funds of the church in question. We want to know whether the money is going for schools, priests' salaries and other legitimate uses or not. Pretty soon we'll have the whole system computerized. Then we could tell any critic exactly where every dollar of bingo profit goes."

Aside from finding Catholic bingo honest, Saxton applauds the use to which parishes put the profits. "I feel [bingo] does the taxpayers of New York a tremendous favor," he states. "By letting pastors supplement school funds, bingo saves the taxpayer from the costs of educating in the public schools youngsters now in parochial schools." Like the diplomat he is, Saxton adds, "and don't forget yeshivas."

Finally, Saxton points out, "Bingo is not only a money-raising function but fills a social and entertainment purpose as well. Lots of people play primarily to meet other people and have a respectable good time. We know of some professionals, women mostly, who follow the game around from parish to parish. Our inspectors call them 'floaters.' They do it mostly for the money: they don't like to lose, they like to win. But even the floaters play partly for the entertainment, too."

This disarming appraisal brings us back full circle to the major subject of our interest, the parish priest as financial man. Having surveyed the various techniques by which pastors and their assistants can raise the money they need, we can move on to consider the reverse role of the pastor: his role as the executive who spends the money of the parish.

In this role as in his role as fund-raiser, the pastor is an amateur, not a professional. Given routines he can follow and rules by which he can be governed, he'll make few serious mistakes. But as we'll see, following the routines and obeying the rules absorb time and energy, and avoiding error is only the most negative kind of administrative behavior.

CHAPTER FOUR

Spending: Does Father Know Best?

When a Catholic church contains a special shrine dedicated to one of the saints or to the Virgin Mary, the altar of the shrine should not merely be part of the fabric of the church. Rather, the foundation of the altar, at whatever expense, should be built firmly on the bare earth itself. Even in the cement precincts of midtown Manhattan, the experts in liturgy of the Archdiocese of New York insisted until not too long ago on the strict observance of this rule.

Those other experts who have designed the parish accounting system of the New York archdiocese are just as insistent on their own rules. In New York as elsewhere, the pastor is supposed to follow the book. With it as a guide, he writes the checks for such ordinary expenditures as those for maintenance, utilities and office overhead. He pays his own salary and those of his assistants. He handles the payroll for any lay employees of the parish (teachers and other school personnel included). The pastor also accounts to the chancery for a host of other significant outlays: e.g., for Federal, state and city payroll taxes; pension and other withheld items on the salary account; taxes on any non-exempt real estate owned by the parish; the cost of books and pamphlets distributed to churchgoers.

And in case the pastor's church does happen to contain a shrine, the cost of the candles for the shrine will be charged to Account #308.

Other liturgical supplies, like the wine and wafers for the Mass, the oil used for the last rites and the candles for the altar of the church itself (these must be at least 51 per cent pure beeswax) are items under Account #309. Outlays for new vestments and sacred vessels, however, are considered extraordinary expenditures.

If we look behind these entries in the accounts of the parish, we see the pastor as the administrator who makes the undramatic daily decisions about which dry-cleaning firm to use for the carpets in the rectory and which brand of sacramental wine to buy.

Above all, the pastor of a parish with a parochial school will be spending the money of his parishioners (and, if necessary, of his bishop) on the school. On the payroll of his lay and religious instructors. On textbooks, supplies and equipment for the students. On the operating overhead of the school plant itself. Nearly 10,000 of the 18,000 U. S. parishes operate schools; and, on average, the schools absorb 60 per cent of the income of their parishes, while bringing in only half that percentage. What this means to the economy of the whole church we'll discuss in later chapters. At the local level, it obviously means that the pastor must add to his other executive burdens the heavy burden of school administrator and purchasing agent. If we peer over the shoulder of the pastor, we can catch him in the administrative act. On any given evening devoted to business, he'll have in front of him on his desk a small pile of bills to pay, the parish checkbooks and a stack of other business mail. (Most of this offers him once-in-a-lifetime bargains in goods ranging from catechetical texts and religious filmstrips to aluminum kneeling rails for the pews in his church and chain link fences for his playground.) In New York, many of the routine bills the pastor pays go not to outside suppliers but rather to the chancery office of the Archdiocese. Through a chancery-run purchasing office, the Institutional Commodities Service, New York pastors can order everything from paint for the rectory dining-room to furnishings for an entire church. I.C.S. handles the transaction through one or another wholesaler and has the merchandise shipped direct to Father, billing the parish itself. "That way," a pastor explains, "we get a quantity discount on almost everything."

In sixty of the 160 U. S. sees, some degree of centralization prevails. But in most areas, each pastor must figure out for himself where to purchase the goods and services needed by the parish. In acting as his own purchasing agent, moreover, a pastor operates at a singular disadvantage. Lest he offend too many of the local faithful, or damage his status in the community at large, the pastor is more or less compelled to buy locally. In terms of his relationships with his parishioners and the non-Catholics he deals with, such a policy undoubtedly does Father a certain amount of good. In terms of money, the parish may be less fortunate and the church—as represented by the diocese—is almost certain to be the loser.

Nowhere is this fact more evident than in the purchase of insurance.

Later in this book, in the section on diocesan finance, we'll examine closely the subject of insurance and its special place in the financial undertakings of every diocese. Still later, we'll view the role of insurance in the affairs of the religious orders and of the institutions they operate. We'll come to realize that insurance, and the set of economic principles insurance embodies, is fundamental in the economy of the church. Here, however, we can introduce ourselves to the topic by looking at insurance as the pastor looks at it, from within the limited context of the parish itself.

As the man appointed by the bishop to be responsible for parish property, the pastor must concern himself with the common contingencies which could lead to financial loss. Like every manager, he must safeguard the property he manages against the hazards of fire, water damage, storms and so on. He must make sure that the contents of church and rectory, school and convent are protected against burglary and theft. Because the property of the parish is institutional property, most of it open to the public, the pastor must also protect the parish (and the diocese as well) against lawsuits claiming personal injury or damage to property. In short, running a parish is a risky business.

So as a matter of course, the pastor must pay attention to the insurance program of the parish. With relatively few exceptions, pastors do so in exactly the same way that everyone else in this country takes care of insurance. They call in local insurance brokers.

Like the accountant Father brings in regularly (or irregularly) to go over the books of the parish, the insurance broker, whatever his other qualifications, is certain to be a Catholic. He may be well known in the community as "the man who handles insurance for the church"—i.e., for several of the parishes and perhaps for the local Catholic hospital or college. Or he may be a loyal parishioner who accommodates only his own pastor. In any case, his task is straightforward. Just like your own insurance man, he: a) draws up a survey of the real estate and the other property to be insured; b) adds up the values involved; c) draws up recommendations of the types and amounts of insurance needed; d) sets about getting an insurance company (or companies) to provide the insurance; and e) collects from the pastor and forwards to the company the premiums for each insurance policy. To these basic services, the conscientious broker will add two more: periodic revaluation of the insurance program, and aid in case of a loss.

In return for this bundle of services, the insurance man earns commissions. These, at the parochial level, might be worth several hundred dollars a year, on total premiums averaging perhaps $3,000 annually. Typically, however, the broker can't claim even this modest a sum as profit. In addition to his normal overhead, the pastor's insurance man is expected to write off against his commissions handsome regular contributions to the church. Some brokers, in fact, are expected to waive their commissions entirely (an illegal act known in the insurance trade as "rebating") and to proffer their services purely out of loyalty. This they do happily enough (if only for the prestige the parish account brings with it), violating at one stroke the law of the church forbidding service for an unjust wage and the state insurance code.

Legal and moral considerations aside, such insurance arrangements rarely yield what every pastor should be looking for: adequate insurance at the lowest possible cost. In their eagerness to cement local relationships and drive shrewd bargains for their parishes, pastors forget—if they ever knew—a basic fact about the insurance business. That is, that almost no local broker has either the skill or the importance to negotiate on behalf of a client for favorable rates, special policies or other advantageous attentions from an insurance company. As a result, the pastor is very often either carrying the wrong kinds and amounts of insurance or else paying too much money, even after kickbacks, for the parish coverage. Specialists in institutional insurance could do for individual parishes what they now do for larger ecclesiastical units. But pastors almost all prefer (unless their bishops order otherwise, and sometimes even then) to "keep the business right here in the parish."

Obviously, not all pastors are short-sighted about the subtleties of buying insurance. Nor are all parish brokers helpless to bargain with the insurance companies they represent. But in insurance as in other essential transactions (e.g., plant-maintenance contracting, printing), the pastor's lack of expertise, coupled with his desire to root his parish in the community commercially as well as socially and spiritually, does often prove costly. To mention one example here while reserving the details for later, a large Southeastern diocese recently (1967) ended the autonomy of the pastors in insurance matters by installing a centralized insurance program. At the end of the first year, the chancery found that it had saved an astonishing $241,000 on the cost of the insurance for its parishes and other institutions. This amount was equal to about 65 per cent of the total premiums the individual pastors and other administrators had been paying.* Given the increasing concern over finances of the average Catholic diocese, it's not surprising to overhear chancellors, and even bishops, talking learnedly of "umbrella policies," "wrap-up coverage" and reinsurance.

What is true for the larger recurrent items of ordinary expense, like insurance, is equally true for the extraordinary expenditures of the parish. Even in those dioceses where new parish construction must be approved by the bishop, the pastor will still have much to say about what his

---

* The centralized plan included diocesan high schools and hospitals as well as parishes; and provided automobile insurance as well as coverage of buildings and contents and liability insurance.

new classrooms—or chapel or rectory—will look like and cost. Which of us isn't aware, moreover, of how hard it is to keep the costs of building and furnishing under control? Everyone can rationalize those extra dollars for construction sturdier than the climate demands. Or for furniture and equipment just a bit fancier than it really needs to be. When the pastor is ready to add to the plant begun by his predecessors, to build, so to speak, for eternity, he too is apt to be more conscious of quality than of cost.

Diocesan control over construction can usually prevent a pastor from indulging a personal predilection for Carrara marble flooring, gilt statuary or other expensive features of traditional church décor. But whether or not the seats in the beautiful new gymnasium should be upholstered is another matter. In some suburban parishes, the school plant outrivals the church itself as an object of pastoral care. (Today, the members of a newly formed Catholic parish sometimes build a school before they start on the construction of the church.) Chancery officials and pastors, like parishioners, are susceptible to the argument that quality is more important than price. Suppliers have long since learned that the way to the institutional heart is to stress the fineness and durability of the goods they sell. So if Father wants upholstery and can produce plausible reasons for installing it, he'll probably get his wish.

In general, although the specifications for new construction and furnishings may be drawn up by architects under the eagle eye of the bishop, and although contracts are awarded only after competitive bids, today's new parish churches, parochial schools, recreation centers and related structures still mirror the special interests of the incumbent pastors. If the pastor likes music, the organ in his church will be an electronic miracle of stops, pipes and keyboards. If he's fond of sports, the ball diamonds and basketball courts of the parish will be specially treated in the construction budget. In almost every parish church, an interested visitor can uncover evidence of the tastes of each of its successive pastors. And in most U. S. dioceses, the independence of the pastors is a major barrier to the development of systematic parish construction programs.

Inevitably, the portrait of the pastor as executive (and of the assistant pastor as junior executive or trainee) which emerges from these pages is far from complete. To give the portrait life, we'd need room for much more detail. In addition to reading this general description of managerial duties and financial responsibilities, we should somehow also be able to watch closely as the priests of many parishes go about their daily business routines.

If we could do so, we'd quickly realize that the missing ingredient in any abstract summary of these routines is a sense of the politics of parish management. By his own testimony, the priest's single most important task is that of "running organizations." In large measure, the skills needed to run organizations are the political skills: personal authority, persuasiveness, insight into others and all the rest. From books like William Whyte's *The Organization Man* and other annals of contemporary management—and from our daily personal experience—we should be familiar with the entire catalogue. Our experience should tell us as well, however, that the imprecise blending of authority and empathy, of aggressiveness and trust in others that marks the successful executive or politician or pastor is impossible to pin down in prose. Only by seeing the priest as he presides over a meeting of the parish school board, for instance, or as he listens to a committee report, can we flesh out our executive portrait. Only by listening to him as he confers with the specialist from the chancery about some project he intends to undertake (or about some delicate question of canon law involving a parishioner), can we see how well he fits into his organization.

We do know enough, nevertheless, to explode some of the familiar myths about the organization and management of the church. The first is the myth that the Catholic priest acts only at the behest of an omnipotent central organization, the diocese (and ultimately the papacy), the orders and policies of which he is sworn to carry out. This myth, to be sure, contains elements of truth. By definition, the Roman Catholic Church—like the Ford Motor Company and The Metropolitan Life Insurance Company—is an authoritarian rather than an egalitarian institution. Diocesan priests do vow obedience to their bishops. In theory, and with the support of canon law, the bishop can exact strict obedience to all his episcopal directives.* In practice, the bishop expects such obedience in matters of religious faith and in the general conduct of priestly life. Thus, the diocesan priest who refuses to accept, say, a particular parish assignment does so at his risk. His bishop possesses the power to deal summarily with the situation. If the bishop happens to be a rigorous disciplinarian, the priest could find himself in an assignment far worse, from his point of view, than the one he had refused. Today, however, few American bishops are absolutists in the exercise of their power over clerical personnel. In most dioceses, a recalcitrant priest would be given the chance to plead his case to the bishop, or to a committee appointed by the bishop. Even if a compromise assignment were not forthcoming, the priest would have had his day in court.

Much more serious to any Catholic bishop is the act of a priest who disobeys in matters of doctrine or faith. Here, because a subordinate is challenging the tenets

* If such a directive seems clearly contrary to Catholic teaching, the priest has the right not to obey. He then has the canonical right to appeal to Rome, through the Apostolic Delegate in Washington, for a ruling on his case. This process is intricate and time-consuming, and, win or lose, most priests know well what happens when a subordinate bypasses a superior in search of fair play. Still, no priest is completely helpless in a dispute with his bishop.

on which authority presumably rests, even moderate bishops will at least threaten to apply, and will sometimes actually invoke, the strongest sanctions available under canon law. One instance will illustrate the whole point perfectly. In February, 1966, Rev. William P. DuBay, an assistant pastor of the Archdiocese of Los Angeles, announced plans to form a labor union of all the Catholic diocesan clergy in the United States. The then Archbishop of Los Angeles, Cardinal James F. McIntyre, promptly relieved Father DuBay of his duties as an assistant pastor, and threatened further disciplinary action. DuBay then told a press conference that he could not accept McIntyre's orders to stop organizing the priests. McIntyre reacted strongly. He first offered Father DuBay "a refuge for contemplation in any of the monasteries of the archdiocese" for thirty days. When Father DuBay ignored this call to self-incarceration, Cardinal McIntyre suspended his priestly faculties (i.e., his rights to celebrate Mass, administer the other sacraments and preach). DuBay appealed the suspension, via the Apostolic Delegate, to Rome. But he lost his case and later left the priesthood. Whether or not the Cardinal's severity was justified is beside the immediate point. (McIntyre was always considered to be the most conservative of all American bishops.) The lesson remains that doctrinal disobedience in the church brings down executive wrath much hotter than that kindled by violations of even the most cherished organizational rules.

Economically, however, the individual pastor is anything but passive. In all but the largest dioceses (and a very few small ones), pastors operate far more freely than do, for instance, the branch managers of banks, manufacturing companies or chain stores. Apart from the occasional letter of advice from the chancery and the required financial report, the pastor is very much on his own. Only the most flagrant incompetence or breach of trust, moreover, can ever cost him his local franchise.

The second of the myths about the Catholic Church to be deflated by our survey of parish economics is the myth of the church as a single super-efficient money machine. Rather, as we've already seen, every one of the 18,000 Catholic parishes in this country is a separate enterprise. Some run well enough; others sputter and backfire; very few purr along effortlessly. And they certainly don't purr effortlessly along together. Scores or hundreds of parishes may be grouped into one diocese. Even so, the pastors still retain independent control of their money and property. Diffusion of wealth, not concentration of wealth, is the rule. What can we say about the economic results of this freedom?

By now, the flaws in the system should almost be self-evident. At the parochial level, the finances and administration of the church are handled by men untrained and uninformed about money and ignorant of administrative techniques. These men are responsible for the entire array of executive functions, from budgeting and planning through the hiring and training of personnel to the purchase of supplies and equipment. Unlike corporate executives, however, the branch managers of the Catholic Church are barred—by tradition and by their canonical code—from delegating authority to subordinates or to outside specialists. They themselves must assume personal responsibility for the success or failure of every project, however minor, acting not only as director but as performer of the assignment. While these duties absorb much of their time and energy, moreover, the executive role is by no means the primary role these men assume. Of far greater personal significance is the conflicting role of religious leader: i.e., of teacher, counselor and spiritual guide.

As for accountability to others, no system of internal control focuses on the continuous executive activity of the Catholic pastor. Within a rigorous but generalized framework of abstract rules, he operates virtually free of supervision from above. His superior places no stress, of course, on his running a profitable enterprise. Rather, the pastor's financial performance is measured in terms of stability and year-to-year solvency. These minimal goals aside, other objectives are left to individual discretion.

To this brief summary of the system, we might add such other drawbacks as: a) promotion based largely on seniority rather than merit; b) near-permanent tenure, with retirement postponed to seventy or beyond; c) low pay; and d) next to no opportunity for advancement.

On paper, the net result is a system so irrational that it gives rise to the question of why the Catholic Church has not long since collapsed into insolvency. Yet this same system, developed over many centuries, has not only worked but has worked wonders for the church. What has kept the system alive and flourishing? And how can we possibly quarrel with its success?

Underlying what we might call the management philosophy of the diocesan church is a theory as old, perhaps, as society itself. Namely, that the best training to give the man destined to hold authority is a broad general education, not a specialized one. If we wish, we can trace the roots of this theory very far back in time: further back, even, than the ages during which priests were the only educated men in Western society. But for a more recent example of this theory in action, we need only recall the days of Victorian England. Then and later, the mother country sent generation after generation of governors and administrators to rule at the perimeters of empire, armed with little more than self-confidence, loyalty and a knowledge of the classics. And for a contemporary instance, we might consider the administration of government in Switzerland, where (as Sybille Bedford phrases it in her classic, *The Four Faces of Justice*)

> [The] farmer is also a locksmith and a vintner and a shipwright and in the evening mends the clocks; the artisan keeps books; the chartered accountant runs a sawmill and the county council; the woodcutter has a chair of modern history.

And where we still find "a sense of the community of citizens . . . and from a humanistic inheritance, a still-living conviction that—outside of science at least—all branches of human activity are open to all men."

Much of this same serene self-confidence permeates Catholic professional theory and training today, just as it has for hundreds of years. Accompanying it is a similar assurance of the special applicability of priestly training to almost every human situation. Surely, or so it seems in the church, the seminarian who is supposed to be able to discourse fluently in a classical language, Latin, can go on to run a parish. Surely the mind that can follow the twists and turns of scholastic philosophy can cope with the daily details of parish finance. And surely, as one modern executive told a trainee eager to study computer programming, "there's no worse way to spoil your career than to clutter up your mind with useless knowledge."

In sum, the management theory of the Catholic Church, to the extent that its ideas of management can be crystallized into theory, is a spirited defense of the generalist.

In some areas of the world and in certain kinds of societies, the church may still be able to justify this theory in practice. Like the British Empire of Victoria's day, the church does have outposts in remote and undeveloped lands, territories where managerial sophistication is simply irrelevant to the mission of the priest. Similarly, in a stable, traditionalist society (one thinks of parts of Germany, and for that matter of Switzerland), where next year's parish routines will differ not at all from those of this year, the pastor's education can be gained from the land. And during the decades in our own country when Catholics were mostly poor, propertyless beginners in society, a parish priest was by definition the best-educated, best-informed man in the parish.

But in this country at least, those days are long gone. American Catholics no longer hunger for the impressive buildings they once longed to build. Nor do they live in a timeless unchanging society. Rather, Catholics in this country—in common with all Americans—face a notably volatile life in a society which is making change a rule. The system which worked so well when, as a retired pastor said to me, "you could count next Sunday's collection from this Sunday's," works far less well today. The training which enabled pastors to raise billions of dollars for churches almost as big as cathedrals doesn't much help their successors contend with inflation. And while many of the professionals in the church agree that the whole system of administration must be changed, the system is so compartmentalized that no one has the power to initiate wide-ranging change ("except the Pope," one pastor commented sourly, "and he lives in Rome, not Pittsburgh").

Among those most aware of the need for administrative change within the church are the bishops themselves and their chosen advisers. It's time we began to meet these senior executives of the church; and to learn their traditions, sample their powers and taste their problems. As we might expect, the Catholic bishop is a far more sophisticated executive than is the Catholic pastor. And as we might also anticipate, he needs to be.

As a parting comment on the parish priest and his problems, we might choose a remark made by a key member of one bishop's staff. The speaker is a former savings bank executive who now serves, without pay, as the financial adviser to an archdiocese with assets of nearly $200 million. His verdict: "The besetting sin of parish administration is amateurism. When we get a pastor whose father was a businessman or an accountant, then Heaven help us. If only the pastors would admit that they don't know what they're doing, we could save a fortune for the church."

CHAPTER FIVE

The Diocese: How Bishops Operate

On the very day of his installation in the cathedral, the bishop of a Roman Catholic diocese must execute a will drawn up by the lawyers of the chancery. In it, he bequeaths to his "successor in God" every iota of the material property he has just acquired, or will acquire, by virtue of his consecration. Nothing is omitted, from the cathedral itself down to the pectoral cross on the bishop's chest and the signet ring on his finger.

The act, of course, is symbolic. It's much like that of the new Pope, who, amid the ceremonies of his enthronement, accepts from an attendant the whiff of burning hemp which signifies his mortality. But the fact of the bishop's will also discloses the singular nature of his involvement with the bricks and mortar, bank accounts and asset balances of the diocese. On one level, he is their absolute owner. In all but the three or four tiniest dioceses of the United States, this automatically makes the bishop a multimillionaire. On another level, however, the bishop is not the master but only the steward of all the wealth he controls. In business terms, his is the task of the corporate officer; in legal terms, that of the trustee. He is to conserve, to improve and—if possible—to increase the value of whatever lies in his care. His rights over his temporal possessions are thus far from absolute.

What are the managerial responsibilities of the Catholic bishop? What exactly does he own? How does he govern his diocese? Above all, is the bishop really the administrative professional he needs to be, and is supposed to be? Such questions lead us away from the economic firing-line of the parish and move us deeper into the finances, laws and politics of the diocesan church. We can expect the search for answers to uncover broader truths as well, truths about power and authority within the church and truths about responsibility and accountability, their limiting opposites. Sometimes, indeed, we'll be grappling with realities which challenge what any of us, Catholic or not, wish to believe about the church.

But before we can focus on the intriguing details of diocesan finance and administration, and well before we evaluate what we see, we must do certain other things. First, we should be sure we know what we mean by the term "bishop" itself, for Catholic bishops are of more than one variety. Then, let us test our awareness of the place of the bishop in the hierarchy, absorbing as we do so some of the essential statistical truths about the diocesan church in this country. Finally, we should understand something of the unique legal framework within which every bishop must operate. Unless we fill in the background with care, our portrait of the individual bishop and the realm he governs will lack definition; and our appraisal of the management of the church will verge on caricature.

So let's proceed with the question of nomenclature. A glance at the *Annuario Pontificio* or *The Official Catholic Directory* (a 1,503 page guide to the church in the U.S.) or any other roster of the hierarchy reveals a puzzling array of episcopal ranks and titles. To pick our way among these, we should bear in mind always that, in the Catholic Church, the concept of episcopacy is *geographical*. In a business corporation, an executive can hold the rank of vice president without being further classified as "Western regional vice president." But in the church, a bishop must be the Bishop of Somewhere. He must, in a word, have a bishopric, or see. The size and importance of his see, moreover, helps to determine his official rank and does determine his status and prestige.

Thus, an archbishop is simply a bishop whose see is large enough or populous enough to be an archdiocese. A diocesan bishop (the proper term is "residential bishop") governs a smaller ecclesiastical territory. So far, so clear. But what of the other episcopal titles that recur in the official rankings? What, for instance, is the status of "The Most Reverend John Francis Smith, Titular Bishop of Tiberias and Auxiliary Bishop of Townville"?

As the name implies, an auxiliary bishop is one appointed to assist a residential archbishop or bishop. Like a corporate manager of public relations or personnel, an auxiliary may be placed in charge of some particular branch of diocesan operations. Or like a regional vice president, he may serve as the ranking hierarch of a subdivision of the diocese. Either way, his job is considered important enough to warrant his elevation to episcopal rank. Therefore, because a Catholic bishop must be head of a see, the auxiliary is granted jurisdiction over some community which—however real it was in the beginnings of the church—today exists in name only. In the Vatican, the consultors of the Sacred Congregation for the Bishops keep the long list of such titular sees. This they must update periodically so that, as promotions are confirmed by the Pope, vacancies are always available. The list reads like a compendium of classical geography. From Abaradira, the titular see occupied by an auxiliary bishop in Poland, to Zuri, the one held by the Pope's diplomatic representative in Thailand, the list includes 1,956 place-names of authentic but vanished episcopal realms. Of these, about one-third are usually vacant.

Besides auxiliaries, other kinds of senior ecclesiastical executives (e.g., Vatican officials, the rectors of Catholic universities) are frequently awarded titular bishoprics. So also, occasionally, are other lesser figures in the church: administrators, diplomats and even some pastors for whom an honorary bishopric is the same kind of symbolic goal as is the earldom for the British ex-prime minister.

Titular sees are likewise granted to coadjutor bishops, those assigned to take over diocesan affairs when residential bishops become ill or are otherwise disabled. Often, but not always, a coadjutor is given "the right of succession" to the episcopal throne of the bishop whose duties he has assumed. When a coadjutor does succeed, and whenever any titular bishop is named to a residential post, he is formally relieved of his titular see by the same papal decree that confirms the new appointment. While every bishop must be the Bishop of Somewhere, no bishop may simultaneously reign over two sees.

Alone among bishops, the residential bishop is invested with special spiritual faculties. Like all priests, all bishops may celebrate Mass, hear confessions, administer the sacraments, impart blessings and preach. But to the residential bishop is reserved the additional authority (which he may delegate to his auxiliaries or to a coadjutor) to ordain other priests and to confirm Catholics as they come of age in their faith. Nor, strictly speaking, is this authority derived from the Pope. As equal successors to the Apostles, Catholic bishops as a body gain their spiritual powers directly from Christ. Although the individual bishop is appointed to his rank by the Pope, to whom he vows obedience and by whom he may be "deprived" or removed, he is by no means merely the Pope's servant. In some sense a bishop is the co-equal of the head of his church. The subtleties of this are continually being debated by theologians and experts in canon law. But always, the first of the titles by which the Pope himself is styled is simply *vescovo di Roma*, Bishop of Rome.

Now, let's extend this process of definition so that it reveals something of the structure of the diocesan church in this country. In Chapter One, we noted that the diocesan church of the United States is divided into 29 ecclesiastical provinces and subdivided into 160 residential sees. In those areas where the Catholic population is most concentrated, a province covers one state. Thus, New York is a single province which includes the Archdiocese of New York and the lesser (or suffragan) sees of Albany, Brooklyn, Buffalo, Ogdensburg, Rochester, Rockville Centre and Syracuse. Where the Catholic population is sparser, a province may include several states and embrace a huge geographical area. The province of St. Paul-Minneapolis, for example, includes nine suffragan sees stretching across three big states: Minnesota, North Dakota and South Dakota.

Each of the provinces has as its capital an archdiocese governed by an archbishop who may also be a cardinal.* In some matters, the archbishop of a province (who is some-

* Contrary to what many people assume, the title of cardinal is not reserved for the highest-ranking officials of the diocesan church. Rather, the title indicates its possessor's membership in the College of Cardinals in Rome, the group which has among its other duties that of the election of the Popes. A Pope may name as a cardinal not only archbishops but any priest, and indeed any male Catholic. As recently as 1882, a layman was created a cardinal by Pius IX.

times termed a "metropolitan") has the canonical right to exercise control over the bishops of its suffragan sees and to act as their official spokesman. The archbishop's authority over his bishops extends in particular to questions of canon law, civil legislation affecting the church and priestly discipline. Otherwise, in the terse phrase of the *National Catholic Almanac*, the archbishop possesses "strictly limited jurisdiction over his suffragans." As we'll discover, however, a strong archbishop has his own extra-canonical means of asserting leadership.

In Chapter Two, we touched lightly on the demography of American Catholicism. We had occasion to discover that the great archdioceses of the Northeast are the havens of the bingo-players and other gamblers for Catholic charity, as they are also vast centers of Catholic educational, philanthropic and social activity. Detailed analysis of the demographic profile of the American Catholic community (which in 1970 numbered more than 48 million members) is clearly beyond the scope of this book. Yet by reviewing a short set of statistics, we can first draw a rough map of the diocesan church, then bring the map to life. Thus, from a report of CARA* we learn that in 1970, 75 per cent of all the Catholics in the United States were dwelling in metropolitan areas; and that 50 per cent were clustered in just 20 of the 160 U. S. residential sees. And our map lights up to reveal these major concentrations of people. In Chicago, 2,511,000 are Catholics; in Boston, 1,914,350; in New York, 1,836,300; in Los Angeles, 1,743,164; and so on down the list to St. Paul-Minneapolis, its 537,535 Catholic residents ranking it 20th in size.

When these twenty centers of Catholic life are all highlighted, we discern at once the shape of the diocesan church. We see that the spread of our Catholic population

* The Center for Applied Research in the Apostolate, a quasi-official research organization sponsored by several Catholic universities.

has swept across lower New England and the Middle Atlantic states into the Midwest and as far west as Minnesota.
In fact, of the twenty sees on the CARA list, seventeen are
located within this heartland area. In the Far West, we immediately identify California as a stronghold of Catholic
activity. In the deep south, New Orleans, 17th on the list, is
another major Catholic community.

But south of Maryland on the Atlantic coast, and across
the entire southern half of the country, the Catholic population is spread much thinner. Thus, in ranking all U. S.
Catholic dioceses by population, I found that Galveston-
Houston, one of the fastest-growing metropolitan areas in
the U. S., ranks only 41st, just below Green Bay, Wisconsin. In the east, Atlanta, also a mushrooming metropolis,
ranks no higher than 129th. Similarly, in the prairie states
and in the Pacific Northwest, the map is only dimly lit and
the population totals low.

From even this short a run of data, we can deduce
many things. If we need reminding, our survey will remind
us of how, historically, Catholicism came to this country.
After a quiet start in the missionary settlements of the
French and in the sober English gentility of Maryland, it
arrived in the hearts of the millions of Irish, who, throughout the nineteenth century, were fleeing their own
impoverished land. And along the canals, turnpikes and
railroads the Irish helped to build, Catholicism migrated
westward. It came also, of course, with the Germans and
Poles who sought prosperity and freedom in Ohio and Missouri, Michigan, Wisconsin and Minnesota after the European upheavals of 1848; and with the Italians who warred
with the Irish for the jobs, the money and the political
spoils of the urban Northeast. But most of all, the American church, and American Catholicism in general, wore the
map of Ireland on its face. And so it still does, to this day.

For the record, we can note if we please an ethnic side-

light of our survey. Of the 138 archbishops and bishops occupying residential sees in the continental U. S., no fewer
than fifty-five bear unmistakably Irish names, names like
Shehan (Baltimore), Scully (Albany), Flanagan (Worcester), Furey (San Diego), Casey (Denver) and Donnellan
(Atlanta). Of the select group whose members rule over
the twenty largest sees, fourteen are of Irish descent, five of
German and one of Italian. Of the nine American cardinals,
eight are of Irish stock.

Within the church and outside, hostile commentators
have pounced joyously on this aspect of the faith. To the
Irish character of the church in America, critics variously
ascribe: a) Puritanism; b) anti-feminism; c) devotion to
the Virgin Mary; d) political astuteness; e) authoritarianism; f) conservatism, and so on through a host of other
stereotypical traits, all supposedly Celtic in origin.
Sometimes this eagerness to make the church wear green is
funny. Occasionally, however, it smacks of the Know-
Nothingism and bigotry of an era we should hope is gone
forever. Much may be wrong with the church, but it's hard
to see its weaknesses as dependent on the ancestry of its
members or on the ethnic background of its leadership.

What is important for our purposes is the economic
image which emerges from the demographic background.
If we could consult a list which ranked the U. S. Catholic
dioceses by size of total assets as well as by population size
(no such list has ever been officially compiled), we'd perceive at once the correlation between numbers and economic strength. Despite some deviations, we'd conclude
correctly that the bigger the see, the wealthier. Further, to
anticipate here what we'll confirm later, within any diocese
most of the wealth takes the form of parish real estate
property and other parish assets. Non-parochial assets are
never more than a fraction of the total. And only toward

the very top of our list does the share of diocesan wealth held in assets other than parish assets become substantial.

Perhaps the quickest way to drive home this point is to state that while all but the poorest residential bishops are nominally millionaires, only the wealthiest archbishops and bishops command resources truly worthy of the name.

These men, inevitably, are the heads of the same great sees which predominate on the CARA census list. Most of them are archbishops. (Of the twenty largest sees, thirteen are archdioceses and the capitals of ecclesiastical provinces.) As we've already seen, their territories lie mostly in the northeastern and Middle Atlantic states and in the Midwest. Only Los Angeles, San Francisco and New Orleans lie outside this central area of Catholic strength.

Inevitably, too, the men who rule over these major accretions of population and wealth are the men who dominate much else in the American church as well. They are its best-known personalities, its setters of personal and executive style and—supposedly—its shrewdest managers. In mundane matters, though certainly not in spiritual affairs, they are (to quote the comment of a priest versed in administration) "little Popes." Their influence extends far beyond their canonical authority and their geographic jurisdiction into the international politics of the church on the one hand and into American secular society on the other.

To understand exactly why, we need only consider for a moment the nature of a large diocese or archdiocese. Within the network of networks which is the whole church, each such major see is an autonomous nerve center, a ganglion where all the strands of institutional Catholicism perforce come together. In each, to begin with, the number of the parishes to be governed is much higher than average. (The Archdiocese of Boston, for example, contains 401 parishes, 22 more than the total number in all the rest of

Massachusetts.) In the small or medium-sized diocese, the task of coping with the needs of the parishes is not too complex. But in a Boston, a Los Angeles, a Chicago or a New York, this task alone requires an entire staff of specialists under the control of the archbishop.

Then, clustered around the parochial nucleus are other organizational cells, the institutions and services linked directly to the diocese itself: the high schools, the hospitals, the orphanages, the homes for the aged, the seminaries and colleges; and the educational and welfare programs. Because the diocesan church relies on the religious orders to staff and operate these institutions, the bishop is brought directly into the affairs of dozens of different orders. Still other orders will have secured episcopal permission to operate their own institutions within the see. In these, too, the bishop will take more than a passing interest. Leaving aside his involvement with the lay public, an involvement with its own special implications, the head of a large see necessarily gathers into his hands the reins of a hundred different kinds of influence, power and responsibility.

As graphic evidence of the human result, consider just one page from the appointment calendar of the archbishop of a major southeastern see. I had glanced at this schedule during our interview and asked later for a detailed explanation. This particular day began for the archbishop at 7:15 A.M., with a communion breakfast of the Holy Name Society of the fire department officers' association. At 8:30, the archbishop met with the diocesan superintendent of schools to discuss the contract demands of the lay teachers' union. My own 10:00 appointment was noted, followed by a 10:30 meeting of the Building Committee. This lasted until noon. At 12:30, the archbishop lunched privately at his residence. At 1:15, he was scheduled to receive a delegation of nuns who wished to discuss a merger of two private girls' schools. At 2:45, he was expected at a suburban junior college for the dedication of a new chapel. He returned to the chancery for a 4:30 meeting with a group of Spanish-speaking priests about a proposed Hispanic adult education center. At 5:15, he conferred with a state senator about a pending school-subsidy bill. This conference he cut short to review a report sent over earlier by the diocesan law firm in time for a 5:45 conference. At 7:30, His Excellency spoke at a banquet for volunteer charity workers. He wanted to be home by 9:30, which would leave time for a couple of hours of dictation into his Dictaphone. "Then," according to his secretary, "he'll catch the late news on TV, read his Office and go to bed."

Sheer stamina apart, what qualities does the church seek in an archbishop, or indeed in any bishop? I've asked this question repeatedly of parish priests, chancery officials, Catholic laymen and even of some of the bishops themselves. Most of the answers were predictable stereotypes about "organizational loyalty" and "being a good administrator," replies as descriptive of the job of bank officer or insurance-company president as they were of being a bishop. But from one priest of vast experience, whose work as a journalist has brought him close to many of the bishops, I heard: "They look for a man with a good safe record who knows how to size up people. Not a holy man especially, but a practical one." And from a lady who, as secretary to a bishop, is an expert of a different kind: "How many times have I heard His Excellency tell people, 'I may not be the smartest person in the diocese, not by a long shot. But they made me the bishop, and, by God, what I say around here goes!'"

In one word, a bishop is supposed to be a Boss. He may be as authoritarian as Cardinal James F. McIntyre, former Archbishop of Los Angeles, who reputedly said, "None of the 'improvements' of Vatican II will be promulgated here during my lifetime." Or he may be as unassertive as Cardinal Terence J. Cooke of New York, who speaks of the need "to think out and then try new ideas . . . to consult democratically." But this is largely a matter of personal style.

At the beginning of this chapter, we saw that, as well as being a boss, the Catholic bishop is the owner of the property he administers. Here, we should ask: On what basis does he own diocesan property? The answer will give us a foretaste of one crucial truth about diocesan administration. Independent he may be, but the bishop, like the pastor, is hedged about by a system of laws and procedural rules far more restrictive than most outsiders, and for that matter most priests, ever understand. In addition to the civil laws governing the operations of every corporate entity, the Catholic diocesan prelate must obey the regulations of his own church. Thus the codes of 2,000 years of canon law (*The Canon Law Digest* alone takes up three massive volumes) have something to say about every single aspect of diocesan management, from the architectural planning of a chancery building to the investment of the funds of the diocese.

Suppose, for instance, that a "non-exempt" religious order (which is subject to the bishop of any diocese in which it operates) wishes to close up a convent dormitory and move its novices into an apartment. Before a ruling can be handed down, the chancery's legal experts must look up the laws covering: a) relinquishment of conventual property; and b) permissible residences for non-exempt nuns. (When something similar actually happened in 1965 in New York, the chancery's answer to the nuns was no. But the reasons were other than legal ones.) Or suppose that a wealthy layman wishes to give money to the diocese for the planting of trees around its cathedral. Again, someone in the chancery must check the canon laws covering the types of property acceptable as gifts. (This, too, happened in New York, when Major Edward Bowes of radio fame offered to pay for trees around Saint Patrick's Cathedral. This offer, made in 1941, was accepted.)

In sum, we must fix in our minds that a diocese, much like a railroad, a gasworks, a bank or an insurance company, is part of a regulated industry; regulated, moreover, from within as well as from without. If we neglect the fact of regulation, we'll find ourselves mystified by the realities —and therefore vulnerable to the myths—of Catholic episcopal power.

In the United States, the diocesan church makes use of two forms of corporate structure, each implying its own type of episcopal ownership. The older of these, with a history rooted in the civil law of the Roman Empire, is called the "corporation sole." Under this curious but convenient arrangement, the bishop himself is a legal corporation. That is, he himself can own property and transact business as an individual, and yet simultaneously enjoy the special legal privileges reserved to corporations, including in particular limited liability in case of financial failure. Where the corporation-sole arrangement is acceptable under local civil law, the bishop is in literal fact a one-man diocesan holding company. Every parish church, school, convent, rectory and bank account, and every other scrap of property in the diocese, belongs to him. Without his express consent (or that of his personal agent), no financial transaction can take place. Thus, if the Archdiocese of Boston wants to borrow money from a bank, Humberto S. Madeiros, "Archbishop and Corporation Sole of the State of Massachusetts," takes out a personal loan.

Not many Catholic dioceses in this country do operate as corporations sole. For one thing, the creation of so picturesque (and so privileged) a legal entity requires a special act of the state legislature. Between fifty and one hundred years ago, a handful of legislatures, especially in New Eng-

land and in the western states, granted such charters, probably either to encourage immigration or to stabilize the
legal position of the church within the state. As recently as
the early 1900's, the state legislature of New Hampshire
granted corporation-sole status to the Bishop of Manchester, whose diocese covers the entire state. Today, for obvious reasons, lawmakers are reluctant to do similar favors
for the church. Only a few of the oldest, best-established
sees are corporations sole: Boston is one, Baltimore another,
New Orleans a third, Los Angeles a fourth.

More important, the church has found that American
corporate law makes it as easy, or easier, to organize a diocese in other ways. A glance at the early history of the diocesan church in the U. S. highlights the interesting origins
of the accepted legal alternative. Surprisingly, the historians indicate, a number of the first American bishops were
experimentalists. Instead of enforcing the old European
episcopal absolutism, they tried to reconcile Catholic
organizational methods with the more open techniques of
American society. Among the departures from traditional
practice which they nurtured was a system of lay trusteeship over church property. Under this system, each parish was incorporated as a separate charitable trust. Laymen,
sometimes appointed by a pastor or bishop and sometimes
even elected by their fellow-parishioners, exercised complete control over the parish property and decided all
money matters for the parish. Similar groups of laymen
were responsible for diocesan property.

This novel technique worked only briefly. A new generation of bishops, alarmed by threats—some real, some
imaginary—to episcopal authority, fought hard against
their own trustees and rebellious pastors. By a combination
of appeals to Rome, engineered shifts in American civil law
and sheer force of personality, the bishops put an end to the
independence of the lay trustees. Each of the fifteen Catho-

lic dioceses, however, was reduced to a legal shambles of separate corporations. To regain control, Archbishop John Hughes of New York fought hard for legal recognition of the rights of Catholic churchmen to control the corporations. He won repeal of earlier legislation and passage of a bill whereby he could set up a diocesan corporation with himself as president and other clergymen as the directors. He then reorganized each parish corporation, making himself the president of every one, with his vicar-general the treasurer and the pastor the vice president and secretary. As directors and trustees, laymen were once again appointed, two to a parish. But because the clerics can always outvote the lay trustees, laymen's duties became strictly formal and the appointment merely a token of the local pastor's esteem. Lay trustees of diocesan corporations were replaced by boards of consultors drawn from the diocesan clergy.

The struggle over lay trusteeship has left scars in the American church which have yet to heal. To this day, Catholic bishops sorely mistrust the idea of lay autonomy in church financial matters. But more to the immediate point, in 1911, the Sacred Congregation of the Council in Rome made the "New York System," of interlocking parish and diocesan corporations, the preferred method of Catholic diocesan organization. Like the corporation sole, the New York System assures the bishop of absolute control over all of his temporalities. This control he exercises through his chancery office.

In Los Angeles, Cardinal McIntyre housed his chancery in a pleasant California-style brick building in an otherwise bleak neighborhood a few blocks west of Wilshire Boulevard. In Baltimore, the archdiocese has erected a twelve-story office tower in the heart of the downtown urban renewal district. The chancery occupies the top floors, while the rest of the building is shared by dozens of Catholic charitable, educational and social organizations. The chancery of Pittsburgh is located in a grimy office building on the northern perimeter of the city's famed Golden Triangle. Rochester's chancery takes up one floor in a curious downtown structure which was originally a commercial hotel financed by the Knights of Columbus and which now serves mainly as a Catholic home for the aged. A rambling mock-Tudor mansion built by P. T. Barnum is the present home of the chancery of Bridgeport. And as millions of New Yorkers and visitors to New York know, the chancery of the Archdiocese of New York occupies part of the majestic structure at 50th Street and Madison Avenue, directly opposite St. Patrick's Cathedral, purchased a generation ago from the estate of publisher Whitelaw Reid.

As we're about to see, styles of diocesan management vary nearly as widely as do the architectural styles revealed by this casual survey. Nevertheless, all Catholic chanceries do have in common a single set of functions. Viewed in the special perspective not of the architect, but. rather of the management analyst, every chancery is: a) the administrative headquarters of the parishes of the see; b) the administrative headquarters of a mixed group of extra-parochial institutions; and c) an independent center of legal, fiscal, financial, promotional and business activity which is the chief economic agency of the diocese.

Admittedly, a chancery official might well blink in puzzlement at so arbitrary a set of distinctions. Like the bishop himself, the diocesan chancellor or vicar general* is naturally much more aware of the linkages between these

---

* In Catholic Church administrative usage, a chancellor (from the late Latin *cancellarius*, one who sits behind the grating, meaning simply "clerk," or someone able to read and write) is the chief official of the chancery. He reports directly to the bishop, organizing and overseeing routine business affairs. A vicar general is an official to whom the bishop has specifically delegated decision-making authority in one or another area: e.g., planning or finance. In the chancery as in a corporate home office, however, official titles may or may not reveal the responsibilities or relative importance of their designees.

three sectors of chancery responsibility. In the smaller dioceses especially, the chancery administrator moves seemingly without effort from the pastor's difficulties with an annex to the rectory to the latest results of a fund-raising drive for the diocesan high schools to the legal resolution of a dispute between the bishop and the superior of a religious order. The ability to be at home everywhere within the administrative maze is in fact the hallmark of the seasoned chancery executive. But while he can view church administration as one familiar labyrinth, we ourselves must work our way patiently through its many corridors to arrive at our goal: a view of the intricate machinery of diocesan financial management.

CHAPTER SIX

Filling the Diocesan Treasury

We've already caught a glimpse of how extraordinarily complex a Catholic diocese can be and enumerated the three major sectors in which the chancery is active. Also by way of preliminary, let's underscore that in each of these sectors the chancery makes use of varying sets of fiscal arrangements (those having to do with the gathering, allocation and spending of money). Similarly, in each sector the diocese is engaged in some or all of the basic operations of finance: banking, investing, real estate and insurance. By the time we're through, we'll know what very few people know about this complicated universe. Indeed we'll understand better than most churchmen how Catholic parishes support and are supported by the diocese; how Catholic high schools and hospitals are governed, and how and where the internal economy of the diocese touches the external economic world in which we live. First, because the basis of any functioning economy is the inflow of its money, we must identify the sources of diocesan income. Once we've discovered how a Catholic diocese obtains the money it needs to operate, we can go on to consider what uses are made of the cash it obtains.

One great supplier of diocesan income is the parish, and from there we'll start our financial exploration. But the income of a diocese stems from other sources as well. From the laity, and for that matter from individual priests and nuns (and non-Catholics), the chancery collects money via annual fund drives and special gift and bequest programs aimed at wealthy donors. In addition, the tuitions, fees and special collections for the seminaries and other diocesan schools must be classified as income. Every diocese, moreover, realizes some income from "investments." * In covering each of these categories of income, we'll be moving from sector to sector of chancery affairs and seeing for the first time operations with which we'll grow steadily more familiar. Equally important, we'll be basing our observations on the hard-cash realities of diocesan finance.

In Chapter Two, we analyzed the financial report which, in one form or another, every pastor in the land submits to the chancery of his diocese each year. On the Bridgeport form we chose as an example, we noted an entry headed *Cathedraticum*. This we defined as the assessment levied, generally at the flat rate of 5 per cent per year,† on the ordinary income of the parishes: the income from regular collections, seat fees and Mass offerings. Virtually

---

* As you'll see, this word can mean something much broader than the portfolios of securities and parcels of real estate it generally implies.
† In some sees, the bishops are raising the rate to 6 or even 7 per cent of ordinary income, but are ending the extra Sunday collections for the support of the seminary, the diocesan missions and other institutions. In others, no flat percentage is charged. Each parish is assessed a quota according to chancery estimates of its ability to pay.

every diocese in the United States charges such a tax. The revenues from it, besides supporting the chancery itself, supply at least some of the funds needed to operate the institutions of the diocese.

Even in a diocese of moderate size, the receipts will be substantial. Thus in one northeastern see with a Catholic population of about 300,000 and ordinary parish income of just over $8 million, the *cathedraticum* was reported in the 1968 auditors' statement as $450,000. This amount included, in addition to the 5 per cent assessment, the proceeds of several special Sunday collections for the diocese. A somewhat smaller New England diocese (Catholic population, 250,000) reported total ordinary income of about $5,400,000 for 1968, with diocesan tax receipts of $273,000. A much larger see, this one an archdiocese ranked just below the top twenty, took in $800,000 worth of *cathedraticum* receipts in 1968. In each of the four or five largest sees, this tax will yield approximately $2,500,000 a year.

On official diocesan balance sheets (rarely accessible and invariably mystifying to the uninformed), the *cathedraticum* receipts are sometimes mingled with current cash assets* or other current receivable amounts. On income-and-expense statements (not quite so rare, but equally baffling to the non-initiate), the *cathedraticum* may be consolidated with other types of income: e.g., income from special collections or seminary assessments. Still, I can state with fair accuracy that in all but the smallest dioceses (where single non-recurring items, for example, large bequests, can confound all percentages), the *cathedraticum* yields approximately 10 per cent of the annual diocesan income.

To the proceeds from the *cathedraticum*, every diocese

---

* Accountants may be scandalized to note an income item where such an item should never be found, on a statement of assets and liabilities. But I've seen diocesan statements where this does happen.

adds certain other tax proceeds as well. To understand these, we must interrupt ourselves just long enough to glance at the intriguing entirety of the internal tax system of the church. Almost nothing about the Catholic ecclesiastical economy fascinates Americans more than this mysterious system. We're at once intrigued and irritated that an institution in our midst can—solely on its own authority—operate a private revenue service. Even today, anti-Catholic sentiment can readily be aroused by the insinuation that "Catholics pay secret taxes to Rome." Yet ironically, many Catholics are themselves convinced that "the Vatican's cut" of the money they contribute to the church is far too generous a slice. As even a brief glance will indicate, the system certainly is fascinating. But the hidden revenues this system produces for the diocese and for Rome are in fact relatively insignificant ones.

As we've seen, the *cathedraticum* is an income tax. Technically, it could be called a tax on a tax, because the individual Catholic is, in strict canonical terms, obligated to "tax" himself for the support of his parish church. Technicalities aside, however, the parish income, not that of the Catholic churchgoer, bears the direct weight of the *cathedraticum*. Then, the chancery also collects taxes on each of the special collections taken in the parish churches of the diocese. These always include the Peter's Pence collection (the annual offering to Rome) and those for the Bishops' Relief Fund (the overseas relief agency of the National Conference of Catholic Bishops); the Holy Places (the shrines in what the church still calls Palestine); the Catholic University of America; and the Society for the Propagation of the Faith (the international missionary wing of the church).

Before forwarding the proceeds of these collections to the appropriate officials in Washington, the chancery deducts the amounts the diocese is entitled to keep. These amounts are small ones, more like fixed handling fees than like real taxes. In one medium-sized diocese, for instance, the chancery tax on Peter's Pence receipts of $36,000 was $400 in 1968. On the Bishops' Relief Fund Collection of $67,000, the levy was only $200. In this same diocese, the total tax on all seven special collections, which in 1968 brought in approximately $260,000, was $2,400. Not quite 1 per cent.

In addition, the chancery collects some fees from individuals. For example, when the local ordinary dispenses a couple from the canonical requirement of posting marriage banns, a set contribution is payable to the chancery. Like the Mass stipend, this sum is a free-will offering. No bishop would refuse the dispensation solely because the couple declined to pay the ten-dollar fee. Other dispensations from canonical rules also involve standardized fees ranging from $10 to $25. Special dispensations which must be secured from Rome carry with them higher offerings. Similarly, marital dispensations granted by the diocese are by rule taxable at modest rates, as are legal appeals from diocesan marriage tribunals to metropolitan tribunals. Only if a marriage case must be appealed to Rome are the expenses apt to rise sharply. I'm told by a former senior official of a metropolitan marriage tribunal that "it can cost $8,000 to get a separation out of Rome."

Here again, the fees realized by the diocese are modest ones which add little to total income. In Chicago, where the yearly *cathedraticum* is close to $3 million, dispensation taxes bring in less than $100,000 per year; and in smaller sees the revenues from this source are proportionately lower. The money thus collected must be used for the support of the chancery office. And dispensation tax receipts, unlike those from the *cathedraticum*, are in turn taxed by Rome. A levy of 10 per cent of the total income from dispensation taxes is collected from each chancery by the Office of the Apostolic Delegate in Washington, D. C. This sum is either forwarded to the Vatican or credited to the domestic account of the Delegate for use in this country.

Buried still deeper within the structure of the church are other taxes payable to Rome. These are absorbed by the separate institutions of the diocese (as well as by the religious orders and their subsidiary institutions). When seminarians are ordained as priests, for instance, the seminary pays the fees due Rome. Or if a priest or a nun withdraws from the professional church, the diocese or the religious order secures a "rescript of laicization" from the Congregation of the Clergy or the Congregation for Religious in Rome and pays a tax. Such fees are small ones. The rescript costs only $16, an amount obviously intended only to cover the clerical expense of preparing the document itself. In fact, most of these inner Vatican taxes, which are indirect in the sense that the individual Catholic layman never pays them (or even knows of their existence), resemble the stamp taxes, license fees and other minor exactions of secular bureaucracies. They're certainly no great siphon of American dollars into the papal treasury. All in all, I estimate that Rome's total revenues from its tax on dispensation taxes, plus its receipts from fees, are less than $250,000 a year, a drop in the bucket of Vatican resources.

With this tax system reduced to its proper proportions, we can refocus on other—and much more significant— ways of bringing in diocesan income. Indeed, there is sound evidence that charity, and not compulsion, is the basis of this flow of funds. We can cite the crucial importance of fundraising within the diocesan church.

At the diocesan level, Catholic fund-raising is no game for beginners. Nor is this game a simple one to analyze. The ground rules, the goals and the personalities of the players vary from location to location and from year to year.

Looked at from the outside, this game is a welter of organizations, institutions, groups and committees, all involved in one never-ending hunt for money. Viewed through the eyes of an insider, diocesan fund-raising, like parish bingo on a gigantic scale, is a social as well as a financial phenomenon. It can be an exercise in intimate cooperation between the ranking clergy and the lay aristocracy of the see. Or it can be a mixture of clerical timidity, lay apathy and mutual misunderstanding. Seen in still another perspective, Catholic diocesan charity is a classic instance of the strengths and weaknesses of big-time charity in America.

Finally, understood as the church would wish, the philanthropies of this country's sees are miracles of human generosity, perseverance and love.

We can simplify our survey by noting in advance that only some of the fund-raising which goes on every day in every diocese is done by the diocese itself. To choose a simple example, in almost every big city passers-by can still see nuns, armed with the wicker basket or the tin can of the solicitor for charity, posted at certain strategic locations. These sisters, members of one or another of the several mendicant orders, are raising a few dollars, both for the support of the order and for that of the institutions it owns and operates. "The practice of begging is not widespread at the present time," *The National Catholic Almanac* says of such efforts, "although it is still allowed with the permission of competent superiors and bishops." Indeed it is; and in a key spot, a begging nun can collect respectable sums. One Passionist sister, stationed at the entrance of 63 Wall Street in New York's financial district, told me that in the three hours a day she devotes to mendicancy she receives "about $25, if the weather is good; and I ask God to bless about a hundred people for their kindness."

By the same token, the fund-raising drives for large

hospitals, universities and missionary societies are almost never run by the dioceses in which these institutions operate.* Rather, these are separate undertakings of the religious orders or the private Catholic charitable corporatons which manage the institutions. To solicit money within any diocese, such non-diocesan organizations must always obtain the permission of the local Ordinary. If possible, they like to feature His Excellency's name on their list of patrons as assurance of his endorsement. As we'll see when we deal with the economics of the religious orders, the need for episcopal approval of fund-raising campaigns is one reason of many why superiors tread lightly in their relationships with diocesan chanceries.

Typically, the fund-raising done by the diocese is done for one of two basic purposes. The first of these is philanthropy in the strictest sense of the term. The second, as we'll see shortly, is construction.

Great or small, every Catholic diocese operates a variety of welfare programs. These range from the familiar baseball leagues and other Catholic Youth' Organization activities through social work and counselling services to medical clinics and services for the aged and the disabled. For the most part housed in existing diocesan facilities, these welfare agencies all need operating funds rather than bricks-and-mortar capital.

As far back as the turn of the century, Catholic churchmen grasped two truths about raising funds for such continuing programs: a) that dozens of separate drives and collections were as confusing and annoying to donors as they were costly to administer; and b) that centralized fund-raising, besides being more efficient, would bring in more money. The organizational answer was the diocesan

* "Never" is a dangerous word to use in discussions of Catholic fund-raising. As a gesture of esteem, a bishop may in fact decide to raise funds personally for a favored institution or cause not connected with his diocese.

charitable corporation. In most U.S. Dioceses, the bishops have set up these Catholic Charities corporations to central-ize the fiscal operations of their welfare works. Like the Community Chests and United Funds so common today, Catholic Charities corporations mount single yearly fund drives, then divide the proceeds among their member or-ganizations.

Collectively, the Catholic Charities corporations of the dioceses add up to one of the biggest and most sophisticated philanthropic organizations in the world. A trade associa-tion, the Washington-based National Conference of Catho-lic Charities, serves as an information center and clearing house for members. The Conference also keeps its eye on tax, antipoverty and other legislation affecting private charity, almost always as an advocate of liberal government support of welfare work. Like so many trade associations, this one faces the delicate task of promoting among its members ideas and causes more advanced than some mem-bers are willing to accept. Since 1966, for example, the Na-tional Conference of Catholic Charities has urged on its membership policies of nondiscrimination against blacks in the hiring and promotion of professional personnel. In gen-eral, the bishops have responded well to this prodding; but in a few Southern dioceses and in at least one in the North, such tactics make diocesan officials very nervous. One Tennessee clergyman said to me, "Why, if we did some of the things the national boards want us to do, we'd alienate our contributors overnight."

In another significant move, the National Conference is encouraging member organizations to coordinate their fund-raising with that of non-Catholic churches and com-munity-sponsored charities like the United Fund. Unfortu-nately, some Catholic Charities leaders (or their bishops) see in these joint fund-raising efforts the thin end of a dangerous wedge. Because they're afraid of a possible loss of Catholic Church control over the money raised, this particular form of ecumenism is highly disturbing to them. "As a matter of courtesy, we wouldn't start a drive on the same day the Community Chest kicks off its own campaign," explained a Catholic Charities worker in Los Angeles. Then he added, "but if we don't watch out now, pretty soon we'll be raising money for Israel!" His nervous little joke speaks for itself.

Locally, Catholic Charities organizations range from superb instruments of philanthropy to mediocre adjuncts of episcopal economic rule. Some Catholic archbishops and bishops are keenly interested in welfare work and exceptionally responsive to the needs of clerical and lay program directors. (The late Cardinal Albert Meyer, Archbishop of Chicago, was known for his encouragement of welfare activities.) In their dioceses, established programs are given budgetary autonomy, and their financial requirements are automatically made part of the Catholic Charities campaign goal for the year. Furthermore, priests are often given formal training in welfare work; and those priests with innovative ideas for programs (e.g., inner-city vocational training centers, summer excursions for ghetto children) can count on the chance to sell their projects to the bishop's charities committee without wasting months in political infighting.

Often enough, however, the local Ordinary regards Catholic Charities as an uninteresting tool of fiscal control over the social work of his diocese. Year after year in many sees, the same episcopal letters are read from the pulpits of the parishes, asking "once again for contributions to sustain this valuable work" but explaining neither the work nor its value to parishioners. Every year, a few posters are tacked up and some modest financial goal is announced (but probably not achieved). And although the needs of the diocese and the community may be expanding, the same few organizations will do well to limp along on their shares of the inadequate proceeds. In those dioceses where Catholic Charities is a neglected operation, the Catholic hospitals, colleges and other independent institutions may sponsor welfare programs of their own. If so, they must do their own welfare fund-raising. This fact helps to explain why the National Conference numbers among its members not only the diocesan Catholic Charities corporations but also hundreds of extra-diocesan institutions (including more than 800 of the country's 871 Catholic hospitals).

Bishops who deemphasize or ignore Catholic Charities are by no means all villains. Today especially, the individual bishop may feel that in *his* diocese the education crisis* takes precedence over every other economic matter. He may even believe—a handful of American bishops do—that it's an economic mistake for the Catholic Church to be involved in the conventional forms of welfare work; that these are better done by nonsectarian agencies or by government organizations. Take the example set by Bishop Fulton J. Sheen. Formerly the national director of the Society for the Propagation of the Faith, Sheen knows as much about raising money for Catholic causes as any mortal in the world. Yet during his tenure as Bishop of Rochester, the diocesan Catholic Charities corporation (which dates back to 1912) conducted no drives for funds. Bishop Sheen asked Rochester's 1 million adult Catholics (nearly 30 per cent of the total population) to contribute instead to the city's Community Chest; and he himself plunged the diocese into inner-city and ghetto support.†

And so obviously, the economic significance of Catholic Charities fund-raising, impressive on a national scale,‡

---

* Of which there's much more in Chapter Sixteen.

† In October, 1969, Sheen resigned as Bishop of Rochester. According to *The New York Times* account (October 16, 1969), Sheen said of his social activism, "I move too fast. I'm a little too progressive."

‡ Total funds raised nationwide are estimated in Washington at over $100 million a year.

varies dramatically from diocese to diocese. Once again, moreover, the major sees are the focal points of this type of money-raising activity. In key archdioceses like Chicago, Boston and New York, support for Catholic welfare work comes from the entire community. In turn, non-Catholics as well as Catholics are eligible for aid from church-run programs. There, the sums raised by Catholic Charities add up to large percentages of the total incomes of the sees. In New York, which possesses a uniquely vigorous Catholic Charities organization, the 1969 fund drive yielded close to 4 million, nearly 30 per cent of the total operating income of the archdiocese.

However, New York is not Belleville, Illinois, or Spokane, Washington. Away from the major centers of Catholic population, diocesan income from Catholic Charities fund-raising may total less than $100,000 a year; and may constitute less than 10 per cent of total income. In such sees, the bishops are less likely to encourage welfare programs. Sometimes, indeed, they don't feel any need for them. Rightly or wrongly, they raise funds for another purpose entirely. And in terms of the truth about diocesan economics, this other purpose is more important.

Traditionally, American bishops have gone into fund-raising so that they could build. In the days of the immigrant church they gathered money for the construction of seminaries and cathedrals. Then, during the three decades after World War I, they campaigned for the dollars with which to build hospitals and diocesan high schools. Only during the 1960's has this emphasis on bricks and mortar, marble and gilt, beds and blackboards begun to slacken in favor of less tangible objectives. Nor will the so-called "era of the Building Bishops" ever vanish entirely. In many U.S. sees, physical expansion continues. Everywhere, essential additions to diocesan plants must still be financed. For instance, in Chicago the archbishop, Cardinal John

Cody, having raised more than $40 million during a two-year fund drive, in January, 1967, announced "Project Renewal," a ten-year program to spend $250 million on the physical rehabilitation of the archdiocese.*

Like their pastors, many bishops have built first, raised the money later. In Boston, the late Cardinal Cushing began a program of expansion right after World War II, raising some funds as he went along but financing much of the construction by means of bank loans and other borrowings. By 1967, Cushing had brought into being scores of high schools, seminaries and other institutions, but the external debt of the diocese stood at $50 million. One story has it that the Cardinal approached his old friends, the Kennedys, for financial aid. The family is supposed to have pledged $5 million to help reduce the debt; and at the same time, to have informed the Cardinal that he could expect no more major contributions, that the Kennedys would instead develop their own private charitable trust, the Joseph P. and John F. Kennedy Foundation. Another account hints that Cushing's longed-for retirement had been blocked by Rome until he could clear up the debt of the archdiocese and leave an unencumbered legacy to his successor. These stories may or may not be accurate. But it is true that Cardinal Cushing called in outside fund-raisers to help him reduce his $50 million burden. Before Cushing's death in 1970, moreover, Boston's Catholics had pledged their archbishop $40 million worth of the total.

Reasons other than the traditional ones also persuade bishops to launch drives for funds. Thus, in the wake of the liturgical and educational renewal fostered by the Second

---

* This sequence is something of a reversal for Cardinal Cody, noted in both his previous sees (Kansas City–St. Joseph and New Orleans) as a fearless borrower who left behind him sizable diocesan debts. Whatever his image among those responsible for repayment, however, in terms of institutional finance Cody may well have been absolutely right to borrow.

Vatican Council, a popular project in many sees is what we can call, for lack of a more exact term, the Catholic community center.* A typical example is the Catholic Center set up in Tulsa, Oklahoma, in 1966. There, the diocese has converted a small factory building into a home for a variety of social and cultural activities. As well as serving Catholic organizations, the center offers its facilities (including a small auditorium and up-to-date audio-visual equipment) free of charge to Tulsa's non-Catholic civic and political groups. The center serves also as a kind of neutral meeting-ground for Tulsa's numerous ecumenical activists. John Shaw, a local funeral director who is a financial aide of Bishop Victor J. Reed, told me: "The construction of the center cost us relatively little, under $250,000, including the price of the original property. But the budget for staff salaries, programs and equipment will be well over $100,000 a year. We have to raise this money." In Tulsa, the answer is the Bishop's Fund Drive. Its objectives are: to raise enough income each year to support the center and an array of other innovative programs; and to channel some new funds every year into an unrestricted endowment fund.

Similar annual fund drives are now being undertaken in at least forty other dioceses. In some of these, physical expansion or debt reduction (actually, two sides of the same fiscal coin) are still undoubtedly the major preoccupations. In many, however, the funds raised will be spent mainly on intangibles or treated as long-term capital rather than poured into additions to the diocesan plant. To go into detail about this shift in financial policy would mean getting ahead of our story. Still, it's not premature to make one point. Today, when even tiny dioceses may be experimenting with their philanthropic programs, American

* During my travels for the research on this book, I visited eleven such centers.

bishops are beginning to discover that the Catholic Church needs a new kind of money. Namely, money free from legal ties or sentimental associations with the familiar pious causes of Catholicism. "We're not campaigning for funds to redecorate the cathedral, though God knows it's a fearful-looking mess," says a diocesan consultor in Pittsburgh. "We're after money so our young hotshots [he means the spirited assistant pastors of the inner-city parishes] can help the blacks in the ghettos."

Whether their purposes are traditional or innovative, Catholic bishops in search of funds very often do what college presidents, museum directors and charity sponsors are required to do. Eagerly or reluctantly, the bishops seek the aid of professionals at the business, or art, of raising money. Where they go for help, we ourselves should follow. By meeting one of the leading professionals on his own home ground, we can certainly learn how diocesan fund-raising is practiced today. Furthermore, we'll acquire some novel insights into the motivations, economic and psychological, of the bishops who are the chief customers of this particular entrepreneur.

Leo J. Laughlin is the vice president of Community Counselling Service, Inc., a seventy-man organization which advertises itself in the ecclesiastical trade press as "the number one Catholic fund-raising firm in the United States." Community Counselling Service, with executive offices on the 73rd floor of the Empire State Building in New York, is probably the only business concern in this country which uses as its trademark a stained-glass window. Laughlin, a fine figure of a man in his late fifties, says candidly of this logotype, "We need to have that thing redesigned. Ten years ago, the window really stood for something. But fund-raising in the church today is a completely different game."

CCS, Laughlin told me, was founded in 1933 by Francis

K. Zimmermann, like Laughlin himself a graduate of the Fordham School of Social Work and a veteran administrator of Catholic welfare programs. "Back in those days," Laughlin said, "diocesan fund-raising was a scandal. Outsiders would come in and offer to raise money for the bishop on a percentage basis. You know, 10 per cent of the take went to the fund-raiser. Lots of times, the guy would get the pledges and the money and either keep most of it for himself or else just skip town with the cash. When Frank Zimmermann started, professional fund-raisers had an awful bad name. And even now, some of the bishops don't trust any of us."

While strange things do occasionally happen ("I know of cases where the bishop raises the money for something and then does something entirely different"), the efforts of Zimmermann, Laughlin and other professionals have thoroughly decontaminated the business of raising money for the church. Thus, CCS and such competitors as Development Direction, Inc. and Guided Giving, Inc. are members of the nonsectarian American Association of Fund-Raising Counsel. Whatever their specialties, these Catholic fund-raisers all operate according to the Association's ethical code. For instance, they all charge predetermined fees for their services, based on the amount of time and the number of people used in the campaign. None will operate on the basis of a percentage of the proceeds. Employees are bonded and financial reports open to audit. And the major firms shun the circuitous approach to charity via the game of chance. ("The sweepstakes approach," Laughlin says, "is expensive for the client, unfair to the giver and undignified for everybody.")

Partly as a result of their diligent self-policing and partly because their methods prove effective, CCS and the half-dozen other large firms have won the respect, if not the affection, of the hierarchy. The client list of Commu-

nity Counselling Service, moreover, solidly justifies Laughlin's contention that his firm is, like Hertz in auto rentals,
Number One. (Of the competition, Laughlin says amiably,
"Most are offshoots of us, where a couple of our fellas have
gone into business for themselves.") At the end of 1969,
CCS was managing campaigns for about a dozen U. S. dioceses, ranging in size from Reno (106th out of 160) on upward through Erie, Green Bay and Scranton to such major
sees as Chicago and Boston* In addition, CCS raises money
for Catholic colleges, hospitals and religious communities,
and does a good deal of parish fund-raising as well.

As you might expect, there is absolutely nothing pietis-
tic about Laughlin's attitude toward his trade. He's proud
to point to a picture of himself with Pope Paul, taken during a visit to the Vatican in 1964. But he commented to me
that his professional reception in Rome left something to be
desired. "Some of the Holy Father's officials [probably including Pope Paul's vicar general for the Diocese of Rome,
Cardinal Luigi Traglia] asked us about a campaign to raise
money for the diocese. Well, we told them that we'd want
to make a survey. Then we found that in Rome the pastors
don't even file financial statements or keep records, so we
had to do some guessing from what little was available to
us. But we put together a preliminary report and submitted
it. That was five years ago, and we haven't heard a word
since."

In this country, CCS has refined its methods into a system applicable to almost any diocesan situation. First,
Laughlin or another senior representative confers with the
local Ordinary or his designee. Then, CCS does some research into the financial condition of the diocese and comes
up with its proposals for the campaign. "Sometimes the
bishop tells us what he needs, sometimes we make the

* Where CCS is managing each of the $40 million campaigns mentioned
on pp. 116–117.

suggestion. Our figure is usually higher—we know we can raise more than the bishop thinks we can—and we compromise." Once the preliminaries are agreed on, the real work begins.

According to Laughlin, a successful campaign requires a mixture of four ingredients. "First," he says, "you have to have a good case: a solid, reasonable cause. Whether it's education or new programs or whatever, people have to believe in the case." Then, he adds, come the three other essentials which the professionals understand but which amateur fund-raisers often overlook: 2) a thorough sifting of potential donors into "advanced, intermediate and general prospects"; 3) an organization of "community leaders and workers"; and 4) the right techniques, including in particular "the right use of the bishop."

"If the bishop isn't willing to be a personal participant at every level," Laughlin finds, "the campaign just won't be successful. We need him first of all to convince the pastors to *lead* the campaign; and you'd be surprised how hard that can be. Then, the bishop has to be willing to spend time with the workers and to give them encouragement. Finally, we need him for some of the key donors." Given a bishop who will thus place himself at the disposal of the professionals, and given also the time and the facilities to organize the workers properly and classify the prospective donors, Laughlin insists that CCS will always either equal or surpass the financial goal set for any campaign. As proof, he points to the record: in Chicago, the goal was $40 million and the CCS campaign raised $43,126,104; in Brooklyn, the goal was $20 million, the amount raised an astonishing ("to the bishop, not to us") $38 million. In Wheeling, Bishop Joseph Hodges needed $2 million and CCS brought in $3,112,348; and so on. "These figures refer to actual cash in hand, not pledges," Laughlin assured me. "Our job isn't over until the money is collected, though not all fund-raisers work our way."

As you listen to Laughlin, you find yourself wondering how any bishop can resist his blend of fiscal logic, expertise and enthusiasm. Yet many obviously do; and with the aplomb of the polished salesman he is, Laughlin ventures several explanations. "First of all, since Vatican II, a lot of the bishops are stressing their pastoral role, and they don't want to come on too strong in appeals for money. Secondly, with all the problems the church is facing right now, the bishops feel that fund-raising will get people even more worked up. Then, of course, some of them feel they can handle the fund-raising all by themselves. In Los Angeles a few years ago, Cardinal McIntyre told me, 'I just finished raising $6 million. It took me two years, I collected on 80 per cent of the pledges and it cost me [in campaign expenses] less than 4 per cent.' I said to him, 'Your Eminence, with due respect, in your diocese we could raise $40 million in two years. We'd collect on 90 per cent of the pledges and the total cost would be less than 2 per cent.' Well, he got furious, naturally, and he hasn't spoken to me since."

Laughlin quickly tries to correct any impression that CCS prefers "one-shot" campaigns designed to produce impressive sums of money. "We are strong believers in the continuing program that increases yearly income. It's better for the bishop, and in the long run it's better for the people. Right now in St. Paul-Minneapolis, we're working on a continuing program to raise diocesan income by $3.5 million a year. Some of this money will go into a retirement fund for priests, some is inner-city seed money, but most of it is for education, specifically for [lay] teachers' salaries."

He confirms that such programs are of growing significance in diocesan finance. "Hell, as fast as we hire and train new men today, the bishops grab them away from us and put them in charge of 'diocesan development.' More power to them, but we'll see whether they can really do the job." Laughlin stresses, however, that the search for sources of current and future income is gradually making "a new ball-game" out of diocesan fund-raising.

Part of this new game is the effort to "upgrade the giving habits" of prospects. Asked whether CCS devised special programs to reach potential large contributors, Laughlin said simply, "It depends on the particular case. If we're raising funds for certain types of projects, we do concentrate on the people who can afford to be generous." As an example, he mentioned one situation on Long Island where CCS identified fewer than fifty prospective donors. "By the time we got near the end, we were down to just five people. One of the five was the person we were looking for": the Catholic who was wealthy enough, interested enough and charitable enough to finance the entire project. But by and large in diocesan fund-raising, a far less specialized approach is called for. "We'd much rather broaden the economic base of the diocese. It's better to move the average person's contribution up by $10 a year than to solicit a few large gifts."

As testimony to the impact of Laughlin's professional methods on the giving habits of some Catholics, we might note that if the CCS campaign in St. Paul-Minneapolis is successful, it will increase diocesan ordinary income by more than 40 per cent per year, from about $5 million to $8.5 million. Equally important by professional standards, the initial campaign has persuaded 75,000 contributors (out of an adult Catholic population of 200,000) to pledge a total of $2,775,000 per year, or an average of $37 each, to the archdiocese.

Clearly, Leo Laughlin and his colleagues have done

much for the economy of the diocesan church. Clearly, also, Laughlin feels that his firm can do much more. To date, the efforts of the fund-raisers have enabled the bishops to add hundreds of millions of dollars' worth of assets to the capital already held by Catholic dioceses in the form of high schools, seminaries, hospitals and other properties. To the extent that such institutions earn income (from tuitions, charges for room and board and similar fees), the professionals are indirectly responsible for part of the diocesan cash flow. But most of this institutional income is immediately reabsorbed in operating costs. By definition, there's little profit to the chancery in a diocesan nonprofit venture.

As for the "new ball-game" of raising money directly for the chancery, it's much too early to know, or even to guess, how well the professionals will perform. If the results of the St. Paul-Minneapolis campaign give a foretaste of what could happen, what actually is happening in diocesan fund-raising is another story, one that's frustrating to this particular pro. Because Laughlin's shrewd appraisal will add zest as well as depth to the telling, we'll meet him again at the end of our diocesan financial study. Here and now, we must move on, for there are aspects of diocesan fund-raising, still largely in the hands of the bishops themselves, about which the professionals are discreetly silent. In particular, let's consider the big gift and the big giver.

It's no more than a wayward coincidence, of course; but on the bookshelves in the paneled study of Cardinal Terence J. Cooke, Archbishop of New York, two books stand side by side in a bay of their own. One is *The Catholic Guide to Expectant Motherhood*. The other is a guide to a very different subject, Cusak's and Snee's *Documents and Data for Estate Planning*, published by Prentice-Hall. This, as its title indicates, is a technical sourcebook. It's full of information about gifts, wills, foundations and the other legal mechanisms by which those who own money or property can transfer their holdings to someone (or something) else, for the maximum benefit of all concerned. Both books together form an amusing—and an evocative—metaphor of the domain the church claims as its own. The second reminds us of the obvious: in addition to all else, the Catholic Church is, as indeed it must be, an expert professional beneficiary.

Every hour of every day in every diocese, we can assume that somebody is making, or preparing to make, a special gift to the church or to one of its institutions.* Sometimes such a gift takes its ecclesiastical recipient completely by surprise. In 1967, this happened in the Diocese of Rochester, when a former resident who had moved to Florida bequeathed $573,424.01 worth of stock in the Eastman Kodak Company to the diocesan corporation. "We had never even heard of the man," an official of the chancery told me. Sometimes the donation comes as the result of months or years of patient persuasiveness, as when Major Bowes bequeathed $3 million to his friend Cardinal Spellman as an endowment fund for Saint Patrick's Cathedral. And sometimes the gift is a coolly calculated philanthropic distribution made by a wealthy man for tax purposes and for reasons of business or personal prestige. Such was the case, I'm sure, when Lewis S. Rosenstiel, retired board chairman of Schenley Industries, whose personal fortune is estimated at $70 million, gave $3.5 million to the Cardinal Spellman Memorial Foundation in 1968.†

How important are these extraordinary gifts and be-

* Perhaps I should use the canonical term "extraordinary" gift to distinguish the kind of donation in question here from the offerings Catholics make to the church as part of their religious lives.
† Rosenstiel, not a Catholic, made his gift through his family foundation which also made large gifts to many other institutions, including the University of Miami, the Hebrew Union College, Notre Dame and Holy Cross.

quests as a source of diocesan revenues? Part of the answer emerges from the official financial figures of the key Archdiocese of New York. Its 1968 income statement indicates that "special donations and bequests to the Archbishop of New York and the central archdiocesan agencies" totaled $5,468,000. This sum represented approximately 26 per cent of the operating income of the archdiocese. Without it, the archdiocese would have run up a deficit of $6,690,000 for the year, instead of the lesser deficit actually incurred.

My analysis of similar financial reports from twenty other dioceses (with a size distribution roughly corresponding to that of the entire list of U.S. dioceses) further emphasizes the importance of extraordinary gifts and bequests. For instance, in Baltimore (23rd largest see), gifts and bequests in 1968 totaled $2 million and equaled about 15 per cent of operating income. In Rochester (ranked 32nd), the figure was $119,000, about 12 per cent. In Bridgeport (40th in size), gifts and bequests came to $857,666.93 and equaled nearly 30 per cent of operating income. Still further down the list, in Baton Rouge (76th in size), the diocese took in $448,700 worth of gifts and bequests, again about 30 per cent of income. And in Tulsa-Oklahoma City (ranked 93rd), gifts and bequests of $379,908 equaled roughly 22 per cent of operating revenues.

By definition, diocesan receipts from this particular source are never predictable. Within any given diocese, one fat year preceded and followed by several lean years is the only apparent norm. Still, on the basis of the figures from financial reports and in the light of discussions with officials in a dozen chanceries, I estimate that diocesan corporations in the U. S. realize about $300 million a year from special gifts and bequests. Of this total, about 40 per cent ($120 million) falls into the category of "restricted funds," those

which can only be used for the specific purposes designated
by their donors.* The balance, $180 million, is unrestricted
money to be used as its recipients see fit. Properly speaking,
only unrestricted funds should ever be counted as operating
income. (To add in restricted funds is a bit like including
your whole savings account, not just the interest, with
your salary on a credit application.) On this basis, I'd guess
further that "current unrestricted gifts and bequests," to
use appropriate accounting terminology, provides between
15 and 20 per cent of the total annual operating income of
this country's Catholic dioceses.

The size and significance of this flow of wealth make
crystal-clear the presence of an estate-planner's handbook
in the private office of a cardinal. Indeed, in every see the
Ordinary, whether he is aggressive or inactive in the
pursuit of gifts and bequests, is (as lawyers say) a "natural
object of the bounty" of others. Because this bounty inevitably takes many forms and is given in many different
ways, the bishop and his staff must be versed in the practical techniques of acceptance. "You can be the greatest go-
getter in the world," one chancellor told me, "but unless
you know what to do with what you get, you're going to
waste a lot of money. So you'd better be a pretty fair tax
man, and a canon lawyer, too." Much of the mundane legal
and administrative activity of any chancery office has to do
with the handling of gifts and bequests. And in my opinion,
the myth of the Catholic Church as a mighty power in the
world of investment arises largely from its routine but unending dealings as a beneficiary.

As a moment's reflection will tell you, these dealings

---

* Examples of restricted funds include money given to pay for Masses
"in perpetuity" (which canonists now take as meaning ten years); funds
for a specific building; seminary scholarship bequests; and countless other
instances, some as absurd as the fund set up to guarantee ice cream twice
a week to undergraduates of Yale.

are shaped primarily by what donors do. "If people just gave us money," sighed the same chancellor quoted a sentence or two ago, "we could relax and take things easy." But people don't just give money to the church. Rather, they give securities ranging from government bonds (domestic and foreign) through listed securities to shares in companies no stockbroker has ever heard of. They give real estate: in forms as simple as the deed to a house in town or to a lot in the country; and as complex as interests in net leases and commercial mortgages. Authors assign to the church the royalties on books not yet written; vintners donate wine from grapes not yet harvested; oilmen will to bishops fractional shares in reserves yet to be proven and wells still to be drilled. Women give or bequeath jewelry and furs, linens and furniture. Collectors donate works of art. In sum, people give what they have; and the list is truly endless.

Nor do people always make outright gifts or bequests. Thus, the securities are given with the proviso that the income from the dividends must be paid to the donor. (Or, contrariwise, the income is given, with ownership of the securities still vested in the donor.) The choice piece of property is offered to the bishop if he will promise to leave the home of the donor intact forever. The antiques are contributed during the lifetime of their owner, but he is to enjoy their physical custody until his death. And so on and on, with each separate contribution giving rise to its own quota of legal, financial and practical questions. Sometimes chancery officials are truly mystified by the problems involved. For instance, what should His Excellency do with a herd of prize Black Angus cattle? With a supposedly genuine Vermeer? With stock in a corporation which controls restaurants and nightclubs?

To these particular questions, and to the simpler ones

raised by the more conventional forms of generosity, the church has one basic answer: sell, and convert the value of the property into cash.

This approach is undoubtedly at odds with the popular image of the Catholic Church as a "Saintly Profiteer" (to echo the gaudy phrase of *The Nation* in a 1929 article); a performance-minded investor with a sharp eye for tax-free gains. But it does conform exactly with the economic and legal realities confronting every residential bishop in the land. Indeed, if we're to understand what the church does do with its money, whether from gifts and bequests or from other sources, we should keep in mind the classic framework within which bishops must operate. The rules present themselves with an almost Thomistic elegance:

1. To sustain its activities, the church needs money. Above all, it needs income rather than cattle or works of art or business assets or other relatively non-liquid wealth.

2. Under both civil and canon law, the Ordinary of a see is required to act as the trustee of the property he nominally owns. He is forbidden to engage in financial speculation and is accountable to his superiors, and very often to the civil courts as well, for the financial transactions he conducts or authorizes.

For a definitive version of the rules covering diocesan investment activity, let's turn to *Investment of Church Funds,* a dissertation written in 1951 by the Reverend Harry J. Byrne for his doctorate in canon law.*

> The Holy See itself has indicated that speculation is a form of business activity prohibited in clerical and religious affairs, and in ruling speculative practice out it used the Italian equivalent of the phrase "playing the market."

* The *Studies in Canon Law* published by the Catholic University of America (of which Byrne's thesis is No. 309) are fascinating source material for anyone who really wants to know how the church in this country is governed.

"Playing the market" is a reference to the purchase of securities with the purpose of deriving, not a regular income from the investment over a long period, but rather a hoped for quick increase in capital value and the consequent profit . . .

Such speculative practices may also work in the other direction through the activity of "short-selling." Short-selling is completely speculative and as such cannot be employed in ecclesiastical property administration.

Speculation is illicit in ecclesiastical administration for another reason, viz., the excessive degree of risk generally present. The purpose for which stable church assets are to be employed is the production of income periodically in support of ecclesiastical activities, and not the reaping of an increase in the value of the assets themselves . . . In a very similar manner and for evidently the same reasons, American civil law has forbidden speculation with funds whose principal must be kept intact for trust purposes.

What lends this statement special interest today is that the Father Byrne of 1951 is now the Right Reverend Monsignor Byrne, one of the two chancellors of the Archdiocese of New York. As such, he's the key decision-maker in matters of ecclesiastical real property. Furthermore, Monsignor Byrne tells me, nothing in the law has changed since his thesis appeared. Bishops and all others with financial authority are still required to behave as conservatively as trustees do.

And so the Black Angus cattle (bequeathed to a southwestern diocese by an oilman who stocked his estate with the critters to turn it into a "ranch" for tax purposes) were quietly put in the hands of a livestock broker by the law firm representing the chancery. The herd reportedly fetched $80,000. The "Vermeer," which turned out to be by a lesser artist of the same period, was auctioned off for the benefit of another diocese. In still another, the nightclub corporation was liquidated and its assets, mostly in restaurant equipment, also went under the hammer of the auctioneer. A similar fate befalls most of the non-liquid properties given or bequeathed to the church.

This is not to say that the diocesan church turns its back on all investments, or that the bears in chanceries always prevail over the bulls. For one thing, even the defensive strategy we've just reviewed is still a strategy. That is, it requires knowledgeability and a sense of timing. Suppose, for instance, that a bequest to a diocese consists of the controlling interest in a closely held business (one in which ownership is concentrated among only a few people). Even if the business is prosperous, the market for its shares is limited. The search for a buyer willing to pay a reasonable price is apt to take some time, and negotiations will undoubtedly soak up still more time. Although the executors of the estate of the donor may be eager to consummate a deal and thus settle the value of the whole estate—and although the chancery would like its money—the process may consume months or even years. During the interim, moreover, the diocese is in the uncomfortable position of owning a business about which it knows little or nothing.* Yet any hastier behavior might either ruin the business or deprive the church of the value of its bequest.

Seemingly similar donations, for instance, of listed stocks or other marketable securities, may well pose problems of their own. Thus, assume that a bishop, having been given such stocks, elects to sell them. Someone must decide when and how the sale is to be made. If the stock market

---

* This contingency raises, perhaps a bit prematurely, a wonderfully yeasty question. Namely, the right of churches and other tax-exempt organizations to own and operate so-called "unrelated businesses." A footnote is plainly not the place to treat so important an issue. But in advance of any extended discussion, it's worth pointing out that, unlike other religious groups, Catholic Church groups avoid involvements in unrelated businesses. They do so precisely because such involvements would leave them vulnerable to charges of tax-free profit-making and hence unfair competition. Where a diocese does find itself so involved, as in the example above, the bishop is apt to be very nervous until the business is sold or liquidated.

happens to be particularly soft at the time, the obvious move is to wait until the market recovers. This in turn means inventorying the securities, keeping track of their prices and making judgments about the market: in short, playing the money game of the professional investor. The conclusion is inescapable. Even a conservative financial policy necessarily involves the church in the universe of Wall Street. Selling as well as buying, after all, is done in the marketplace.

What has so far served as background to the handling of gifts and bequests will serve also as introduction to the next of the sources of diocesan income: investments. Here, our story broadens rapidly; for as well as being a generator of operating funds, the investments of the diocesan church are the very fabric of the Catholic ecclesiastical economy. In the splendid old term of the canonists, the various investments we're about to consider are the "patrimony" of the church; and their proper administration is a crucial economic function of the diocese.

"Investment," states Father Byrne in *Investment of Church Funds*, "has been canonically defined as the expenditure of money for acquiring productive real estate, or the change of a sum of money into another form of ownership, e.g., into stocks or bonds of states or commercial corporations." As we'll see, the diocesan church does do a good deal of this kind of investing. Every diocesan corporation, and most of the institutional dependencies of each diocese, hold some stocks and bonds, and may even own some income-producing real estate. As we explore the subject of investments, we'll be able to ascertain whether or not the Catholic bishops really do own the vast stockholdings and realty empires they're supposed to own. But if we confine our own definition of investment to the official definition given by Father Byrne, we'll be making a serious error. In fact, we'll be overlooking a class of investment which yields at least as much income as all the securities portfolios and real-estate deals put together, and which absorbs far more capital. I refer to the complex, fascinating and crucially important *internal* investments of the diocesan church: in particular, those derived from the private banking activities of the dioceses.

CHAPTER SEVEN

Bishops as Bankers

My own first-hand education in diocesan banking, and, indeed, in the other mysteries of diocesan financial administration, began with a visit to the chancery office of the Diocese of Manchester, New Hampshire. My instructor there was the Right Reverend Monsignor Albert W. Olkovikas, Chancellor and Vicar General for Administration.

Bespectacled and slightly rumpled, Msgr. Olkovikas neither looked nor sounded like a man elbow-deep in financial affairs. But the Victor adding machine on his desk did give his office a hint of the right atmosphere, and his enthusiasm for the facts and figures he spread before me was that of every seasoned administrator who finds he has an audience. After a few moments of preliminary conversation, Msgr. Olkovikas said briskly, "But you want to know all about money," and he did his best to tell me. What follows is my distillation of his comments and those of the many other chancery specialists who have elaborated on the economic patterns he first explained.

In an ideal world for the Catholic diocesan administrator, every parish in the diocese would be a self-sustaining economic unit. Ordinary income would cover ordinary expenses. The contributions and pledges of the parishioners would enable the pastor to embark confidently on a building program or to undertake any other needed project. When it came to negotiating a loan or financing a mortgage, the credit of the parish would assure Father deferential treatment at the local bank. A modest cash surplus tucked away in a savings account would serve as a cushion against emergencies. The unpleasing voice of the bingo-caller would never be heard in the land.

Within any diocese, some of these idyllic parishes do in fact exist. But in Chapter Two we saw conspicuous evidence of the unevenness of parochial financial administration. Even in the most affluent communities, there are pastors who simply can't balance their books. Year by year in their parishes, outgo exceeds income. Every year, despite pleas and special collections, the parish debt mounts a little bit higher; and interest charges sop up more of the cash that does come in.

In poor communities, moreover, the problems of amateurish administration are intensified by a double strain on the pastor's economic resources. On the one hand, the spiraling costs of goods and services afflict the pastor at least as sorely as they do the businessman and the housewife. But where the merchant can either increase his prices or cut back his operations, and where the housewife can at least hunt for bargains, the pastor cannot retrench. Come what may, his church must stay open, his school must still operate, his services must still be freely offered. On the other hand, an outward migration of parishioners will narrow the income base of the parish precisely when income is most needed. Caught in this crossfire between economic inflation and depopulation, the urban pastor in particular may well be unable to lay his hands on enough cash to run the parish.

Small wonder that bankers are less eager now than they once were to lend money to parishes. At one bank in Rochester which handles millions of dollars' worth of church deposits (and which logically should be sympathetic to requests for credit), a loan officer told me bluntly, "We can make much more profitable loans elsewhere. In conscience, we can't charge a church 12 per cent a year. Besides, how the hell can you foreclose on a parish?"

In Manchester and in many other U.S. dioceses, the answers to these problems have long been sought in what the church calls "central financing" arrangements. As we'll see, the specific details vary from diocese to diocese. But although economic conditions have changed radically, the basic technique is still the same as that introduced in New York by Cardinal Spellman as far back as 1939. This letter, introducing central financing to his pastors, still stands as a good first example of the system.

> There are . . . some parishes which are weighed down with debts that they are absolutely unable to carry. These situations are due to unforeseen and unforeseeable circumstances, such as the depression and losses in the number of parishioners . . . It is clear that the accumulation of such situations has resulted in the creation of a diocesan problem, the solution of which requires the wholehearted cooperation of all of us who are in a position to help. . . . I shall, therefore, welcome the practical cooperation of the pastors of any parishes who have [bank] deposits of more than five thousand or ten thousand dollars. I invite the pastors of such parishes, who contemplate no immediate building or extensive repair programs, to come to my assistance in helping me to help others. At the present time I do not intend to make this a matter of obligation. . . .

In brief, Spellman "invited" those pastors who could lay
their hands on surplus funds to turn the money over to the
archdiocese, which would redirect it into parishes badly
overextended or hopelessly in debt. As an inducement,
Spellman offered to pay interest of 1 per cent per year on
these advances. (In 1939, savings banks were paying very
little more.) Pastors who needed money, either to pay off
their debts to the banks or to finance parish expansion,
could borrow from these funds (with chancery approval)
and pay interest of 1½ per cent a year. The difference
was retained by the archdiocese.*

Since its genesis, this neat technique of borrowing from
rich parishes to help finance the poorer ones has spread
widely within the diocesan church. After three decades of
refinement, it has in fact become the chief instrument of diocesan financial control. A closer look shows us how useful
this tool of episcopal administration can be.

Purely in terms of money, central financing means first
of all a way to clean up the Augean stable of parish debt.
Instead of fumbling with a scrapbook of bank notes, mortgages, personal notes and other encumbrances—all falling
due at different dates, payable to various parties and, invariably, costing too much money—the individual pastor
borrows from a single source, pays less interest and forgets
his nightmares about foreclosure. And for those pastors
who do have extra money, loans *to* the diocesan central
fund are safe, licit and fairly productive investments. Mul-
tiply both situations by the number of parishes in a diocese
of average size (by, say, 200), and you'll see that central
financing can save the laity thousands of dollars' worth of
loan interest every year. At the same time, central financ-

* In New York, the ½ per cent "profit" was, and still is, turned over to
the central financing agency, the Archdiocesan Reciprocal Loan Fund, to
increase the loan capital available. Elsewhere, the profit is added to
income each year.

ing brings out of bank accounts and into the hands of the bishop astonishing amounts of parish capital.

Moreover, this is only the first step.

As every corporate comptroller knows, efficient internal financing is one of the keys to gilt-edged credit status. If you manage your own money shrewdly, so lenders reason, you'll do well with ours. The bishop who frees his parishes of a tangle of local debt also frees his diocese to bargain for money on a larger-scale, and hence less costly, basis. "The local bank branches did do some grumbling when we took the parish debts away from them in 1966," Msgr. Porter J. White, Chancellor of the Archdiocese of Baltimore, told me, "but the senior executives understood. In fact, they said we should have done it twenty years ago."

Cardinal Spellman was one of the first of the bishops to understand that a fiscal housecleaning at the parish level increased his own financial bargaining power. He used his knowledge initially to cut the interest cost of the $28 million diocesan debt he inherited from Cardinal Hayes. By borrowing from banks and insurance companies in New England, his official biography reveals, Spellman raised funds to repay the higher-priced New York banks. This strategy created some unhappiness in New York, but saved the archdiocese nearly $500,000 worth of interest a year. Then, the Cardinal proceeded toward his real goal, the retirement of the entire debt of the archdiocese.

Other bishops, for many reasons, stop short of Spellman's goal. In practical terms, few dioceses possess the "earning-power" (i.e., either the numbers or the eagerness of contributors) of the Archdiocese of New York. Also, economic times have changed, so that external indebtedness is no longer as abhorrent to the bishops as it once was to the Cardinal. Finally, not many bishops are gifted with the virtuosity in fund-raising which made one professional, a charity organizer for the United Jewish Appeal, say, "Ah, Spellman was the greatest *schnorrer* [beggar] of us all."

For instance, in Manchester a look at the confidential annual report of the diocesan central fund reveals that of the total capital of approximately $5.5 million in 1967, nearly $2 million came not from the parishes but from banks. Clearly, Bishop Ernest J. Primeau was using the external borrowing power of his diocese to buttress its internal financial resources. This in turn suggests two facts about the diocesan economy: a) that its central financing is relatively new (the Fund began operating in 1962); and b) that at the moment the need for expansion is outpacing the ability of the combined parishes to generate capital. As Msgr. Olkovikas confirmed, it will take time and careful planning for the diocese to finish internalizing its debt. But the timing of borrowings and the pattern of expenditure for debt service and repayment are now under firm control. All in all, the Catholic laity, on whose shoulders the whole financial burden ultimately rests, can be well satisfied with the quality of financial management in Manchester.

Similar central financing programs around the country are well worth noting here. In the Archdiocese of Louisville, according to Archbishop Thomas J. McDonough, "the largest financial operation . . . involves borrowing money from parishes which have accumulated savings and in lending this money to parishes building new churches, schools or other facilities." At the end of 1968, Louisville's central fund held deposits of about $6 million, plus approximately $2 million worth of loan proceeds, against parish borrowings of about $7 million. The much larger Archdiocese of Baltimore set up a central fund in 1966. By November, 1968, internal deposits to the fund were worth about $8 million, to which must be added approximately $12 million worth of external bank debt (the parish debt assumed and refinanced by the archdiocese) for a total capital of $20 million. From the proportion of external to internal borrowing, we can deduce that Baltimore, like Manchester, is in the early stages of a drive to internalize its indebtedness.

Under an exceptionally astute chancellor, Msgr. James P. Devine, who was an accountant before he entered the priesthood, the Diocese of Bridgeport is likewise laboring to refinance its parish debt. So far, a diocesan central fund has accepted about $1.5 million in deposits from the parishes. With diocesan aid, the parishes themselves are retiring more than $1 million worth of their external debts every year. New borrowing is being handled directly by the diocese.

As a final example, in 1968 Archbishop (now Cardinal) John F. Dearden of Detroit announced that his archdiocese, the seventh largest in the U. S., would begin operating a central fund by seeking "voluntary deposits" of up to 10 per cent of annual parish income.

Throughout the U. S., varying forms of central financing are in use in about three-quarters of the dioceses. Some are mandatory systems. Others are looser arrangements under which a diocese backs the credit of the parish at a bank instead of lending it money directly. In a few sees, the *ad hoc* informality of the pre-Spellman days still prevails: the bishops simply lend money from the diocesan reserves to whichever pastors seem most in need of aid. Because there are so many and such varied methods of central financing and because diocesan accounting is so often vague, the total volume of central financing activity is hard to estimate. But the sums of money involved are substantial. Thus, the archdioceses of New York, Chicago and Los Angeles alone have more than $150 million worth of capital tied up in central financing arrangements. In 1970, New York's Reciprocal Loan Fund held parish-loan assets of nearly $80 million. Chicago's central financing program has lent $47,668,000 to 180 parishes and seven other church agencies. In Los Angeles, the program has made loans totaling approximately $30,000.

The five sees mentioned above, Manchester, Louisville, Baltimore, Bridgeport and Detroit, run central financing programs worth a total of $32 million. Reports and off-the-record statements from officials in twenty-three other sees make it reasonable to estimate that, in all, central financing programs absorb between $1.5 billion and $2 billion worth of church capital in the U. S.*

At an average rate of return of 5 per cent per year, the bishops are thus bringing in from $75 million to $100 million yearly from this source. They must of course pay their depositors. If they do so at an average rate of 4 per cent, then $60 million to $80 million a year goes back into the treasuries of the parishes. This leaves a 1 per cent net profit of between $15 million and $20 million a year for the chanceries.

If these 120 operations were ever consolidated into a single "bank"—to say the least, an unlikely prospect—the bank would command considerable attention in financial circles. By comparison with the real giants of the commercial banking business, its size would be modest. As we noted in Chapter One, the Bank of America (the California bank which the Jesuits must surely wish they *did* own) is worth more than $21 billion. The second-ranking Chase Manhattan Bank controls assets of nearly $18 billion. Still, a bank of the diocesan church would rank comfortably high on the *Fortune* list of the 50 largest commercial banks; somewhere between 20th and 35th, if my estimate of total assets is correct. Needless to add, however, dioce-

* I'm assuming, of course, that new loans are balanced by the sum of new deposits, repayments and interest income, a situation which is far from universal.

san "banking" (which is merely a form of private institutional mortgage financing) poses no threat whatever to our friends at the friendly Chase.

What of the remaining one-quarter of the Catholic dioceses? We may well wonder why a time-lag of thirty years should separate Cardinal Spellman's first successes with central financing from the parallel developments now just beginning elsewhere. And why do so many bishops still disregard the obvious practical advantages of this system? Is this simply a matter of institutional inertia and unresponsiveness to innovation? The answers are revealing. Some of the holdout bishops are reluctant to challenge the financial autonomy of their pastors, who can be stubborn opponents of any change. Others hesitate to jar the established relationships between the parishes and their local banks. "When a bank branch manager has nursed a parish through depression, war and a new school plant," an assistant chancellor says, "and when he's a good loyal Catholic who heads the list on Sundays, you'd be inhuman to cut the ground out from under him."

Still other bishops feel that help from the chancery saps the native independence and fiscal ingenuity of the pastor and thus eventually produces a less generous laity. "They got themselves into debt, let them get themselves out," is a refrain still heard in chanceries.

Finally, there do remain dioceses fortunate enough to have been spared the need for this form of financial reorganization. If the banks are treating the pastors magnanimously, if the parishes themselves are prospering and if the few "problem cases" are responding to lectures from the chancellor and occasional direct subsidies from the episcopal checkbook, then the bishop may see no need to quarrel with success.

Fewer and fewer of the bishops, however, are completely disdainful of the virtues of central financing. Today, most do understand that the retirement of external debt is only the first of the advantages this money technique offers. Like Cardinal Spellman (and others) before them, they are discovering that hand in hand with the centralization of parish finance goes much firmer administrative control of all other diocesan affairs. To assert such control, the essential step is to do what Spellman did in New York as far back as 1943: *require* pastors to apply to the chancery for all long-term financing, with no exceptions made even for pastors of wealthy parishes.

Once this step is taken, not only formal permission to build or otherwise expand but also budgeting and supervision of the program rests with the bishop. Given a chancery staff trained in accounting and reasonably adept at construction management, the bishop can put an end to heedless planning and slipshod execution at the parish level. In theory if not always in practice, the chancery can make sure that the pastor doesn't wind up with some parishioner's least-wanted piece of bargain real estate. No longer must construction contracts and subcontracts be awarded solely on the basis of who puts the most money in the collection envelopes. Nor must future generations of parishioners and pastors be enslaved to the mortgage on Father Dolan's Folly. On the contrary, a building commission (a group of chancery representatives and senior pastors with the bishop as chairman) can if necessary force sensible decisions on the Father Dolans of the see.

Furthermore, because the chancery can compel each pastor to take his place in line, the bishop who so desires can do some real administrative planning for the diocese. Instead of being a jumble of unrelated local schemes, the parish building and maintenance programs can be pulled together with diocesan construction projects in one master plan. Land for expansion can be purchased in advance, often at low prices, and stockpiled until needed. Complex real estate trades (e.g., of urban diocesan property with high commercial value for suburban or rural acreage) can be worked out quietly and advantageously. Contractors can be hired to work on more than one job at a time. Guarantees of continuing work on a sizable scale mean that the big, well-financed contractors will compete for church projects, which in turn means reductions in bids and actual costs. Church furnishings, school equipment and other items can similarly be bought in quantity at discounts. Insurance, a mare's nest in most parishes, can be untangled and consolidated. Whenever circumstances dictate a slowdown or a halt in plant expansion, the chancery can redirect the flow of funds from depositors into other worthy projects.

In sum, central financing brings with it the budgetary, scheduling and forecasting tools which most executives take for granted, and which Catholic bishops badly need.

Plainly, this pivotal topic has eased us away from the production of diocesan income and into the new area of internal financial administration. Indeed, we're due to discover how the bishop who sets up a central fund can use it to ease his managerial burdens in areas other than parish expansion. As illustration, and also as the prologue to a broader survey of diocesan management, we might glance at the current list of outstanding loans made by the Central Fund of one eastern diocese. Of the 71 loans on this particular list, 59 were made to parishes. These range in initial amount from a few thousand dollars up to one item of more than $400,000, a loan made to the pastor of a brand-new parish for the down-payment on land and plant construction.

Other loans on the list, however, were made not to needy parishes but to *diocesan* organizations. Several, totaling about $1.3 million, represented the outlay for the construction of high schools. In this see, the high school building program is more than a decade old. As the schools have opened and have begun to generate tuition income, much of this original Central Fund indebtedness has been repaid.* We also note such other items as a loan of $442,000 to the Development Fund; one of $26,000 to the Mission Fund; and a loan of $10,000 to the "Blue Cross/Blue Shield account" of the chancery office. Each of these transactions is worth a closer look.

The diocesan Development Fund was originally set up to seek money for an adult center of religious education and for the accompanying program of instruction. Because this particular bishop feels that such a center is an urgent requirement, he anticipated the sum a Development Fund drive would produce by borrowing the needed cash from the Central Fund. By publicizing the center and its goals, by doing some fund-raising and by charging fees for the use of the new center, the bishop can begin the repayment process after the project is completed. To be sure, in arranging the initial loan, the bishop is in the pleasant position of being able to dictate, within canonical limits, the terms under which he becomes both lender and borrower.

The Mission Fund, through which the chancery aids some parishes with cash to support church activities in outlying areas, has similarly borrowed in anticipation of income from the annual special parish collection. Lastly, the total cost of the Blue Cross/Blue Shield and major medical insurance for the priests, nuns and lay employees of the diocese is close to $45,000 a year. "Most years," the chancellor admitted to me rather sheepishly, "the pastors are late in forwarding their premiums. They forget the notice in the parish bulletin. And to tell the truth, sometimes we don't remind them in time." If all the money hasn't come in by the date the premiums are due, the bishop takes what cash

_____

* One of the high schools, however, has been forced to borrow, this time from a bank, to repay its Central Fund obligation.

he needs from the Central Fund, repaying it a few weeks or months later.

On the other side of the ledger, the parishes of the diocese have deposited in the Central Fund approximately $1.5 million of the $5.5 million total. As in many sees, external bank financing supplements the internal deposits to the Fund. Also, however, we note among the depositors the Catholic Charities unit of the diocese (which has put more than $500,000 into the Fund) and many other nonparochial organizations.

This bishop, who deserves his reputation as a shrewd manager of diocesan money, has obviously made of his Central Fund something more than a repository of construction money for the parishes. Indeed, he's using the Fund almost as he would a regular bank, for short-term as well as long-term financial dealings. In the process, he's solving one of the major administrative problems of the Catholic bishop, the problem of gaining immediate access to wealth already accumulated but sequestered in one or another of the many crannies of the diocesan economy.

At first glance, this may not seem like much of a problem. As the legal owner of all diocesan assets, doesn't the bishop have the right to lay his hands on whatever money or property he needs for legitimate ecclesiastical reasons? Perhaps surprisingly, the answer is no. Here, as in other areas of diocesan government, the bishop himself is governed by seldom invoked but ironclad legal regulations. To delve deeply into the canonical limitations on his fiscal powers is well beyond the scope of this book. But we should be aware of the basic rules with which the bishops all must contend. Thus, in Catholic usage, every institution of the church—whether a parish, a convent, a hospital or an intangible enterprise like a foundation or a charitable trust—is considered to be a "juridical personality." That is, an independent entity with its own special purposes (its "ends," as canonists say) and its own legal rights, including the right to acquire and hold property.

The alphas and omegas of episcopal authority over such entities are these: a) a bishop can create new juridical personalities; and b) he may—in fact, he must—administer the property of the juridical personalities under his control *in keeping with their special purposes.* Conversely, however, c) the bishop may not summarily dissolve an existing juridical personality; nor d) arbitrarily expropriate its money or property for use elsewhere.

The logic behind the rules certainly seems unassailable. The canons safeguard subordinate diocesan institutions against the overefficiency (or the rapacity) of the powerful administrative figure who might otherwise swallow whole any faltering organization. And yet, given the exigencies of running a diocese today, such protective legislation can be a serious administrative hazard. In every diocese, the chancery will know of pockets of wealth which, because of the canons, are literally sealed off from use. Even if the financial needs of the bishop are desperate and the property in question superfluous, slow-moving and intricate legal processes must be set in motion in order to free the assets in question. And needless to add, while the case is *sub judice,* the property might as well be on the moon.

Rather than entangle himself in such time-wasting maneuvers,* the canny bishop will choose another, much easier alternative. He'll simply arrange a loan transaction, with the given institution as the lender and the diocese itself as the borrower. The fact of the loan completely changes the legal situation. Instead of challenging the rights of an established juridical personality, the Ordinary—in his role as

* "It's amazing," commented one bishop to me, "the shabbiest, most neglected and worst-run nursing home or pious program will turn out to have a protector in Rome who's a real hothead. He can tie you up for years. They call it the Eternal City because it takes forever to get anything done there."

trustee—is authorizing it to make an investment, an absolutely proper act of administration. At the same time, he is liberating a chunk of previously restricted capital for presumably more productive uses. As long as the bishop observes the terms of the loan, which must be reasonably fair to the lender, his legal position is invulnerable.*

Therefore, by using diocesan credit as a lever, a bishop can if he wishes pry open coffers which in most dioceses have remained locked for generations. To uncover a pluperfect example, let's return to the ledger of the diocesan Central Fund we were examining a few pages ago. On the list of depositors (those lending money to the bishop), we find an entry headed "P/C Funds," and a corresponding deposit of more than $800,000. These initials stand for "Perpetual Care"; and, as a word or two of explanation will make clear, their presence offers convincing evidence of this bishop's financial acumen.

As many Americans undoubtedly know, cemeteries are uniquely lucrative enterprises. To put matters succinctly, the cost of a final resting place is almost never low. In most cemeteries, moreover, including Catholic cemeteries, the cost of the actual burial plot is only a fraction of the total outlay. Because cemeteries do cost money to maintain, and because people not unnaturally prefer nice tidy graves, the cemetery people add in substantial sums to cover the cost of so-called perpetual care. Especially for the millions of families whose funerary traditions require what cemetery salesmen style "the memorial approach," the price of this care is very high; higher than the price of the plot itself. Accordingly, many of us—just how many, nobody knows for sure—are forced to prepay the expenses of a last lodging a little bit at a time on the installment plan. So by sim-

---

* Some canon lawyers question whether or not the deposit of money at interest is truly an investment. The current view, as far as I can figure it out, is that long-term loans are investments while short-term transactions (e.g., savings-bank deposits) are not.

ple commercial logic, every cemetery not already filled up is the recipient of a steady cash income, one always in excess of its current needs. Whether the cemetery is a business venture catering to all creeds, like California's fabled Forest Lawn, or a nonprofit burial place owned by a church or synagogue and operated by a board of trustees, the economic principle is exactly the same. The time payments of those still living add up to more than enough to care for the graves of the dead.

What happens to the surplus money?

Reassuringly, in the eyes of the civil law no funds are more sacrosanct than the funds in the treasury of a graveyard.* Everywhere, stringent state statutes govern the handling of these trust funds. An impressive panoply of legal controls over cemetery fiduciaries (separate bank and investment accounts, periodic audits and financial reports) is the rule. While cemetery owners or trustees may invest the money as it comes in, their choice of investments is generally restricted to corporate bonds or listed common stocks with good dividend histories. The protection of capital, not the financial growth of the fund, is the mandatory goal. So it is that the funds held in trust to cover cemetery perpetual care rank—though on a more modest scale—with the legal reserves of life insurance companies as unassailably solvent pools of capital. Not that the aggregate sums involved are minuscule. For example, according to Fred S. Suthergreen, director of the Division of Cemeteries, New York State Department of State, the perpetual care endowments of the 2,000 "membership corporation" cemeteries in New York (excluding cemeteries operated by religious corporations) total approximately $85 million. Another $45 million is held in trust to provide per-

* In most states the church follows the civil statutes which govern cemetery operations.

manent maintenance of cemetery grounds apart from the grave sites themselves.

In the diocesan church, cemetery administration is a specialty of its own. Almost without exception, diocesan chanceries place ranking officials in charge of cemeteries. Their jobs cover everything from keeping pastors informed of changes in the canons of Catholic burial to conducting labor negotiations with gravediggers' and maintenance-workers' unions. Some of the cemeteries they supervise were originally founded by bishops and thus came under chancery jurisdiction from the start. Others began as adjuncts to parishes and only later came under diocesan control. Still others, and these constitute the vast majority, remain parish cemeteries under the direct control of the pastor.

As usual, no statistical information has ever been released; but a diocese-by-diocese scrutiny of the 1970 *Official Catholic Directory* yielded some significant figures. According to my count, Catholic dioceses currently operate 459 cemeteries; and the cemeteries connected with parishes number 6,192. On the basis of rather sketchy reports from eight dioceses out of 160, I estimate that the average size of the perpetual care fund of a Catholic cemetery is $50,000.* This means that spread across the country, the perpetual-care endowments of Catholic cemeteries are worth something like $350 million today.

So far, almost all of the bishops have left these cemetery funds strictly alone. For instance, in New York the two archdiocesan cemeteries (Gate of Heaven in Westchester and Calvary Cemetery in Queens) are owned by a corporation entirely independent of other archdiocesan corporations. Despite occasional looks of longing cast at

---

* The endowments of the huge diocesan cemeteries are worth many millions of dollars. But most Catholic cemeteries are small and only lightly endowed.

the endowment funds ("Wouldn't we love to get our hands on that working capital," a chancery assistant acknowledged), no transfers of money between this corporation and the Archbishopric of New York have ever been made.* The lawyers for the cemetery corporation insist that its investments be confined to the types of listed securities specified by state law. "The credit of the archdiocese is great," says John Hoyt, who is one of them, "but it's not a public company." Therefore, the cemetery corporation will make no "investment," via loan or other means, in archdiocesan projects.

The bishop whose Central Fund has tapped the cemetery trust funds is thus something of an innovator. His chancellor is matter-of-fact about the transaction. "Certainly we asked our lawyers, and they told us that under our state laws a diocesan loan was a perfectly sound investment for our cemetery corporations. After all, pastors have been borrowing from cemetery funds for years. [A practice also forbidden in most sees but widely if surreptitiously pursued.] We see every reason to open up these funds for the benefit of the whole diocese."

Leaving this particular debate to be settled by the bishops and their lawyers, we can underscore the point the cemetery-fund situation illustrates. Used creatively, central financing is not just a way of consolidating and controlling parish debt, or a modest source of investment income for the see. Much more important is its administrative value as a means of moving money around; of getting income to flow from sector to sector of the diocesan economy; of unblocking restricted capital; of enabling bishops to utilize all their financial resources; of establishing fiscal controls.

Properly speaking, then, further consideration of cen-

* Because both cemeteries were originally those of the parish of Saint Patrick's Cathedral, The Trustees of Saint Patrick's Cathedral, Inc. is their owner. The Archbishopric of New York is the legal title of the archdiocesan corporation.

tral financing should wait until we deal with the key subject of diocesan financial administration. We'll later see that in some dioceses, centralized mortgage financing has been accompanied by the centralization of such other crucial financial operations as purchasing, insurance-buying and the planning of benefits for priests and lay employees. And we'll explore each of these specific areas in detail.

Here, we began by viewing central financing as a form of internal investment; one of the many sources of diocesan income. Let's now continue our survey of how dioceses bring in money by doing full justice to a seemingly more colorful topic. This one, indeed, casts a peculiar spell over every observer, bemusing equally the expert in finance and the expert in religion, obsessing equally those connected with the Catholic Church and those resentful of it. The topic in question is the investment portfolio of the diocesan church.

CHAPTER EIGHT

Stocks, Bonds and Bishops

During the first stages of my research for this book, a friend of mine, a securities analyst, met me for lunch one day in the Wall Street area. As we strolled toward the restaurant, my companion nudged me and pointed out a priest who was hurrying, briefcase in hand, down lower Broadway. "See that?" he muttered darkly. "He comes down here every day from the Power House [a favorite nickname of New Yorkers for the chancery of their archdiocese]. The black bag is full of stock certificates. He's the messenger who takes them to the Chase bank." I was duly impressed by this glimpse of the Eternal Money Game until I buttonholed the priest and learned: a) that he was one of those in residence at Our Lady of Victory, the church at Pine and William streets which serves the financial district; b) that he was rushing not to be late for a special Mass; and c) that his briefcase held devotional, not financial literature. Unhappily, my friend's credibility quotient sank still further when I later learned that although the Chase Manhattan Bank does do some business with the Catholic Church, it does not handle the investment account of the Archdiocese of New York.

At about the same time, I came across a comment, first printed in 1959 and since widely quoted, by Dr. Eugene Carson Blake, General Secretary (now President) of the World Council of Churches, a liberal Protestant organization which strongly supports interfaith activity. Said Dr. Blake:

> When one remembers that churches pay no inheritance tax (churches do not die), that churches may own and operate businesses and be exempt from the 52 per cent corporate income tax, and that real property used for church purposes (which in some states are most generously construed) is tax exempt, it is not unreasonable to prophesy that with reasonably prudent management, the churches ought to be able to control the whole economy of the nation within the predictable future.

If my securities-analyst friend was the casual transmitter of a fable about the investment prowess of the church, the respected Dr. Blake clearly accepts a much more sweeping version of the same story.* Is there any truth to his contention? Could the churches really take over the American economy?

As I've already indicated, one purpose of this book is simply to find accurate answers to questions like these. Now, part of the way through our study, a direct rejoinder in terms of the Catholic Church may well seem unnecessary. I myself feel that the myth is a myth. To put matters

* In a collection of essays published in 1966, Dr. Blake reiterated his concern about the wealth and power of the churches.

bluntly, the notion that the Catholic Church (presumably in combination with all other churches) could engineer an economic takeover of this country seems to me even sillier than the notion that a Catholic president would get his political orders from the Pope.

Still, if part of our purpose is to dispel the myths, another part is to uncover the truths about the economy of the church and to open up the issues these truths raise. Editorializing on the subject is thus undoubtedly premature. A better strategy, at least for the moment, is to leave Dr. Blake poised, however precariously, on the brink of his own startling prophecy. We ourselves should keep on with our quest for the actualities of church financial power.

Let's do so by asking the broad basic question: What do we mean by the "assets" of the diocesan church? For instance, when we learn from a financial report that the Archdiocese of Boston is worth precisely $648,074,468.51, what form does this wealth take?

Obviously, much of it is in real estate; and specifically in what realty experts term "single-use institutional property"; meaning, of course, the parish churches, chapels, rectories, convents and schools; and the diocesan hospitals, high schools, seminaries and retreat houses of every see. This in itself is no revelation. What is significant, however, is the ratio of these fixed assets to other diocesan assets. Thus, in Boston and in each of the twenty-two other Catholic dioceses I've surveyed, *this institutional real property accounts for 90 per cent or more of all diocesan asset values.* In the smaller dioceses, the ratio tends to fluctuate a bit, ranging from 85 per cent up to 95 per cent.

Before we focus on the 10 per cent of diocesan assets held in property other than institutional realty, let's be certain we understand the investment value of ecclesiastical bricks and mortar. First of all, measured in dollars and cents, the productivity of these physical assets is always low. Very often, in fact, productivity is negative. To illustrate, a Catholic hospital or other diocesan service institution might conceivably, by dint of heroic effort, break even at the end of a given year without the benefit of outside aid. But I know of no parochial school in the land which today sustains itself on its tuitions and fees alone. All Catholic schools need, in addition, the direct support of their parishes and the indirect subsidy which takes the form of low-cost labor on the part of teaching priests and nuns. On the question of productivity, Msgr. Porter J. White of Baltimore sums matters up neatly when he says, "We'll never operate at a profit, not until the end of time."

Next, it's true that the fixed assets of the 160 dioceses, like those of business concerns, are worth money.* To the businessman, in fact, the mere existence of his plant and equipment means an addition to his supply of dollars. Even in a bad year, he can count on a flow of cash from tax allowances for depreciation. In contrast, the bishop luxuriates in a tax-free income. But he enjoys no extra benefits from the wear and tear on his properties. Nor is there any reason why he should, given today's tax structure.

The commercial value of church real estate naturally depends on the type and location of the given parcel, as well as on the state of the market itself. Occasionally, a chancery can make a lot of money on a sale of diocesan property. For example, early in 1969 the Archdiocese of New York sold its forty-three-year-old Cathedral High School for Girls to realty developer Samuel Rudin for $8.5 million in cash. Rudin coveted the property because its location, at the corner of 50th Street and Lexington Avenue, is absolutely ideal for an office skyscraper. The Archdiocese, which fifty years ago paid less than $1 million for the site, is equally pleased. Out of its gains, the chancery can: a) relocate the school on a more appropriate site (the

* In Chapter Ten we'll analyze in detail the valuation of realty assets.

one chosen is at 55th Street and First Avenue, on property already owned by the church which is out of the midtown melee); b) build a bigger, more modern plant; and c) perhaps even have funds left over to reinvest.

Not very many diocesan properties, however, are to be found in Gold Coast neighborhoods conveniently near favorable sites for relocation. In fact, the properties least needed by a given see are almost invariably those with the poorest market values. This is the point of a comment by Robert F. Borg, president of the Kreisler-Borg Construction Company in New York, which does much building work for the church. "What commercial operator wants to buy a stone mausoleum in an out-of-the-way, decaying neighborhood? To get at the land, he'd have to demolish the thing. It's cheaper to knock down a couple of tenements on the same block, and still cheaper to stay away entirely."

Furthermore, Catholics in the old neighborhoods become deeply attached to their churches, and are fiercely resentful of chancery efforts to close them down or put them on sale. One bishop who made this discovery the hard way was Fulton J. Sheen of Rochester. In a well-meant gesture of charity, Sheen attempted to donate the physical plant of St. Mary's, an underpopulated parish in the heart of the city, to the federal urban-renewal authorities. But the protests of the 150 furious parishioners and their pastor were so heated that the embarrassed Sheen was forced to withdraw his offer.* "Sell church property?" a Rochester priest laughed when I raised the question, "Hell, our boss can't even give it away!"

So it may be correct to conclude that the imposing presence of the institutional properties of the church is evi-

* I suspect also that the canon lawyers in Bishop Sheen's chancery warned him against this form of alienation (i.e., transfer of ownership away from the church) as contrary to Canon 1531, which governs the question.

dence of solid financial strength. But only an innocent could see in such properties a machine for producing profits or a huge generator of dividends. On the contrary, these weighty assets are, with few exceptions, not really productive assets at all. From the administrative point of view, they are costly—if indispensable—liabilities. The economic and managerial implications of this curious economic fact will unfold as we go on, and we'll consider its full significance later. Right now, the thing to keep in mind is that, for better or for worse, most of the wealth of the church is frozen in stone; and that money, not granite or marble, begets money.

A few pages ago, I stressed that according to my survey of reports from twenty-three dioceses, only about 10 per cent of the assets of any see qualify as liquid assets. Sometimes, indeed, the percentage is surprisingly lower. For instance, in Boston, the liquid assets (including cash, accounts receivable and the value of all parish and archdiocesan securities) totaled just over $40 million in 1969: about 7 per cent of total assets. If similar ratios prevail in all sees, as I'm certain they do, then the next question is: what fraction of this fraction constitutes commercial investments of the types which so disturb Dr. Blake? Once again, to anyone who wants to see the church as a mill for producing profits and rolling out capital gains, the answer will be disappointing. My sampling indicates that only about one-fifth to one-quarter of the liquid assets of the average diocese is held in stocks, bonds and income-producing realty.

If liquid assets equal no more than 10 per cent of total diocesan assets, simple arithmetic will tell us that in most sees only a small fraction of total assets, *perhaps 2 to 3 per cent*, take the form of commercial investments.

The best way to validate this key assumption is to list some of the representative American sees, their total assets and their investment holdings.

See	Rank[1]	Total Assets	Investment Assets	Percentage
Boston	3	$648,074,469	$14,538,900[2]	2.24
Baltimore	23	216,000,000	5,200,000	2.40
Miami	25	85,968,211	856,918	1.00
Joliet	46	77,548,990	2,765,762	3.00
Tulsa	93	40,000,000[3]	2,508,195	6.26
Spokane	119	5,929,400	154,000	2.50
Rapid City	136	7,313,437	600,000	8.50

1. By size of Catholic population.
2. Includes cash as well as investments in general and restricted funds.
3. Estimated based on published financial data.

Because the reports from which these figures are taken are not all current (though only one dates from before 1968), I cannot claim that this listing exactly represents today's situation. But the figures do give us a good idea of the ratios between investment assets and total assets typical within the diocesan church. (It's worth noting that the exceptionally high ratio of investments to all assets in Rapid City was due to the receipt of securities as a gift to the cathedral building fund.) And reports from the other dioceses substantiate that productive commercial investments take up correspondingly little room on their official balance sheets and financial statements. In fact, most of the liquid assets of the dioceses surveyed take the form of plain cash, kept either in checking accounts or in bank savings accounts. For instance, in analyzing the financial report of one New England see, I found that it owned securities worth more than $800,000, but that $4.3 million was being held in dozens of separate savings accounts at four local banks. Short of keeping his money in a cigar box, the bishop could hardly have devised a less sophisticated (or a lower-yielding) investment technique.*

* Some of the bishops have discovered that "c/d's," bank certificates of deposit, are just as safe as savings accounts and pay higher interest.

While the commercial investments of the 160 dioceses may be low in proportion to total assets, a small percentage of a huge total still must add up to a lot of money. How much money? Once again, the hazards of projecting nationwide totals from limited information should not be discounted. But on the basis of current figures from twenty-three U. S. dioceses (including three of the four most populous), I feel secure in stating that the bishops in this country own stocks, bonds and commercial realty with an aggregate value of between $900 million and $1 billion.

For the sake of comparison, note that the endowment funds of Harvard, Yale and Princeton universities are worth, all told, about $1.5 billion. The investment assets of the University of Texas are valued at $544 million; of the University of California, $250 million. And the endowment funds of the Ford Foundation add up to $850 million. In terms of the productive investments of secular educational and philanthropic enterprises, therefore, the investment holdings of the diocesan church are certainly not outlandishly large. No one diocesan investment portfolio (not even the combined portfolios of all institutions of the Archdiocese of New York, which I value at about $20 million) even comes close to matching the holdings of one of the above-named giants of American education or charity.

Who owns these diocesan commercial investment assets? As we might suspect, ownership is widely spread, not only among the different dioceses but within each diocese. Only recently, in fact, have diocesan chanceries gone into investment markets with the funds at their disposal. When they do so, moreover, they usually use as channel a separate legal entity, a foundation or development corporation. Thus, the Spellman Memorial Foundation in New York, the Catholic Foundation in Tulsa and dozens of other foundations and Bishop's Development Funds serve both as receptacles for contributions of securities and as investment media. Such foundations are shrewd fund-raising devices as well as handy vehicles of investment activity. Unconnected with specifically Catholic religious institutions, the foundations can attract money from non-Catholics as well as from Catholics interested in the nonsectarian welfare programs, charities and educational works of a diocese. The mushrooming growth of these "secularized" foundations is one sign of what a lay diocesan financial aide in Baltimore calls "our endeavor to convince people that money is ecumenical."

Aside from watching over the growth of foundation endowments, however, the chanceries themselves stay away from the investment markets. As we've seen, traditional chancery practice, whenever feasible, is to convert receipts of securities and other commercial property into cash. This process necessarily involves the bishop and his financial officials in planning and even direct negotiation with lawyers, bankers, brokers, realtors and other outside financial advisers. In terms of diocesan investment policy-making, these relations are extremely interesting and highly important ones. Shortly, we'll be measuring their effectiveness. But in terms of investment ownership, the professionals who serve the Catholic chancery are almost always selling for the account of the bishop, not buying.

Episcopally sponsored foundations aside, the ownership of investments within any diocese is diffused over the entire range of church organizations, from the parishes on upward through the hospitals, seminaries, colleges, cemeteries and other subsidiaries of the see. A quick survey will indicate where the ownership of investment assets is spread most thinly, and where major concentrations of investment assets are to be found. Thus, at the parish level, the ownership of securities and other investments is rare today and growing rapidly rarer. For one thing, the actual investment of parish funds in stocks and bonds is strongly discouraged, if not forbidden, by most bishops.* For another, the chanceries, exercising the bishops' legal control over parish assets, are pressing pastors to turn over all surplus funds to the diocesan central administration. So the few shares of stock or the thin sheaves of corporate or government bonds which parishioners donate to their parishes find their way almost automatically into diocesan brokerage accounts for eventual sale, with the proceeds credited to the central fund accounts of the parishes.

Once in a while, the pastor of a parish which has received a gift or bequest of securities is allowed to keep it for use as collateral on a construction loan or for some other approved purpose. And once in a while, a pastor will keep secret the receipt of securities, simply because, as a pastor in Connecticut insisted to me, "those *monsignori* in the chancery aren't going to tell me what to do with the money *I* raise." But by and large, pastors report what they bring in, and parish involvement in the investment process is minimal.

Such separate diocesan institutions as high schools, hospitals and homes for the ill or aged are much more likely than parishes to list investment holdings among their assets. Because these institutions are generally run by religious orders exempt from diocesan supervision, or else owned by quasi-autonomous Catholic charitable corporations, they are islands of self-government within the diocese. Typically, their boards of trustees are mixtures of laymen and professional religious. The members of their finance committees are picked for their investment acumen as well as for their fund-raising abilities. As a result, their endowment funds, while rarely large, are often better handled than the invest-

* The Ordinary can legally do this because, in canon law, investing is an act of "extraordinary administration" which requires episcopal permission.

ment funds of chancery-run trusts. One reason is that the trustees of diocesan institutions aren't required—though they're frequently requested—to trade their stocks and bonds to the bishop in exchange for central fund credits which pay relatively low interest and yield no capital gains.

Apart from these institutions, the most important holders of commercial investments within a see are the various trust funds which control the capital of the seminaries, Catholic Charities corporations, Mass trust funds and other "pious foundations" and cemeteries. Merely to identify these investment media is to gain an idea of their character. Thus, by tradition, Catholic seminaries charge nominal fees or none at all. The seminary of a diocese is a favorite object of parish charity. Not only is an annual Sunday collection allotted to the seminary in most sees, but parish fund drives raise additional money to further seminary education. Especially popular is the "burse" collected in honor of a veteran pastor and presented to Father at his twenty-fifth (or his fiftieth) anniversary celebration. He turns the money over to the chancery which adds it to the burse, or permanent endowment, of the seminary.

Other donors to diocesan seminaries, naturally enough, include the families of seminarians and of priests. And priests themselves, as loyal alumni, also give or bequeath money to their seminaries. In addition to increasing permanent endowment capital, such gifts may be directed into student aid funds. These funds cover part of the cost of seminary training. The seminary student aid fund as well as the burse will thus control some capital, in the form of restricted funds from which the income alone is available for loan purposes.

Similarly, the Catholic Charities corporation of a see will accumulate in the course of its fund-raising gifts and bequests of securities which come with strings attached. For example, the donor may specify that the income from the securities be paid only to a Catholic orphanage, or that the securities themselves may never be sold. Over the years, any Catholic Charities corporation builds up a whole portfolio of such securities. Its value is frequently much greater than that of the total income being funneled into participating charities each year. "If they knew this, the laity would probably be scandalized," says a Catholic Charities spokesman in Los Angeles. "They'd accuse us of holding back on charity. But what can we do? We don't want to turn down the capital. And if we sell our stocks, we'll be violating the civil law." *

> Five hundred poor I have in yearly pay,
> Who twice a day their wither'd hands hold up
> Toward heaven, to pardon blood: and I have built
> Two chantries where the sad and solemn priests
> Sing still for Richard's soul.

Thus Shakespeare versifies the acts of remorse of Henry V for his father's slaying of Richard II. And the poetry reminds us that the endowment of prayers and Masses in memory of the dead is an age-old pious custom of the church. (It is as well the ancestor of almost all of today's charitable foundations, endowments and memorials. Indeed, the term "foundation" stems from a verb meaning "provide for," and an "endowment" originally referred to the "dowry" paid to a monastery for the maintenance of a nun.)

Today, of course, the tradition of founding chantries or leaving money to the poor in return for prayers and Masses has been supplanted by other types of memorial gifts. The completion of a Mass card and its accompaniment by an offering assure the Catholic that an obligation to pray for the dead will be honored. Nevertheless, on a modest scale,

---

* When I suggested that direct disclosure, coupled with a straightforward explanation of the facts, might be the best answer to "scandal," this priest shook his head. "They'd never understand," he said.

Catholic families do give funds to the church in order to endow Masses "in perpetuity." The endowment, moreover, constitutes a gift not so much to the parish or the diocese as to the international church. As a rule, the income from Mass endowments is sent, along with a directive to celebrate the requisite number of Masses, to a mission church in Asia, Africa or Latin America. There, the priests perform the Masses, scrupulously notifying the originating chancery of their completion (a bookkeeping job of no small proportions). The stipends are used to support the mission. So as well as being a pious act, a Mass endowment is a form of foreign aid. But the income only is sent abroad. The principal of the endowment constitutes a restricted gift in trust. It must be invested, but it may not be spent.

Lastly, we've already seen in some detail how a cemetery trust fund grows out of the maintenance and perpetual care contributions of parishioners.

This catalogue of the diocesan entities which may own commercial investments should suggest even to a skeptical reader that diocesan investment power is both fragmented and held in check by civil and canon law. We can summarize the real situation as follows: a) the investment capital of the diocese is split among dozens (and in a large see, hundreds) of separate trusts; b) as chief trustee, the bishop is primarily responsible for the safety of the capital and only secondarily for its growth; c) the diocese, like other fiduciaries (e.g., banks, life insurance companies) tends to be a highly cautious investor, as both law and logic dictate.

Now that this groundwork is laid, we can focus on some of the interesting specifics. For instance, we can ask such questions as: What types of stocks, bonds and other investments do diocesan institutions like to own? What criteria govern the selection of these investments? Who advises whom on financial matters in the diocesan church?

Better than any abstract discussion, an actual listing of

diocesan securities answers the first of these questions. The example I've chosen is the portfolio held at the beginning of 1968 by the Student Education Fund of the Diocese of Oklahoma City-Tulsa.

Corporate stock	No. of shares	Market value[1]	Book value[2]
American Motors Corp.	801	$ 10,713	$ 11,314
Anaconda Co.	40	1,895	1,970
Beryllium Corp.	5	221	219
City Stores Corp.	151	3,001	3,001
Federal-Mogul, Inc.	161	6,581	5,333
International Mining	20	635	635
Int'l. Silver (preferred)	30	915	1,050
Int'l. Silver (common)	396	13,068	19,948
Northern States Power	100	2,875	3,063
Okla. Gas & Electric	1,065	28,222	26,758
Pennzoil Co.	100	12,400	11,600
Scotten Dillon Co.	115	1,150	1,150
Screw & Bolt Corp. Amer.	450	4,331	5,512
U.T.D. Corporation	242	8,531	6,927
White Motor Co.	858	42,900	46,332
Fresnillo Co.	250	9,125	7,187
Universal Marion Corp.	200	4,900	3,800
Wentworth Manufac. Co.	200	1,000	900
American Gen'l. Life Ins.	2,010	44,471	51,004
Gulf Life Ins. Co.	73	1,624	1,643
Lamar Life Ins. Co.	20	690	830
Insurance Securities Inc.	9	68	54
Affiliated Fund	82	713	759
Channing Common Fund	5,180	11,603	12,280
Canadian Fund	105	1,873	2,210
Fundamental Investors	540	6,334	7,176
National Securities	527	4,121	4,242

Corporate stock	No. of shares	Market value[1]	Book value[2]
Du Pont	166	26,311	26,145
General Motors	167	13,694	13,945
Texas Gulf Sulphur	50	6,350	7,300
Canadian Grain	727	727	727
Farmers Co-op Assn. Sayre	4	4	100
Galveston-Houston Co.	200	200	400
Mid-Continent Co-op.	1	1	1
Panhandle Co-op.	0.5	1	25
Trout Mining Co.	4	4	4
		$271,252	$285,544

1. On December 31, 1967.
2. Value at time of acquisition.

You need not be an investment expert to see in this portfolio the fruits of a highly conservative investment policy. According to a bank trust officer who reviewed the list for me, "Except for a few oddities like those co-op shares, it's a classic trust portfolio. All listed stocks, with blue chips like Du Pont and GM, lots of industrials and utilities, lots of insurance companies. If your grandmother were unusually timid, this is what she'd do with her money. There's not a computer stock or a hot space-age issue in sight."

One feature of the list, indeed, reflects ultraconservatism. Of the thirty-six issues owned, six are mutual funds. These are not the "no-load" funds favored by more sophisticated purchasers, moreover, but the "contract" funds bought by individuals from sales representatives. The basic principle of the mutual fund, of course, is diversification of investments and thus presumably of financial risk. But these are goals which any professional money-manager knows how to achieve. By including these funds in the portfolio, the trustee who handles this particular trust is only redoubling his cautiousness (at the price of the sales commissions and management fees involved). "Whoever chose the funds was clearly looking for safety and freedom from worry," my banker friend commented. "Or else the bishop's brother is a mutual-fund salesman."

This same banker stressed that many of the stocks on the list are income stocks, noted more for their steady dividends than for their price performance. "For a trust fund, this is as it should be," he said. But he still wondered how, during a year when all stock prices increased by 6.77 per cent and industrials rose in value by 8.31 per cent, the trustee could have allowed the total worth of this diocesan portfolio to *decrease* by nearly 5 per cent.

"Conservatism is one thing, but in 1967 a loss of absolute value took real ingenuity. It certainly proves that the Catholics aren't the swingers they're supposed to be."

If we examine the securities held by other diocesan trusts, we naturally discover variations in market orientation and performance. Yet the results are almost always unspectacular. For instance, in Oklahoma City-Tulsa the seminary burse. funds include investments in a common stock portfolio consisting mostly of oils and utilities. At the beginning of 1968, the total value of the portfolio was $108,370, a gain of only $1,068 over the value at the beginning of 1967, or less than 1 per cent.

Such specific lists of securities holdings are almost never released by chancery officials or lay trustees of diocesan institutions.* The few I've seen, however, do bear out my contention that the diocesan church in general is hypercautious about the stock market, though not necessarily unconcerned about gains. One New England diocese I visited, not a large one, seems recently to have tailored its

---

* Bishop Victor J. Reed of Oklahoma City–Tulsa is one bishop who believes in full public disclosure. He is unique among the bishops in this respect.

investments to today's market conditions rather better than the average Catholic see has done. All told, its various trust funds are invested in a combined portfolio of only twenty stocks. (According to most contemporary money-men, it's much better to work with a small list than to diversify too broadly.) The portfolio includes such blue chips as RCA, AT&T and Standard Oil, but nearly 40 per cent of its total value is concentrated in the stocks of two companies, IBM and Sears, Roebuck & Co. The 151 shares of IBM owned by the diocese were acquired at a cost of $37,107 and in early 1971 were worth about $47,000. A block of 800 Sears, Roebuck shares which originally cost $14,000 had a value of $64,000. The solid gains from these investments, plus modest gains from lesser holdings, more than offset losses on holdings in Insurance Company of North America (a favorite diocesan investment) and Globe Union. In all, the diocese has realized total long-term profits (on paper) of nearly $60,000 on stocks acquired for an aggregate of $151,000. "That's a better result [than Oklahoma City's record]," my banker friend told me. "But it's still a ten-year average gain, including dividends, of less than five per cent a year."

Although he would not dream of disclosing the specific holdings of the various archdiocesan portfolios, Msgr. Joseph P. Murphy, vice-chancellor of the Archdiocese of New York, confirms that investment policy is conservative. "Less than 10 per cent of our investment income is income from stocks, bonds or other commercial investments," he says. "Most is loan interest from the Reciprocal Loan Fund and other sources." The 1968 archdiocesan financial report shows total income "from marketable investments, royalties* and interest on notes receiva-

---

* Like several other sees, New York is a participant in private oil and gas syndications which yield royalty income. I could not ascertain the exact amount of this income.

ble" as $3,064,000. According to Msgr. Murphy, who handles all financial matters for the chancery, commercial investment income (including dividends and the proceeds of securities sales) comes to $300,000 or less per year. This in itself is a sign, Murphy pointed out to me, "that we're not in business to make money on the market." Nor, he believes, is any other major see.

A preference for blue-chip stocks, a concern for safety rather than growth, and obedience to the canons forbidding speculation hardly add up to an institution intent on a takeover of the economy. Furthermore, the other types of investments favored by diocesan chanceries and institutional trustees are even less oriented toward expansion. For instance, take the bond market. On the surface, corporate bonds and the various types of federal, state and municipal issues available to investors seem ideal for churches. All the investment features of bonds, as well as the low prices and correspondingly high yields they offer in today's tight money market, should make them tempting to chanceries. Yet from what I've seen, Catholic dioceses pay little attention to bonds. The shrewder chancellors occasionally do put payroll money and other operating cash into short-term government paper (notes issued by the U. S. Treasury on a 30-, 60- or 90-day basis). And as one chancellor put it, "We've all got a few thousand dollars in Defense Bonds lying around somewhere." But typically, at the end of 1967, Oklahoma City-Tulsa held only $10,000 worth of U. S. government bonds, and $36,100 worth of municipal and corporate bonds. Most of these, moreover, were the short-term obligations of their issuers, not the long-term indebtednesses we usually associate with bond financing. The fact suggests that such holdings were merely a temporary interest-bearing haven for diocesan cash which would be needed not immediately but within a few months.

One species of bond, however, is widely held by

Catholic chanceries and other diocesan institutions. It goes by the intriguingly simple name of "religious bond." Both its current role in the economy of the church and its broader significance as a tool of ecclesiastical investment justify detailed treatment here.

What exactly is a religious bond? Before we answer this question, let's be certain of some basic facts about bonds in general. At the risk of belaboring the obvious: every bond is a credit instrument which obliges the issuer to repay to the bondholder money borrowed from the original purchaser. The purchaser and the bondholder may of course be one and the same party. But because bonds do very often change hands, I've drawn the possible distinction between the two. To offer its bonds to the public, the issuer must comply with a host of legal and practical requirements. In a prospectus, a descriptive brochure couched in careful legal language, the bond issuer must spell out the precise loan arrangements: the total amount to be borrowed; the length of time the loan will be outstanding; the interest to be paid to lenders; and the provisions for the repayment of the principal. The prospectus will also contain information about the purpose of the loan, the financial condition of the borrower and the property (if any) pledged as security on the debt.

Companies sell bonds to borrow funds for the construction of new plants, the purchase of new equipment or any of dozens of other business reasons. Governments offer bonds to finance roads and schools, peace programs and wars. The primary buyers of bonds are our huge financial institutions, the insurance and trust companies, mutual funds and pension funds with billions of dollars to invest each year on behalf of their policy-owners, depositors, shareholders and beneficiaries. Individuals, too, put money into bonds, seeking investments which offer: a) safety; b) a predictable rate of return; c) eventual repayment of principal; and d) in the case of state and municipal bonds, an income exempt from federal and state taxes.

This is no place to describe the delicate intermediary processes by which issuers and buyers are brought together in the marketplace. Nor should we try to analyze the methods by which professional underwriters representing the borrower form syndicates of other professionals which first buy the bonds at auction, then resell them at a profit to institutions and private investors. We need only note that the bond market is one of the great sources of sustenance for the entire American economy. In 1968 alone, the market moved nearly $61 billion worth of cash into the hands of business and government borrowers, in exchange for hundreds of bond issues, each one a different type of promise of repayment. This amount is roughly fifteen times the value of all the new stocks issued during the same year. Truly, the workings of the bond market deserve to be better known.

Knowing what we have learned thus far, however, we should be well able to understand religious bonds and the operations involved in their creation and marketing.

Religious bonds are those which can be issued by the parishes, sees and diocesan institutions of the church; and by any of the thousands of other Catholic religious corporations in the U. S. and Canada. To get an idea of the institutions and projects involved, let's look at a few actual examples. In 1966, the Diocese of Joliet, Illinois, issued $2 million worth of three-year bonds. According to the prospectus, "the net proceeds . . . will be used for improvements, additions and expansions of parishes of the Diocese . . . and for the refunding of intra-Diocesan obligations to certain funds in the custody of the Bishop." That is, for parish construction and for repayment of parish loans to the central fund. In 1967, the Sisters of St. Francis of the Congregation of Our Lady of Lourdes, a re-

ligious order with headquarters in Sylvania, Ohio, floated a
$2 million bond issue. The prospectus revealed that the
proceeds were meant "to pay in part the cost of the new
. . . addition" to Holy Cross Hospital in Detroit, an institutional property of the order. In 1961, Mary Queen of
Heaven Congregation, a parish corporation in Milwaukee,
Wisconsin, offered $80,000 worth of serial notes (bonds on
which a fraction of the principal is repaid each year) to
finance a new parochial school. Every year, dozens of similar borrowings are set in motion by Catholic institutions.

To all but a tiny handful of specialists, the very existence of religious bonds is unknown. If you ask about them,
most bankers, brokers and even bond dealers reward you
with a puzzled stare. Yet in an obscure corner of the bond
market—so small a corner that three or four companies
handle 95 per cent of all such transactions—the institutional
obligations of the Catholic Church* are regularly bought,
sold and traded. By comparison with the multimillion-
dollar daily activity of the bond market as a whole, the volume of business in religious bonds is minuscule. In 1968
(the most recent year for which figures are available), the
total worth of new Catholic Church bond issues was less
than $100 million. But while this volume may be insignifi-
cant in terms of the total national economy, it's a sizable
component of the economy of the church. In the aggregate, moreover, Catholic religious bonds are anything but
insignificant. Over the past fifteen years, in fact, one firm,
B. C. Ziegler and Company of West Bend, Wisconsin (a
suburb of Milwaukee), has sold over $600 million worth of
bonds on behalf of church corporations.

Among the purchasers of these ecclesiastical obligations
are banks, trust companies, life-insurance companies, private individuals and—most important—a great many of the

* Other church organizations (e.g., the Lutheran congregations) also
issue bonds, as do some hospitals and universities.

institutions of the church itself. Thus, in addition to owning the portfolio of common stocks listed on pp. 168–169, the Student Education Fund of the Diocese of Oklahoma City-Tulsa also held the following religious bonds:

Issuer	Interest rate	Maturity	Value
Bishop Noa Home for Senior Citizens	5⅛%	1974	$ 33,000
Diocese of Joliet*	5%	1973	30,000
Bishop of Miami, Florida†	5%	1972	10,000
Diocese of Oklahoma City-Tulsa	5½%	1975	82,000
Holy Name Church, Chickasha, Okla.	5%	1970	5,000
St. John Evangelist Church, McAlester	5⅛%	1975	10,000
Archdiocese of Santa Fe	5⅜%	1975	25,000
Sacred Heart Church, Oklahoma City	4⅝%	1968	1,500
St. Anthony Hospital, Oklahoma City	6¼%	1980	15,000

$211,500

In fact, the Fund's portfolio of religious bonds is not too much smaller than its $285,000 portfolio of common stocks.

And so, there actually exists a money market in which two firms can a) transform the private debts of the Catholic Church into publicly held securities; and b) persuade the church to become its own best bond customer for these obligations. Plainly, this system of finance deserves more attention.

In terms of background, nobody knows for certain who first decided that the same technique of borrowing which works so well for businesses and government bodies would also work for the church. According to a 1963 article on B. C. Ziegler and Company in a magazine called *Let's See*,

* Not the same series of bonds as those mentioned in the text above.
† Because the diocese of Miami is a corporation sole (*v.* pp. 99–100), the bishop is considered the issuer of the bonds.

Bernard C. Ziegler, the founder of the firm, should be given the credit. At the turn of the century, Ben Ziegler ran a small real-estate and farm mortgage agency serving the country town of West Bend, Wisconsin. In 1913, his personal friend, Reverend Peter Stupfel, pastor of Holy Angels parish, asked Ziegler to lend him $30,000 for a new church. This homespun arrangement, the article states, was the first venture of Ziegler and Company into its chosen financial specialty.

A rather different account was given to me by a senior executive of Dempsey-Tegeler & Co., Inc. (which until its liquidation in 1970 was Ziegler's only major competitor in religious bonds). His story has it that a gentleman named J. Festus Wade, an officer of the Mercantile Trust Company in St. Louis, first devised the concept of formal offerings of debt securities by church corporations. By the time of the 1929 crash, the bank was actively soliciting religious bond accounts. In 1933, however, federal laws were enacted to prohibit banks from engaging in bond underwritings. This left two young employees of Mercantile Trust, Tim Dempsey and Pat Tegeler, "with a long list of contacts—and no jobs." With little to lose, the two bond specialists teamed up, took over Wade's idea and went into business for themselves. They worked both sides of the street, cultivating local church officials in need of money and also lining up prospective buyers of the bonds the company underwrote.

Because business expansion was at a virtual standstill during the Depression, and because states and municipalities were faced with financial troubles of their own, the bond market was very slow indeed. But Dempsey and Tegeler gradually created an institutional market for religious bonds. A number of life-insurance companies (which, in good times or bad, must invest the money flowing in from premiums on policies) were willing to trust the credit of

the Catholic Church. Some of the insurance-company investment specialists who bought religious bonds were Catholics sympathetic to the needs of the church.* Catholic or
not, however, these executives had the interests of their
companies at heart. In a stagnant economy, religious bonds
seemed to them an eminently safe investment yielding a
better-than-average profit.

Meanwhile, Ziegler and Company was finding that its
Wisconsin neighbors, the prosperous dairy farmers of the
region and the small banks which held their money, also
thought well of the church as an investment risk. As well as
soliciting institutional buyers, Ziegler's president, Delbert J.
Kenny, built up a list of individual prospects. Both Ziegler
and Dempsey-Tegeler found that hard work paid off in
modest prosperity. By 1940, the total sale of Catholic religious bonds had reached an annual level of $20 million.

Whichever version of the development of religious
bonds is correct, both stories illustrate the same point. The
use of this special method of financing was at first, and still
largely remains, a regional affair. As we've just seen, marketing religious bonds began as an effort of personal salesmanship; one that combined with investment banking many
of the elements of Catholic charitable fund-raising. As the
two competitive firms in the field gained experience, they
did broaden their markets to include church institutions as
well as investors outside the church. But this step was inevitable. Any bishop or superior of a religious order who
had launched a successful bond issue of his own became
ipso facto a natural customer for the bonds of other bishops
or superiors. To such ecclesiastical administrators, who by

---

* Naturally enough, bond houses guard the identities of institutional buyers with care. One key figure in life insurance who did approve purchases of religious bonds—and who has done much else for his church—
is Harry C. Hagerty of New York. Now retired, Hagerty was for many
years in charge of the bond portfolio of The Metropolitan Life Insurance
Company.

tradition love to see the church as self-supporting, the cleverness of the bond concept as well as its fiscal soundness held particular appeal. During the decade after World War II, when churchmen were giving top priority to physical expansion, both Ziegler and Dempsey-Tegeler were able to involve chanceries and the motherhouses of religious orders in bond-buying on a national scale. Today, Ziegler operates offices in key cities across the country.

Nevertheless, the religious bond business still retains much of its early regional flavor. The major reason has to do with the basic economic situation of the church in this country. We've noted more than once that the diocesan church is strongest economically in the Northeast, mid-Atlantic and Midwest regions, weakest in the South, Southwest and Northwest. In the great sees of the East Coast and Midwest, the Ordinaries have always been confident of their ability to sustain their economies with a minimum of external borrowing and to base investments on measurable standards of merit. West of the Mississippi and in the other less developed sectors of the church, the bishops and religious superiors have never enjoyed any such sense of economic security. Nor, especially in the real Bible Belt areas of the country, have Catholic prelates been able to rely on sympathetic local bankers for financial aid. "When the three local banks told me what they'd charge us for a million-dollar loan," said the financial assistant of one bishop in the Southwest, "I got on a plane and went straight to Chicago for the money." Precisely because they lack both internal financial resources and ready access to cash, the smaller dioceses of the South, Southwest and Far West are the chief issuers of religious bonds, and their most enthusiastic purchasers as well.

The marketing of the bonds themselves reveals that Ziegler and Dempsey-Tegeler still operate in an informal, almost folksy, style, one a million miles removed from the sophistication of Wall Street. "Dear Friend," begins a Ziegler and Company letter addressed to prospective buyers:

> The enclosed circular describes a loan of $1,800,000 which B. C. Ziegler and Company is making to Providence Hospital, Portland, Oregon.
> This is an excellent loan, and we recommend it as a sound investment for your available savings. Interest rates have been set at 6½% to 7%, and the Notes are rated "AA" by Fitch Investors Service.
> You can see from the picture that Providence Hospital is an impressive looking structure. . . .

And the letter goes on to sing the praises of the religious order of Sisters of Charity as experts in hospital management. It closes: "I am confident these Notes will sell out very quickly, and I suggest you promptly call our nearest office with your reservation."

Casual or not, this approach has worked nicely. In 1963, Delbert Kenny of Ziegler was quoted as saying that he could recall only two "slow issues where we've had to get out and ring doorbells" to get the bonds sold.* Nor have the bond underwriters starved. If we assume average commissions of about 0.75 per cent of the total face value of annual offerings, a figure in line with compensation in other areas of the bond market, then between them Ziegler and its competitors are bringing in about $750,000 a year from religious bond sales. In addition, they earn sizable incomes from other financial services (insurance, general investment counseling) to the church.

Certain special features of these bonds, moreover, keep the costs of marketing them very low. Thus, as obligations

---

* But beginning in 1966, tight money and inflation have made all bonds harder to sell and more expensive for borrowers. Ralph M. Zitzmann, formerly in charge of religious bond marketing for Dempsey-Tegeler and now an independent agent, tells me that religious bond activity has been held back by these factors.

of nonprofit corporations, religious bonds need not be registered with the Securities and Exchange Commission in Washington. This in itself means a sizable saving in legal fees and administrative overhead. Also, unless the total number of prospective buyers exceeds some statutory limit (generally twenty-five), religious bonds are usually not subject to clearance by state regulatory agencies.

Partly as a result of these exemptions, and partly because the customers for Catholic Church bonds tend to be trusting souls, the bond prospectuses can be informal indeed. For example, in Catholic religious bond literature unaudited financial reports are commonplace. Partial rather than complete disclosure of assets, liabilities and net worth is the rule. Special covenants for the protection of bondholders (e.g., agreements to guarantee proper insurance coverage on properties pledged as security) are notable for their absence. Such omissions are perfectly legal and aboveboard; and they do save the bond underwriters a good deal of the money they'd otherwise be spending on research and consultation with clients.

Some of the savings are passed on to ecclesiastical borrowers in the form of lower interest charges on their bonds. Indeed, the price of the money is perhaps the most startling feature of the religious bond trade. As evidence, take the figures from the prospectuses themselves. I've checked nearly 150 of these proposals for bonds issued since 1960, and this survey reveals that the interest rates are consistently lower than those paid for money raised via bonds by the major American business corporations. For example, as recently as 1968 the Carmelite Sisters of the Divine Heart of Jesus, a religious order located in Milwaukee, were offering to pay a maximum of 7 per cent on $1 million worth of ten-year hospital bonds. The same year, the Sisters of St. Joseph, in Orange, California, sold $750,000 worth of their hospital bonds, also at 7 per cent. Yet in

1968, all corporate bonds rated AAA (the highest rating) by Standard & Poor were priced to yield an average return of nearly 9 per cent a year. On the evidence of these figures, the credit rating of the Catholic Church is seemingly far superior to that of Du Pont, General Motors or U. S. Steel.

But neither lower underwriting costs nor an impeccable credit record explain why church organizations can sell their bonds so cheaply. A mixture of other reasons enters this picture. Taken together, these add up to the matter of buyer psychology. Thus, just as diocesan pastors can be persuaded to accept 4 per cent interest on their deposits to the central fund, so can bishops and other purchasers of religious bonds be persuaded to accept lower-than-average returns on bond investments. How? Although a spokesman for Dempsey-Tegeler heatedly denied the fact, the magic concept that "it's for the benefit of the church" is nevertheless the most potent weapon in the arsenal of the religious bond salesman. Along with the appeals of financial safety and regular return, the appeal to motives of charity is hard to resist. Everybody, bishops included, loves to do good and make money at the same time.

Furthermore, to ecclesiastical administrators (though certainly not to insurance-company bond buyers and other professional investors), high interest rates connote speculation and undue financial risk. The Wall Street Journal may tell us that the cost of borrowing money depends on the interaction of impersonal economic forces, but priests— being priests—don't always believe it. In Catholic chanceries, it's somehow morally right for all interest rates to be low; and it's wrong to make too much money and even worse to make it at the expense of others in the priesthood.

Finally, the church official who purchases religious bonds today knows well that he may have to offer bonds of his own tomorrow. He naturally wants to be sure that his fellow prelates will be willing to lend him money at rates he can afford. To assure himself of a stable market when his own turn comes to sell, the bishop decides to accept (or the underwriter convinces him that it's shrewd to accept) a lower profit than economic logic would dictate.

So it is that a blend of charitable feelings, moral concerns and self-restraint on the part of lenders helps to make this particular market for money a lower-cost market than any other I know of in America.

But before we congratulate the Catholic Church on its ingenuity in cornering a supply of cut-rate capital, let's take a look at the other side of the coin. As a medium of investment, religious bonds certainly do have serious drawbacks. In today's inflationary economy, the most serious drawback is simply the growing indifference of professional investors to a low-yield, fixed-income security. Bishop may lend to bishop for twenty years at 7 per cent, but not many insurance companies or banks will do so. Present-day unrealistic pricing sharply restricts the flow of outside capital into the Catholic ecclesiastical economy; and makes of the religious bond business nothing more than an ingenious device for shuttling church money from one sector of the church to another.

Another drawback related to the first is lack of liquidity. One essential property of commercial and government bonds is that, during the period before they mature, they can be freely traded. Naturally, the prices at which such bonds are bought and sold do fluctuate, mirroring their quality on the one hand and the prevailing demand for money on the other. Still, if you need cash, you can always sell your industrial, utility or government bonds. But if few outside investors will buy a *new* 7 per cent bond from a bishop today, no professional will pay 100 cents on the dollar for a 4 per cent bond issued eight or ten years ago. Right now, not even the most charitable of the bishop's peers in the church will lend him money at 4 per cent.

On occasion, one or the other of the underwriters will assume the burden of providing liquidity by "making a market" in a given religious bond. This involves purchasing for cash the supply of the bond held by one customer and negotiating its resale to another. But neither Ziegler and Company nor its competitors relish the task of making a market. It ties up too much of the firm's cash for too long, and it uses up too much good will.

And so, while the ingenuity and versatility of religious bonds have made them highly useful in some sectors of the church, their low profitability and lack of liquidity have sharply limited their usefulness. In 1964, before inflationary pressures on the money supply began to grind away at bond prices, it did seem as if the rather static market for religious bonds might expand dramatically. That year, Ziegler successfully marketed the first $10 million worth of bonds in a three-year, $40 million loan-financing program for the Archdiocese of Boston. This was by far the largest bond issue ever launched by a Catholic religious corporation and the first ever undertaken by a major Eastern see. As such, it was a tribute to the energetic salesmanship of Ziegler and Co. and an optimistic sign of potential growth. Unfortunately for both Ziegler and its client, however, the rapid tightening of the money market dampened investor enthusiasm. Although Ziegler's representatives are close-mouthed about the ultimate result of the underwriting, I suspect that Cardinal Cushing had to pay much more for his $40 million* than the 5½ per cent advertised in the original prospectus. And since 1966, when the last Boston

* It is to pay off these bonds that the Archdiocese of Boston embarked on the fund-raising drive mentioned on p. 121. Note that this has meant paying two sets of professionals to bring in one large sum of money.

bonds were marketed, no similar financial program has brought the bond underwriters into the big leagues of Catholic diocesan finance.*

The fact that there is a going market—however limited —for the bonds of the Catholic Church, I myself find fascinating. Whatever other lessons it teaches us, the religious bond market testifies to the sheer inventiveness of ecclesiastical economic operations. But cleverness aside, the mechanics of the purchase and sale of church debt offers a fine illustration of the real truth about church investment: its extreme unaggressiveness. Surely it's obvious that no institution intent on economic gain will set up a money market solely so it can borrow from itself at low interest, thereby tying up funds which could earn much more money elsewhere. Nor will such an institution base investment decisions on moral directives (some of which date back to medieval canons outlawing usury) about just and unjust rates of interest. All in all, despite the beliefs of the myth-makers about the investment aims of the church, the workings of the market for its bonds display a fine disregard for the principles of financial profit.

The operations of the religious bond market also shed light on a broader aspect of the investment activity of the diocesan church: the actual process by which all investment decisions are made. Although the powers of the Catholic bishop are very wide, no bishop makes his investment decisions alone. "We have no Howard Hugheses in the hierarchy," said Bishop John J. Wright of Pittsburgh (now Cardinal Wright of the Sacred Congregation of the Clergy in Rome) when I asked him about the bishop's role in the investment process. His quip is in fact an understatement. On all sides of his throne, the bishop is surrounded by those with a voice in investment-making.

* In 1970, almost 90 per cent of all religious bond offerings were hospital bonds of the various religious orders.

CHAPTER NINE

The Rules of the Chancery Money Game

As a matter of canon law, an Ordinary must place major investment questions before the Diocesan Council of Administration. This includes the bishop himself, the chancellor and the heads of the various diocesan administrative departments, as well as one or more laymen from the law firm representing the chancery. Because most of the members of the council are priests appointed by the bishop himself, the council may be, and very often is, merely a rubber-stamp group which automatically ratifies the moves of its chief. But in many sees, the bishops expect their senior executives to air their joint opinions about specific investments, if not to formulate policy. Rarely will any bishop anywhere insist on making an investment which his council members seriously mistrust.

187

Part of the job of being a bishop, of course, is to ensure that so awkward a situation never develops, that the diocese is kept out of debatable investments. Before he submits any major investment proposal to his Administrative Council, His Excellency will have had his chancellor, vicar general or other chief financial aide consult lay professionals about the merit of the proposal. If the matter is significant enough, moreover, it will be the bishop himself who sits down with the bankers, lawyers and brokers to discuss the details and make the real decision.

Who are these laymen and what are their backgrounds? On what basis does a bishop select the professionals he needs to assist him with investment-making? To what extent are *they*—and not the bishops themselves—responsible for the investment policies of the 160 U. S. sees?

By now we know that where money and its management are the issues, generalizations about the church are dangerous. Nevertheless, I think we can risk a series of generalizations about the laymen who handle investments for the diocesan church. In fact, I think we must. Because they so strongly influence the managerial thinking of the priests with whom they work (and every bishop is first of all a priest), we have good reason to want to know who and what these laymen are. And because the laymen in question undoubtedly do run to type, we can single out some of the key traits, professional and personal, which they tend to share.

Almost universally, the laymen who place their professional skills at the disposal of the bishops are themselves Catholics, and Catholics of a particular kind. They are, to begin with, products of the Catholic educational environment, from parochial school right through to the colleges, law schools and business schools where they receive their professional training. In their 1966 study, *The Education of Catholic Americans*, sociologists Andrew M. Greeley (who is a priest) and Peter H. Rossi offer an apt summarization of their attitudes.

> Sunday Mass, monthly Communion, Confession several times a year, Catholic education of children, financial contribution to the Church, acceptance of the Church as an authoritative teacher, acknowledgement of papal and hierarchal authority, informality with the clergy . . . are [some of] the apparent effects of Catholic education.

This does not mean that all bishops arbitrarily exclude non-Catholics from their innermost financial circles, but rather that most of them automatically include only Catholics, never thinking to seek elsewhere for assistance. For instance, during a discussion in 1969, Bishop Walter W. Curtis of Bridgeport mentioned that he was considering a lay financial board to help him with diocesan money matters. I suggested that he name one or two non-Catholics to the board, on the ground that the move would assure a diversity of views and would also greatly please the local business community. Even after I explained my reasoning, Bishop Curtis seemed puzzled. Then he said, "I wonder whether any non-Catholics would really be interested in giving us a hand." His tone was dubious, not defensive. But clearly Bishop Curtis had never before considered the notion that a non-Catholic financial expert might be flattered to be asked for advice, and might even in some ways be more objective than a Catholic about church money.

I'm certainly not suggesting that devout Catholics are by definition poor financial advisers to the church. No one could believe such a suggestion who has dealt with laymen like John Shaw of Tulsa, a consultant to Bishop Victor J. Reed; John J. Kennedy of Baton Rouge, executive secretary to Bishop Robert E. Tracy; and J. Early Hardesty of Baltimore, formerly financial vice president of Black & Decker, Inc., the power-tool manufacturer, and now consultant to Cardinal Lawrence Shehan. We can take for

granted that dozens of other lay Catholics bring to the work
they do for the bishops equal skill and equal objectivity.

And yet, I'm convinced that the fact of the religious tie
sometimes does complicate the business relationship between a Catholic bishop and his exclusively Catholic financial counselors.

Ironically, the party most sensitive to the presence of a
problem may be the bishop himself. When I asked one
bishop how he made use of lay experts in investment, he
confessed that wherever possible he interposed his chancellor between himself and the laymen. "When they're with
me, they're too deferential," he said ruefully. "I always
worry that they're telling me only what they think I want
to hear." But be this as it may, the consensus among American bishops is still that only Catholics are loyal enough to
be entrusted with the responsibility for executing the investment requirements of the church.

More surprising and more important, few of these lay
experts are specifically experts in investment. Rather, the
bishop's advisers are almost invariably bankers and accountants. They are thus money generalists whose concepts
of the investment process are not those of the so-called
professional investor: e.g., the full-time portfolio manager
for a financial institution, the investment counselor who
serves private clients and the financial executive on Wall
Street. Again, this is not to suggest that all bankers and all
accountants are ignorant about investments or mystified by
the daily behavior of the securities markets. Nor would a
bishop necessarily be better advised by a performance-
minded portfolio manager than he is by the bank official or
the CPA on whom he now relies. As we'll shortly discover,
both the banker and the accountant do much more for the
bishop than offer him investment advice. Each has a key
role to play in the wider realm of diocesan administration.

In theory, each is better situated than the investment specialist to relate investment-making to all the other financial activities of the see.

Still, the preeminent virtues of banking and accountancy are orderliness, cautiousness and devotion to routine. Given these virtues, you'd expect to find the bankers and the accountants reinforcing, not reversing, the financial conservatism which is bred into every Catholic bishop from his first days as a seminarian. And in diocese after diocese, this is exactly what you do find: enough competence in the mechanics of investment to win for one or two laymen the complete confidence of the bishop, coupled with a mistrust of genuine investment flair and a professional indifference to the specialized skills needed to run a portfolio.

Even in the one see where, according to legend, investment sophistication prevails, the reality demonstrates a deadly conservatism. In New York, all of Wall Street is available to the archdiocesan chancery. Here, in fact, Cardinal Spellman did establish as his chief financial adviser John A. Coleman, a specialist trader on the floor of the New York Stock Exchange who has for decades been one of the best-known members of the investment fraternity. Coleman is a trustee of the Catholic Charities corporation of the archdiocese. He is also on the board of The Trustees of St. Patrick's Cathedral, Inc., an archdiocesan corporation which not only administers St. Patrick's but also watches over the two large archdiocesan cemeteries. If any one lay investment expert in this country has access to a Catholic chancery, John Coleman does.* Yet the investment funds of the archdiocese, including both restricted funds and nonrestricted investment capital, are firmly in the hands of

---

* But Spellman's successor, Cardinal Terence J. Cooke, relies also on the advice of his own personal friend, stockbroker T. Murray McDonnell, former owner of McDonnell & Co.

banks. Ever since Cardinal Spellman's first years as archbishop, the two banks which have controlled most of the money are Bankers Trust Company and the Manufacturers Hanover Trust (of which Coleman is a director). The investment committees of the bank trust departments thus make the actual investment decisions. The brokerage firms favored by the banks do whatever buying and selling of securities is to be done. As a trustee and a bank director, Coleman is several management layers removed from the process at which he is an acknowledged expert. Not even he can coax the chancery into an effort to do better at the Money Game.

On our way to a summary of this strangely passive investment policy, we owe ourselves a look at one more aspect of diocesan investment management. This we might call the moral aspect. We can best approach this facet of investment affairs by asking two related questions: 1) is there such a thing as a favorite stock or bond or other investment of the diocesan church? and 2) do diocesan investment specialists ever apply moral criteria to their selection of investments?

To the best of my knowledge, no one stock is ever singled out as an investment target by numbers of Catholic dioceses. At least, none recurs repeatedly on the lists of holdings shown to me privately by chancery officials, or on those few lists which have been made public. Furthermore, we've already determined that the legal doctrines governing church trust funds dictate the strict isolation of one fund from another. From what we've learned of such financial separatism (and on the evidence of some horrified comments from chancellors), I find it impossible to believe that the bishops and their advisers ever cross diocesan lines to join investment forces. The notion of forming such interdiocesan alliances to take a position in the stock of one company, much less to gain management control, is quite literally *anathema maranatha* to the church.

Nor, according to all the evidence I've seen, do Catholic sees ever pool their investment resources to gain any of the straightforward advantages of large-scale investment. By these, I mean the reduced commission costs, the negotiated "third-market" prices and the rapid service available on transactions involving large blocks of shares. For better or for worse, in the diocesan church the state of the art of investment has not advanced even this far.

In looking over lists of investments, I have come across what appear to be preferred groups of stocks and favored sectors of investment. But far from revealing any profound market strategy, these rather suggest a prosaic interest in the industries most basic to the economy: food, retailing, petroleum, chemicals, metals. As we noted earlier, absent from the typical diocesan portfolio are the shares of electronics companies or of others in advanced-technology industries. For instance, although Rochester is the home of Xerox, I learned that the Diocese of Rochester held only forty-five shares of Xerox stock in 1969.

If any one area of investment is in fact strongly favored by the diocesan church, this must surely be the insurance industry. On each of the securities lists available to me, I found at least one insurance stock; and I'd venture that every diocese, large or small, owns shares in one or more insurance companies. It's easy enough to guess why the insurance industry has found favor with the diocesan church. For one thing, the bishops themselves are familiar with the products and the operations of insurance companies. Chanceries buy a lot of insurance. For another, the insurance industry is comfortingly stable and safe. Its financial strength is unassailable. Its wares are needed by every consumer. In the sense that insurance relieves people in distress, the industry is a benevolent institution. And because its growth is based on such certainties as the increase of population and the yield on conservative investments, the industry's future is secure. Indeed, in many respects the American insurance industry bears a startling resemblance to the church itself.

The evident fondness of diocesan investment aides for the shares of insurance companies hints at the answer to the second of the questions asked a few paragraphs ago. Similarly, the workings of the religious bond market add flesh to the proposition that moral considerations do affect the process of investing diocesan money. True, nothing in canon law requires that church funds be invested in "good" —i.e., socially beneficial—corporations. Nor can I imagine an American bishop saintly enough to reject a gift or a bequest of stock in a "bad" corporation (for instance, one which harshly exploits its labor, or which pollutes the environment). But many Catholic bishops do instruct their bankers to stay out of controversial investments. Several, I've learned, have sold their Dow Chemical stock because the company manufactured the napalm used in Vietnam. Moreover, the laymen who handle investments for the dioceses know without being told that, today especially, they should keep the church away from such nasty corporate citizens as the firearms manufacturers, the strip-mining companies and the producers of DDT.

One or two recent examples illustrate the specific moral pressures which sometimes do influence diocesan investment policy. In 1967, Matthew Ahmann, a Chicago layman active in the civil rights movement, and James Norris, the lay director of the Catholic Council for Interracial Justice, began a vigorous campaign among the bishops. Their primary objective was to persuade the hierarchy not to do business with companies known to practice racial discrimination. They further urged the bishops not to authorize investments in the securities of such companies. So far, their efforts have met with fair success, especially in the Midwest and the North.*

In New York, however, another campaign has been much less effective. This is a behind-the-scenes drive aimed at gaining the withdrawal of Catholic Church funds from the First National City Bank and the Chase Manhattan Bank. The reason is that both these institutions lend money to the Union of South Africa, which practices apartheid. Since the banks claim with some justice that their loans actually finance trade between the Union of South Africa and the emerging black nations of the continent (and since every other major bank will have similar moral skeletons in its vaults), the church organizations using First National and Chase Manhattan have not responded to this attempt at moral suasion.† Nor are they likely to do so.

As I've observed before, Catholic bishops naturally prefer to do good as well as to make an adequate return on their investments. As long as they can be safe in sinking funds into morally acceptable enterprises, they will attempt —informally and haphazardly, but sincerely—to remain on the side of the angels. The American economy, diversified as it is, offers ample opportunity to select "good" investments and to avoid those which are morally suspect. Accordingly, the official posture of the U. S. church for a long time to come will be one of enlightened capitalism. At times, the American bishops seem uneasy about their roles as the custodians of wealth, and specifically of investment wealth. Nevertheless, they accept the powerful argument that to liquidate the wealth would mean also dismantling the charity of the church in America.

Having made this final point, let's recapitulate what we

* Ahmann and Norris have encountered some resistance from chancellors and bankers who insist that "white lists" of companies which discriminate are impractical and inaccurate.
† But the Protestant National Council of Churches has withdrawn $55 million from the Chase Manhattan Bank.

have learned of diocesan investment. Then, let's place in proper perspective the entire process of investment as it affects diocesan economics. Thus:

1. I find that 90 per cent of the assets of Catholic dioceses take the form of institutional real estate;
2. Of the remaining 10 per cent, the liquid assets, most is held as cash and constitutes the operating balances of the sees;
3. Perhaps 2 to 3 per cent of all diocesan assets take the form of commercial investments, including stocks, bonds, realty and money in savings banks;
4. All told, the commercial investments held by Catholic bishops may be worth as much as $1 billion.

Given these estimates, we went on to discover that the ownership of diocesan investment assets is split among thousands of individual Catholic institutions and trusts, with the bishops and their designees as the trustees. We noted the canonic and the civil legal limitations within which church financial trustees must operate. We saw in particular that these rules forbid the "commingling" of trust assets with other assets and the pooling of separate trust funds; and that they also restrict the types of securities allowable as investments.

We next considered the actual results of this highly regulated investment procedure. We reviewed diocesan portfolios and examined the most specialized investment available to a churchman, the religious bond. We learned that bankers and accountants, not investment specialists, are the lay advisers closest to most of the bishops. And we've just seen that diocesan investment philosophy, already conservative, is rendered more cautious still by the moral imperatives to which Catholic bishops give heed.

These discoveries force us toward one conclusion. Taken together, our findings mark the diocesan church as perhaps the least effectual investment institution in this

country, if not in the world. Its investments are character-
ized by low yield, poor planning, lack of creative management and mistaken priorities.

And so, rather than agreeing with Eugene Carson Blake
—and many other critics—that corporate immortality and
tax advantages make the churches too powerful, I feel that
the truth of the argument lies in exactly the opposite direction. As later chapters will demonstrate, the Catholic
Church today is only barely strong enough economically
to keep its promises and to sustain its spiritual mission. Un-
skilled investment-making has been only a minor factor in
the economic decline of the church. Still, so low is the investment efficiency of even the well-managed Catholic see
that its investments add little or nothing to its economic
strength. Unless radical changes in policy are made soon,
investments, instead of bolstering the economy of the
church, will become mere lumps of unproductive asset
value. Such unproductive assets may enhance diocesan
balance sheets. But they neither forward the dynamic purposes of the institutional church nor help church executives
meet their critical economic needs.

By "radical changes," I don't mean a switch to the
brand of investment philosophy which has led some Protestant groups (and a very few nondiocesan Catholic organizations) into the direct ownership of businesses. No reasonable investment advisers would advocate that Catholic
bishops should all follow the lead of, say, the Cathedral of
Tomorrow. This Ohio Protestant church, according to
journalist Alfred Balk's brief book, *The Religion Business*,
owns "a shopping center, an apartment building, an electronics firm, a wire and plastic company, and the Real
Form Girdle Company." Catholic bishops have wisely kept
away from commercial ventures like these. Reversal of this
policy, in my judgment, is no sort of answer.

At the heart of the problem, rather, lies the Catholic ecclesiastical concept of trusteeship. As we've repeatedly seen, the episcopacy itself is by law and by tradition a great trusteeship, safeguarding the property and the money of the church from the potential foolishness or greed of the mere men who become church leaders. But the safer the trusteeship, the more rigorous—and the less flexible—its terms. Today, the bishop who seeks to be innovative in investment practice may well find himself in legal difficulties, not so much under civil law as under the much more inhibiting canonic code. Indeed, such an Ordinary would almost certainly be violating the terms of hundreds of trusts, each of which is written as if it were the only legal arrangement binding on him. As Catholic canon lawyers freely admit, better investment performance (no less than more meaningful liturgy and more responsive tribunals) hinges on change in the massive legal system. In two areas especially, the system badly needs an overhaul.

First of all, the canons should be rewritten* so that a bishop may, without penalty, pool together small trust funds to form a single larger investment fund. Such a change would enormously simplify the bookkeeping and banking routines now essential just to keep track of diocesan money. It would also encourage productive investment rather than the present futile accumulations of tiny increments on small amounts of capital.

Far more important, the canonists must do something about the problem of episcopal accountability. In civil law, there are typically three parties to every trust: the donor, the trustee and the beneficiary for whose benefit the trust is set up. Behind the entire concept of the trust is the age-old legal doctrine of accountability. As the party responsible for the assets of the trust, the trustee must supply

---

* A complete revision of the canon laws, the first since 1914, is now being undertaken by commissions of laymen and priests from all over the world. Modernization of the canons governing investments is thus a possibility.

the beneficiary with written evidence of the trust's financial status. The beneficiary is regularly entitled to such accountings; and the courts are always there to see that he gets them.

Like all other churches, however, the Catholic Church is privileged in the eyes of the American civil law. Because of its status as a religious institution, the church is allowed what amounts to a partial exemption from the laws of fiduciary responsibility. Thus, a Catholic can legally set up a civil trust (for instance, under the terms of his will) in favor of any institution of a diocese; and he may name the bishop as a trustee. The civil law will overlook that the bishop, as the legal owner of every diocesan institution, is therefore also the beneficiary of the trust. To say the least, this blurs the third-party or "arm's-length" relationship that is basic to trusteeships in general. It means that the Catholic bishop is legally accountable only to himself and to his superiors in Rome. Those who actually benefit from the trusts under his charge, the people of his diocese, are legally entitled to no accounting at all. Largely out of the fear that the facts and figures will be misconstrued and that they themselves will be attacked ("either because we're too rich or because we're not richer," said former Bishop John J. Wright of Pittsburgh), most of the Catholic bishops in the U. S. take full advantage of their legal position. They rest content to leave their flocks, and, for that matter, their priestly subordinates, totally unenlightened about investments.

Whether or not lay Catholics are morally entitled to know the details of diocesan investment operations is a question for Catholics themselves to debate. But in crudely practical terms, our society holds that a trustee whose record is subject to outside scrutiny will be better at his job than a trustee immune from such scrutiny; and I believe so, too. Certainly, the mandatory reporting required of trust companies, insurance companies and other public fiduciaries has helped rather than harmed these institutions. Nor is it coincidence that those universities which consistently publicize their finances are the ones with the largest, healthiest endowments. Such institutions take for granted that accountability increases public confidence and public support.

Like all other Americans, American Catholics today are well enough informed about investments (and disturbed enough about church financial problems) to want to know what their church is doing with the money it invests. Increasingly, therefore, the bishop whose investment policies are made clear to his laity will be financially better off than the bishop still committed to secretiveness and mystery. Apprised of the exact truth about investments, Catholics everywhere will be more responsive to appeals for new funds and less mistrustful of the financial competence of the hierarchy. In their turn, the bishops will be placed under pressure to make every investment dollar count. But such self-imposed pressure will free them at last to formulate investment strategies more positive than the medieval strategy of hoarding. They will learn that, well within the framework of their trusteeship, they can vastly improve diocesan financial performance.

The consequences of a canonically sanctioned decision to "go public" * sweep beyond investment into other areas of diocesan financial administration. To dwell on these consequences here would mean getting ahead of our story. Instead, we should pick up the main thread of the story itself. Up to the point where the subtheme of investment demanded attention, we had mainly been studying the flow of money into the chancery. We discovered where the funds

* This notion of the process of financial disclosure I owe to Rev. Eugene J. Quigley, S.J. We'll meet Father Quigley later, in his official role as Director of Financial Planning of the New York Province of the Society of Jesus.

of a diocese originate. In many sees, we noted, central financing arrangements enable the bishops to control the circulation of money within the diocesan economy and to reduce external debt. We saw also that central financing allows Ordinaries to extend financial support to hospitals and other quasi-independent institutions; and gives chanceries an opportunity, at least, to gain administrative control.

By now, we may be wondering about the efficiency of all of this elaborate economic machinery. The lackluster reality of diocesan investment is certainly enough to make us wonder. However much we appreciate the ingenuity of the existing system, we may well suspect that the Catholic bishop today needs managerial tools of an altogether different order if his see is to go on flourishing. But before we subject diocesan management to any further appraisal, we should complete our yet-unfinished picture. To our study of how money comes into a chancery, we should add a survey of how it goes out.

CHAPTER TEN

How the Bishop
Spends His Money

In chanceries as in all corporate headquarters, the struggle to make the most of the available financial resources is climaxed every year by the battle of the budget. Economically, the superintendent of the diocesan schools, the rector of the seminary, the administrators of the hospitals and the welfare agencies and the heads of all of the other diocesan institutions are dependents of the bishop. All must submit to the bishop their budgetary proposals. Only the parish pastors are free to plan their finances as they see fit.

Although laymen may (and very often do) help to draw up these separate budgets, only the priests in charge take part in the maneuvering for favorable consideration. Only these priests—so they themselves tell me—can hope to understand how the bishop reaches his decisions. And even these ranking diocesan executives may never know. Of all the priests holding administrative office, only a tiny minority of perhaps two or three key aides will share with the bishop his full knowledge of diocesan resources and the demands being made on them.

The task of spending the money of the diocese lays bare the problem of the ecclesiastical administrator, whose task it is to fill and keep filled the bottomless bowl of charity. To the neediest clients of the church, the sick, the poor, the aged, the schoolchildren, every penny does indeed count. To those in charge of the philanthropic and educational programs of a see, budgetary compromises are painful and slashes in funds are demoralizing defeats. When I asked one bishop how he managed to set up priorities among the many urgent works of his diocese without antagonizing his administrators, he answered simply, "I pray."

In actual fact, of course, a bishop can do much more. He can compel any institutional supervisor to accept a smaller slice of the general diocesan receipts. Or he can lavish diocesan income on a favored project. His power to shift money from sector to sector of the diocesan economy is also the power to regulate institutional income. For example, a bishop can always advance funds to a high school or a home for aged priests, the loan to be repaid out of a future income which the institution would never develop without the loan. Or a bishop can place the credit of the diocese at the service of an institution seeking to borrow from a bank. By thus making capital available, the bishop can finance what he hopes will turn into new sources of income. He can in fact behave like a venture capitalist within the church, something he would never do on Wall Street.

Note that there are limits even to the authority of a bishop. He cannot, for instance, deny all support to a major institution (e.g., a school or a hospital), thereby forcing it to close its doors.* Nor can he dip into diocesan capital to keep afloat an institution unable to pay its way and unlikely ever to do so. To rid his see of an unwanted institution, a bishop must resort to canonical rather than financial weapons.

More important, the political and social realities of the American church necessarily govern the bishop's broad economic decisions. While every bishop can manipulate the budget, no bishop can safely ignore the budgetary requests of his most powerful administrators. And while we may never know exactly why Msgr. Smith of St. Thomas's Seminary won an increase while Msgr. Kelly of Our Lady of Sorrows High School lost 5 per cent of his last year's subsidy, we can discover in general how the money of the Catholic diocese is spent. We can also learn how, in practice, the bishop uses his authority in the interest of maintaining financial control over his see.

Let's explore these matters by using as a representative example the Diocese of Pittsburgh. In many ways, Pittsburgh is typical of the sizable Catholic see. Its Catholic population (915,179 in 1969) ranks it tenth in size in the U. S. Its location is in the demographic heartland of American Catholicism. Yet Pittsburgh is not so immense that it becomes unique. Its finances are nothing like as complex as those of Boston, Chicago or New York. Thus, in 1969 the ordinary income of Pittsburgh's 319 parishes was about $22,300,000. The total value of diocesan assets I estimate at approximately $265 million. As further background, we might note that the diocese is staffed by 753 priests and 4,570 nuns; that it operates one seminary, five hospitals and eleven high schools; and that it subsidizes, as do all large sees, dozens of other institutions belonging to various religious orders.

---

* See pp. 147–148 for a summary of the bishop's powers over these and other "juridical personalities" within the church.

According to a confidential report prepared for Bishop Vincent M. Leonard by the accounting firm of Arthur Young & Company, chancery receipts in 1968-69 were $3,431,430. (Chancery accounting in Pittsburgh is on an April-to-April rather than a calendar-year basis.) A separate diocesan development fund realized $1,104,583. Another fund, this one for the maintenance of the diocesan high schools, received $1,191,692. In all, the diocese took in $5,727,705.

The report meticulously documents the expenditures of the diocese. It duly records even so small an item as a gift of $854 sent to Rome as "aid to Lithuania." Only by reproducing all twelve of the report's pages of figures could we do full justice to the information it contains. Still, by following a summary given in the report and by doing a bit of extra arithmetic, we can see clearly where the money in Pittsburgh is going. In 1968-69, the funds of the diocese were used as follows:

Community improvement	$ 340,219
Education	
For seminarians and clergy	588,467
For the laity	433,089
College buildings and endowments	353,507
High school maintenance	1,491,092
Extra-diocesan expenditures	562,216
Outlays for diocesan properties	233,378
Grants to various organizations	591,506
Administration and planning	479,276

Without getting deeply entangled in the details, let's find out what each of these categories of expenditure contains. Under "Community improvement," we note the diocesan grants to Catholic Charities ($177,932), C.Y.O. and other exclusively Catholic organizations. Also included are such items as a $17,792 contribution to the Pittsburgh Human

Relations Commission, a gift of $11,280 to Project Equality and modest donations to other non-Catholic and nonsectarian welfare agencies.

Expenditures for "Education—laity" include outlays for the CCD (Confraternity of Christian Doctrine) program of religious instruction aimed at adults and at students in the public schools. Under this heading, the accountants have also grouped the diocesan grants to the Holy Name Society, the Council of Catholic Women, the college chaplaincies, the liturgical music commission and the dozen or so other organizations loosely related to education.

"Extra-diocesan expenditures" cover a contribution of $173,797 to the Bishops' Relief Fund, a Peter's Pence collection for the Pope of $101,588 and the proceeds of the other special Sunday collections for the church abroad.*

"Outlays for diocesan properties" range from a contribution of $117,345 to a high school to the $14,739 cost of a piece of property "for future parish development."

"Grants to various organizations" heads a list of dona tions to thirteen special groups. Of these, three were parishes, two were schools and one a religious order. Other beneficiaries include such disparate organizations as Interfaith Housing, Inc., a developer, and the nonsectarian Church Planning Board of Western Pennsylvania which received $5,000.

Finally, under "Administration and planning," we locate such items as the disbursement for the diocesan tribunal ($36,585), a $16,202 payment for an "administrative study" and the outlay for the salaries of the bishop and his two auxiliaries ($10,500). We also find that in 1968-69 the maintenance of the bishop's residence cost a healthy $32,861, and that the travel and entertainment expenses of the bishop himself ran to another $26,805.

* See p. 44 for a brief discussion of these special collections.

Apart from all of these intriguing particulars, what else is to be learned from an analysis of diocesan expenditures? Most important, certainly, we gain a sense of the demands being made by Catholic education today on the resources of the Catholic see. All told, the outlays of the Diocese of Pittsburgh for educational activities added up to $3,256,500 in 1968-69. This sum is fully 57 per cent of the entire diocesan budget. Later, when we focus on the multiple economic crises overtaking the teaching church, we'll find that the situation in Pittsburgh, far from being unusual, is the absolute economic rule. For the moment, we should realize how supremely strong is the hold of education upon the minds—and the purse-strings—of the American hierarchy.

If education is obviously their first budgetary priority, the Pittsburgh report suggests (and a mass of other evidence confirms) that the bishops recognize no equally obvious second priority. It's significant that in Pittsburgh more than sixty non-educational institutions of the diocese received some money from the chancery. But none of them except the Catholic Charities corporation was given more than a modest $55,000. Indeed, the $562,216 "exported" to Rome and elsewhere outside the diocese exceeded by more than $200,000 the total amount of money expended on welfare programs. This eagerness to benefit the universal church at the expense of the local see is extraordinary. It's probably only characteristic of a bishop who, like John J. Wright of Pittsburgh, anticipates being made a cardinal and who therefore wishes to display his munificence to the church at large.*

But even after making allowances for so special a situation, we can see from this one report that the clear-cut

---

* In this context, the exceptionally large Peter's Pence collection reported for 1968–69 in Pittsburgh is explicable. I suspect that Bishop Wright (who was indeed created a cardinal in March, 1969) added to the proceeds of the parish Peter's Pence collected as much as $50,000 worth of diocesan funds.

planning of priorities is alien to the diocesan church. Once we get past education, we sense that instead of receiving any advance notice of financial support, the various lesser diocesan agencies are actually competing with one another for the economic favor of the bishop. The diocesan budget is thus what an accountant would label a retrospective, not a prospective, document: a record of the personal financial skirmishes won and lost by the diocesan functionaries.

After studying the Pittsburgh report, we can believe the tales told of former Bishop Wright by his constituents in Pittsburgh. "In money matters, he was completely unpredictable and quixotic," a close acquaintance of Wright's told me, "with the appetite for power of a Renaissance prince." We can also accept as containing at least a grain of truth other legends about the bishops as dispensers of money. One of the best-known in church circles is that of the generosity of the late Cardinal Richard F. Cushing of Boston. According to report, his visitations to parishes all ended—after tea in the parlor of the convent—with the question: "Sisters, is there anything you need?" Whatever the answer, the Cardinal would say, "Well, I think you could use a new refrigerator [or sometimes a new TV set: it depends on which priest is telling the story]." He then would turn to an aide and ask, "Monsignor, have you got any money on you?" If necessary, Cushing would take up a collection from his entourage to buy the grateful nuns their new appliance.

This may sound like something out of *The Last Hurrah*. But the facts as well as the legends confirm that the Catholic chancery is never the apex of a tidy economic pyramid, but rather the center of a busy disorganized hive. Even in very large sees, we'll find that budgeting is casual* and that

* In six out of the ten largest sees, no centralized diocesan budget is ever put together. The rule seems to be that the Ordinaries first approve the budgets of the high schools, then of the chancery office itself. They

the other available tools of organized management are either neglected or misapplied. For example, we saw earlier that the process of fiscal centralization begins with chancery control over surplus parish funds. In most dioceses, this process has gone not one step farther.

Thus, like three-quarters of all the U. S. sees, Pittsburgh does have a central fund, which the chancery calls a "Loans-in-aid" program. According to the official report, its exclusive purpose is

> to provide funds for parish building programs. Loans are made to the parishes at an interest rate of 3½ per cent . . . As of April 30, 1969 there were outstanding loans to parishes in the amount of $27,539,696 . . . Interest of 3 per cent per annum is paid to all depositors.

The ½ per cent spread between the interest charged the borrowers and the interest paid the depositors yielded $253,352 (after expenses), a nice addition to total chancery receipts. New parish construction must be approved by the Diocesan Building Commission, which also supplies architectural and contracting services. Parish participation in the central funding program, however, is not mandatory. Although pastors are "encouraged to deposit excess working funds with the program," they are not required to do so; and the very low interest paid to depositors offers them correspondingly little incentive to put the money in the fund.

(On this issue, much light is shed by the remarks of the chancellor of a very large Eastern archdiocese, which really do deserve repeating here. Quizzed on the problems of central funds, he told me: "If you make [the pastors] take part, you're liable to get them sore, especially the rich ones. So you have to pay a decent interest rate, like 5 per cent, to sweeten the situation. But then you have to charge

---

next allocate funds to Catholic Charities and other quasi-independent welfare agencies. Lastly, they handle the requests of the smaller organizations on an informal basis.

borrowers more than you'd like, and they're poor enough
to begin with. Trouble is, if you make the program voluntary, the rich pastors won't come in at all. And if the archbishop really puts personal pressure on them, they're liable
to start hiding money away." What's the answer? "Well,
frankly, an appeal to their self-interest. We tell them they
may want to borrow money some day." An unspoken
thought in the chancellor's mind and in mine was that this
situation, multiplied thousands of times across the country,
partly accounts for the terrible disparity between the prosperous Catholic churches of our suburbs and the impoverished but vital churches of inner-city neighborhoods.)

Finally, the Pittsburgh financial report we've been
studying makes clear that there, as in most other sees, the
central fund is used only as a source of loans for parish
construction. The full potential of central financing as the
chief instrument of diocesan-wide money management* is
thus ignored. Nor does it seem, from the other evidence
I've gathered, that the bishops currently operating central
funds are planning to extend these operations beyond the
parishes. "It's enough just to get the banks off the backs of
my pastors," was one bishop's explanation to me.

Let's let this remark stand as a temporary valedictory to
central funds and their applications, and turn to other
efforts aimed at pulling together the internal finances of a
diocese. Of these, one of the most interesting is the centralized purchasing arrangement. Especially in a far-flung organization, the virtues of such an arrangement speak for
themselves. By funneling routine requests for goods and
services into a single office which does the actual buying,
the local administrator saves himself time and energy. The
organization saves money. In the church, some types of
purchasing have automatically recommended themselves to
even unbusinesslike Ordinaries. Because the curricula of the

* Illustrated in detail earlier, pp. 144–149.

parochial schools are everywhere established by chancery-level school boards, the textbooks used by the children are almost always ordered in quantity by the chancery. The pastor or his school principal requisitions the texts he needs and advances the money for them, later billing the families of the individual students. Sometimes, in fact, the chancery will contract with authors and printers for workbooks and other supplementary teaching materials, publishing these itself and selling them to the pastors at a modest profit.

Except in this one area, however, the centralization of purchasing at the diocesan level has proceeded with striking unevenness. At the one extreme, we note the broad and relatively sophisticated procedures of the Archdiocese of New York. There, Cardinal Spellman set up a special corporation, the Institutional Commodity Services, as a purchasing agency. An official description of its activities claims:

> It generates savings for institutions and parishes by the pooling of their purchase volume and the application of professional buying techniques. It enables the institutions and parishes to economize on the major purchase of a variety of commodities ranging from the complete furnishing of new buildings to food, fuel oil, and most equipment and supply items used within the institutional field.

Headed by a priest, Msgr. William J. McCormack, and staffed by laymen, I.C.S. buys goods worth about $16 million a year from outside suppliers. It estimates that it saves pastors and institutional administrators nearly $2 million a year on such purchases. Yet not all diocesan organizations use I.C.S. ("They take too long to get delivery," a Westchester pastor commented, "and you have to buy what's in their catalogues.") And despite the obvious need for I.C.S. professionalism, the archdiocesan high schools (which posted a deficit of $2,160,000 in 1968) do their purchasing independently.

As in the case of central funding, other sees are gradually following the example of New York. As an example of the kinds of savings that tight chancery control over purchasing can mean, consider the budget devised by Msgr. James P. Devine, Chancellor of the Diocese of Bridgeport, for new convents. (The specific figures given are for the convent housing the teaching nuns of St. Margaret Mary Parish, Shelton, Conn.)

14 cells @ $8,000 per cell	$112,000
Architect fees	7,000
Furnishing	20,000
TOTAL	$139,000
Contingencies	1,000
TOTAL BUDGET	$140,000

Despite its terseness, this set of prices is all Msgr. Devine needs to discuss convent design and construction with architects and contractors for the diocese. "Of course, Monsignor worked on those figures for months, with sisters from all the religious orders, and with the architect, builders and decorators," said Irene Green, Msgr. Devine's administrative assistant. Mrs. Green also explained to me that, in a contemporary convent, a cell is by no means the grim abode the name implies. "It's a combination sitting-room, bedroom and study," she said. "Sisters need space for studying and schoolwork as well as for living, eating and entertaining visitors. To put all of this into one building which is cheerful and comfortable, and then to budget the costs accurately, you have to be a real expert." One testimony to the expertise of Msgr. Devine is that the convent of St. Margaret Mary's, budgeted at $140,000, was completed at an actual cost of $136,958.28. And as corresponding evidence that such expertise is in short supply

within the church, there's the fact that Cardinal Terence
Cooke sought out Msgr. Devine in Bridgeport to serve on
Cooke's own Archdiocesan Committee for Education in
New York.

Of the sixty attempts to centralize the institutional
purchasing of the Catholic see, the most curious I've encountered is the one set up in the Archdiocese of Baltimore. There, the chancery—for all the world like some ecclesiastical Diners Club—has decided to sponsor its own
private credit card.

During an interview with Msgr. Porter J. White, the
chancellor, and J. Early Hardesty, lay financial adviser to
the chancery, I mentioned central purchasing. Msgr.
White* immediately slipped from his wallet a neat plasti-
cized card with the raised lettering we associate with
charge cards everywhere. But this one bore the official im-
print of the Archdiocese of Baltimore. Fascinated, I asked
for an explanation. "Every priest in the archdiocese is issued one of these," Msgr. White said, "and some lay employees have them, too. We can use the card to buy just
about everything, from shaving cream to automobile tires.
The chancery has made arrangements with fourteen leading Baltimore retailers to accept our card. Their bills are
sent directly to the chancery for payment, and we mail our
own monthly statements to the pastors and other cardholders."

Knowing something of who commercial credit-card
systems work, I assumed that the archdiocese would run its
system the same way and for much the same practical purposes. I saw that, like a bank, a travel company or any
other financial organization, a chancery could offer a re-
tailer two special attractions: 1) large purchasing volume;

---

* In addition to being the chief administrator of this major see, Msgr.
White is a distinguished theologian who was instrumental in formulating
policy at the Second Vatican Council.

and 2) immediate, guaranteed payment of bills. Such irresistible terms would persuade the fourteen approved retailers to offer handsome discounts, thus lowering their prices by even more than the 10 per cent traditionally granted to individual clergymen. It next occurred to me that the chancery might bill its cardholders at prices somewhat higher than those it was actually being charged. The resulting difference would be large enough to cover the cost of operating the system.

But when I tested these assumptions on Msgr. White, he looked puzzled. "No," he said, "we don't get any volume discounts from the retailers. We certainly don't charge cardholders more than we ourselves have to pay." Then it was my turn to be puzzled. When I learned that the chancery has had to hire two billing clerks and a supervisor, at a total payroll cost of $17,000 a year, just to prepare the monthly statements and to keep the rest of the paperwork straight, my puzzlement deepened. And when I finally asked Msgr. White if the whole system wasn't very costly in terms of the convenience it offered, there was an embarrassed silence.

Msgr. White finally replied that the credit-card system "helped keep track of what the priests were buying." But the use of the credit card is voluntary. A Baltimore priest can just as easily either open his own charge accounts or pay cash for what he buys. Furthermore, he can do his shopping anywhere. So the fiscal controls of which Msgr. White speaks seem to me illusory. The Baltimore credit card could undoubtedly be an ingenious way of reconciling local purchasing with centralized financial administration. It could give pastors in particular the independence they want (and which the chancery wants them to have) and at the same time save the real bill-payers of the archdiocese, the parishioners, scores of thousands of dollars a year. But as things stand, the credit card is merely an appealing gimmick, and the system an incomplete—and therefore a self-defeating—fiscal stratagem.

Even so, Baltimore is light-years ahead of most sees. In general, the individual pastor, school administrator or other institutional supervisor does his own purchasing without any aid from the local chancery. According to Leo V. Ryan, C.S.V., a brother of the order of St. Viator and a prolific writer on school management, in a parish "almost everyone becomes a purchasing agent, in fact if not in theory."

> Purchases are made for the rectory, convent, school, church, parish hall; purchases are made by the pastor, the assistants, the superior, the principal, the teachers, the custodians, and the parish housekeeper. Unless a system is developed and agreed upon, chaos can easily result. . . .
>
> A system for standard purchasing lists, requisitioning, securing bids and quotes for selected vendors, for ordering, for receiving, for receipting, for inventory control, for internal distribution, and for payment must be agreed upon. . . . Many practical guidelines have been developed. . . .

And Brother Leo refers the reader to a list of his own articles in the trade magazine, *Catholic Property Administration.*

The comments of Brother Leo underscore that few Catholic chanceries are even monitoring, much less actively managing, the inflow of ordinary goods and services into the diocesan economy. (If there were tighter controls, Brother Leo's admonitions might not be needed.) Naturally, not every parish, school, hospital and seminary is wasteful about its purchasing; and not every administrator is at the mercy of venal suppliers. But with localization carried to such extremes, it's almost inevitable that the provisioning of the church will cost the church more than it should. In an area of management in which more than $300 million is being spent every year, the absence of control is bound to be costly.

Purchasing is only one area in which managerial half-heartedness seems to be a major problem, and in which the sense of partial but never complete commitment to good management becomes almost haunting. At first, it seems picturesque that a diocese will rigidly centralize the purchasing of such items as altar-cloths, holy oils and candles. You're amused—and impressed—to overhear a chancery aide demand from a religious-articles purveyor the maximum discount and the most favorable credit terms. But when you learn that, even in a New York, the bulk of the procurement is handled by nonprofessionals leagues removed from the chancery, the picturesqueness rapidly vanishes. Instead, you're left with the uneasy feeling that the priorities have been reversed; that the chancery is busy being efficient about minutiae at the expense of what really matters; and that the men who manage a diocese are strangely ambivalent about the techniques they attempt to master.

This brings us once again to the subject of insurance.

We first discussed insurance many pages ago, in the section of the book devoted to the pastor as administrator. We noted then that running a parish is a risky business, and that obtaining proper coverage was an obligation no pastor could neglect. We saw also that for a variety of reasons, pastors prefer to buy their insurance locally, giving preference to the insurance broker or agent who is a loyal, active parishioner.

From every standpoint except that of sentiment, this is the worst possible way to meet the insurance needs of the parishes and thus of the dioceses. First of all, the price an individual pastor pays an individual broker for coverage is far higher than it needs to be. The parish's broker may be an able insurance man. But the rates he quotes his customers are those he finds in an insurance company manual (or obtains from an insurance rating organization). These are weighted to cover the fixed expenses and margins of profit on individual policies and are not subject to negotiation. Secondly, the favored broker may *not* be an able insurance man. But this the pastor only discovers when the broker tells him that he's sorry, but the theft of the trunk containing the parish basketball equipment is not covered. Or, more seriously, when the rectory boiler springs a leak, floods the basement and causes thousands of dollars' worth of uninsured damage. Thirdly, the broker's insurance company may one day decide to cancel Father's insurance.* If this happens, a local broker doing only a limited amount of business with the company is in no position to argue. Either he has to place the parish coverage with another company or the pastor has to call another broker, at the cost of time, money and embarrassment.

This list of problems could be lengthened almost indefinitely. From the point of view of the bishop, a diocese with, say, 200 separate parish insurance programs is a diocese with 199 possible trouble-spots. So obvious are the drawbacks of non-uniformity, and so evident the possibilities for improvement, that insurance on church properties has long been made an objective of standardization. As far back as 1889, in fact, a group of bishops met in Omaha to contend with their insurance problems. It's likely that they were having trouble in obtaining fire insurance from Eastern insurance companies on the wooden churches being constructed in the railroad towns and other communities of the frontier. It's also possible that anti-Catholic feeling in the East played some part in their difficulties. At all events, the bishops decided that the answer was to form an insur-

* The cancellation of parish insurance, especially in urban neighborhoods, is becoming a serious problem in Newark, Detroit, Cleveland and other major sees.

ance company of their own. Because canon law forbids churchmen to engage directly in any profit-making activity, they set up the company as a mutual company, the Catholic Mutual Relief Society of America.* Managed by laymen, but with a board of trustees composed of eighteen bishops, the company is still operating today. According to its advertisement in the 1971 *Official Catholic Directory*, Catholic Mutual Relief's assets "have now approached the four million dollar mark. . . . The Society has no outside ownership and its funds are in a very real sense Church funds sequestered for a specific use."

Although $4 million sounds impressive, by insurance company standards this sum is modest. (By comparison, the assets of a really large mutual company in the property and casualty insurance field, Atlantic Mutual of New York, were worth more than $130 million in 1969.) And although Catholic Mutual Relief states proudly that it "serves over 165 Dioceses and Religious Orders located in all parts of the country," a glance at the geographic distribution of the sees headed by its trustees puts this claim in proper perspective. Among the trustees are the bishops of such dioceses as Sioux City, Wichita, Duluth and Yakima: none of them, obviously, of major size. The largest see represented on the board is St. Paul-Minneapolis, ranking 21st in the U.S. by size of Catholic population. The easternmost is Harrisburg, ranked 69th.

This tells us plainly that Catholic Mutual Relief still is today what it was orginally organized to be: a regional company. Like the religious-bond firms discussed earlier, the insurance venture of the bishops was meant to answer an economic need of those sees in the Midwest and Far West which lacked access to the financial services of the

---

* A mutual insurance company is one legally owned by its policyholders rather than by shareholders. Financial gains are shared by the parties insured (as in a cooperative).

East. Now, of course, the economic vacuum is well filled, and such services are available everywhere. In insurance, the big companies sell their products and operate their claims and other service offices nationwide. As a result of this growth, Catholic Mutual Relief (like dozens of other local and regional insurance companies) has been pushed out of its primary business, the underwriting or acceptance of insurance risks. It survives basically as a sales agency serving a special clientele. The company may in fact underwrite some insurance. Policies are issued in its own name. But most of the coverage its representatives sell is reinsured: i.e., turned over to other, larger companies which assume most of the financial risk and receive all but a small percentage of the premium.*

The limited scope of this one Catholic Church insurance "subsidiary" suggests that most sees have had little difficulty in obtaining insurance from commercial companies. Whatever the situation in the late nineteenth century the physical properties of the church have for decades been considered excellent insurance risks, literally "as safe as a church." Even today, when all types of institutional property are exposed to great hazards, Catholic Church organizations are prized as customers.

How does the diocesan church buy its insurance? As usual, statistical information is nonexistent. But on the basis of a survey of thirty sees, I estimate that in one-third to one-half of all dioceses, insurance is still bought locally. That is, the individual pastors or institutional administrators do business with individual insurance brokers. Of the twenty largest sees, however, at least nine and probably as many as fifteen or sixteen have developed centralized insur-

* The advertisement quoted above also states that "the combined assets of our professional reinsurers total more than two billion dollars" and claims that "this Society places vast amounts of Church insurance in the large reinsurance market." The "vast amounts" are not specified.

ance programs.* Others which have done so range in size from Baltimore (23rd) down to tiny Yakima (132nd).

Regardless of size, the principle of centralization is the same: to insure all diocesan properties in one company (or group of companies) under the supervision of one man or one brokerage firm. And the decision to centralize comes whenever, in a given see, the Ordinary determines to "straighten out the insurance mess." Indeed, some bishops have made a preoccupation with insurance a hallmark of their reputations as administrators. This was true of Cardinal Spellman of New York, who found time within weeks of his installation in 1939 to appoint two priests "to supervise all transactions concerning insurance." Spellman also advised his pastors to carry liability, workmen's compensation and boiler insurance in addition to the fire insurance customarily carried.† This same interest in insurance is true today of Cardinal John Cody, who has revamped the coverage in each of the three sees he has headed: Kansas City-St. Joseph, New Orleans and Chicago.

The first move toward centralization involves the selection of a lay diocesan insurance adviser to work with the bishop and his aides. Sometimes the layman is the personal friend of the Ordinary, or the member of a firm known to chancery officials. For years in New York, Spellman relied on the brokerage firm of Corroon & Reynolds (now Corroon & Black) for insurance advice. In Baltimore, Cardinal Shehan's decision to centralize led J. Early Hardesty, the lay financial consultant to the chancery, to recommend a friend, Thomas Murphy, as insurance counsellor. Mr. Murphy, a retired specialist in casualty insurance, designed an archdiocesan program which saved Baltimore nearly a

---

* The ones of which I'm certain are Chicago, New York, Los Angeles, Brooklyn, Detroit, Philadelphia, Rockville Centre, New Orleans and St. Louis.
† Gannon, *The Cardinal Spellman Story*, p. 252.

quarter of a million dollars worth of premiums in the first year of operation. As consultant and broker on the insurance account of the Archdiocese of Chicago, Cardinal Cody employs David Wilson, a St. Louis-based insurance man who is Cody's nephew. The Gallagher-Basset Insurance Service of Chicago administers the account, which costs the archdiocese $1 million a year.

The insurance man for a Catholic diocese does exactly what he'd do if the bishop were a business client. He first collects from the pastors and other administrators the separate policies under which their properties are insured. On the basis of the information he gleans from these, he next develops a comprehensive plan of property protection. This typically includes fire insurance on church buildings and on their contents; insurance against water damage, windstorm, explosion and related hazards; and protection against damage due to "riot and civil commotion." In theory, the insurance broker should then "market" the insurance—that is, solicit bids from several insurance companies on the program he is proposing.

But for several reasons, this rarely happens.

One reason is that the job of preparing the proposal itself is too complex for the average diocesan broker. If he happens to own or to represent a sizable firm, he can call on his own experts in property insurance to assist in such essentials as the analysis of the existing policies and the verification of the insurance rates on individual structures. But few bishops pick insurance brokers because of the resources at their disposal. Thus, in a small see, the diocesan insurance man will simply rely on the information in the policies he's replacing. And if the situation is too complicated, or if the broker finds that he needs aid, he turns to an insurance company.

In most dioceses, the insurance company and not the broker does all the work of appraising property, recording the data and designing the property-insurance "package" for the diocese. The broker is simply the contact man between the insurance company and the chancery. "On Mondays, Wednesdays and Fridays, he's the bishop's errand boy," said an official of one huge insurance company (who declined to be identified). "On Tuesdays and Thursdays, he's ours."

Because so few brokers can handle the burden of putting together a centralized program, the insurance companies take over. And this explains why certain insurance companies have risen to dominance in the market for Catholic ecclesiastical insurance. "The local broker for the diocese falls on his face," said Brian Black of the Insurance Company of North America. "So we move in, meet the priests and set up the plan. Our field men [salaried representatives who assist the brokers] deal directly with the church personalities. Our underwriters learn how to rate church policies. Our adjusters get good at settling the value of the altar when a church burns down. After a while, we become known as the experts."

And so, while no one insurance company monopolizes church property coverage, several do dominate the field. One such leader is the $2 billion giant for which Brian Black works, the Insurance Company of North America. Among the dozen or more major sees insured by INA are the Archdioceses of Philadelphia and New York and the Diocese of Bridgeport.

Another big insurance organization active in the diocesan insurance market is the Fund Group. Of the several companies in the Group, the Fireman's Fund, the oldest and largest, is the property-insurance unit. So large is its volume of Catholic Church business that the company prints inventory and other forms especially for diocesan administrators. The inventory form for pastors is similar to the one your own insurance broker hands you for listing the household items you want covered. But this form asks the pastor for the numbers and values of a lengthy list of items no householder keeps on hand. The list includes "altars (non-affixed),* organ (non-affixed), baptismal font, candelabra, catafalque & pall, credence table, ciboria, chalices, confessionals (non-affixed), crucifixes, missals, monstrances, pedestals, paintings (commercial & prints), pulpit, stations [of the Cross] (non-affixed), statuary, reliquaries, registers, sedilla, candles, wine, votive units, vestments, copes and linens." This marvelous catalogue reminds us—if we need reminding—that every Catholic church is a repository of ceremonial wares. To assess the value of even one church is a laborious job. To add up the total values of all the church property in a diocese is a major proposition. As a rule, the insurance company setting up a centralized program will ask the bishop to hire professional appraisers to do this task.

As soon as the information is gathered, the company's underwriters determine (often in concert with industry rating organizations) the premium rates for each type of property insurance to be carried. When a broker plays an active role in developing the program, the bishop will reap the benefits of competitive bidding by several companies. Or even if only one company is asked to bid, a good broker can negotiate for favorable rates and extra services (e.g., safety engineering surveys on the basis of which risky structural weaknesses can be removed and insurance costs lowered). Most of the time, however, the insurance company is under no such pressure. It simply studies the figures and sets a cost for the program. And most of the time, the chancery accepts the company's offer and the program is launched.

---

* If the altars and other structures on the list are "affixed," or built in, they'd be classified as part of the church building itself and insured at a different premium rate.

There's much more to be said about the price the church pays for its centralized program; and more than one form of insurance to consider. But for the moment, let's dig deeper into property insurance and its ramifications. In particular, we should study the crucial question to which this insurance is the key. That is, the question of valuing the property assets of the church.

To set the stage, let's consider the most familiar insurance example of all, your own. When you decide, or when your insurance man persuades you, that it's time to do something about your household insurance, your first question is: how much insurance should I carry on my house?* As you may recall, the answer is a bit more complicated than you thought it would be. If you borrowed money to buy the house, the bank or other lender will insist on being protected up to the present limit of the mortgage loan. You yourself will want enough insurance to cover your own equity, whether it's large or small. The total—the loan plus the amount you've got invested—gives you one possible figure for your insurance, a minimum figure.

Your house may very well be worth more than this amount, which is what you paid for it originally. But the insurance company doesn't care. On the contrary, no insurance company will allow you to make money on a fire that destroys your home. The best the company will let you do is break even. So your broker will advise you to work out the so-called "actual cash value" of your house: i.e., its replacement cost at today's prices *minus an amount for depreciation* during the time you've owned it. If you're willing to pay extra, you may be able to cover the full replacement cost without subtracting a sum for depreciation. However, because the chances are slight that you'll ever suffer a total loss, you probably won't even insure the

* If you live in a rental apartment, you begin with the contents of your home, not the dwelling itself. But the principle is exactly the same.

house for its actual cash value. Rather, you'll carry fire insurance of 75 or 80 per cent of this amount.

Having ordered the insurance, you'll rightly feel safe. And yet, the whole transaction does leave unanswered a second question: how much is my house really worth? Whatever I paid for it? What I might get if I put it on the market? What it's insured for? Or some compromise amount? If this personal puzzle leads you to ponder the intangible and elusive aspects of putting a price on all realty, so much the better. You're in exactly the right frame of mind to understand the situation within the diocesan church.

My own introduction to this situation I owe to Bishop Ernest J. Primeau of Manchester. Bishop Primeau valiantly attempted to explain to me, a non-initiate, the mechanics of diocesan finance. When the question of depreciation came up, His Excellency commented, "I've got a brother who works for Uni-Royal. One of the things they do there is keep very accurate schedules of the values of all their plants and equipment. They have to, for tax reasons. Otherwise, they couldn't claim depreciation. But we pay no corporate taxes. So we don't go through all of that routine." Because diocesan property values aren't constantly being adjusted for depreciation, Bishop Primeau was saying, chanceries need not assess the properties too carefully in the first place.

Only a Howard Hughes or an Aristotle Onassis, I thought to myself, could really be this casual about his real estate. So I asked the bishop, "Suppose you need to borrow money? When the bank asks you for your financial statement, what do you use to show how much your property is worth?"

"The insurance figures," was Bishop Primeau's answer. And in every other see from which I obtained information,

I was told the same thing. In all accounting statements, whether they're for internal use or for the information of lenders and other outsiders, *the asset value of the diocesan real estate is simply the value of the insurance on the property.* When you recall that this realty constitutes an estimated 90 per cent or more of the value of all diocesan assets, you can see why insurance is of vital importance to the bishops and to the church. Because the amount of money a bishop can borrow externally depends on the strength of the diocesan financial statement,* the credit of the diocese ultimately rests on its property values: i.e., its insurance values. And because the amount of *internal* financing a bishop can arrange usually depends on his ready access to outside money, the entire debt structure of the diocese—and thus its entire capital economy—may be based on the financial story the insurance schedules tell.

How accurate is this story?

The best answer to this question I've ever seen appears in a confidential study prepared in 1969 for Cardinal Terence Cooke of New York. Members of Cooke's blue-ribbon Committee on Education produced the study, which analyzes the finances of the archdiocesan school system. Later, we'll learn more about this study, which is a milestone in church management. Now, let's merely sample its comments on the valuation of archdiocesan assets.

> When the parishes file their financial statements with the Archbishopric of New York, the entry "fixed assets" is supposed to be comprised of the following ingredients:
> 1. Land is supposed to be included at assessed valuation. The taxing authorities in New York City generally assess tax-exempt properties at 64 per cent of their presumed market value.
> 2. The buildings are supposed to be booked at their ap-

---

* Credit depends also, of course, on the lender's evaluation of the diocesan cash flow, past borrowing record and potential ability to repay.

praised value in keeping with an annual insurance appraisal . . . This appraised value is 80 percent of estimated *replacement* cost.

Except for one feature, the evaluation practices of the Archdiocese of New York are identical with those of all the other sees I've visited or surveyed. The one exception is New York's requirement that land be valued separately from buildings. In most of the parish financial reports I've seen, land and buildings are lumped together. Note, by the way, that churches, unlike most private dwellings, are insured for their full replacement cost, not their "actual cash value" (replacement cost minus depreciation). To go on with the New York report:

> Thus, we see some important conclusions regarding the stated fixed assets of the Church.
> 1. Land values are understated by at least 36 per cent in New York City. In fact, it appears that *land is not even included in the fixed assets reported by some of the parishes.*
> 2. *The value of buildings is fictional.* The value of buildings is not stated at original cost, or at depreciated original cost, as might be supposed under rules of good accounting. They are stated at 80 per cent of the theoretical cost in today's economy of reproducing the cubic footage of the facility. [Italics added.]

The report is telling you what you already know in terms of your own house and your own insurance, that insurance values are very crude indicators of the actual value of property. But another bombshell is yet to come:

> We find from an examination of the insurance records, parish by parish, that the Churches are reporting their fixed assets in ways which are inconsistent, unreliable, and frequently inaccurate.

And the report notes that out of thirty-five parishes on Staten Island, eight have "*insured* values (80 per cent of replacement value of buildings and contents) higher than the total booked (i.e., reported) values of all the fixed assets including land." That is, the pastor is telling the chancery one thing and the insurance company another.

One of these eight Staten Island parishes reported the value of its buildings *and* land as $188,000, when it was carrying insurance (which of course covers only buildings) of $684,000. Another parish reported its fixed assets as worth $250,000 when it was insured for $844,000. A third filed a valuation of $634,00 for buildings and land, although its insurance policy read $910,000. And one hapless pastor declared the value of his parish property to be $73,000 when, according to the insurance records, it was covered for $1,106,000!

What's happening here? Are the pastors of Staten Island conspiring to conceal from their own chancery the realty treasures they've got hidden away?

The best evidence to the contrary is simply that in the Archdiocese of New York, all pastors arrange their insurance and pay their premiums not through an outside broker but through the chancery itself. (A separate corporation, the Archdiocesan Service Corporation, run by priests, is the broker.) Since the annual financial reports also go to the chancery, pastors are hardly likely to be attempting any deception. Rather, as the report explains:

> It appears that a pastor is just not apt to call up the local taxing authority each year to ask what market valuation is presently placed on his Church's land. He is not apt to contact insurance people to ask what replacement value is currently assigned to his depreciable assets. The value of his fixed assets has nothing to do with his annual operating problems. Liquidation of a parish is unthinkable to him. He does not think like an economist; he does not think about fixed asset valuation at all in many cases.

And indeed, how could he? The rueful language of the report confirms everything we've learned about the administrative skill—or rather, lack of skill—of the Catholic priest. We can almost hear Father Wittenbrink in Washington saying again what we first heard him say in Chapter Two: "They want the theology of love, not how to balance a checkbook."

But the errors and the misrepresentations of some pastors, however revealing as symptoms, are not the main issue here. As the New York report makes baldly evident, the real problem lies in the system itself. In truth, the splendid churches which earlier generations of priests and parishioners have left behind were expensive enough to build. To replace them today would obviously cost double, treble or even quadruple the original price. To insure them for what it would take to replace them, thereby protecting today's worshipers against financial catastrophes, is sensible administrative practice.

Nevertheless, the custom of valuing all diocesan fixed assets in terms of insurance is certain to produce a confusing (and sometimes a wildly inaccurate) notion of what these assets are really worth. To confirm the fact, simply glance at the mixture of realty assets typical of any see. Clearly, some of these properties will be worth at least as much as the insurance schedule says they are. In particular, the up-to-date parish plants occupying prime land in suburbia fully meet their insurance appraisal values. The land, though probably not the buildings, tempts the developers. But in the decaying neighborhoods, the slums and the little-visited corners of the diocese, stand many more churches which will never again be as valuable as they once were. These properties cannot possibly be worth what their insurance makes them appear to be.

Therefore, the net result of the accepted valuation method is to overinflate the fixed asset values of the diocese. This in turn distorts the balance sheet. If the bishop is a sophisticated executive—and some bishops are—he'll attempt to discount the exaggerated evidence of his net worth. But bishops no less than bankers are at the mercy of the figures they read. Although these leave the bishops uncertain about the real financial conditions of their sees, even the most management-minded bishops remain unperturbed by the lack of exact information. Like Bishop Primeau, many dismiss as unnecessary the labor involved in making accurate estimates of values. And the average Ordinary, comfortably sure that his property is worth many millions of dollars, is happy to accept the misleading figures which assert that the property is worth still more.* As James P. Shannon, now no longer a priest but until 1969 an auxiliary bishop of St. Paul-Minneapolis, put it to me: "He knows enough to think he's in pretty good shape, and that's all he wants to know."

And so, ironically, the myth of unlimited church wealth seems nowhere to find more eager acceptance than in the Catholic chancery.

How dangerous to the ecclesiastical economy is this distorted self-image of diocesan wealth? If you keep in mind the comment of the New York report that "the value of his fixed assets has nothing to do with [a pastor's] annual operating problems," you can guess why the bishops worry so little about the accuracy of their balance sheets. Like their pastors, the bishops are men preoccupied with daily managerial routines. They concentrate on what they consider the essentials, and leave the Big Picture to others. In this, the mentality of the bishop more closely resembles that of the salesman than that of the auditor. If we do a good job with our services—so goes the reasoning—then

---

* The New York report suggests what I believe to be true of all but a very few sees, that the currently accepted values of diocesan properties are overstated by as much as 200 per cent.

our income will be steady and we can sail ahead to new growth. To any administrator who thinks this way, a handsome balance sheet is an open invitation to expand.

And there, I think, is the crux of the problem. As if hypnotized by the growing values in the left-hand columns of their financial statements, the American bishops have continued to invest heavily in the physical plants of their sees. Despite inflation and its effect on both costs and income (and despite the fund shortages pleaded by the bishops themselves), the almost mechanical conversion of scarce liquid assets into bricks and mortar still proceeds apace. Thus, according to the authoritative trade journal *Catholic Building and Maintenance*, in 1968 the diocesan church in the U.S. completed approximately 1,350 construction projects at a cost of more than $900 million. These included 450 new churches, 304 parish halls and religious education centers, 190 rectories, 95 convents, 108 elementary schools, 39 high schools and 38 other diocesan buildings. In 1969, another 304 churches, 300 parish centers, 200 rectories and 100 elementary schools were added to the inventory of parish realty. Most of these structures were financed by diocesan central-fund mortgage loans. Other diocesan building activity stayed level with that of 1968.

In March, 1969, the New York study group recommended to Cardinal Cooke that:

> a moratorium should be called upon all discretionary capital expenditure as far as the parochial schools, the parishes, and the regional high school system are concerned until it is sure that operating income needed to cover operating expenses is not used to fund expansion which can then not be supported.

But while the report calling for a check on new construction was being prepared, the U.S. diocesan church was adding to its physical plant the equivalent of two archdioceses the size of the Archdiocese of New York. In part because they're deceived by their own bookkeeping, the bishops seem to be bricking themselves into a prison from which there's no escape.

It's ironic that the effort to centralize property insurance, an effort at better management, has helped to convince the bishops to go on with their building. If centralization hadn't made those huge, misleading asset totals so available, their impact on chancery thinking might have been less strong; and perhaps by now the flow of money into new construction would be better controlled. But let's not be too hasty in our search for ironies. The same centralization programs which undoubtedly have encouraged overbuilding are, potentially at least, essential to more rational allocations of diocesan resources. In insurance, centralization is saving individual sees much money and will save them much more. Central financing, so far used primarily to reduce external debt, could become the instrument of internal fiscal control. If they can learn to use such managerial tools correctly, the bishops still have enough time to master their sprawling economies.

In fairness, we should note that some Catholic bishops are already sharpening their construction-management skills. Cardinal Patrick J. O'Boyle of Washington, D.C., is keeping his promise of 1968 to observe a three-year moratorium on new construction pending a complete reappraisal of diocesan priorities. In 1969, Cardinal John F. Dearden of Detroit completely reorganized his chancery, placing building and maintenance services in the hands of lay specialists. In January, 1970, Cardinal John J. Carberry of St. Louis published a financial statement which includes a $1,035,576 depreciation write-off on the $25,055,305 archdiocesan high school plant. True, the last official act of Cardinal James F. McIntyre before his retirement as

archbishop of Los Angeles was the dedication of the new
$3.5 million Church of St. Basil on Wilshire Boulevard.
Archbishop Joseph T. McGucken, to the dismay of his
own pastors, has insisted on completing his $11 million ca-
thedral in downtown San Francisco. But the New York report from which we've been quoting was commissioned by
a far more influential prelate. And as we'll see, Cardinal
Cooke is quietly acting on some of its most critical recommendations.

   After drawing so near to so huge an economic problem
as this one of overbuilding, it may seem anticlimactic to refocus our attention on the particulars of diocesan insurance.
But only by fitting together the smaller pieces of our complicated puzzle can we at last set the big pieces into their
proper framework. Accordingly, let's complete our scrutiny of the insurance practices of the diocesan church.
These do indeed shed a light of their own on the larger
issues we've been uncovering.

   To most of us, a Catholic church is a quiet neighborhood sanctuary. But to a seasoned property and casualty insurance man,* a church is a particularly horrifying collection of hazards to life and limb. Take for example the stone
steps leading to the portals, well-worn by generations of
worshipers and the ideal place for wedding parties to pose
for their photographs. Instead of such pleasant visions,
however, the insurance man sees when he looks at the steps
a rainy day, an elderly churchgoer, a sudden loss of balance
and a serious accident. Or consider the gleaming marble
floors of so many church interiors. No matter how se-
renely elegant their patinas, these mean only trouble to the
insurance expert. "What kid going to choir practice can resist taking a running slide down the aisle?" one casualty

* Casualty insurance is the generic term which includes all forms of
liability insurance, workmen's compensation coverage and accident expense insurance.

agent asked me. "All he has to do is skid the wrong way
and bang! you've got a big problem. And don't think for a
minute that Catholic parents won't sue their own church."

Not only parish churches but rectories, convents and
especially schools are what the casualty insurance underwriter thinks of as high-risk locations. If anything, the insurance companies serving the church are closer-mouthed
than the church itself about the casualty insurance claims
which arise against the individual parishes and dioceses each
year. But it's safe to assume that, across the country, thousands of claims alleging personal injury and damage to
property are filed against the church. Furthermore, the lay
employees of Catholic sees and of their individual institutions number in the hundreds of thousands. (In 1969, Catholic schools, colleges and universities employed more than
100,000 lay teachers alone.) From gravediggers in the
cemeteries to secretaries in the chanceries and rectories,
these employees suffer their share of injuries and add their
workmen's compensation claims to the total.

As you might expect in a society which believes the
Catholic Church to be rich, church institutions are targets
for big claims. "We've handled some whoppers," said a representative of INA. "People figure the church can pay anything, and then they assume that because the church is a
church, it will be a soft touch. We do our best to disillusion
them." In self-defense, individual pastors and those sees in
which casualty insurance is centralized generally carry high
liability-insurance limits. The Diocese of Baton Rouge, for
instance, takes no chances on such insurance. According to
an audit report prepared for Bishop Robert E. Tracy in
1968 by Hannis T. Bourgeois & Co., the diocesan accountants:

> Firemen's Fund Insurance Company's Policy No. TP69504
> . . . includes Comprehensive General Liability on all prop-
> erties with Bodily Injury coverage in the amount of

$100,000 per person and $500,000 per accident, as well as Property Damage in the amount of $100,000.

The Diocese is also properly covered under workmen's compensation insurance together with an Automobile Policy covering Liability with limits of $100,000 for each person, $500,000 each accident and $50,000 Property Damage.

For larger dioceses and archdioceses, such blanket coverage has become increasingly difficult to obtain, a sure sign that claims have been on the rise. Thus, when J. Early Hardesty of Baltimore asked his friend Thomas B. Murphy to secure blanket liability insurance for the archdiocese, Murphy found no domestic bidders at all for the coverage. Part of the reason, I'm sure, was the "custom-tailored" coverage on which he insisted. Feeling that a Catholic see needs truly enormous amounts of insurance, Murphy proposed coverage of up to $10 million for each incident. To keep the premium from being prohibitive, he suggested a $10,000 deductible for each separate diocesan structure. (In effect, this means that on claims of less than $10,000—and most claims are settled for less—the archdiocese acts as its own insurance company.) According to Hardesty, no U.S. insurance company would consider underwriting such a policy, not even the CNA group, which provides the property coverage. Only Lloyd's of London would accept the insurance.* But even though Lloyd's rates are substantially higher than those of domestic insurance companies, Murphy's efforts lowered the casualty insurance premiums from $390,000 to $149,000 a year.

Those dioceses which are centralizing liability as well as property insurance are doing so just in time to avoid serious

* When I mentioned this situation to a New York City insurance broker who handles insurance nationally for a number of Catholic religious orders, he smiled sardonically. All he would say was, "We know about the Baltimore situation." But the message was unmistakable: Murphy could have obtained the insurance in the U.S. This broker added that his firm "wouldn't go near" diocesan insurance operations. "Too much of a mess."

cost difficulties. For the past ten years, liability insurance
rates have been rising steadily. The upward trend reflects
not only increases in the numbers of claims (and higher settlement costs per claim) but the struggles of the insurance
companies to cover their own spiraling expenses and still
make money. "We can handle the big industrial [casualty
insurance] lines," said a company representative on this
subject. "But the churches can't pass on premium increases
to their customers." Then he added, "Of course, the
churches aren't alone." In some states—New Jersey is a notable example—insurance companies are actually refusing
to renew the liability policies of such institutional clients as
local school boards and branches of the state university.
"With all the violence that's going on," says Walter Samples of the American Insurance Association, "our member
companies just don't want the business. So far, the church
has been very fortunate." Plainly, over the next several
years the bishops will need to be shrewd insurance managers to contend with the rising premiums and tightening
standards of the casualty insurance industry.

One of the special features of the blanket liability policies now being sought by chanceries is their coverage of the
automobiles owned or driven by priests, nuns and lay employees of the see. In Baltimore, the diocesan policy covers
every one of the more than 5,000 cars in use. The individual owner (which may be a parish or other institution) secures from a local broker basic liability coverage of
$10,000 per occurrence. The owner is also responsible for
collision insurance and theft coverage on the car. The diocesan policy serves as so-called "excess" insurance over the
$10,000 basic coverage up to the $10 million limit. Similarly, the more conventional blanket insurance program of
Baton Rouge includes auto liability insurance. "It's a good
deal for Father," says a Catholic insurance expert. "You
have to remember, priests are usually lousy drivers.

They're like doctors, driving along with something entirely different on their minds." Perhaps so; but in any case it's comforting, and less costly, for the pastor to be protected by the enfolding wings of the chancery insurance program.*

Property insurance (which includes fire, burglary, theft and vandalism coverage) is no less of a problem for the church. Thus, a story in the insurance trade paper *Business Insurance* (August 31, 1970) was headlined, "Churches [Are] No Longer Seen As 'Sacred Insureds.' " The report went on, "In the age of the dope addict, and the revolutionary, churches stand as the oldest, sometimes wealthiest and easiest to hit symbols of the American Establishment." And property losses have risen accordingly. For instance, in 1968 (the most recent year for which figures are available), the Catholic Church in this country was plagued by nearly 1,500 fires. Some were large, some small, but the total dollar loss was about $10 million. Apart from the very real threat of arson, the main reason seems to be the characteristic construction of the churches themselves. *Business Insurance* quotes Deuel Richardson, head of the insurance-company-backed National Fire Prevention Association as commenting that "the construction of a church is almost identical with that of an incinerator. Stairways are often unprotected and the high ceilings and towers act just like draft flues." Another expert, a representative of the New York insurance brokerage firm of Corroon and Black, told *Business Insurance* that "The companies used to love to see church brokers coming, but now we're the bad guys."

Before we go on to consider other types of personal insurance on churchmen, we might ask: how much does the

---

* Such auto coverage is good business for the chanceries, too, because they know they'll be made parties to any injury or damage suit arising from an accident involving a priest, nun or lay diocesan employee.

diocesan church spend on its property and casualty insurance each year? Even in those sees which have fully centralized their insurance, the premiums are invariably broken down into subtotals for billing to the individual institutions and the parishes. So the chanceries may or may not add up the diocesan totals. True, the year-end reports of "experience" (i.e., of the relationships between total premiums paid, claims settled, financial reserves held by the insurance companies and expenses) would tell us what we want to know. But diocesan brokers and the chanceries file these documents away very carefully indeed.*

Then, too, some parishes and institutions pay their premiums once a year, some only every three years. (The latter method entitles them to a discount.) But few pastors indicate in their annual reports any distinction between one-year and three-year premiums, or between the premiums for the different types of insurance. So we can't add up the totals accurately from this end of the system, either.

"Don't worry about being confused," says one layman who works in the accounting department of an archdiocesan chancery in the East. "Monsignor [his boss, the vicar-general] is confused. And His Eminence [the archbishop, a cardinal) is completely mystified. So we're all in the same boat."

The most significant fact about insurance for the diocesan church is this prevailing confusion over its costs. But on the basis of the figures I've combed out of financial reports and coaxed out of insurance specialists for several sees, I'd place the total national expenditure for diocesan property and casualty insurance at about $150 million a year. Other types of insurance, like workmen's compensation coverage for lay employees, and coverages like Blue Cross-Blue

---

* Some brokers carefully edit for their diocesan clients the experience reports they receive from the insurance companies. Others simply lock such confidential documents away in the office safe. I doubt whether more than a few of the bishops know that such reports are available.

Shield which are not technically considered insurance, add perhaps another $25 million to the bill. How much of this money could be saved by more effective accounting methods and by further centralization is anybody's guess. But one representative of a leading national insurance brokerage firm has said to me, after surveying the insurance of several diocesan institutions, that insurance costs could probably be cut by 25 or 30 per cent.

As an appropriate finale to this analysis of fiscal centralization, one more item recommends itself. This one is the provision made for priests who grow old or ill in the service of the see.

Until relatively recently, the costs of supporting the aged or the disabled priest never showed up at all on the books of the church. A priest who fell ill would either remain at home in the rectory or enter a Catholic hospital or nursing home. Either way, the parish paid the doctors' bills and the nursing care was free. As for retirement, the concept was totally alien to the priesthood. In truth as well as in legend, the church, from the top down, was—and still is —run by elderly men.* Especially in the major urban sees, where a priest is lucky to be made a pastor by the time he reaches sixty,† the problems raised by the combination of seniority and longevity are thorny indeed. The pastor who achieves his rank at an age when most men are happy to think about retirement traditionally insists on running his parish for as long as he himself can survive. Only when old age makes him too infirm to live in the rectory will Father

* Though in this respect as in so many others, the truth is less damaging than the legend. Thus, it's true that of the 133 cardinals living in 1970, fully fifty are older than seventy-five, while four are ninety or older. But most Catholic cardinals (thirty-four, in fact) are between sixty-five and seventy; and thirty-seven are younger than sixty-five. The average age is almost exactly seventy. The oldest of the American bishops is eighty-seven, and the average age of the bishops is a "young" sixty-five.
† In 1969, the *average* age of the pastors of the Archdiocese of New York was sixty-two.

even consider moving to a home for retired priests. To this day, rectories in and around the big cities are occupied by priests too old to serve actively but too proud to leave. "Pastors *emeritus*, they're called," said a young assistant pastor, "and they can drive you crazy."

In his book *America's Forgotten Priests*, the Jesuit priest and sociologist Joseph Fichter reports that of the 2,000 assistant priests polled for this study, "about half are not on a first-name basis with their pastor and about three out of ten give a negative appraisal of their manner of communicating with him." Fichter quotes a Massachusetts curate in his late forties on this subject:

> In a well-established diocese like ours, a good portion of the assistants have become functionaries who obediently perform routine duties defined by the pastor. In my own case I find it hard to see the will of God in the will of my pastor who is well over eighty years of age and whose ideas and ways of acting belong to another age.

In general, Fichter's findings document that in rectories as everywhere else, the generation gap is a wide one.

The bishops are well aware of the personnel and management problems posed by the ancient tradition that a priest should serve in his post for life. Indeed, Pope Paul has himself acknowledged these problems.* A few of the bishops know that the common practice of "retiring" chancery officials by assigning them to parishes as pastors has merely compounded the difficulties. But only a very few bishops have gone so far as to devise and put into practice formal retirement programs.

Instead, in most sees the bishops maintain and subsidize special funds for the diocesan clergy. These are used by the

* The Pope has at least required the officials of the Roman Curia to submit their resignations from active duty when they reach age seventy. He has also suggested that bishops retire at seventy-five. And no cardinal older than seventy-five will be eligible to vote in the consistory which elects Pope Paul's successor.

Ordinaries for a variety of purposes, including that of paying cash allowances to priests no longer able to serve actively. In a large see, the annual contribution to the clergy fund is likely to be substantial, and the fund itself to be worth several million dollars. In Baltimore, the chancery added $85,000 to its "Infirm Priests Fund" in 1969. In New York, the 1969 contribution was $200,000. Most of the money put into clergy funds is drawn from diocesan ordinary income (*cathedraticum* receipts or special parish assessments). Some dioceses also collect personal contributions from the priests themselves, and clergy funds are favorite beneficiaries of priests who bequeath money to the church. The bishops use the income from these funds to take care of medical bills, retirement allowances and funeral expenses as the need arises. The money needed to pay for the treatment of the occasional "problem cases"—the alcoholic, emotionally disturbed or homosexual priests whose illnesses are discovered by the Ordinary—is quietly taken from these funds. Clergy funds are also tapped for other purposes. Thus, when a diocesan priest is granted the title of monsignor, the bishop may make a gift on his behalf to Rome from the fund. The expenses of travel on quasipersonal business may be covered (for instance, if a group of diocesan priests makes the trip to Rome to see their Ordinary created a cardinal). And memorial tablets honoring deceased members of the clergy are paid for out of the clergy fund.

Almost without exception, the Ordinary himself makes all the decisions involving the clergy fund. In the past, this has meant the type of casual personal benevolence we associate with paternalistic management everywhere. The ailing priest whose illness was called to the attention of his bishop might suddenly find himself in the hands of the leading medical specialists, with all costs borne by His Excellency. Through the kindness of the bishop, the aged curate might be given a trip to Florida, or enough pocket money to keep him in books, brandy and cigars. When the church was a smaller, clubbier organization (as it still is in some dioceses), such personal attentions were adequate substitutes for better salaries, insurance programs, retirement plans and other formal financial benefits.

Now, however, things are different. Sees which numbered their priests in the hundreds only a few years ago now number them in the thousands. Of necessity, the professional church (in particular the urban church) is becoming a more impersonal milieu. Today, a bishop has little enough time to deal with his pastors in business matters, let alone to socialize with them. He's unlikely to know even the names of the assistant pastors of his see. To be felt at all, the benevolence of a bishop toward his clergy must be planned and formalized. In small sees as well as large ones, this shift toward systematization of aid to the clergy is gaining momentum today.

A striking instance of what such a transition can involve is the situation which developed about five years ago in the Archdiocese of Chicago. To understand what happened, we need a bit of background. Under two gifted archbishops, Cardinals Samuel Stritch (1939-58) and Albert Meyer (1958-65), Chicago had become a great center of liberal Catholicism. Although the pastors of this largest of American sees were by and large conservatives, the younger diocesan clergy anticipated the great changes in the faith which Vatican II was later to legitimatize.*

One of the elder heroes of this liberal movement was the senior auxiliary of the archdiocese, Bernard J. Sheil, famed since the early 1930's as a supporter of organized labor, and later a crusader for civil rights and a specialist in

---

* For a brief but evocative account of the "Whiz Kids" of the Chicago priesthood, see Chapter VIII, "The Chicago Experience," of *The Catholic Experience*, by Rev. Andrew M. Greeley.

Catholic Youth Organization work. In addition to his friendships with union officials, politicians and lay liberals, Sheil, a man of great charm, took care to stay on excellent terms with his fellow-priests and members of the hierarchy. As proof that his friends within the church were influential ones, we can note that Sheil, though only an auxiliary, was appointed in 1959 to one of the very few titular archbishoprics given to anyone outside the Vatican.

When John Cody succeeded Cardinal Meyer as archbishop of Chicago in 1965, one of his first moves was to press for the retirement of those pastors he deemed too old for active service. During his first two years in office, Cody is said to have demanded the resignations of 250 of his 460 pastors. Sheil, meanwhile, had established the headquarters of his network of CYO and other organizations in the rectory of St. Andrew's Church in central Chicago. Repeated suggestions from Cody that the seventy-five-year-old auxiliary step down from his post (and thus lead the way for others) were ignored. Finally, Cody, accompanied by Msgr. John Quinn, his choice as Sheil's successor, went in person to interview Sheil. The archbishop found his auxiliary living in luxury while the four assistant pastors of St. Andrew's made do belowstairs. While Cody was still wondering what to do, Msgr. Quinn abruptly demanded the parish books. He then asked, "How much will you take to get out of my parish?"

"Twenty-five thousand dollars a year," Sheil snapped.

"I'll give you ten thousand dollars and not a penny more," said Quinn, and the funds of the Chicago Priests' Retirement and Mutual Aid Association were used to finance the arrangement. Sheil promptly moved to Arizona, where he died a year later, in 1969. Cody has proceeded with his program of mandatory retirement, and is reportedly developing a formal pension program.

For most of us, a retirement program is a basic benefit

that goes along with a job. The design of such a benefit program, however, is a complex specialty. For a corporate client, the pension specialist must answer dozens of questions about the legal, actuarial, financial, tax and social aspects of the plan. For instance: will the levels of the retirement benefits be realistic in terms of future living costs? Does the plan discriminate in favor of the higher-paid employee (in violation of Treasury Department regulations)? Should the employee who quits his job be given the legal right to take with him any part of the money the employer has contributed to fund his retirement? As a necessary offshoot of our drive for the security represented by retirement plans, a whole industry has arisen to deal with questions like these.

For the Catholic bishop, these questions pose no problems. Because the church is tax-exempt, he's free from any need to qualify a priests' retirement program as tax-deductible under Treasury rules. Furthermore, the bishop need not make his program competitive with those of other employers, simply because priests are free neither to bargain for money nor to sell their services to another, higher bidder. Finally, because a priest receives only a nominal cash salary, his income from a retirement plan can likewise be made minimal.

So it's logical to wonder why any bishop should set up a formal retirement plan for priests in the first place. Why not simply go on granting cash allowances to needy priests out of the existing priests' funds? The answer is simple. A program which first sets up rules for retirement and also makes clear the benefits to be received is a powerful tool of personnel management. Such a program gives His Excellency a means of enforcing retirement, and thus of opening the way for the promotion of younger priests. And it makes clear to present incumbents what they can expect in the future.

Of the relatively few formal programs in being today, I'm familiar with three, those of the Archdiocese of New York and of the dioceses of Newark and Bridgeport. The Newark program is typical of the others and of plans now being recommended elsewhere. Under this plan, according to a *New York Times* report (November 29, 1968):

> Priests will receive benefits of $300 to $600 a month. . . . The program does not require contributions from the priests. The costs will be met by monthly contributions from the parish or institution the clergymen serve.
> Priests may apply for retirement between the ages of 65 and 75. Those continuing to live in a rectory will receive smaller allotments than those living outside.

The report goes no further into the program than these visible features. But by making certain estimates about the ages of Newark's 252 pastors and 592 other diocesan priests, and by accepting as average a retirement age of seventy and a $450-a-month retirement income, I was able to obtain from a pension actuary estimates of the cost of the plan. Depending on which of several possible methods of payment the Newark chancery adopts, the annual outlay could range from $150,000 all the way up to about $550,000.* The higher the annual chancery contribution, the larger the amount of actual cash being set aside for each priest each year and the safer the benefits in case the plan is discontinued.

The benefits promised by the Newark plan are considerably more generous than those payable to retired priests

---

* The differences hinge on whether or not the pension plan is to be "fully funded": i.e., whether or not the money for each priest's pension is to be accumulated by the date he retires. If not, the benefits—for some or all plan members—can be paid out of current income. Smaller contributions are then needed to keep the plan current; but a financial disaster could deprive the members, retired or not, of their pensions. Also, the interest earnings of the fund dictate the size of the yearly contribution. Higher interest earnings mean lower contributions, and vice versa.

in New York, where the priest who lives on in the rectory after he retires gets $200 a month and a retired priest who lives elsewhere receives $400 a month. In terms of the salaries of nonretired priests (though not in terms of the cost of living), neither plan is illiberal. But the significant point is that the servants of these two adjacent sees are treated so very differently. In pensions as in the many other financial arrangements we've surveyed, the only reason for the difference is that even neighboring Ordinaries think and feel differently about the problem, or are in different stages of their attempts to solve it.

What happens to the priest whose superior, lacking a retirement plan, either refuses financial aid or forgets about the priest's needs? The classic instance actually concerns not a pastor or a curate but a titular bishop, the Most Reverend Bonaventure F. Broderick. The background is fascinating. Originally a priest of the Diocese of Hartford, Bishop Broderick had studied in Rome at the turn of the century, taught in an American seminary and returned to Italy as a pastor. After the Spanish-American War, Broderick was sent to Havana to assist the church in settling claims for damages against the U. S. Government. So successful was he that Pope Pius X appointed him a special delegate "to organize and promote in each diocese of the United States the Peter's Pence collection."

The assignment proved disastrous. The American hierarchy, angered at what it considered a Vatican affront to its loyalty (and solvency), brought so much pressure to bear on Pius X that the Pope rescinded Broderick's appointment. Broderick, furious in his turn, wrote repeatedly to Rome for aid, stating finally that his situation "without a place to go or to work as a Bishop would be a scandal in America." Rightly or wrongly, the Pope interpreted Broderick's letter as meaning that Broderick would *cause* a scandal. From then on, Broderick heard no more from the papal palace.

Only after thirty years did the Vatican pick up this dropped stitch of the church. On November 27, 1939, the newly installed Archbishop of New York wrote to Archbishop Amleto Cicognani, the Apostolic Delegate:

> Your Excellency will remember that you told me that there was a Bishop living in the Diocese who was not living as a Bishop but instead was conducting a business establishment for the sale of automobile accessories and gasoline.

Archbishop Spellman went on to describe his visit to the home of this presumably lapsed bishop in Millbrook, a small town in Dutchess County, about eighty miles from New York. There he learned from the parish priest where the bishop lived; and he promptly paid a call.

> I knocked on the door and it was opened by a man of about seventy years of age, dressed plainly in rough clothes, and I took it for granted that it was the Bishop. I said, "Good afternoon, Dr. Broderick [so the townspeople styled Broderick]. I am Archbishop Spellman and I heard that you were here and I thought I would come to see you and ask you if there was anything I could do to help you." Immediately and spontaneously came his answer. "I have been waiting for thirty years for someone to say those words to me."

After listening to (and carefully substantiating) Bishop Broderick's bizarre story, Spellman asked Broderick "if he would be willing to return to his duties as a priest."

> He told me that gladly would he do so, and the only reason that he was eking out his existence by conducting a little business was because the One Hundred ($100) Dollars pension which the Holy See had graciously granted to him thirty years ago and still continued was not enough for him to live on.

Reinstated, Bishop Broderick was given duties as a hospital chaplain in the Bronx. Until his death in 1943, he was, according to Spellman's biography, "a familiar figure in the cathedral and at religious functions throughout the archdiocese."

The singular case of Bishop Broderick throws into melodramatic relief the entire problem of retirement in the diocesan church. Of all the world's private organizations, perhaps only the Catholic Church could forcibly retire an executive, sentence him to thirty years of running a gas station (in violation of the rule forbidding profit-making activity) and then restore him to active status. And not even the church wants to operate a system so absentmindedly that it becomes heartless. But the fact remains that in many sees dozens of priests who have served loyally all their lives are "eking out an existence" as dependents of the bishop. They need and deserve the type of formal planning which leaves them dignity and a measure of financial independence. Younger priests are demanding such arrangements of their chanceries. To me, diocesan expenditures for retirement plans are justifiable on human as well as financial grounds.

CHAPTER ELEVEN

The Future of
an Archaic Economy

We began our exploration of Catholic diocesan finance by learning how a diocese raises money. We've learned also how the bishops and their financial aides treat the money that comes in. We know now how this money is used administratively to support church activities. We've discovered some surprising truths about diocesan investments and the management of investment funds. And we've noted the efforts of bishops to maintain, by means of budgets and other tools of fiscal management, the necessary control over their financial affairs.

How do we evaluate what we've seen?

Indeed, how can we evaluate any institution as vast, as diversified, as unevenly managed and as unique as the diocesan church? Making such a judgment cannot be taken lightly. Simply because the church is the church, almost every argument about effective management can be matched by a convincing counter-argument.

For instance, on the basis of what we've seen, we may be convinced that the investment strategy of the typical Catholic see is so defensive as to be harmful. In some cases, we can even prove that the total yield of the diocesan portfolio is too low to cover the costs of investment-making (e.g., bank trustees' fees, brokerage charges). Over the years, such negative returns waste the money of the church.

But what about the theory that, for the church, commercial investment gains or losses don't really matter? That the real "investments" of the see should be investments in the church itself; in the land, buildings, equipment and personnel needed to broaden religious, educational and charitable services? According to this theory, stocks and bonds— aside from being just a little bit sinful—are all poor investments. Even the profitable ones deflect into the secular economy funds which would be more productive in the ecclesiastical economy. If you carry this theory to its logical conclusion, you find yourself proving that the diocese with the smallest and worst-managed investment portfolio is in fact the best-managed diocese of all.

In other key areas of diocesan finance, similar paradoxes confuse our judgment. Suppose a bishop plunges deeply into debt to build for his diocese the schools he and his educators think it needs. Surely this places a weighty burden on future generations of parishioners, one which they themselves might never willingly shoulder. As those yearly development drives bite into their pocketbooks, they may well curse His Excellency's extravagance. And yet, if the schools aren't built today, the cost to build them tomorrow may be so much greater that future parishioners will damn the bishop for his penuriousness.

Or take the most useful financial tool of all, central financing. By means of his central fund, a conscientious bishop can enable the poor parishes of the see to improve their facilities and extend their services. Because the cost of money is thus brought within the means of the "have-not" congregations, whole neighborhoods benefit. (In New York and elsewhere, for example, such low-cost financing means that thousands of nonwhite youngsters can go to local parochial schools.) But to operate a central fund, a bishop must demand the surpluses of some pastors and parishioners who have struggled to make their parishes self-supporting. And the bishop asks himself: is it my duty to penalize thrift and good management, even on behalf of the poor?

I offer these examples as evidence that to measure fairly the quality of diocesan management, we need more than the efficiency expert's stopwatch and slide rule. We need also the wisdom and the wariness of the truly sophisticated management specialist. I myself feel that the managerial perfomance of the diocesan church today is startlingly— sometimes even shockingly—poor. In plain truth, the facts and figures mustered in these pages do not reveal the church as a professionally managed institution making the most of its available resources. But this is no reason to substitute for the myth of the church as a rich, powerful, greedy threat to our economy another equally silly fantasy, that of the church as an ineffectual establishment on the brink of economic collapse.

Let's also be mindful of two other facts about the economic life of the church. The first is simply that Catholic sees, however badly run, are in general no worse run than many other American institutions, from the Congress of the United States through the New York Stock Exchange to our local public libraries. For reasons far too complex to catalogue here, our society (and other societies as well) is faced with an increasingly serious decline in the efficiency of its institutions. Like so many other Americans, the Catholic bishop is as much a victim of this crisis as he is a chief perpetrator. In particular, the bishop shares with the university president, the hospital administrator, the foundation director and all the rest of nonprofit officialdom the critical economic problems arising from inflation. Even the most brilliant manager can find these problems nightmarish. And a bishop's robes and powers are no defense against rising costs and depreciating dollars.

The second truth is that the Catholic bishops of this country, albeit slowly and belatedly, are beginning to do something about their management problems. Very soon, we'll be seeing what strategies the bishops are adopting to help them reform the administration of the church. Whether or not this one generation of Catholic leaders can mend the flaws in the system is highly problematical. But the question is still open and there still may be enough time.

Let's begin our own appraisal of the system with the perceptive comments of an insider. Rev. Ernest Bartell, C.S.C., is a priest of the Order of the Congregation of the Holy Cross. Father Bartell teaches economics at Notre Dame. As far as I know, he is the only professional economist either within or outside the church to focus his special skills on the church itself. In a paper prepared for a 1967 symposium on Catholic education, Father Bartell observes that "the contemporary American Church economy could still be described [as] a rudimentary laissez-faire free-enterprise economy," one remarkably like that of an underdeveloped country in Asia, Africa or Latin America.

> The [U. S.] is divided into over 150 financially independent dioceses, while the dioceses themselves are divided into parish units that from the point of view of [Catholic] public finance are relatively independent. Tax and transfer mechanisms for redistributing resources among dioceses

and among parishes within dioceses are relatively under-developed. . . . The pricing mechanism typically used in the market structure within the Church . . . still resembles those [sic] in a classic model of underdevelopment.

This, as far as it goes, is a shrewd summarization of what we ourselves have been studying in detail. Obviously, the diocesan church appears just as disjointed economically from Father Bartell's vantage-point as it does from our own.

But Father Bartell, unhappily, ascribes the economic weaknesses of the church to just one feature, "simply the fact that the Church lacks the sanctions possessed by the state in order to raise general revenues through taxation":

The fact that Church finance is so dependent upon voluntary contributions for general revenues is sufficient reason to explain the relative lack of tax and transfer mechanisms to effect socially desirable programs of income redistribution within the Catholic community.

At this point, the scholar has left the platform and the politician has taken over. Not too subtly, Father Bartell is easing the responsibility for weaknesses in the diocesan economy away from the system itself and the men who run it. Instead, he seems to blame these weaknesses on the status of the church within the state. Without the civil legal right to tax American Catholics for the support of their church, Father Bartell implies, the church will never have enough revenue. And because of this chronic shortage of money, the American diocesan economy is forever doomed to its present imperfection.

The interior logic of this argument leaves much to be desired. If the diocesan economy were suddenly flooded with tax money, would its flaws then automatically repair themselves? Would Father Bartell's "socially desirable programs"—whatever these may be—magically come into being? On the evidence of such well-financed and desirable social institutions as Operation Head Start and Medicare (both of which are in serious management trouble), the observer should know that money alone never greases the wheels of administration. Furthermore, our own scrutiny of the church should at least make us dubious of Father Bartell's thesis. Are the bishops managing their present assets so brilliantly that their success with still more money is a certainty?

Even more important, Father Bartell insists that the "voluntary contributions" of American Catholics will never yield enough revenue to support the diocesan economy. In so insisting, he absolutely disregards what seem to me the basic economic issues. Suppose Father Bartell is correct. Suppose the contributions of the Catholic laity are indeed inadequate to finance the diocesan church. Then surely the bishops in charge of the ecclesiastical economy should be modifying their plans—even to the point of cutting back existing services—so that expenditures can be brought in line with revenues. To do anything else would presumably endanger the whole structure of the church. Yet Father Bartell, far from urging such fiscal responsibility, never even mentions the case for economic retrenchment.

But is Father Bartell correct in the first place? Is it true that this country's 48 million Catholics will never be able to support their church? One Catholic who vehemently disagrees with this view is Leo Laughlin. He's the fund-raising professional we met earlier whose firm, Community Counselling Service, specializes in diocesan revenue drives. Laughlin believes that traditionalism and the lack of information about the laity stand between the diocesan church and its goal of greatly increased revenues. "From the 1890's through the 1930's," Laughlin says, "we were the nickel church. That's what people put in the collection basket every week. Then, in the 1940's and 1950's, we were the dime church. Today, we're the quarter church—and we should be the dollar church." Outraged, he adds, "You know why we're not? Because the bishops still think we're the 'church of the poor.' Poor, hell; we're at least as affluent as any other religious group in the country."

According to Laughlin, the whole "solicitation base" (the group from which most revenue is derived) is kept too narrow by professional churchmen. "By and large, the church only goes after the easiest prospects, the weekly Mass-goers. But millions of people attend Mass much less often, and yet they still consider themselves good Catholics. But the only way they get asked for money is if some religious order sends them a piece of begging mail."

The evidence suggests that Leo Laughlin is quite right, and that the base of support of the diocesan economy is far less broad than it could be. For example, in the Archdiocese of New York a 1968 study indicates that out of 1,260,000 adult baptized Catholics, about 756,000, or 60 per cent, consider themselves practicing Catholics. Of this smaller number, not more than 529,000 (70 per cent) attend Mass regularly.* If a similar situation prevails nationwide—and Laughlin assures me it does—then the Sunday collections and appeals which already bring in more than $2 billion worth of ordinary income a year are bypassing millions of potential regular donors. Laughlin feels that the systematic solicitation of these overlooked Catholics (their total number may be as high as 6 million) might mean as much as 40 per cent more annual revenue for the diocesan church. "Then," he says, "you'd really have a new ball game."

Laughlin, salesman that he is, may well be overly optimistic. Nevertheless, his firm's successes in widening diocesan financial support are one more reason for rejecting

* The percentage may be as low as 40 per cent, which would mean that only 302,400 of New York's adult Catholics attend Mass regularly.

Father Bartell's contention. A shortage of income cannot be blamed for the flaws of the diocesan economic system. Too much of what we see points to exactly the opposite proposition: that the flaws in the system are to blame for the absence of stronger lay financial support.

What are some of these flaws, and what do they reveal about the system itself? The gravest weakness in the diocesan economic structure, and the one which causes the most serious administrative problems, is the shortage of usable, useful information. Because of this shortage, the diocesan church simply doesn't know enough about itself to operate efficiently. A few examples drawn from various sectors illustrate the extent of the trouble:

- In the Diocese of Des Moines, the 70 parish pastors, as recently as 1969, were not filing financial reports with the chancery;
- In Los Angeles, the Advisory Board of Education confirmed in 1969 that the chancery "had no up-to-date information on tuition levels or total revenues in the parochial schools";
- In Atlanta, a 1967 survey revealed that pastors had been overstating Mass attendance by 25 per cent;
- In Cleveland, the accountants hired in 1967 to centralize diocesan bookkeeping had not completed their task by early 1970;
- In Rome, Cardinal Egidio Vagnozzi, ordered by Pope Paul to gather financial data from all Vatican institutions, has met resistance from many officials. He confided to an American priest in 1970 that "the accursed job will take an eternity."

Throughout the entire church, we can find similar evidence of a famine of information. Sometimes the famine is caused by the lack of raw data. Until 1966, for example, the archdiocesan chancery in New York knew nothing whatever about the *parents* of the 165,000 children who go to the parochial elementary schools. Although data about the ages, educational levels and economic backgrounds of the parents obviously has bearing on their ability to meet the costs of parochial education, no one had ever bothered to obtain such data. Even by 1970, moreover, only school parents in Manhattan, the Bronx and Queens had been surveyed, although the archdiocese also includes Westchester, Rockland and portions of other outlying countries. And as far as I know, no other Catholic see in the country has even tried to accumulate similar data on its own.

As often, however, the information shortage is a shortage of *processed* data. As we've seen, the diocesan church loves to keep minute records. Every memorial Mass card is faithfully recorded to make certain the Mass is actually celebrated. Every Sunday contribution is entered on the books of the parish. In every Catholic rectory and in each of the chanceries, the files bulge with material of monetary significance. But because the facts and figures are almost never sorted out, organized and studied, the material might just as well not exist.

One reason why so much potentially valuable data goes unexamined is that the processing—whatever there is of it—must be done by hand. A couple of personal experiences should suffice to illustrate the state of the art of data-processing in the diocesan church. I can still recall my surprise at discovering that the first diocesan financial records I ever handled, the parish debt records of the Diocese of Manchester, were penciled accountants' ledger-sheets. I was even more startled to learn that Msgr. Albert Olkovikas, the chancellor, had prepared these and all the other records himself, a job which cost him hours of his time. Nor can I forget the embarrassed smile this good administrator and good priest gave me when I asked innocently,

"Why not run these off on a computer?" He so obviously wanted me to accept that, in the church, machinery is an extravagance and human labor cheap.

Then, too, I remember being taken on a tour, in 1968, of the brand-new Catholic Center of the Diocese of Baton Rouge. My guide, John J. Kennedy, had had much to do with the development and construction of the Center, which combines under one roof the chancery, the bishop's residence, a boys' school and extensive facilities for public gatherings. Near the end of our tour, Kennedy proudly showed me an air-conditioned basement room with the special flooring and ducting needed for electronic equipment. "Some day," he said, "we'll have our own computers, and I want to be ready for them." But thus far, he added disconsolately, Bishop Robert E. Tracy and the diocesan consultors had vetoed acquisition of a computer. "The $12,000 a year for the unit I wanted was too expensive for them. So we do most of our record-keeping the old way."

In New York, the archdiocese does have a computer, a Univac Model 9400 acquired in 1970. But before the chancery leased this machine, the only computer in the whole see was an IBM 1407 at Cardinal Hayes High School in the Bronx. This was used to train students in commercial-diploma classes. Until 1968, in fact, the chancery had never used computers at all. In that year, part of the archdiocesan education study from which I quoted earlier involved the computerization of the parish financial records. The computer programs developed for this purpose yielded a rich trove of new information about the schools, the parishes and the archdiocese itself. By 1971, only some of this information has been digested, and the programs may or may not be used regularly in the future. But the chancery knows that it must learn to live with the computer.

Still another cause of the information famine in the diocesan church is that usable information, when it does appear, is almost never widely enough circulated. Granted, in the church as in Monsanto or General Motors, access to certain types of information must be restricted. For example, we can see why the personnel records of diocesan priests are locked away in the triple vaults which canon law requires be built into every chancery. We can understand why an official like Msgr. Joseph P. Murphy, vice-chancellor and treasurer of the Archdiocese of New York, is reluctant to lend even to other officials his special black notebook containing all of the financial data of the see. But such reasonable instances aside, too often the report—or the study or proposal or fiscal analysis—which could solve the problem of Msgr. A will never leave the desk of Msgr. B, who gathered the material.

It's not that Msgr. B makes a fetish of secrecy. After all, Msgr. A is a fellow-insider. It's rather that, as a specialist, Msgr. B naturally thinks in terms of his specialty alone. So if he's a hospital administrator he may honestly not understand how his colleagues in schools or cemeteries could benefit by a sharing of information. One seasoned chancery executive, Patrick O'Meara (a St. Louisan now working on education problems for the Archdiocese of New York), has the appropriate image for the situation. "We're all perched on top of separate mountains," he says. "We can hear each other yodeling, but we can't make out the words."

In particular, as we've been seeing all along, the information famine within the diocesan church extends to the laity. If it's true that the Catholic layman knows less than he should know (and less, I've found, than he wants to know) about the workings of his own church, it's equally true that the professional church is starved of socioeconomic information about the laity. To be sure, the individual pastor may know a great deal about the patterns of social and economic behavior within his parish. The diocesan educator or hospital administrator may have commissioned research into the "market," so to speak, for a new school or hospital. But the knowledge of the pastor, intuitive rather than reasoned, never finds its way into his annual reports to the chancery. And although the researchers may be conducting interviews right in Father's parish hall, the results of chancery-sponsored research rarely trickle back down to the rectory.

And so, as Leo Laughlin is only one of many to confirm, too many bishops base their economic decisions on such generalities as "we're the church of the poor" and "my people are already giving all they can give."

Closely related to this first weakness in diocesan operations is another flaw, the absence of comprehensive planning. On this problem, Msgr. Joseph P. Murphy of New York is well worth consulting. As well as being the key financial official of a major archdiocese, Murphy is a thoughtful, sensitive theorist of diocesan management. According to him, planning in the diocesan church is necessarily very difficult. "After all, we're a church, not a business," he says. "We can't just research an area, then throw resources into it knowing in advance that if we put in so much money, we'll earn such-and-such a return. Our decisions have to be based on what people need, and on circumstances we ourselves don't control."

To some extent, certainly, Murphy's argument is a valid one. Like all other service enterprises, the church is a product as well as a shaper of circumstance; it is less free than, say, Procter & Gamble to perceive its goals in the distance and then to march upon them. But as Murphy himself agrees, the difficulties of planning and forecasting are no justification for hostility to the planning concept itself. "We could be doing much more in the way of research and development," he allows, "but we're already moving in that direction in certain areas."

Again, Murphy is correct. In New York and in some other major sees, the belated recognition of the need to plan has begun to produce results. Notably in education, where the big archdioceses in particular are facing apparent financial crisis, research and diocesan-wide planning are being greeted as possible aids to salvation. We have already sampled the forthright contents of the report on the Catholic schools of New York (pp. 227–229). During 1968 and 1969, similar studies were launched in Boston, Brooklyn, Pittsburgh, Chicago and New Orleans among the larger sees and in such smaller dioceses as Louisville, Davenport and Omaha. Moreover, because the financial and managerial problems of the schools are affecting all other aspects of diocesan economics, many of these studies call into question the broader practices of diocesan management as well.

So far, however, not much has actually happened. Even where the research has been completed, the results are being withheld or "re-evaluated." Only carefully edited versions of completed reports are being circulated among the pastors or released to the lay public. One reason for this chancery reticence is the old deep-rooted secretiveness of the church. Another is the worry that full disclosure of the difficulties of the schools will "disturb the laity" and therefore worsen the situation. Still another reason is political. The bishops and their aides are using the evidence of their research to develop support (among non-Catholic educators, philanthropists and businessmen as well as among legislators) for state aid to Catholic education. This lobbying they wish to do quietly. But the most important reason why the various school studies are being treated so delicately is that the bishops themselves are uncertain about what the facts and figures really mean. As we'll discover in Chapter Sixteen on the issues of education, the fate of the Catholic schools rests today in decidedly unsteady hands.

There's yet another sign that modern management

planning has begun to recommend itself to the American hierarchy. In a sense, this one is even more revealing than the upsurge of interest in educational research. As if they were so many troubled industrialists or baffled bankers, the bishops are now turning for counsel to those civilian priests of private enterprise, the management consultants.

As a matter of fact, this involvement of the church with the liturgies and rites of efficient management is not quite brand-new. As far back as 1948, Jackson Martindell, president of an enterprise which styled itself the American Institute of Management, offered his professional services and those of his experts to the Vatican. Martindell's specialty, which he had already succeeded in selling to a number of American corporations, was the management analysis and "efficiency rating" of a customer's organization. The analysis was done by interviewers in the field. According to an article in *Fortune* (November, 1956), the efficiency rating was handled by Martindell himself and a group of his senior associates. The article stated that they generally did this job after dinner in Martindell's New York town house on East 38th Street, aided by such tools of evaluation as vintage brandy and Havana cigars.

Probably because Pope Pius XII was himself a devotee of efficiency (his most famous move was to install timeclocks in the offices of the Vatican), Martindell's proposal was considered and accepted. As *Time* magazine reported the story years later (January 30, 1956):

> For a full year, 200 researchers worked away in Rome, swarming through the Vatican's archives and offices, codifying, correlating, questioning. They were aided by hundreds of other researchers, working in 30 languages throughout the world.

The results of this "codifying, correlating, questioning" apparently took eight years to evaluate. And the final judgments of the American Institute of Management, given to the world in a twenty-six-page report, still present themselves as a masterpiece of unintentional comedy.

First of all, the AIM gave the Catholic Church a grade of 88 per cent in "management efficiency," which ranked the church a percentage point above Time, Inc. and only two points below Standard Oil of New Jersey. Next, Martindell's group rated the church in terms of "average Catholic zeal" (higher than it was 100 years ago but "only half" of what it was in the beginning). Other ratings included an award of 650 points out of a possible 700 for "efficiency" and one of 1,000 points out of 1,000 for "social function." Not that the AIM's findings were all favorable. For instance, on public relations:

> Having first used the word propaganda, the Holy See has failed to utilize the best talent available in the field. Time and again it puts its worst vestment forward when the best side could easily be shown.

On trusteeship:

> The College of Cardinals is the nearest approach the Church has to a Board of Trustees. Its effectiveness is not as high as it could be because of the advanced age of the Cardinals, and the fact that they so largely seem to represent an Italian clique.

But by and large, the American Institute of Management was very pleased with the Roman Catholic Church.

The profound silliness of the AIM effort to rate the church requires, I'm sure, no further comment. Fortunately, Mr. Martindell's Institute has long since ceased to interest either professionals in management consulting or their clients. When I mentioned the AIM to one top specialist, Jon Gundersen of McKinsey & Company, he just groaned, "Are those guys still around?" But every so often I do encounter a Catholic pastor or a chancery official with a good memory who still refers proudly to "that management report on the church."

In another category entirely are the more recent contacts between churchmen in the U.S. and the management consultants. One of the very first of these contacts was the work of Cardinal John F. Dearden of Detroit. Not long after his installation as archbishop in 1959, Dearden met Kenneth Vatner, a teacher of courses in management at the University of Michigan. At Vatner's suggestion, Dearden commissioned a management study of the Detroit chancery from the noted consulting firm of Booz Allen & Hamilton Inc. Guided by this study, in 1967 Dearden set about overhauling his archdiocesan administration. As a first step, the title of chancellor was abolished. The traditional chancery bureaus and offices Dearden grouped together in broad departments. To handle archdiocesan fund-raising, budgeting, purchasing and construction, he set up a separate Office of Administrative Services under a lay accountant, Leo G. Schulte. Another lay specialist heads an Office of Planning and Research. Probably because these shifts were in progress when my request reached him in 1969, Dearden has declined to comment for this book on the results of the reorganization. (By mid-1970, the task was still not completed.) But this streamlining will almost certainly improve chancery management in Detroit.

In his role as president of the National Conference of Catholic Bishops, Dearden has promoted the use of consulting aid with much vigor. On his recommendation, Booz Allen & Hamilton was retained (for a fee of $75,000) to study the permanent secretariat of the Conference in Washington, D. C. A set of findings and recommendations was submitted early in 1968 for consideration by a three-bishop Committee on Personnel and Administrative Services. But before Booz Allen's specialists arrived on the scene, the secretariat, under its own skilled administrative head, Bishop

Joseph L. Bernardin, had already begun to modernize its operations. Partly for this reason and partly because the Booz Allen & Hamilton study contained serious flaws, the study seems to have been shelved. Nevertheless, its commissioning has encouraged the bishops to summon the consultants for aid in the managements of their own sees.

So far, the aid requested has taken the specific form of advice on fiscal matters. And instead of choosing such general consulting firms as Booz Allen & Hamilton and McKinsey & Co., the bishops have been favoring the major public accounting firms. For example, Arthur Andersen & Company does regular audits of the books of several sees in New England and the Midwest. Like most other large accounting organizations, Arthur Andersen also offers consulting services in financial management. Other prominent firms of CPA's are being brought in locally to do their best with the primitive bookkeeping typical of most sees. But by far the most popular of the major firms doing work for the diocesan church is Peat, Marwick, Mitchell & Company.

In 1967, Peat, Marwick was summoned by Archbishop Gerald T. Bergen of Omaha to do a survey of the cost of operating the Omaha Catholic schools. This survey, which cost the archdiocese $45,000, was the first of its kind ever undertaken in a Catholic see, and the first to be released to the public. Its conclusions, according to a National Catholic News Service report, were that "the rising cost of operating schools within the Omaha archdiocese is threatening the ability of the archdiocese as a whole to maintain a balanced financial position."

Impressed by the preciseness and thoroughness of the Omaha survey, other bishops began to call in Peat, Marwick. In particular, Cardinal Cooke of New York turned to the firm for management advice on the formation of a new Educational Financial Office. And an *ad hoc* committee of bishops working on diocesan finance for the

National Conference selected Peat, Marwick to handle a special project: the development of uniform guideliness on financial reports to the public for use by all 160 Catholic sees. This project, begun in November, 1969, is only now gaining momentum. Peat, Marwick expects its study to take at least one year and possibly several to complete. Then, the bishops' committee will submit the guidelines to the whole membership of the National Conference. If all the bishops approve, these guidelines (in the form of a procedural manual) will be the accepted norms on which to base individual diocesan financial reports. Of course, approval of the Peat, Marwick recommendations will not make financial disclosure mandatory. Nor will approval mean that those bishops who do issue financial reports must adhere to the guidelines. Neither the National Conference nor any other Catholic episcopal conference can impose such a fiscal policy on its membership.

Still, the National Conference has brought in an expensive consultant. (For this assignment, Peat, Marwick's initial fee is $67,000.) The fact indicates that the bishops see the sad state of diocesan accounting as a pressing national problem. Such official concern will undoubtedly persuade many of the bishops to modernize their bookkeeping. As a result, the quality and the timeliness of their fiscal information will improve. Whether or not this improvement in turn leads to better financial planning depends—as so much else depends—on the individual bishop. As for the diocesan church at large, the effect of Peat, Marwick's labors may not be measurable for many years.

And yet, in my opinion the bishops have not too many years left in which to reform their flawed systems of finance and administration. And given the economic pressures under which the leaders of the institutional church are already operating, an archaic economy is the very last thing they can afford.

By an archaic economy, I mean one not in gear with the mechanisms by which the broader secular economy is guided. Take the crucial example of inflation. In the "real" world, so to speak, inflation is the overriding fact of current economic life. As such, it is both taken for granted and planned for by business managers, economists and governments. But the economic behavior of the individual bishops, far from being effective against inflation, is rather enabling inflation to plunder the church. To see how, bear in mind that the decay in the value of the dollar (or for that matter, of the franc, the mark and the lira) automatically jeopardizes the income of all institutions like the church. On the one hand, as churchgoers themselves feel the bite of inflation, their contributions to the church tend at best to remain level. Sometimes they even decrease. And by definition, during periods of inflation the value of a level income actually lessens each year. On the other hand, the cost of operating the church, like the cost of running anything else, continues to rise. Plainly, the best strategy to adopt during inflation is one which will: a) increase revenues from all possible sources; and b) hold overhead expenses down.

Instead, trapped by their own traditions, the Catholic bishops have for years been doing exactly the opposite.

By marking time in the effort to increase lay support, and by neglecting such additional sources of revenue as commercial investments and more realistic charges for services (especially education), the bishops have done little better than hold their incomes level over the past five years. And by continuing to invest money in a new physical plant, which is expensive to build and even more expensive to maintain, the bishops have saddled themselves with drastic increases in operating expenses. As a result of these perverse economic activities, inflation is rendering it more and more difficult for the dioceses to meet current expenditures out of current revenues. Already, the bishops of some major sees (Baltimore is one, Boston another) are dipping into scarce liquid capital to cover their obligations as they fall due. To do so, of course, is the equivalent of cashing in the bonds you meant for your children's education to pay for the house you can't really afford.

With better fiscal planning, this economic crisis could have been eased. Institutions other than the church have found themselves threatened by inflation and have contrived to hold their own economically. Now, the question is whether greater sensitivity to economic reality and less nostalgia for the past will enable the church to regain its equilibrium.

Nostalgia seems to me to be at the very heart of the economic problems we've been considering. And there, along with nostalgia, we find the almost palpable force of ecclesiastical tradition. Indeed, because so much of what is wrong or inadequate today is rooted in yesterday, we do well at this point to catch a glimpse of the diocesan church against the background of its past history.

For the American church, yesterday is sometimes no more remote than the 1940's and the 1950's, when the Catholic population was exploding in size and ripening in prosperity. Then, the logic of bricks and mortar and physical expansion quite literally spoke for itself. As the pattern of American life changed, turning city dwellers by the millions into suburbanites, so by reflex action did the Catholic Church also seek the suburbs. In the process, the church tested the willingness of its laity to finance new growth, and discovered a seemingly endless generosity. And although the first voices of reform were already being heard, there had as yet been no Vatican II, nor any Good Pope John to awaken the entire church with his call for *aggiornamento*, renewal.

Or yesterday may be no older than the Depression,

when the collection-basket dollars were fewer but when every one of them was worth 100 cents. Even though money was scarce during the 1930's, a good solid church was cheap to build, cheaper still to maintain and the only secure investment in a treacherous economic world.

I think we can trace back to these relatively recent decades some of the economic weaknesses (and, of course, some of the strengths) of today's diocesan church. During those decades, many of the present bishops gained their training and their pastoral and administrative experience. During the Depression, they learned to be economic conservatives: dreaders of debt, believers in a stable currency and men deeply suspicious of the investment markets. After the war, these same men, as pastors and chancery officials, learned to believe in building as the key to a flourishing church. Only today are they discovering that it's possible to be too conservative with money and too liberal with real estate.

But within the church, yesterday can also be much more than one generation old. Of the things we've seen, some of the strangest hint at the nostalgia for a far more distant past. For example, consider the ties of favoritism which link so many bishops to their privy counselors in banking, insurance, accounting and realty. Today, business suits have replaced gowns of audience, and profit rather than preferment is the obvious motive. Yet such ritualistic relationships still have too much in common with those between the needy princes and the helpful commoners of earlier days. Finally, look again at the cumbersome mechanics of the diocesan inner economies. In such anomalies as internal banking, the religious bond and the quota system of parish taxation, I detect traces of the age when the Catholic Church was in truth an independent, self-sustaining economy. These vestiges still remain because, in theory and to some extent in practice, they are still useful in the government of the church. But more practical mechanisms would accomplish the same goals at far less cost. These others are perpetuated primarily because they remind some Catholics of the glory of a church which once owned almost everything.

This sense of the weight of the past makes it hard for us to blame today's bishops for the economic flaws we find in today's diocesan church. We realize that, for all their power, the bishops are prisoners of their own system. And to say the least, the church is not an easy system to reform. Furthermore, economic reform, however urgently needed, may not relieve the real pressures on these men who are struggling to make the system work. Thus, full financial disclosure is no certain way to the heart of a discontented layman, or to his checkbook, either. The reordering of financial priorities is no assurance that the needs of the poor, the sick and the oppressed will be better met. Nor is a generous retirement program any guarantee that today's disheartened priests will remain loyal to the institutional church.

Nevertheless, the bishops must attempt economic reform, for the obvious reason that they have no alternative.

As we move on into other areas of the Catholic ecclesiastical economy, we'll see that sweeping reforms are in fact being made, and made successfully, by church organizations everywhere. Within the religious orders, for instance, traditions as old and as revered as any to be found in the diocesan church are simply being cast aside as inappropriate. In many ways, the supposedly unworldly nuns, priests and brothers who belong to religious communities are better able and freer than the bishops to contend with economic change.

One minor incident seems to me to sum up metaphorically almost everything we've been discovering abut the diocesan economic universe. Earlier, I mentioned being given a tour of the new, modern Catholic Center of the Diocese of Baton Rouge. The building itself has won prizes given for ecclesiastical architecture, and deservedly so. Its openness and elegance are the antithesis of the Victorian gloom of so many chanceries. And its comforts, including a thirteen-room suite for the bishop, are almost too comfortable. In any event, my tour concluded with a trip to the sub-basement. There, I was shown the heating and air-conditioning plant, and there also I visited the office of the building superintendent. Against one wall of the office stood a gleaming console. Made by Honeywell, this was the computerized control center of the whole heating-cooling complex. Changes in the climate of even a single room were automatically recorded via thermostats, and the computer immediately adjusted the temperature accordingly. I found the gadgetry fascinating. It seemed to me perfect evidence of the modernization I expected in the church. Then, as we turned to leave, I caught sight of another piece of machinery on another wall. It was a cuckoo-clock from the Black Forest. And it was ten minutes slow.

CHAPTER TWELVE

How Rich Is the American Church?

In his 1968 book, *Should Churches Be Taxed?*, D. H. Robertson, Associate Professor of Religion at Syracuse University, comments: "There is no one person or agency, including the government, with exact knowledge of the value of church property in the United States." Robertson covers at some length what he calls "the story of rough estimates" of church wealth. He cites various local efforts to determine how much real estate the churches of a given community own. He notes the labors of the U. S. Bureau of the Census, which between 1890 and 1936 questioned religious bodies about their ecclesiastical realty. Robertson concludes his survey with an approving nod at the approach taken by Dr. Martin A. Larson. Larson's own most recent book, published in 1969, is juicily titled *Praise*

*the Lord for Tax Exemption: How the Churches Grow
Rich While the Cities and You Grow Poor.*

Larson's method of estimating the wealth of the
churches is to pore over the property-tax rolls of various
U. S. cities. To the resulting tabulations of data about tax-
exempt church real estate, he adds snippets of information
about church construction projects, commercial investments and, especially in the case of the Catholic Church,
the unrelated businesses in which "all dioceses and numerous parishes" supposedly engage. After 192 pages of this
mixture, Larson states:

> We may therefore declare as established fact that Prot-
> estant and miscellaneous properties used for religious pur-
> poses and exempt from taxation are now worth well in
> excess of $40 billion; Jewish, not less than $8 or $10 billion;
> and Roman Catholic at least $60 billion.
> And all this, of course, does not include a great deal of
> real estate owned by churches. . . . Nor does it take into
> account all the vast reserves of church wealth in the form
> of cash, stocks, bonds, land contracts, mortgages and busi-
> ness corporations or ventures of infinite variety . . .

But despite Larson's assertiveness, I find that his estimates
fall somewhat short of being "established fact."

Like most other books about church wealth, Larson's
book is based on a double argument: a) that in a society
which legally requires the separation of church and state,
the churches are subtly using their privilege of exemption
from taxes to grow rich, so rich that they threaten the
state; and b) that in any society, the proper economic status
of churchmen is that of voluntary poverty. Neither one of
these contentions is unworthy of consideration. But in his
zeal to prove them both, Larson seems to have forgotten
even the simplest truths of economics.

Thus, although he piles up church asset values with a
will, he never suggests that churches also accumulate lia-

bilities. Although he tells us about all the money churches derive from their commercial investments, unrelated business endeavors and dubious tax deals, we never do learn where the money goes. As for the Catholic Church, Larson still wants us to believe that the Jesuits own the Bank of America. (He deliberately falsifies the facts of their denial.) We're told that in New York "complete financial reports . . . have never been made in the history of the archdiocese," although a fairly detailed report of archdiocesan receipts and expenditures was published in May, 1969. We learn that the Knights of Columbus possess assets worth nearly $300 million. But Larson never mentions that these assets are the mandatory legal reserves held by the Knights of Columbus to pay life-insurance claims. Other errors of fact and other distortions of truth are multiplied almost endlessly.

Unfortunately, instead of pursuing his argument and in place of what his introduction calls "a definitive work on the status of religious tax exemption," Larson has given us a work of anticlerical propaganda.

In company with those others who fabricate the myths about the wealth of the churches, Larson seems never to grasp the obvious. In the United States, the reason the churches and the clergy are as affluent as they are is that the country itself is rich almost beyond measure. Rightly or wrongly by Larson's standards, millions of churchgoers have used the ballot as well as the collection-basket to make the religious establishment prosperous. And although some clergymen are sharply questioning the right of the churches to material riches, most of those who operate the religious establishment still sincerely believe that their institutional wealth is a vital tool of God's good work on earth.

Nor do the Larsons of the world understand that in the face of the real dangers to our society today—racism, militarism, violence, commercial greed, fear—the danger of church economic power is trifling. For example, note that in 1970 our military expenditures totaled $80 billion. Even if we believe Larson, we spent more money on armaments in this one year than the Catholic Church in the U.S. has ever accumulated. Speaking personally, I find in our defense statistics a threat far more disturbing than the threat supposedly latent in the economic power of religion. Or take another one of Larson's estimates. The total income of all the churches of this country, he guesses, is $22 billion a year. I myself think his estimate is high by about 30 per cent, though no one can say for sure. But even if Larson is correct, what has he told us about ourselves? According to the *Statistical Abstract of the United States*, we spend on one commodity, gasoline, $24 billion a year: $2 billion more than the religious establishment takes in. Our cigarettes and liquor cost us $21 billion a year. To speak for myself once again, it seems to me that the threat to our lives and our environment posed by our habits as consumers is more worrisome than that posed by our habits as worshipers.

Truly, in a land which every year produces goods and services worth a *trillion* dollars, the economic might of all the churches put together scarcely even registers.

In terms of what we ourselves are scrutinizing—namely, the dynamics of the Catholic ecclesiastical economy—an estimate of the total wealth of the church is of only marginal value. As we've seen, the individual bishops have no very clear idea of what their diocesan assets (in particular, their institutional properties) are worth. We'll shortly discover that the Catholic religious orders also suffer from primitive bookkeeping and from inadequate knowledge of their own resources. And because neither the dioceses nor the religious orders ever pool their capital or act in economic concert, the aggregate wealth of the church is never wielded as a single economic instrument.

Nevertheless, adding up the available totals does seem to me worth the effort. For one thing, it's natural to be curious about how much wealth the church has, or thinks it has. For another, an estimate based on official figures may help to counterbalance the exaggerations about church riches.

I've thus obtained from 20 of the 160 Catholic sees the asset-value figures on which the chanceries base their current (1968 or 1969) balance sheets. Some of these figures were given to me verbally during interviews. Others come from published financial statements. Still others I've taken from confidential financial reports made available to me by church officials. A few are derived from the figures contained in church bond prospectuses, adjusted for growth since the prospectuses were issued and verified by officials of the sees. Only one, that of the Archdiocese of New York, has not specifically been confirmed by archdiocesan officials.

As far as I know, no similar group of confirmed asset-value totals has ever before been assembled. Before presenting these figures, I should mention that in all cases property values are based on insurance appraisals of replacement cost. Securities are valued at their market price at the time of acquisition. And the value of parochial properties as well as that of directly owned diocesan institutions is included. First, let's look at the figures themselves. To present them, I've simply listed the sees involved, ranking them by the size of their 1971 Catholic populations, then giving the total values of reported assets.

How should we interpret these figures?

In number, the 20 sees listed represent approximately 12.5 per cent of all U. S. Catholic sees. More important for our purposes, they contain 14.2 per cent of the total U. S. Catholic population. According to my figures, the aggregate value of the assets held by these 20 sees is $4.1 billion.

Rank	Location	Diocesan Assets (in millions)
1	Chicago	$610(000,000)
2	Boston	654
3	New York	700
9	Newark	260.5
10	Buffalo	240
11	Cleveland	261
20	St. Louis	250
23	Baltimore	196
25	Miami	108
32	Rochester	225
40	Bridgeport	145
44	Youngstown	95
46	Joliet	82
49	Manchester	99
72	Omaha	50
76	Baton Rouge	47
77	El Paso	43
93	Oklahoma City	40
119	Spokane	20
137	Rapid City	7.5

If the relationship between population and assets found in this sample is constant for all sees, then by simple ratio we can value the total assets of the U. S. diocesan church at $28.6 billion.

However, our sample does contain a disproportionately large group of the biggest, wealthiest sees and a correspondingly small number of the less populous, less prosperous dioceses. Thus, of the 20 largest sees, seven are included above; but of the 40 smallest, I've obtained figures from only two. To correct the imbalance, I think we should lower the total-asset figures by about 10 per cent. We can then safely estimate that the 160 Catholic sees are worth collectively between $25 billion and $26 billion.

Earlier I cited figures which indicate that, in the typical Catholic see, about 90 per cent of the total assets are in the form of institutional real estate. Cash and commercial investments constitute the remaining 10 per cent. Applied to our estimate of national diocesan wealth, these percentages mean that of the $26 billion total, $23 billion is the value of Catholic parochial and diocesan physical property. The balance, $2 billion, is held in liquid assets.

To this $26 billion we must add another figure, the lesser total of the assets controlled by the nearly 500 religious orders active in this country. In the chapters to follow, we'll be learning of the operations of this economic sector of the church; and I'll substantiate in detail my estimate of $8.2 billion for the value of the assets the orders control. Once again, we'll find that most of this total takes the form of institutional realty. But we'll also see something of the other (and highly diversified) assets of the religious orders. These include such religious "service businesses" as retreat houses, bakeries for sacramental wafers and statuary factories. They also range from agribusiness ventures in cheesemaking, wines, preserves and similar comestibles all the way to communications companies like the Paulist Press and commercial radio and television stations WWL-AM, FM and TV, these last owned by the Jesuits of the Province of New Orleans.

But let's first finish our appraisal of the total wealth of the church. And let's also spend a moment to consider the significance of this appraisal. Thus, taken together, my estimates of the value of all diocesan assets and of all assets held by Catholic religious orders add up to a final total of $34.2 billion.

In terms of the sheer bulk of holdings, this ranks the Catholic Church as something less than an equal of the two largest U. S. commercial banks, the Bank of America and the Chase Manhattan Bank, combined. Between them, these banks control about $41 billion worth of deposits. (Most of this money, of course, belongs not to the banks themselves but to their depositors.)

Nor, in the same terms, is the Catholic Church on an economic par with the American Telephone & Telegraph Company. AT&T owns assets worth about $39 billion. Collectively, moreover, the four largest U. S. industrial corporations overshadow the church. Together, these giants (General Motors, Standard Oil of New Jersey, Ford Motor and General Electric) own assets worth about $43 billion. And when we turn to the American life-insurance industry, we find pools of assets so large that the industry leaders easily dwarf the church. The combined assets of the two biggest life-insurance companies in the U. S., the Metropolitan Life and the Prudential Insurance Company of America, amount to more than $50 billion. And the life-insurance industry as a whole holds assets worth well over $200 billion.

Such billion-dollar comparisons can be made to mean almost anything. For a Martin Larson, they plainly mean that the Roman Catholic Church is an economic menace to American society. For the Catholic who seeks reassurance of the strength and stability of his church, the huge asset figures are undoubtedly soothing. For the Catholic of another stamp who longs to change the church, the figures represent a scandal, a pile of treasure which should never have been accumulated and which should be liquidated forthwith on behalf of the poor.

For us, with our special awareness of the truths behind the totals, none of these responses is entirely adequate. We know, first of all, that the balance-sheet assets of the church are drastically overstated. In terms of liquidity, the church possesses far less than our summary suggests. We know also that the assets of the church are neither machines by which merchandise is manufactured nor stocks of merchandise waiting to be sold. Nor are these assets the money from the sale.

In short, we know that the Catholic Church is neither a General Motors nor a Bank of America. And we might summarize what we know in a couple of complementary notions. In large measure, the art of managing business concerns like GM and the Bank of America is the art of deploying their assets to produce suitable earnings. The art of managing the church is that of raising enough money to support the assets successfully.

To be sensitive to these differences is to be wary of comparisons between the church and its secular corporate counterparts. More important still, it is to be unaffected by the mystique of the wealth of the church. As we've documented, both the churchmen and their critics, dazzled by this mystique, have for generations been behaving like men entranced. On their part, the bishops have built and built. How many marble high schools we owe to their ignorance of their own economies, God alone knows. Meanwhile, on such key issues as the financing of education and the taxability of the churches, the arguments of the critics are blurred by a vision of gold. For the sake of both sides, the economic truth should prevail.

And the truth, after all, is not so very obscure. The wealth of the Catholic Church—and the economic and political power which, in our society, accompanies great wealth—undoubtedly does give the church a voice in the conduct of this country's affairs. A voice, moreover, which few other churches possess. But amid the many voices raised in our country, that of the church is only one, and never one of the loudest. Indeed, among the blocs and alliances and special interests which, in Washington and elsewhere, contend for real power in America, the Catholic

Church is a minor competitor. Its lobbyists carry away from Congress or the White House no lucrative special legislation or profit-laden executive orders. Its promoters acquire no gigantic contracts from the Department of Defense, no offshore drilling permits from the Department of the Interior. Even in legislation affecting health and education, the influence of the church is hardly visible compared with that of organized labor or that of the public education establishment.

Even on state and local political levels, the "legendary" power of the church is far less significant than critics of the church like to believe. For a perfect example, take the struggle over legalized abortion in New York State. Despite its implacable opposition to liberalization of the abortion laws, the church found itself almost helpless early in March, 1970. On March 6, a bill legalizing abortion, supposedly bottled up in legislative committee by the "loyal" chairman, suddenly exploded out of committee onto the legislative floor in Albany. One story has it that the churchmen in New York City (the archdiocesan capital of the Province of New York) were so unprepared for the emergence of the bill that those in charge of rallying its opponents had only seventy-two hours' notice of the impending vote. Much of the time they spent in a frantic search for the parish maps which would indicate who among New York pastors and prominent laymen should be asked to contact the individual state assemblymen. By the time the maps were found, the time had run out and the law had gained enough support to pass.

I cite the incident not to reprove the church for its stand on abortion. Obviously, the right to take a stand on legislation is, or should be, inviolable in America. Rather I mention it to substantiate that, in local politics, the church is not the force so many commentators believe it to be. In our city halls and statehouses, the utilities, the insurance companies, the banks and the construction interests (to list only a handful) lobby far more effectively than does the Catholic Church.

We could go on still further, to point out that because the wealth of the church is so decentralized, the political power of the church is more fragmented still. This I think is true, and indeed self-evident. But we've seen enough to reach a conclusion without the need to frame that argument.

The fact is that the mystique of church wealth is far more dangerous than the wealth itself could ever be. Because so many churchmen have believed in the infinite resources of the church, the ecclesiastical economy today is seriously overstrained. In particular, the ability of this economy to sustain Catholic education is in doubt. And because so many lay Americans, Catholic and non-Catholic, subscribe to the same myth, the severity of the crisis is underestimated and the consequences (for the church and for the country as a whole) are misunderstood. What we've seen so far should convince us to set aside the myths; as we go on, we'll consider the religious orders, which are today both cause and victim of this economic crisis. We'll see more and more distinctly that $40 billion falls short of being economic security.

CHAPTER THIRTEEN

The Jesuits and Others: The Economics of the Religious Orders

In Rome, the telephone exchange for the Vatican is 698. The exchange itself serves 2,000 telephones within the Vatican and handles an average of 18,000 incoming calls per day (25,000 at Christmas time), including several hundred to the Pope's private extension, 3101.*

The delicate task of deciding who gets through to the Pope, and the bigger job of running the Vatican switchboard, is shared by six operators who are Brothers of the Don Orione Society of the Small Works of Divine Providence. They are supervised by two priests of another religious order, the Pious Society of St. Paul. This order was

* All calls to the Pope are intercepted and held while another, secret number is dialed. As writer Curtis G. Pepper tells us in his book, *The Pope's Back Yard,* "that's how the Pope is protected against cranks or someone dialing the wrong number."

founded in 1914, specifically to do work in what the *Annuario Pontificio* calls "the apostolate of editing: press, cinema, radio, television, recordings."

There's something amusing about this example of specialization within the church. Perhaps it's that the zeal to serve God contrasts so oddly here with the particular nature of the service. Quaintness aside, however, the way the Vatican's telephone system is managed can tell us something revealing about the special world of the Catholic religious orders. Within this world, we're reminded, diversity, differentiation and specialization have been the norms for centuries. A few more examples will make the point obvious. Thus, again in Vatican City, the small pharmacy near St. Anne's Gate is run by six Brothers of the Order of Hospitalers of St. John of God. This order, known also as the *Fate Bene Fratelli* (literally, the Do-Good Brothers), specializes in pharmaceutical work and emergency medical care. In this country, an order of nuns, the Sisters of Jesus Crucified, conduct hospital cytology laboratories for the early detection of cancer. And the missionary priests of the Society of the Divine Word operate an equally specialized service. From their seminary in Techne, Illinois (on the outskirts of Chicago), they sell to priests all over the country what their illustrated catalogue describes as "the latest in liturgical vestments. Benediction sets, solemn sets, albs, stoles, surplices." In the design and manufacture of these, moreover, the Divine Word priests count on the aid of still other professional religious. To quote the catalogue, "Our Vestments are made by the Holy Spirit Missionary Sisters in Tokyo, Japan. All are HAND EMBROIDERED and beautifully executed by the Sisters with the help of 15 Japanese girls."

As these examples testify, one major economic role of the Catholic religious orders is that of the supplier of goods and services to the rest of the church. Indeed, some orders subsist entirely by marketing tangible products to the diocesan church, to other orders or to the laity. Thus, in many sees the communities of cloistered contemplative nuns make their livings solely by baking and selling communion wafers to the parish churches.* This they generally do under a contract with the local chancery. And as I mentioned in the previous chapter, the Order of Cistercians of the Strict Observance, better-known as the Trappists, derive most of their income from the cheese the order makes, then markets via direct mail advertising.

Other orders, even though their main work may lie in teaching, healing or preaching, bolster the income they receive for this work by dealing in church supplies, publications or other specialties. In a sense, their members are doing what the pastor does by running bazaars, cake sales and bingo games for the support of his parish. But most of the religious orders, including the largest and the best known, gain their economic support by marketing their labor. In particular, they sell their professional skills and services in one (or more) of three great areas of Catholic Church endeavor: education, health care and missionary activity.

Later, we'll be studying in detail the operations of a number of the Catholic religious orders. Chief among them, at least in size and reputation, will be the Society of Jesus. Because the Jesuits do play a vital part in the economy of the church, and because their "riches" have long been the subject of legend, we must deal at length with the actualities of Jesuit wealth and Jesuit power. Also, we'll be exploring the economies of such orders as the Marianists, the Sisters of Mercy, the Dominican Sisters of St. Catharine of Siena, the Maryknoll Fathers and the Religious of the

---

* Cloistered contemplatives are the members of those orders which restrict their activities to the work which can be done inside a monastery or convent. The apostolate—i.e., religious mission—of the contemplative order is generally that of prayer.

Sacred Heart of Mary. Behind the evocative titles of these orders are equally evocative questions of finance and administration. Some of these questions are seemingly simple ones. For instance, I've always wondered (along with many others, I'm sure) how much money a nun's costume, or habit, costs. In due course, we'll find out. In so doing, we'll discover that practical as well as spiritual reasoning underlies the "new look" in nuns' fashions—as it underlies even more striking changes in life-style.

Other questions we'll be answering are more complex. They'll involve us once again in canon law, economics and institutional finance. Through these questions, we'll be moving toward an understanding of the most challenging questions of all: how is it that the religious orders, whose members all take the vow of poverty, can nevertheless accumulate billions of dollars' worth of assets? How—and how well—do the orders manage their assets? How do the changes in the church affect their economies?

Perhaps the best way to begin is simply to cite the current statistics. Better than a prose account, these reveal the astonishing results of those first impulses which drove Christians into the desert to seek a holy life. The facts and figures, moreover, do something else. Read dispassionately, they make clear in advance the special problems we face in our hunt for economic truths about the religious orders.

In the 1970 *Annuario Pontificio*, 421 orders of priests and brothers are listed. Worldwide, 144,960 priests and 199,052 seminarians and lay brothers belong to these orders. Of the orders of men, by far the largest is the Society of Jesus, with 33,828 members. Second in size is the Franciscan Order of Friars Minor, with a membership of 26,666. The Salesians (21,905) are third; the Brothers of Christian Schools (16,187), fourth; the Franciscan Capuchins (15,291), fifth. These five account for approximately 60 per cent of the membership of all male religious orders. According to the 1970 *Catholic Almanac*, 62 of the male orders claim 1,000 or more members. Collectively, these orders enroll 90 per cent of all Catholic male religious.

As a matter of interest, the very smallest of all the orders of men is a medieval order, the Canons Regular of Windeshelm, in Austria. (The term "canons regular" signifies that the order was originally a group of secular priests in charge of one large church or cathedral who elected to live in community and to observe a religious rule. The famed monks of St. Bernard, those who rescue snowbound Alpine travelers, are another order of canons regular.) Founded in 1386, the Canons Regular of Windeshelm now has only eleven members.

For the orders of women, no such neat statistical summary is possible. So numerous and so diversely arrayed are these orders that they defy all classification. Even the experts avoid the subject. To prove the point, we need only plunge into the *Annuario Pontificio*. This official publication does offer a list of "religious institutes [of women] with autonomous houses," a title unusually vague even for the Vatican. From this list, we learn that the largest single group of women religious is the Discalced Carmelites, with a total membership of 11,075. However, there is no one "Order of Discalced Carmelites." "Discalced" means unshod or barefoot. Like "Franciscan" and "Benedictine," this term is used generically. It designated those orders of nuns of Our Lady of Mount Carmel which observe the constitutions drawn up in 1543 by the reforming saint of the Carmelites, Teresa of Avila. (St. Teresa reinstated the ideal of personal poverty among her nuns, hence their description as barefoot. In actual practice, the sisters were permitted to wear sandals.) There are nineteen orders of Discalced Carmelites. The biggest, the Carmelite Sisters of Charity of Vedruna, has 3,366 members. The Discalced Carmelite Sisters of Rapallo, Italy, with a membership of sixty-six, is the smallest.

The *Annuario*'s numbing roll-call similarly reveals that the Claretians, the followers of the Rule of St. Clare and St. Francis, rank second in numbers. The *Annuario* counts 105 separate orders as Claretians, and gives their total membership as 10,020. Mind you, these Franciscan Claretians are not to be confused with the Capuchin Claretians, the Colettine Claretians or the Urbanist Claretians, which are altogether separate smaller groups.

The Benedictines rank third, with 7,534 members belonging to ten orders. Again, however, dozens of orders following some variant of the Benedictine Rule are not included in this group. The Visitandines, whose official title is the Sisters of Charity of St. Vincent de Paul, are fourth (6,584 nuns, six orders). The Dominicans (5,660 nuns, thirty independent congregations) rank fifth.

Of all of these groups, only the Benedictines and the Dominicans are in any way internally cohesive. In each of these two groups, the orders have formed loose federations. Like professional or trade associations, these function mainly as clearinghouses for information. But in general, the only link between orders belonging to one of these groups is the observance of the given Rule. In organization, administration and economy, every one of the religious orders of women (as of men) is a separate entity. The fact is reflected in the next of the lists of women's orders in the *Annuario Pontificio*. This one simply gives in alphabetical order the official title, the address of the motherhouse and the total membership of each of the orders. According to my count (no official figure is made public), there are 1,108 orders of women. Their aggregate membership, which the *Catholic Almanac* does report each year, was 1,053,632 in 1970.

Even as we narrow our focus to the religious orders at

work in the United States—and this we must now do—
we're faced with the problem of sheer numbers. As I noted
above, 103 orders of priests have established themselves in
this country. Their 1970 membership total is 21,920. In addition, twenty-four "third orders" of lay brothers operate
here, with a total membership of 11,623. And Sister Mary
Hester Valentine states in her book that 484 orders of nuns
are active in the U. S. These orders have a current total
membership of 160,931.

These statistics underscore that for the orders as for
every other sector of the church, the organizational
principle is one of total decentralization. By definition,
we're already afloat once more on the sea of independent corporations, localized administration and miniaturized
economics. In what follows, moreover, we'll be reminded
repeatedly of what Rev. Ernest Bartell, C.S.C., says the
Catholic Church really is: "a rudimentary laissez-faire
free-enterprise economy."

Also by definition, we can deal in detail with only a few
of the orders. Nor, except in passing, can we spend time on
the picturesque. Among the nuns, for example, the orders
of cloistered contemplatives are those with the most curious and appealing economies. These are literally medieval,
complete with posts like that of Procuress (the senior nun
entrusted with the keys to the food cupboards). Furthermore, the cloistered contemplative communities are generally run with Spartan efficiency. But because these play so
small a role in the economy of the church, we can't dwell
on their finances. Conversely, because the major active (as
opposed to contemplative) orders are crucially important
economically, their operations demand the most careful in-
spection. For a first instance, we do well to choose the Society of Jesus.

Of all of the priests in the U. S. who belong to religious
orders, nearly one-quarter are Jesuits. With 4,992 ordained

members, 1,989 scholastics (members in training, most of them candidates for the priesthood) and 685 lay brothers in 1970, the Society is today the largest Catholic order in this country, as it is throughout the world. Its size, moreover, is matched by the variety and scope of its activities. By all odds, the most conspicuous and the most impressive of the Jesuit endeavors is education. All told, the Jesuits operate nineteen universities and nine colleges in the United States. These range from institutions as well known as Fordham, Georgetown, Boston College and Marquette to such local establishments as Le Moyne College in Syracuse, New York, and Spring Hill College in Mobile, Alabama. Many people, I find, assume automatically that the Jesuits also run the most famous of all American Catholic universities, Notre Dame. Actually, Notre Dame is operated by the Congregation of the Holy Cross. But the Jesuits do run Holy Cross College in Worcester, Massachusetts, a fact which undoubtedly contributes to the confusion.

According to the *Catholic Almanac*, in 1969 the total student enrollment in the Jesuit-run colleges and universities was 139,341. This ranks the Society of Jesus as the largest private purveyor of higher education in the U. S. Nor is the Jesuit involvement in education solely at the college level. The order also operates fifty-seven private* high schools, many of them academically outstanding. As we'll see, the focus of the Jesuits on education sharply conditions both the economy and the management philosophy of the order.

Rivaling education as a Jesuit concern is missionary work. In 1969, more than 600 American Jesuit priests were serving in domestic and foreign missions. The number is

---

* In the broad sense of the term, every one of the Catholic schools in this country is of course a private (i.e., non-public) school. But Catholic educators use the word as I use it here, to refer to those Catholic schools which are not part of the parochial and diocesan school systems of the various sees.

equivalent to about 12 per cent of the manpower of the Society in the U. S. Jesuits from this country staff missions in areas as remote as the Fiji Islands and Nepal, and serve in a total of thirty countries. But most of their foreign activity is concentrated in such traditional outposts of Jesuit service as India, Japan, Taiwan and the Philippines. In American territory, 134 Jesuits were working as missionaries in 1969. Thirty-five served in Alaska, in the schools and medical stations for the Eskimos. Twenty more were assigned to missions in Puerto Rico. And another forty-nine were continuing the teaching and counseling of American Indian tribesmen which has been a Jesuit specialty for 400 years.

Missionary services on this scale are both complex and costly. To coordinate the flow of personnel and to raise money, the Jesuits of this country adopt a technique already familiar to us from earlier chapters of the present book. As an administrative organ, they use an entirely separate corporation, Jesuit Missions, Inc., of New York. In this, the Jesuits are doing much what a local Ordinary does when he sets up a diocesan development fund. Like the hospital and welfare work of the diocese, the work of the missionary (especially in medicine and in secondary education) is very often nonsectarian. By detaching such activities from those which are specifically religious, the bishops and the Jesuits—and those other orders which follow suit—find it easier to attract outside financial support.

Having come this far, we must now look more closely at the organization and management of the Society itself. The world headquarters of the Jesuits is of course located in Rome. It is housed in a modest building at No. 5, Borgo Santo Spirito; "not too near the Vatican," as one American Jesuit observed wryly after a papal scolding in 1966. There the General of the order, Father Pedro Arrupe, has his office, along with those of the four Assistants General who help him manage the affairs of the Society worldwide. The

American Assistancy, which includes Canada, the U. S., Latin America and the Philippines, is the operational division with authority over Jesuit activity in this hemisphere.

In the United States, the Jesuits have established ten provinces.* Each of these is governed by a provincial appointed (for a six-year term) by Rome. He in turn appoints as personal aides a *socius*, or confidential assistant, and a secretary; and he may also add to his staff several assistant provincials to supervise the colleges, the high schools and the parishes† of the province. These officials plus a treasurer make up the top-management echelon.

As we might expect, every province is administratively and financially autonomous. Like the residential archbishop or bishop, the Jesuit provincial is an independent chief executive officer. However, there is a major difference between the diocesan Ordinary and the Jesuit official. Unlike a bishop, a provincial can never own the properties he administers. Because the provincial's personal vow of poverty prohibits such ownership, the legal title to Jesuit property within his province must be vested in a civil corporation. Moreover, this must be a so-called "membership corporation," one set up without stock or any other instrument of individual ownership. Indeed, this question of who owns the property of a Catholic religious order is a curious one. We'll shortly discover that the question is central to present-day Jesuit economic strategy.

Below the provincial level, there are in each province the separate Jesuit communities. Such communities are al-

---

* In order of their founding, these are: Maryland (1833), Missouri (1863), New York (1879), New Orleans (1907), California (1909), New England (1926), Chicago (1928), Oregon (1932), Detroit (1955) and Wisconsin (1955). The Jesuit provinces should not be confused with the ecclesiastical provinces of the diocesan church.

† Like many other religious orders, the Society staffs a number of parishes, chiefly in areas where there is a shortage of diocesan clergy but also in choice districts. In all, Jesuit priests ran ninety-two parishes in 1969.

most always associated with the specific institutions run by
the Jesuits of the province. For example, in the New York
province, the Jesuits run (according to the 1970 *Official
Catholic Directory*): "parishes 8; university 1; colleges 3;
high schools 9; houses for laymen's retreats 2; houses of
study 2; novitiate 1; community houses 5; interdiocesan
major seminary 1." From what we already know of the
church, we can be sure that every one of these thirty-two
institutions is an independent entity and a separate civil
corporation. But we must also realize that the various Jesuit communities which staff these facilities are themselves
independent. The communities are each headed by a superior who reports to the provincial of the province. And to
point out here what will take on special significance later,
the superior of a given Jesuit community may or may not
also be the official in charge of the institution that community serves.

A quick recapitulation of this organizational arrangement will lay bare for us the economic structure of the Society. Worldwide, the entire order is divided into four
Assistancies; and these in turn are divided into provinces.
Within each province, independent Jesuit communities are
set up as needed to supply manpower to a variety of Jesuit
institutions. Depending on the nature and function of the
given institution, a community may be large or small,
known to the public or inconspicuous. But the Jesuit community will always be an entity in its own right.

The economics of the arrangement thus become
straightforward enough. In any province, those Jesuit communities which run the public institutions of the Society—
its parishes, its universities, its colleges, its schools, its
retreat houses—derive their own financial support from
these institutions. To some extent, moreover, a local community can tap the revenues of the institutions in its charge
for the benefit of the province. Conversely, the communi-

ties of Jesuits which operate the novitiates, houses of study and seminaries of the Society are dependent for support on the province. (Only rarely do these internal institutions generate much income of their own.)

And so, to penetrate the supposed mysteries of the Jesuit economy, we must first explore the finances of the external institutions the Jesuits operate. We must next examine the internal finances of the community and the province. We'll then be able to see how these separate economic systems are linked; and we'll likewise be able to reach some factual conclusions about the wealth of the Society.

For most of us, the economics of higher education are anything but mysterious. If only because we're the targets of the fund-raising efforts of our own schools and colleges, we grasp without conscious effort that all educational institutions operate in much the same way. That is, they derive current income from such sources as tuition charges, grants from private or government donors, receipts from athletic and cultural programs and earnings from endowment funds. And this income is used to meet the standard current operating expenses: faculty and administration salaries, plant maintenance and upkeep, departmental overhead and the like. We know also that the private colleges and universities in particular are always seeking money to add to permanent endowment funds, because such capital can either be used to finance physical expansion or else invested to yield useful income. If you're running a university or a college, your economic strategy is the same whether your institution is a Harvard, a Montana State or a Holy Cross. Each year, you try to meet current expenses out of current income by making adjustments on both sides of the ledger. If you're successful, you finish the year with a modest surplus which you transfer to an endowment account. If you're not, you end the year with a deficit. This you attempt to wipe out by means of a fund drive or by some other money-raising technique. If all else fails, you dip guiltily into your endowment capital for the money you need.

This familiar pattern is as characteristic of the schools and colleges and universities of the Jesuits as it is of those run by ministers of other denominations—or by laymen of any persuasion. To see how the pattern works itself out in practice for the Jesuits, let's study in some detail the finances and the administration of one major Jesuit institute, Saint Louis University.

To native St. Louisans, the university which bears the name of their city has long been a familiar institution. Its charter dates back to 1832, and its administrators are proud to point out that this Catholic institution was the first university founded west of the Mississippi. Its size (a student enrollment of over 11,000; a faculty of 848 full-time and 921 part-time teachers) makes Saint Louis University one of the two largest in a large city. And its scope is unchallengeably that of a university. In addition to its college of arts and sciences, the university operates separate schools of engineering, aeronautics, commerce and nursing for undergraduates. On the graduate level, advanced degrees are awarded in sixty-four areas of study. Both the law school and the medical school, moreover, are nationally ranked as first-rate establishments.

Like most of the large Catholic colleges and universities, Saint Louis University is firmly nonsectarian, welcoming non-Catholic students and teachers. Nevertheless, Saint Louis University insists on its Catholic identity. In the words of an official statement of March 21, 1970:

> The University is specifically a Catholic university and has a special obligation to the Catholic public and to their institutions. These Catholic concerns provide one set of criteria in developing the Academic Plan of the University.

However, the observance of these criteria is in no sense to result in a closed intellectual ghetto or a closed campus community. On the contrary, the University is completely open to the whole of modern culture and recognizes the value of other traditions, even other religious traditions.

The university's president, the Very Reverend Paul C. Reinert, S.J., readily conceded to me that this is a narrow path to tread. But in our long interview, Father Reinert stressed his own feeling that Catholic tradition and full educational freedom could be—and must be—reconciled on his campus. Furthermore, the respect of non-Catholic educators in St. Louis for the city's Catholic university persuades me that intellectual narrowness is no problem there. (Like almost every college president today, however, Father Reinert does have his other problems. For instance, when I first telephoned his office for an appointment, his secretary apologized for his absence and asked me if I'd please call back later. "Father has a racial crisis this morning," she explained politely.)

Fiscally speaking, Saint Louis University is a considerable establishment. In 1969, the book value of its physical plant (the value based on cost) was $72,133,000. This total ranks the real estate assets of the university on a par with those of a medium-sized diocese. (One, say, like Portland, Maine, which has a Catholic population of about 270,000 and assets of approximately $80 million.) According to the official financial statement for 1968-69, the total revenues of the university were $37,505,851. Total expenditures equaled $36,520,065, which left an apparent surplus of nearly $1 million to please the university's trustees.

But a closer look at the figures reveals no such happy financial outcome. Indeed, the fact of the matter is that in 1968-69, Saint Louis University suffered an operating loss. To give a simplified summary of the true situation, the university's general education revenues totaled $31,444,144 (including tuition receipts of $13,786,237, government grants, research subsidies and revenues from the university's hospitals, clinics and other services) fell short of current expenditures by nearly $3 million. Additional expenditures for student aid brought the deficit to just over $5 million. Receipts of $4,567,443 from the university's so-called auxiliary operations (athletics, residence halls, bookstores, cafeterias and parking lots) just about equaled the expenses of running these operations. And while endowment income made up part of the $5 million operating loss, only the use of the $4.4 million worth of gifts received during the year enabled the university to keep itself in the black. And the gifts, once spent, can of course never be added to the university's store of capital, its endowment.

This same perilous situation is to be found today at many other Jesuit universities and colleges across the country; and perhaps at all of them. To judge from the balance sheets I've seen (nine out of thirty) and from conversations with university officials, only a very few are able to match current expenditures out of current revenues. For years, such major institutions as the University of Detroit and Georgetown University have operated at deficits. Private gifts, foundation grants (the Ford Foundation in particular has been generous to the Jesuit schools) and federal funds have helped to make up these losses. But even the wealthiest of the Jesuit universities have been hard-pressed. In New York, Fordham University, with its 10,450 students and a physical plant worth $57 million, is on the edge of financial disaster. Its troubles began a decade ago, with its amibitious but ill-fated educational venture at Manhattan's Lincoln Center for the Performing Arts. Fordham's showcase campus there was to have cost the university $3 million to build. But the actual cost of land acquisition and construction came to nearly $8 million. Later, promised New York State aid for staffing and maintaining the

Lincoln Center Campus failed to materialize; and enrollments and course offerings had to be trimmed sharply. So costly has this project proven that it has drained the university of funds and weakened its credit. During the spring of 1969, in fact, Fordham was forced to borrow money to meet its payroll. If a loyal alumnus, Thomas Cahill of the Pfizer Chemical Company, had not advanced the trustees $2.5 million, the entire university might have come to a halt.

Not all Jesuit institutions have thus been dogged by misfortune. But all are laboring under the same economic problems. On the one hand, their costs are rising alarmingly (especially their faculty salary costs). On the other, student and parental demands for more modern facilities (and the needs of graduate and professional students for up-to-date equipment) make retrenchment impossible. The resulting economic crisis is not confined to the Jesuit-run colleges alone, nor even to Catholic colleges as a group. Indeed, every university and college in the country faces comparable difficulties. Most colleges and universities meet the spiraling costs of operation by the simple strategy of raising tuition charges. Over the past decade, these have climbed at the rate of about 8 per cent per year.

But Jesuit institutions find themselves less able than other private colleges to adopt this strategy. Historically, the Jesuits (and other religious orders as well) have seen their role as that of the supplier serving a special market. Their mission has been to educate American Catholics supposedly too poor to bear the full cost of the education. By tradition, the tuitions of the Jesuit colleges have been kept low. And a look at current tuition levels suggests that this tradition has yet to be abandoned.

Of the twenty-eight Jesuit colleges and universities, only five, Boston College, the University of Denver, Fordham, Georgetown and Holy Cross, were charging as much as $2,000 a year in 1970. At the smaller colleges, the charges were markedly lower. The University of Seattle, for instance, charged only $1,300 a year; Gonzaga University, $1,410; Creighton College, $1,550. These tuitions contrast startlingly with those being charged by non-Catholic colleges. (For example, Bucknell and Rensselaer Polytechnic Institute each charged $2,425 in 1970. The Ivy League colleges averaged $2,553. Swarthmore, another expensive college, pegged its tuition at $2,510 a year.)

At Saint Louis University, E. J. Hellman, the vice president for financial administration, commented on the 1969 financial report: "To have covered [the $5,010,288] deficit out of tuition, it would have necessitated raising the tuition from $1,600 per year to $2,200 per year or 36 per cent. Tuition in the past ten years has increased from $800 per year to $1,600 per year." Hellman's remark sums up admirably the chief concern of Jesuit educators. Having raised tuitions by 100 per cent over the past decade, they now fear that further increases will price them completely out of the Catholic student market.

For these same educators, an accompanying economic handicap is a critical shortage of permanent endowment capital.

By now, we know enough about the church in this country, and enough about the economic thinking of Catholic ecclesiastics, to see very clearly why the Jesuit colleges suffer from chronic capital starvation. The fundamental reasons are matters of history. First, by comparison with many private colleges, the Jesuit institutions are newcomers. Only one was founded before 1800 (Georgetown, established in 1789), and only six date from before 1850. Eighteen were opened between 1850 and 1900, and another six have been founded during this century. Clearly, then, the sheer longevity which has helped the Harvards, Yales and Columbias to accumulate great sums of capital has not yet been granted to the Fordhams, Xaviers and Holy Crosses.

Furthermore, from the beginning, the richest of the American private colleges have been the handmaidens of the American Establishment. Its favored sons have been their students, its leaders their alumni and its wealth theirs by gift and bequest. But the Jesuit institutions have served a very different constituency. Only recently have American Catholics begun to prosper on an equal basis with other Americans. In no small measure, Catholic universities in general and Jesuit universities in particular have contributed to this prosperity. But thus far, these institutions have not in their turn reaped the full benefits.

Finally, the Catholic university president, Jesuit or not, has much in common with the Catholic bishop. For him as a priest, money exists to be used. In the past, this has meant two things: a) good, solid bricks and mortar; and b) scholarship aid. Whatever money he could raise for purposes other than new buildings he has spent on his students—on would-be doctors, lawyers and engineers, I might add, as well as on the promising athletes of legend. But the fact remains that not much money has ever been left over. Neither the Jesuits nor other religious orders in the costly business of higher education enjoy the luxury of substantial capitalizations.

Even if we know the background, it still comes as something of a shock to learn that, at Saint Louis University, the total income from unrestricted endowment was $419,240 in 1969. At 6 per cent interest, this sum represents the earnings on capital of $6,987,333. For a university of national reputation already 140 years old, $7 million is a wretchedly meager endowment fund. Furthermore, although Father Reinert gave me no exact figures, he did make clear that not all of that $419,240 was pure income. A sizable fraction was an amount transferred from capital.

The double lesson is obvious. First, the university's endowment is even smaller than $7 million. Secondly, this lesser amount is being further reduced each year as the university dips into capital to meet current expenditures.

Other evidence indicates that the financial plight of Saint Louis University is far from the exception among the Jesuit universities. For instance, according to the official financial statement, the total restricted capital of the University of Detroit was $3,997,552 in April, 1968. Four and a half years earlier, this total was $4,539,852. Study of the statement reveals that the decline is the direct result of transfers of capital funds to the current income account. This university, too, has been forced to "dissave" out of its skimpy endowment. Members of the boards of trustees of two other Jesuit universities, Georgetown and Fordham, have told me that their institutions, too, are deep in the throes of deficit financing. Other Jesuit institutions (e.g., Gonzaga University) are being forced to borrow funds for expansion.

So it is that the Jesuit higher education establishment, with a total current income of at least $250 million a year, faces financial crisis.

The first question that comes to mind is: why doesn't the Society of Jesus come to the rescue of its colleges and universities? In response, Father Reinert states flatly: "Impossible. Our order doesn't have the resources." If he's speaking the truth, then one of the dearest of the myths of Catholic Church wealth has suddenly lost its potency. Can the Jesuits in fact be poor?

To test Father Reinert, let's turn to the internal finances of a Jesuit province. And let's choose the largest, the 1,300-man New York Province of the Society of Jesus. Its provincialate, or headquarters, is housed in Kohlmann Hall, an impressively gaunt Victorian structure on the campus of Fordham University. There Rev. Eugene J. Quigley, S. J., the treasurer of the province, discussed with me its fiscal affairs and made available its most recent financial documents.

These certainly justify Father Reinert's contention that the money problems of the Jesuit educational establishments are far too weighty for the provinces themselves to solve. Indeed, the provinces have money problems of their own. Thus, for the New York province the total receipts in 1967-68 were $1,635,817. Of this sum, $346,844 was the proceeds of a "province tax" levied on the various houses, the Jesuit communities, of the province. Another $79,950 was realized from fund-raising drives for Jesuit seminaries and missions. Legacies and gifts accounted for $125,876 and $171,947, respectively. Dividends and interest yielded $648,520, and other income amounted to $262,680.

By far the largest of the expenditures of the province was the $1,321,210 spent on the "upkeep of personnel in training." Its central administration cost the province $188,649, while new construction absorbed $616,893 and other expenditures came to $405,641. In addition, the province laid out $53,311 on care for the sick (including medical insurance), $31,034 for special projects, $37,524 on "Assistancy projects" and $57,827 on what the financial statement labels succinctly "Alms." In all, the 1967-68 expenses were $2,712,089. In that year, the province operated at a deficit of $1,076,272. To cover the deficit, the provincialate dug into its own capital (then worth about $16 million) to the tune of $1,090,708. This transaction cost the province nearly 25 per cent of its unrestricted capital assets, $4,408,538 of the $16 million just mentioned.

In this financial report as in so many of the others we've seen, a number of items can stand clarification. Father Quigley's own comments (in a letter to me dated March 16, 1969) shed exactly the light we need.

The Province Tax is an $1,100 charge on [every] one of our institutions for each working member of the Province. The point of this tax is that each working member of the Province should be contributing to the support of his eventual replacement. Due to financial problems, this tax has been reduced in the high schools to $600 and some of the houses have not been able to contribute anything.

The Upkeep of Personnel is our cost for: 2 years of novitiate, 2 years of classical & language studies, 3 years of philosophy, 4 years of theology, 1 year of spiritual and pastoral training, and for a number of men, graduate studies leading to a doctorate. Nothing is asked of the men by way of support from their families nor is anything required when admission to the Province is sought.

Examples of Province and Assistancy Projects would be as follows: the theological school for laymen in California, the commission for Mass Media, the commission for Intergroup Relations, the Cambridge Center for Social Studies, the Higher Achievement program for underprivileged youth, the mission to the Indians in South America, the cooperative in the Caroline Islands.

Examples of Other Expenses would be: subsidies to our high schools, gifts to Father General [in Rome] for his works, gifts to other provinces in need.

These specifics draw us a clear picture of the Jesuit province as a going concern. And the movement of cash through the provincial economy shows us that the province has two major functions. The first is simply that of executive headquarters and administrative center. The second is that of manpower development: the selection, training and placement of personnel.

Further analysis makes the picture even clearer. To start with the income side of the ledger, nearly two-thirds of what the province brings in ($1,026,293 out of $1,635,817 in 1968) is charitable income. That is, income from current gifts and bequests, earnings from the accumulated donations of past years and cash from yearly fund-raising campaigns. The remaining one-third of its income the province derives, directly or indirectly, from its individual members. Some money comes in from the province tax. This, as we'll see shortly, is a tax on earnings. The balance trickles in from such miscellaneous sources as royalties on publications, fees for speeches and other public appearances and private sums voluntarily paid over to the province by those of its members (there are always a few) who have inherited money or property.

As for expenditures, in an average year the province spends approximately three-quarters of its receipts on the development of its own younger members. This pattern, Father Quigley tells me, is the norm in most American Jesuit provinces. Outlays for administrative services and for the various "Province and Assistancy Projects" catalogued above must be made every year. But because manpower is the lifeblood of the Society (as it is of every religious order), the cost of supporting and educating new men is the one vital expense which can never be trimmed. And as Father Quigley writes:

> In looking at our expenses the only area for flexibility that we have is in Construction and Other Expenses. We can always delay construction and to a lesser extent we could take on less help of [i.e., assume less financial responsibility for] our schools and other Provinces. This latter is hard to do since they are in need.

These are hardly the comments of a financial executive who has at his disposal the unlimited wealth that legend attributes to the Jesuits. They're rather the phrases you'd expect from the treasurer of any organization which has an unpredictable income, substantial fixed expenses and modest capital resources.* Like his counterparts in the nine

---

* In 1968, the New York Province of the Society of Jesus held current assets worth $16,128,089. Of this total, $11,719,501 was restricted capital. (Only the income of such capital can be used.) According to Father

other Jesuit provinces, Father Quigley can certainly keep the sheriff from the door. But the door itself opens on no vast chamber full of treasure.

On the one hand, then, we find that there are scores of Jesuit religious and educational institutions; each of them independent, each with its own economy and its special economic problems. On the other are the Jesuit provinces, their finances geared to the training of new men for the Society, their funds too limited to afford the institutions more than token support. As in the diocesan church, the organizational principle here is one of extreme decentralization. But despite this deliberate separateness, there does exist an economic link between the Jesuit province and the institutions within its boundaries.

In essence, the link is a labor transaction, an exchange of manpower for money. The province acts as the supplier of trained personnel. The various institutions undertake the financial support of the men assigned to them and, in addition, indirectly compensate the province for its services as an ecclesiastical employment agency. This seems straightforward enough. But this seemingly simple internal exchange is more complex than I've made it sound. Furthermore, the same transaction is central to the economy of every major religious order. Because of its importance, we must consider it in detail. And because the Jesuits, in tune with a changing church and a changing society, are at this moment devising new forms of this ancient transaction, they are the ideal model for study.

To begin, let's look at the unit of labor involved: the individual Jesuit with his vow of poverty. Economically

---

Quigley, these funds are held in trusts managed by the Chase Manhattan Bank. Until the late 1960's, the province owned about $2 million worth of commercial real estate: "apartment houses near Prospect Park in Brooklyn." But these properties were sold and the proceeds turned over to the Bank to invest because "we didn't want to be landlords."

speaking, exactly what does it mean for a man to have taken this vow?

On the personal level, we already know at least part of the answer. The Catholic religious who vows poverty is voluntarily renouncing the right to material possessions. Whatever he or she wears or uses, down to the very last shoelace, thus belongs not to the individual but to the religious community, to the order as a whole and ultimately to God. Indeed, one of the first rules the Catholic novice learns is that the word "my" must be banished from his ordinary speech. Sister Mary Hester Valentine tells us that the rule leads many a young religious into such touching grammatical absurdities as "our toothbrush" and even "our feet."

Here we might note that the church makes an interesting canonical distinction between the "simple" and the "solemn" vows of poverty. The members of most religious orders today take the simple vow. Under this vow, the rights of ownership of property are sharply restricted but not entirely forfeited. For instance, the votary may continue to be the legal beneficiary of a trust fund. He may legally inherit money or property and in turn bequeath money or property to his own heir. (Legend to the contrary, moreover, he need not name his own order as the legatee.) However, the religious who takes the simple vow may never receive any personal benefit from being the legal owner of property. If the property is a trust fund, the income must be reinvested or distributed to another. If property is inherited, its yield in rent or other income must likewise be directed elsewhere. In sum, what canonists and civil lawyers term the usufruct (from the Latin *usus fructum*, meaning "use of the fruits" of property) is prohibited under the simple vow of poverty. Under the solemn vow, however, not only the usufruct but the right even to passive ownership of property is renounced. As far as property is concerned, the solemn vow is the legal equivalent of death. Only those religious who have demonstrated (by their length of service and their dedication) total indifference to externals are encouraged to take the solemn vow.

Also on the personal level, the obverse of the vow of poverty is that the basic economic needs of the individual will always be met. He can therefore pursue his vocation unconcerned by money matters. This other aspect of the vow was clarified for me by an expert, Rev. William R. Walsh, S. J. Father Walsh heads an excellent library, open to the public, which the Jesuits maintain at their parish of St. Ignatius Loyola in Manhattan. With the ease of someone used to being questioned on the subject, Father Walsh explained: "The vow of poverty doesn't mean we have to live in squalor. We're supposed to live decently in terms of the standards around us. Here, for instance [St. Ignatius is located on Park Avenue in the fashionable East Eighties], if I need an overcoat I don't go to a secondhand store. I ask our superior and he says, 'Okay, if you really need one, get one. Don't get the cheapest, but don't get the most expensive, either.' And I send the bill right here to the community. But if I'm assigned to a poor community, I either do without or borrow one from somebody else." What's true of Father Walsh's overcoat is true of other personal requirements. To free its members from material concerns, every order provides whatever they need to subsist and to do their jobs.

But when we move from personal economics to the impersonal economics of labor, the vow of poverty assumes a broader significance. For in professing poverty, the Catholic religious relinquishes not only the control of property but the control over his own labor as well. Whether he's a surgeon, a scholar or a scrubber of floors, the Jesuit priest (or the Franciscan brother or the Sister of Mercy) has given to God and to his order his work and its economic value. The order gains the absolute right to use this productivity for its own purposes. The superior of a religious community can, and often does, employ the members of the community in its workshops, kitchens and gardens. Or he can hire outsiders to do the domestic work of the community and, with the consent of his own superiors, "contract" to other organizations the labor at his disposal.

In practice, of course, the religious superior does both. Typically, the novices of an order share in the physical maintenance of the novitiate; and every member of every community has his household chores. But in the active orders, all but the very youngest and the very oldest members of each community do their main work outside the monastery walls. Wherever there's a market for their labor, their services are sold.

Sometimes the labor transaction is an external transaction. Although it does take place within the church, the purchase and sale of services are negotiated between entirely unrelated organizations. The commonest and most important example is that set yearly by the dozens of orders of teaching nuns and brothers. Their provincials and superiors bargain at the local level with the officials of the 160 dioceses for teachers to staff the parochial and diocesan schools. Together, the parties work out such essentials as the numbers of sisters and brothers to be supplied, the rate of compensation per individual, the specific schools to be staffed, the allowable proportions of lay teachers to religious teachers in the schools and the living accommodations to be provided. When an agreement is reached, the two sides execute a written contract.

Most of the time, the arrangements are concluded amicably on the basis of years of previous understandings. But on occasion, the give-and-take between an Ordinary and his "good sisters" becomes as acrimonious as the battle between management and union at the industrial bargaining table. The classic recent instance arose in Los Angeles in 1966. Cardinal James F. McIntyre, then the archbishop, was negotiating with the California Institute of the Sisters of the Most Holy and Immaculate Heart of the Blessed Virgin Mary for teachers to serve in the archdiocesan high schools. The Institute, under the leadership of the brilliant Sister Anita Caspary, was preoccupied with a program of modernization. This program called for some of the sisters to withdraw temporarily from teaching so that they could study for advanced college degrees. The reduction in the number of available teachers (coupled with such other reforms as the abolition of traditional dress and the relaxation of convent rules) greatly disturbed the Cardinal. So angry was McIntyre, in fact, that he expelled the I. H. M. sisters from the schools and forbade them to teach anywhere in his see. Because adjacent sees welcomed the sisters despite McIntyre's disapproval, this threat to their security failed to cow them. Furthermore, the Institute falls under papal, not archdiocesan, jurisdiction. As Sister Anita Caspary said to me in the spring of 1968, "This made His Eminence's intervention not only ungentlemanly but illegal." The sisters promptly complained to the Sacred Congregation for Religious in Rome. When the influential McIntyre hotly contested the complaint, the Sacred Congregation—after months of investigation and delay—issued a compromise ruling in the winter of 1968. The sisters were to slow down their reform program and McIntyre was then to rescind his ban.

Cardinal McIntyre has since retired and the Institute is once more represented in the school system of the archdiocese. But the Institute is no longer the same. In March, 1970, 315 of its 372 members, led by Anita Caspary, resigned to form a new community. The Immaculate Heart Community admits married couples as well as single men and women to its membership. Unlikely ever to receive official sanction, this most novel of religious orders faces serious difficulties in its fight for survival. (The sisters will support themselves by teaching, but new members may choose other specialties.) Plainly, this struggle has left its scars. But to hundreds of other communities of religious, the result represents a triumph. It marks the end of the long era when, in the words of another former Institute nun and charter member of the new community, ex-Sister Mary Jean, "the bishops could treat us all like slave labor."

To return to the Jesuits, their essential labor transaction is not external but internal, a fact which has so far spared them from open disputes on the labor issue. Like the many other orders engaged in private Catholic education (and also in hospital work), the Society has in effect created its own market for its manpower; the market being, of course, the institutions which the Jesuits themselves have founded. Still, even though Jesuit is negotiating with Jesuit in this marketplace, certain economic factors make the bargaining between province and institution for labor a genuine bargaining process, not merely a bookkeeping matter.

In theory, these factors are simple enough. As the executive responsible, the provincial knows what it costs the Society to turn out a unit of manpower. He knows that the "2 years of novitiate, 2 years of classical & language studies, 3 years of philosophy, 4 years of theology, 1 year of spiritual and pastoral training and [possible] graduate study" outlined by Father Quigley represents a sizable investment in the individual. Because the Jesuit-in-training lives in a community under rules, his style of life and the training itself can be standardized. So it does cost less money to educate a Jesuit than it would to give comparable training to an outsider (or, in the private language of the Society, an "extern"). In fact, throughout the 1940's and 1950's and into the mid-1960's, the provincials could use as their norm in computing the cost of both training and support the modest figure of $1,200 a year. But even at this low rate, an education which requires at least twelve years to complete, and which may well last longer, costs the province a minimum of $14,400 per man.

To this sum, the provincial must add other charges as well. From the day he joins the Society as a novice until the day he dies, the individual Jesuit receives any needed medical care at the expense of his province. The province likewise bears the cost of supporting members who become disabled and members who are retired. The individual's share of the cost of these "fringe benefits" is easily worth another $20,000.

From the viewpoint of the personnel executive, which is what every provincial must be, the Society thus sinks into each individual about $35,000 worth of its funds. If the economic stability of the province is to be preserved, this much money at least must be recovered from every individual during his working lifetime. Then, too, every Jesuit must generate from his work enough money to pay for his daily support. If these basic economic goals can be met, the provincial is satisfied. To be certain they are met, he makes certain other assumptions. On these, he bases his negotiations with the heads of the schools, colleges and other institutions which are his market for the labor he controls.

He assumes, for instance, that because Jesuit training does take so long, the individual will be thirty years old or older before he begins his active career. In business, so late a start would shorten a man's career. But we've already learned that in the Catholic Church, mandatory retirement at sixty-five—or, indeed at any other age—is still a startling notion. So the provincial takes for granted that the average Jesuit, like his counterpart in secular society, will have a working career of about forty years. Simple arithmetic tells the rest of the story. To recapture its $35,000 investment in the man over a forty-year period, the province will require yearly return payments of $875. For his personal support, the man himself will need perhaps $1,200 a year.

And so, for the services of every Jesuit on its staff, an institution will be asked by the province to allocate $2,075 a year.

These figures naturally vary from province to province and from institution to institution within each of the provinces. Moreover, conditions are changing. As averages, however, the figures I've just given still do represent the reality in many Jesuit institutions. When we wonder how the Jesuit schools, colleges and universities have survived for so long on such low tuition charges, the mathematics of the labor equation solves part of the mystery. For decades, the institutions have been paying bargain prices for the services of key members of their faculties and administrations.

As for the mechanics of the labor transaction, these, too, are simple. Each institution carries on its payroll the Jesuits assigned to it, at the agreed-on rate of compensation per man. But instead of writing every individual a periodic paycheck, the institution sends to the head of its Jesuit community a single monthly check for the services of all Jesuit staff members. In his turn, the rector of the community writes one check to the province each year to cover the obligations of the individuals in the community. This is the "province tax" Father Quigley mentions in his explanatory letter. In an average year, this tax brings in about 15 per cent of the total income of the province.

Now that we know how the system works, let's probe a bit deeper. Let's first consider the ideas which underlie the labor economics of the Jesuits and of all other religious orders. Next, because these ideas are being challenged today as rarely before in the history of the church, we need to know what the Jesuits and some others are doing in response to the challenge. The varying reactions we encounter will shed light on an even broader final issue: the economic future of the religious orders in America and the possible fate of the services they have been rendering.

A moment's thought makes clear that the economic structure of the religious order rests on two postulates. These are: 1) that the human economic environment is basically orderly, stable and predictable; 2) that there will always be large numbers of new religious to take the places of those who resign, retire and die. I suspect that if we tried, we could trace these beliefs back to the very beginnings of Catholic monastic history. I myself think that they matured during the long centuries when Western society was primarily an agrarian society; when a static subsistence economy did wed generation after generation to the unchanging land; and when ecclesiastical poverty offered the individual no worse a material life than did secular poverty. But we really need no such historical speculation to persuade us that even now, in today's post-industrial society, these same two ideas still anchor monastic economics. What we've seen so far is proof enough. Today as in 1500 or 1700, each generation of monastic labor is supposed to produce just enough of a surplus to pay for the training of the next. Like medieval manors, modern monastic institutions are expected to sustain themselves from within. From year to year and from decade to decade, every religious order strives to preserve a perfect economic balance.

But today, both of these postulates are being contradicted by reality. As I've mentioned repeatedly, the economic forces at work in our society are making us pay for material progress in the hidden but very real coin of inflation. And no organization is more sensitive to the effects of inflation than is the religious order. In the case of the Jesuit universities, we've already seen that spiraling costs are a serious threat to solvency. What is true for the satellite institution is no less true for the parent province. A training institution in its own right, the province, too, must today raid its own capital for the cash it needs to meet current expenses. Furthermore, the labor transaction between institution and province is breaking down under the economic strain. It's easy to see why. At the traditional rate of $800 or $900 per man per year, the province tax, which once brought in enough money to cover most of the cost of training new manpower, now no longer even comes close. But if the provincial raises the rate, the institutions, already in trouble, are simply not able to bear the increase.

The current situation in the Jesuit province of New York illustrates graphically the breakdown of the system. Earlier I cited the official figures for 1968, which showed that in that year the "upkeep of personnel in training" cost $1,321,210. In 1968, the number of scholastics in the province was 377. So for each man, the year's training cost $3,504: nearly triple the average cost of a year's training a decade earlier. Also in 1968, the province tax per working Jesuit was $1,100. But even at this rate, which was nearly 30 per cent higher than it had been in 1958, the tax yielded only $346,844: a sum equal to about one-quarter of the outlay the tax is meant to cover. As Father Quigley noted for us, moreover, the $1,100 rate could not always be met. "Due to financial problems, this tax has been reduced in the [9] high schools to $600 and some of the houses have not been able to contribute anything."

What inflation is doing in New York it is doing to Jesuit provinces, institutions and communities across the country. And what inflation does to the Jesuits, it does in worse measure to other religious orders. As a grim example, consider the financial predicament of the 290-man American Province of the Society of the Divine Saviour and of its companion order, the Sisters of the Divine Saviour. In 1955, the Salvatorian Sisters (to use their customary title) retained as a financial consultant a Washington, D. C., attor-

ney named Victor J. Orsinger. Because inflation was jeopardizing the missionary activities of the sisters, Orsinger
told them that they should increase the yield on their $3
million worth of mission trust funds. His chosen investment
vehicle was real estate. Orsinger lent the funds to a realty
company then promoting Parkwood Homes, a high-income
residential development in the Washington suburbs.

Attracted by what seemed to be a safe investment and
high, inflation-beating interest yields, the Salvatorian
priests, too, turned over to Orsinger funds for Parkwood
Homes. Most of the $4,418,000 they invested was held in
trust for the 1,100 members of a charitable annuity program run by the province. Suddenly, in 1965, Parkwood
began to turn sour. First, the company defaulted on its
repayments of principal and interest to the two religious
orders. Then, Parkwood filed a petition of bankruptcy.
Orsinger, it turned out, had been the actual owner of the
realty operation itself. And according to the S. E. C., his
methods had been something less honest than those required of a fiduciary. (He is now serving a three- to nine-
year jail sentence for fraud.)

But the Salvatorians were in dire financial trouble. With
most of their liquid capital tied up in a bankrupt company,
their own obligations were steadily harder to meet. To
stave off a crisis, the order turned to the religious bond
market. Through bonds and through personal appeals, the
Salvatorians borrowed a total of $1.1 million from other
church institutions. These included 93 of the religious orders and seven dioceses and archdioceses (New York, Boston, Chicago, Newark, Trenton, Milwaukee and St.
Paul-Minneapolis). When they advanced the funds, the
lenders did know that the order was pressed for money.
But by agreement, a deadline of November 1, 1970, was set
for repayment of the loans. When the deadline came, the
Salvatorians were unable to meet it. On November 3, 1970,

the order filed a voluntary petition of bankruptcy in the federal bankruptcy court of Milwaukee, listing debts of $8,603,000 which it could not pay. For the first time in the history of the Catholic Church in this country, a church institution had become legally insolvent.*

But inflation and its consequences are not the only aspect of what must be called an economic crisis for the religious orders. The other aspect is perhaps even more critical. Today, the second as well as the first of the two economic postulates outlined above is being called into question. In the once-steady stream of religious manpower there is a slackening. To put it in the language of the professional ecclesiastics, the orders are suffering from "a shortage of vocations."

That the stream is slackening is confirmed by the church itself. In April, 1969, a study group reported to the National Conference of Catholic Bishops that during the three-year period ending in 1968, the total number of Catholic seminarians in the United States had dropped from 45,267 to 33,065. The most recent figures available, those for 1970, reveal a further decline, to 25,710. These totals cover diocesan seminarians as well as students in the seminaries of the religious orders. My own analysis of the figures published each year in *The Official Catholic Directory* indicates that this shrinkage in numbers affects the religious orders even more strongly than it does the diocesan church. According to these statistics, between 1965 and 1970 enrollments in the seminaries of the orders declined by more than 50 per cent, from 23,000 to 10,723.

Because of the time lag before the seminarian joins the active ministry, the full impact of the shrinkage on the

* The creditors of the Salvatorians will ultimately be repaid in full, according to a Salvatorian spokesman, Father Ramon Wagner. The assets of the order are worth $16,910,168. If these can be liquidated at anywhere near that value, the province will of course be solvent. Meanwhile, the educational and charitable work of its members is to be continued.

priesthood has not yet made itself apparent. But for several years, the edge of the problem has been visible. Over the thirty years leading up to the mid-1960's, the number of Catholic priests in this country had been growing steadily at the rate of about 400 a year. In 1966, this total stood at 59,892. Since then, however, the count has been decreasing ever so slightly each year: to 59,803 in 1967; 59,620 in 1968; 59,192 in 1969; and 58,161 in 1970. Again, the religious orders have suffered from this nibbling at their numbers more severely than has the diocesan church. From its maximum of 23,021 in 1966, the total number of religious priests has slipped to 21,141 in 1970.

No comparable year-by-year figures are available by which to chart the trend among the postulants and novices of the orders of women. But the available figures do testify to a similar sharp decline. According to a "Sister Survey" completed early in 1967 by Sister Mary Augusta Neil, S.N.D., in 1966, 958 women left their religious communities before pronouncing their vows. This figure represents about 6 per cent of the total population of novices and postulants in U. S. religious communities of women. Studies now (1970) in progress are expected to reveal more dramatic losses, through declines in new enrollments and through increases in "pre-votive departures." For the total population of women religious, the trend is likewise downward. In 1965, there were 181,421 nuns in the United States. By the end of 1970, their ranks had been thinned (by deaths as well as by departures) to 153,645.

Why, after generations of growth, has the Catholic Church in America suddenly begun to lose its professional manpower?

CHAPTER FOURTEEN

The Economic Crisis of Catholic Higher Education

The question of manpower shrinkage has certainly had more than its quota of answers. Pope Paul has urged Catholics here and elsewhere to pray for an increase in vocations. In its 1969 report, the National Conference study group (composed largely of churchmen) listed as causes of the decline "the growing acceptance of a materialistic value system in modern society, exaggerated personalism, and a growing rejection of values of close-knit family life." After two thousand years, it seems, worldliness has at last conquered the seminary. The report also speaks of the "uncertainty of a large number of sincere Catholics with priestly and Religious life" and of the "departure of priests and Religious from the Church . . . and dramatization of this in the press." Nowhere in this marvelously grumpy catalogue of external reasons does the group even hint that the church itself could be doing something wrong.

As for the secular press, its response, too, has left something to be desired. There has been a freshet of articles with such titles as "Should Seminarians Date?" and "Why Priests Want to Marry" (two actual examples). But apart from these efforts and from occasional fashion-page interviews with former nuns about their troubles with mini-skirts, not much has been published, dramatic or otherwise. In a cover story archly entitled "Priests and Nuns: Going Their Way," *Time* (February 23, 1970) did describe the situation as "the most notable mass defection of priests (and nuns) from the service of the church since the Reformation." But the story had little to say about the reasons except that: a) the church is too authoritarian; and b) things may be better some day.

This question surely demands—and deserves—a better answer. Our immediate concern, however, must be not the spiritual and social causes but rather the economic consequences of the manpower crisis. As I pointed out a few paragraphs ago, the full effect won't be felt for another several years. By the mid-1970's, the numbers graduating from the seminaries will be falling very short of replacing the numbers of priests lost through death, disability, resignation and retirement. By then, the shortage will have become crippling. Even now, the economic pinch is badly hurting the whole church. And on the Catholic educational establishment, the manpower shortage exerts excruciating pressure.

The reason is obvious. Every time a Catholic school loses a teaching priest, nun or brother, it loses services for which it pays at most $2,500 a year. Unless the school can dispense altogether with these services, the teaching religious must be replaced. But this has never been easy. (Catholic educators like to point out that for years before the present drastic decline, the church had faced a milder but chronic shortage of religious manpower.) Today, the typical Catholic institution finds it impossible to replace one priest or nun or brother with another. The choice is therefore between no replacement and a lay replacement. Herein lies the economic disaster. Instead of costing $2,500 a year, the lay teacher even in an elementary school will cost the school at least $5,000 a year. To replace a priest who teaches in a high school or college with a comparably trained layman means paying $12,000 or more a year.

What this fatal choice has meant to the nation's parochial schools, we'll find out in detail in a later chapter. Suffice it to say here what every Catholic parent knows. For the past twenty years, as more and more of the teaching sisters have left the schools, pastors and bishops have hired the lay replacements to keep the classrooms open. But in so doing the pastors and bishops have crippled the economies of parishes and of whole sees. And the education of Catholic schoolchildren is still a divisive, polarizing national issue.

The private Catholic schools and the colleges and universities have as a rule fared better. For one thing, these institutions (unlike the parochial schools) have always charged tuitions. For another, the religious orders which control them have never attempted to put a religious teacher in every classroom. In the colleges especially, lay teachers have been welcomed and their salary requirements accepted as a normal budgetary expense. As a result, the shortage of religious manpower has been less of an economic threat in this sector of the church than has been the inflation we discussed earlier.

Now, however, the combination of the two problems is persuading the private educators that they must change their ways. Led by the Holy Cross Fathers, the Jesuits and some enterprising communities of nuns, many orders have decided that they can no longer afford to own the institutions they worked so hard to establish. The financial burden is too great; and their present members see ownership of property as alien to the religious calling. So in a series of unprecedented moves, some orders have already begun to divest themselves of their schools, colleges and universities. As we'll see, the process is complex—and the motivation neither simple nor entirely selfless. But if the legal and financial advantages of divestiture are in fact what they now appear to be, most of the other orders in private education will eventually follow the leaders.

The first and biggest step has been the laicization of the institutional boards of trustees.

Throughout the history of the Catholic Church, the great management axiom has been that churchmen, not laymen, must own and control all ecclesiastical property. In the U. S., the nineteenth-century struggles of the diocesan hierarchy against lay trusteeism (see Chapter Five) convinced church officials never to relax such control. To this day, a minority of the orders (e.g., the Vincentians, who own and run three universities: De Paul in Chicago, Niagara in Buffalo and St. John's in Queens) still insist that the governing boards of their institutions be composed entirely of priests. For most of the orders, however, simple majorities of their priests on the boards seemed sufficient insurance against the loss of operating control. Generous alumni and other useful members of the Catholic laity could then be awarded trusteeships. But "lay intervention" could never become a problem and the "Catholic character" of the institution would always be guaranteed.

As the problems of operating and financing church educational institutions grew more complicated, the shrewder religious administrators welcomed the assistance of lay trustees. These laymen, most of them seasoned businessmen and all of them loyal Catholics, showed no signs of challenging priestly control. Their presence, moreover, attracted others. During the 1950's and the early 1960's, the Catholic colleges were forming all sorts of advisory boards and special committees of laymen "to help the good Fathers" (or the good Sisters) with their fiscal, legal and political difficulties. Still, the possessive fist of the clergy remained tightly clenched. As far as I know, before 1967 no religious order in this country had ever relinquished control of an institution to a lay board or to a lay majority on a mixed board of religious and lay trustees.

But in January, 1967, the tradition was broken. That month, Sister Jacqueline Grennan, S. L., announced to the press that her order, the Sisters of Loretto, would transfer to a lay board the ownership and control of Webster College. Webster is a small college (1970 enrollment, 1,048 students) in suburban St. Louis, Missouri; Sister Jacqueline herself was then president. Already celebrated as a Catholic liberal, Sister Jacqueline told reporters on this occasion: "It is my personal conviction that the very nature of higher education is opposed to juridical control by the Church." She did not mention (or at least the news media did not report) certain other facts of the situation, namely: a) that the main reason for the transfer was economic, not academic; b) that the transfer had the support of Cardinal Joseph Ritter, the Archbishop of St. Louis; c) that the lay board was to be made up entirely of Catholics; and d) that the Sisters of Loretto would continue to supply teachers to the college. These additional details cast no doubt whatever on Sister Jacqueline's sincerity,* but they do make obvious

* At the same press conference, Sister Jacqueline also announced her decision to withdraw from monastic life. Her career in education continued, and in 1969 (after her marriage) she took over the presidency of Hunter College in Manhattan, a job in public education traditionally reserved by New York City political leaders for Catholics.

that laicization is not synonymous with the casting aside of all Catholic influence.

Jacqueline Grennan's verve (she once dazzled an audience of New York magazine space salesmen convening in Arizona with a speech on the unlikely topic—for a nun—of imagination in business) undoubtedly dramatized what would otherwise have been a minor change in an obscure Catholic college. But bigger news was to come. On January 27, 1967, the provincial chapter of the Indiana Province of the Congregation of Holy Cross met in South Bend. By huge majorities, the forty-two-man chapter voted to approve what *The New York Times* called "greater lay participation in [the] government and control" of its two universities. One of these was the University of Portland, in Portland, Oregon. The other was Notre Dame.

In laicizing the boards of these institutions, the Holy Cross Fathers were accepting the recommendations of another remarkable Catholic educator, the Rev. Theodore M. Hesburgh, C. S. C., president of Notre Dame. And because the technique devised by Father Hesburgh and his aides sets a pattern for other religious orders to follow, we should glance at his plan. According to *The Times*:

> The changes at Notre Dame call for the present six clerical trustees of the university, all members of the Holy Cross teaching and missionary order, to select six laymen to form with them a new body, the Fellows of the University.
> The Fellows, operating on a two-thirds voting rule, will adopt the [new] statutes and bylaws governing Notre Dame. They will also select about 30 other laymen to form with them the Trustees of the University. The Trustees will make most of the decisions on operating policy under the statutes.
> Father Hesburgh said that the 27 members of the present board of lay trustees [an advisory body] would probably fill most of the new positions.
> He said that the lay trustees had been closely consulted

by university officials in the last few years in all major policy decisions.

From this outline, we can see that the legalities of a transfer of control were scrupulously observed. But it's equally obvious that the Holy Cross Fathers intended to retain considerable authority in university affairs. Once again, we find that in Catholic educational philosophy, laicization means something far short of complete secularization.

Two years after Father Hesburgh's laicization scheme was approved, journalist Thomas J. Fleming wrote an entertaining article about Notre Dame's dynamic priest-president ("Hesburgh of Notre Dame," *The New York Times* Magazine, May 11, 1969). In his article, Fleming catalogued Hesburgh's economic achievements for the university since his appointment to its presidency in 1952. Among them: a $66 million construction program; a quadrupling of the operating budget to $43 million annually; a $6 million grant from the Ford Foundation; a $5 million National Science Foundation award; and a seventeen-year increase in endowment from $5 million to $72 million (which makes Notre Dame by far the wealthiest of all Catholic universities). Hesburgh is quoted as saying: "Since I became president of Notre Dame, money is all I think about." While this is obviously untrue, Hesburgh certainly does think about money—and especially about secular financing—on the grand scale. According to Fleming, the president's dream is to make Notre Dame the Catholic equivalent of a Princeton. And this will require funds in amounts which only the largest non-Catholic foundations can afford. Hence Hesburgh's move to end direct church control of his university.

Of the laicization of Notre Dame, Fleming remarks:

> Hesburgh and the Holy Cross Order turned the university over to a board of trustees, the majority of whom are laymen. But . . . most of the trustees were selected by

Hesburgh. One of them, for instance, is [Hesburgh's] Special Assistant George M. Shuster,* an arrangement even he admits is "a little peculiar." The day when a lay revolt might conceivably oust a Notre Dame priest-president is 20 or 50 years off, if it ever comes at all.

This, I think, is fair comment. Moreover, it helps us to sum up the situation. Like so many other Catholic educators today, Hesburgh wants to be able to say that his university is controlled not by priests but by laymen. Yet it's plain that at Notre Dame the *de facto* control has never left the hands of the Catholic religious. In seeking to eat his cake and have it, too, is Hesburgh involving Notre Dame (and the entire church educational establishment) in some sort of Catholic academic conspiracy? The question is a critical one; but before we answer it, let's study another laicization move, one that stands in sharp contrast to Hesburgh's maneuverings.

Like Notre Dame's Holy Cross Fathers, the Jesuits of the Society's Missouri province voted to laicize their major university in 1967. But the Jesuit approach to laicization made forthrightly clear that Saint Louis University was still to be a Jesuit institution. According to the new bylaws:

a) The University will be publicly identified as a Catholic university and as a Jesuit university.

b) The University will be motivated by the moral, spiritual and religious inspiration and values of the Judaeo-Christian tradition.

c) The University will be guided by the spiritual and intellectual ideals of the Society of Jesus.

Under the Saint Louis University laicization formula, a thirty-two-man board of trustees was to inherit control

---

* Shuster is well known in American education circles as a spokesman for the view that Catholic education and academic freedom are compatible. Before becoming Hesburgh's assistant at Notre Dame, Shuster served with distinction in Jacqueline Grennan's present post as head of Hunter College in New York.

from the previous board. On the new board, no fewer than eleven members were to be Jesuits, no more than twenty-one could be "laymen or laywomen." Of the lay members, eighteen could be "persons recognized locally or nationally as leaders in their respective professions or businesses or civic affairs." Four could be "educational leaders chosen from institutions, agencies or organizations not directly identified with Saint Louis University." At least four were to be "alumni or alumnae of the University." Nothing requires lay trustees to be Catholics.

Of the eleven Jesuit members of the board, not more than six may be active in the university's administration. The other five must be outsiders.

This sounds as if the Jesuits mean business. And other changes at Saint Louis University strongly persuade me that they do. For example, the university's Jesuit community has been separately incorporated and has been made to set up its own budget. Its finances will no longer be intermingled with those of the university. Indeed, the community pays rent to the university for the building which houses the Jesuits. Furthermore, each of the sixty-five Jesuits on the faculty now handles his own negotiations with his department and with the administration on matters of rank, salary, tenure and teaching commitment. Most of the department heads are laymen, and they treat their Jesuit professors exactly as they do the lay members of the faculty. Even the fringe benefits the Jesuits receive have been made parallel with those of the lay teachers. So that the individual Jesuits won't incur personal income-tax liabilities, their salary checks are paid directly to the Jesuit community each month. From this income, the rector draws what he needs for the community's financial support. Each year, most of the surplus is returned to the university in the form of an unrestricted cash gift from the community. In 1970, this gift was worth about $450,000.

The money is to be used as the board of trustees, not the community, sees fit.

I detect a marked difference between the Saint Louis version of laicization and the Holy Cross version at Notre Dame. The Jesuits seem to me to be making a serious attempt to redefine the relationship between a Catholic university and its founding religious order. The Notre Dame arrangement looks much more like an effort to blur the fact that such a relationship exists and will continue to exist. The official responses of those in charge of the two programs also suggest a difference. Asked by the press why Notre Dame had decided to increase the role of the layman in the government of the university, the Rev. Howard J. Kenna, C. S. C., superior of the Holy Cross province of Indiana, said only: "It has long been evident that this is a trend which has been going on for some 50 to 75 years, is still in progress, and will continue. It is a trend which is to be found in most Catholic institutions of higher learning in this country." After listening to this official nonsense, it's refreshing to consult Father Reinert of Saint Louis University on the same issue. "Laicization is bringing all sorts of advantages," he told me. "The stress on independence makes the Jesuits on our faculty work harder. They can earn salary increases and they see that this benefits the Jesuit community and the province. It's better for the university, too. With private education in so much financial trouble today, federal aid is already crucial. We used to have all sorts of problems explaining the status of our men who applied for federal grants. Now, we simply write it all down—salary, status and everything. And of course we want to be ready and qualified for more aid when it comes."

Federal aid, current and future, is the major reason why the private Catholic colleges and universities are reconstituting themselves as lay institutions. There are other rea-

sons. The professional religious who have for so long conducted these institutions do indeed feel that the nature of
their involvement must change. Their spokesmen are quick
to admit that laymen, after all, make better administrators
and add badly needed skills to the governing process. One
such spokesman is Sister Roberta Schmidt, C. S. J.

Sister Roberta is president of Fontbonne College, another small Catholic college (826 students) located in suburban St. Louis, Missouri. In January, 1970, the Sisters of
St. Joseph of Carondelet transferred legal ownership and
control of Fontbonne to an eighteen-member board which
includes ten laymen. Sister Roberta made no sweeping
statement about the evils of church control. Instead, she
said: "Studies have shown that the inclusion of lay men and
women of varied backgrounds supplements the expertise of
religious administrators. It negates the possibility of a college planning in isolation and without a firmly established
timetable." Still, in summing up, the reporter covering the
story of the Fontbonne transfer for the *St. Louis Review*
(one of the best diocesan newspapers in the country) puts
the question of laicization in exactly the right perspective.

> Such changes in Catholic higher education have been
> viewed as both philosophic—to give lay people a voice in
> the church—and economic—to assure federal grants are not
> endangered by religious ties which might violate church-
> state separation laws.

In essence, laicization is a legal process with a double
purpose. And if we look further into the question, we learn
that behind the present wave of laicizations is a startling
legal theory. This theory was first put forward in 1968 by
John J. McGrath, an associate professor of law at the Catholic University of America, in a study entitled *Catholic Institutions in the United States: Canonical and Civil Law
Status*. In his opening pages, McGrath asks all the puzzling

questions that the lawyers for the church—and for our secular governments—must now try to answer.

> Since the close of Vatican Council II great changes have been taking place in the colleges, hospitals and other institutions conducted by the Catholic Church. Laymen, both Catholic and non-Catholic, have been added to the governing boards of our institutions in such numbers that they are often in the majority. . . . If laymen constitute the majority of the governing board, is the institution still Catholic? Is Church property being alienated when a majority of laymen are elected to the board and thus have effective control of the institution? In attempting to fulfill the mandate of Vatican Council II to use lay people in their proper role in our institutions, are we not violating the canon law of the same Church? Who really owns our Catholic institutions? What law governs them, canon law or civil law?

So intriguing are McGrath's answers, and so central to the theme of economic support, that I feel we must pursue his argument further. McGrath first explains that certain types of ecclesiastical establishments (e.g., parishes, sees, religious communities) are "juridical personalities" under canon law.* These may or may not also be civil legal corporations; although in the United States, as we've seen, they almost always are nonprofit or charitable corporations chartered by the various states. But whatever its civil-law status, a juridical personality can only be created by the competent ecclesiastical authority. Depending on the particular case, this may be the Holy See, a cardinal, a local Ordinary, a religious superior or some other officer of the church. Unless the appropriate official does act, moreover, a given Catholic institution does not acquire canonical sanction. Even though it exists as a corporation under civil law, it does not become a juridical personality and thus part of the fabric of the church.

* For a discussion of the concept of the juridical personality, see p. 147.

McGrath next tells us that Catholic colleges, universities and hospitals may indeed be founded as juridical personalities. "However," he continues, "a survey of these institutions in the United States reveals that it has not been the policy to erect them as canonical moral persons [one form of juridical personality]." They are therefore civil-law corporations only, and their Catholic status is a matter of tradition, not of canon law.

From this premise, McGrath reasons ingeniously in two directions. On the one hand, the state-chartered Catholic colleges, universities and hospitals owe their existence to the "contract with the public" implicit in their charters. As long as these institutions render services to the public, their status as educational and charitable enterprises is unassailable. On the other hand, this status has nothing whatever to do with the fact of their sponsorship by religious orders or other Catholic Church organizations. In particular:

There is no question of dealing with ecclesiastical property when speaking of the property of Catholic hospitals and higher educational institutions in the United States. The canon law is clear that property is ecclesiastical only when it belongs to some ecclesiastical moral person. Since the institutions under consideration have not themselves been established as moral persons and, since no other moral person in fact holds title to the property of the institution, their assets are not ecclesiastical property.

And later:

Charitable and educational institutions chartered as corporations under American law are not *owned* by the sponsoring body. The legal title to the real and personal property is vested in the corporation. It is the corporation that cares for the sick or grants academic degrees. It is the corporation that buys and sells and borrows money. If anyone *owns* the assets of the charitable or educational institution, it is the general public.

If we believe McGrath, then hundreds of the colleges, universities and hospitals founded by the Catholic Church in this country are not legally part of the church. Catholic priests and religious may run them and serve in them. They may cater largely to lay Catholic constituencies. Economically, they may have been treated as subsidiaries of Catholic ecclesiastical organizations. But this Catholic orientation is strictly a matter of "sponsorship." The institutions themselves are public institutions. Like public parks, public libraries and public schools, the Catholic institutions of the country serve the general public. They therefore deserve public support.

To me, McGrath's theorizing, bold as it is, smacks a bit of the old jingle: "When the devil was sick/The devil a monk would be;/When the devil is well/Devil a monk is he." For more than two hundred years, the church has been busy in America, founding and expanding institutions of the type we're discussing. During this entire span, churchmen have prided themselves on the growth of auxiliary institutions designed not only to educate and to heal but also to preserve and to propagate the faith. Until now, not one word has ever been spoken about the "public" character of such institutions. On the contrary, their private character has been the issue. In courts and legislatures across the land, the church has zealously sought and ruthlessly defended its absolute right to operate its own institution in its own fashion, free from "lay interference." Only now, when the ecclesiastical economy can no longer sustain its institutional superstructure, has the attitude changed. Only now, when church officials are urgently seeking public funds and federal support, have the canonists been turned loose on the curious legal question of who owns what in the church. And the resulting discovery that in this country the Catholic institutions are really not Catholic is too convenient.

There is another side to the story, it's true. McGrath, to do him justice, is sincere as well as clever. He does stress that if laicization is to be effective in the eyes of the law, it must be genuine.

It has been repeatedly emphasized throughout this study that our Catholic institutions of higher education and public health are institutions of *public trust*. Their task is primarily one of service to the general public, and all the groups served by these institutions should be represented on the board of trustees: the local civic and business community, interested professional groups, and alumni.

If we were to ask McGrath whether non-Catholics as well as Catholics should be asked to serve on Catholic institutional boards, I'm certain that his answer would be yes. To date, this is not the answer being given by the Hesburghs of the church.

As another indication that the theory of laicization has so far outrun its actual practice, consider McGrath's comment on conflicts of interest in the choice of trustees.

Under no circumstances should employees of the institution except the president or administrator be elected to the board of trustees. An insoluble conflict of interest results when any member of the staff of an institution sits in judgment of the senior executive officer as one of the trustees.

In the light of this strong statement, I wonder what McGrath thinks about Father Hesburgh's selection of George Shuster, Hesburgh's own assistant, as a trustee of Notre Dame. Or about the compositions of the boards of most other "laicized" Catholic institutions.

The foregoing must make me sound like an implacable enemy of laicization, of progress in the church and of federal aid to church-related institutions. But in fact, I'm opposed to none of the three. If laicization really does signify a widening of authority in the church and is not merely a legal fiction masking continued clerical control, well and good. Laicization can indeed bring into Catholic institutions the professional management philosophies they so badly need. As for federal aid, such aid is already so vital to the finances of the Catholic colleges, universities and hospitals that to take a stand against it at this late date seems to me simply naïve.

As evidence of the importance of existing federal aid, let's note some of the most conspicuous examples. Under such enabling laws as the 1946 Hill-Burton Act, the 1963 Higher Education Facilities Act and the 1965 Elementary and Secondary Education Act, billions of dollars' worth of direct federal grants and low-cost loans have been made for the physical improvement of educational and health-care institutions, sectarian and nonsectarian. Federal dollars have thus financed the construction of Catholic hospitals, paid for dormitories at Catholic colleges and built classrooms for private Catholic schools. Other federal funds purchase lunches and provide milk for Catholic schoolchildren in all fifty states. Using federal "flow-through" dollars, state education agencies buy textbooks, films and other study materials for loan to pupils and teachers in Catholic schools.

In addition, there are the thirty-five aid-to-education programs of the Department of Health, Education and Welfare; the education and job-training allowances for veterans at Catholic institutions under the original G.I. Bill and its successors; and the student loan funds administered by most Catholic colleges and universities under the 1958 Defense Education Act. Moreover, Catholic as well as non-Catholic colleges, universities and hospitals compete aggressively for the research funds disbursed each year by the Department of Agriculture, the Department of Defense, NASA, the National Science Foundation and dozens of other federal departments and agencies.

How much money does the federal government make available to Catholic institutions every year? God alone knows. Neither the government nor the church keeps track of the totals.

Hostile estimators naturally peg the amounts as dizzyingly high. For instance, in *Praise the Lord for Tax Exemption*, Martin A. Larson fools around a bit with the aggregates for the entire country and comes up with a total of $6.08 billion as the yearly amount the federal government turns over to all churches and church-related institutions. Perhaps half of this, he estimates, goes to Catholic organizations. My own estimate is dramatically lower. On the basis of the same official aggregates, I'd say that Catholic institutions are currently receiving about $1.2 billion worth of federal funds a year. To know the extent to which the institutions themselves benefit from this income, we'd have to be able to distinguish among many different classes of funds. To take one example, Catholic religious orders receive government money for hospital construction. How much of the money comes in the form of outright grants and how much takes the form of mortgage loans? Unless we know, we can't measure the direct involvement of the government in the subsidization of these Catholic institutions.*

In any event, the flow of federal dollars into Catholic institutions is so substantial as to be a major source of their income. At Saint Louis University, for example, the 1968-69 budget included $9,196,542.23 worth of expenditures under federal grants, contracts, student loan programs and

---

* In this discussion, I've deliberately omitted mention of the millions of federal dollars disbursed by Catholic welfare organizations as agents of the government or used by Catholic dioceses or orders to finance government-approved housing programs.

construction programs. Among the government organizations paying for these projects were the U. S. Army, Navy and Air Force, NASA, AID, OEO, the Office of Education, the National Science Foundation and the U. S. Public Health Service. The money spent on the projects constituted more than 30 per cent of the university's total operating outlays for the year.

No one familiar with the growth of federal involvement in higher education will be shocked at these figures. They're typical of those to be found in the financial report of any major university. Students and some others are disturbed (rightly, I think) about certain aspects of this involvement. But all of us who sense what the government's commitment to higher education has meant to our country should also accept that the 292 Catholic colleges and universities have earned their measure of public support. Since the first federal funds began to trickle in two decades and more ago, these establishments have contributed thousands of graduates to a society which has sorely needed college-trained people. Moreover, the quality of the academic training they deliver has markedly improved. Indeed, largely because of federal aid, scores of Catholic institutions have become much more than the narrow, religion-ridden, let's-go-to-early-Mass-for-the-football-team schools they once were. And hundreds of non-Catholic denominational institutions have likewise broadened their horizons.

Are these government support programs constitutional? Regardless of their value, do they obey or do they violate the great clause which stands first in the Bill of Rights: "Congress shall make no law respecting an establishment of religion, or prohibiting the free exercise thereof"? To give this question the attention it warrants would require both a separate book and a panel of constitutional lawyers to do the writing. Still, so crucial an issue can't be dismissed as peripheral. What we must do—and what I think will serve our purpose here—is survey the current legal situation. Apart from its own intrinsic interest, this survey will give us another (and a final) vantage-point from which to view laicization and its significance for the church.

By the time this book is published, the United States Supreme Court may well have placed on its docket one case which could decide, once and for all, whether or not the United States Government may legally extend aid to the institutions of churches in this country. This case has three titles. In the records of the U. S. District Court for the District of Connecticut, the court of first hearing, it is listed simply as Civil Action No. 12767. In the customary shorthand of court reporters, lawyers, judges and other legal specialists, the case is called *Tilton v. Finch*. But to the legal historians, professors of jurisprudence and scholars of church-state relations, the case is already known by a special name, "The Connecticut Colleges Case." *

In *Tilton v. Finch*, the Tilton of the title and fourteen other Connecticut residents who are federal taxpayers filed suit on September 25, 1968, against the Federal officials responsible for administering Title I of the Higher Education Facilities Act of 1963. Also named as defendants were the chairman of the Connecticut state commission which shares in the administration of the program and four Catholic colleges and universities in the state. These schools are Fairfield University, Sacred Heart University in Bridgeport, Albertus Magnus College in New Haven and Annhurst College in South Woodstock. All four had received federal construction grants under the Title I program: the total value of the grants was about $1,870,000. The basic legal contention of the plaintiffs is that the defendant schools are "sectarian institutions" and that public financial assistance

---

* I owe this account of the case to a report presented to the Commission on Religion in Higher Education of the Association of American Colleges by Charles H. Wilson, one of the lawyers for the defendants.

to these schools—and all other similar sectarian institutions
—is impermissible aid to religion under the Establishment
Clause of the First Amendment.

As evidence of the landmark quality of the case, we
might note that both sides are represented by nationally famous lawyers. Leo Pfeffer, who is chief counsel for the
plaintiffs, is considered a legal authority on church-state
matters. In fact, Pfeffer's pleading of an earlier case, *Flast
v. Cohen*, before the U. S. Supreme Court (June 10, 1968)
paved the way for Tilton and his co-plaintiffs to bring their
taxpayers' suit against the federal government. As their
chief attorney, the defendant colleges and universities have
retained an even better known personality, Edward Ben-
nett Williams. Famous as a trial lawyer, especially in criminal cases, William is considered by his colleagues to be also
one of this country's great masters of appellate law.

In support of their suit, the plaintiffs have put together
a two-part argument. First, they rely on a key phrase in the
Supreme Court ruling on an earlier church-state classic,
Everson v. Board of Education. In this 1947 case, the Supreme Court upheld a New Jersey statue which authorized
the state to repay the parents of parochial school pupils for
the cost of sending their children to school via public transportation. In their ruling, the Justices declared:

> The "establishment of religion" clause means at least [that]
> no tax . . . can be levied to support any religious activities
> or institutions, whatever they may be called or whatever
> form they adopt to teach or practice religion.

In *Tilton v. Finch*, Pfeffer and his fellow-attorneys are
claiming that the Catholic colleges involved are primarily
institutions which "teach or practice religion" in the sense
of indoctrinating their students in a particular religious
faith.

To determine whether these (or any other) institutions

are "sectarian" in this sense, the plaintiffs wish to apply a test derived from still another court case. This one, *Horace Mann League v. Board of Public Works*, was decided in 1966 by the Court of Appeals (the highest court) of the State of Maryland. The *Horace Mann* case, even though a state and not a federal case, seems to have precipitated the present constitutional test. According to the commentary of Charles H. Wilson:

> At issue in the *Horace Mann* case were grants of public money made by the Maryland legislature to four church-related colleges. Two . . . were Catholic and two were Protestant. The public funds were . . . to assist the construction of classroom and dormitory facilities. The Maryland Court of Appeals ruled that all four grants were valid under the *state* constitution, but it invalidated three of the four grants under the Establishment Clause of the First Amendment because the recipients were—in the words of the Maryland court—"legally sectarian" . . . according to criteria proposed by the taxpayer plaintiffs [and accepted by the court].

These criteria were minutely detailed tests of religious affiliation.

> For example, under the category of the religious character of the college's personnel, the Court inquired into whether there is a religious qualification for appointment to the . . . governing board, administrative staff or faculty, or for admission to the student body, the religious composition of [these groups], and whether there was "religious control" of the college's governing board. Under the category of the college's relationship with religious groups, the Court examined the extent of ownership of the college by a religious group, the degree of financial assistance received . . . from a religious group . . . and the extent to which the college's facilities are used for supplementary religious purposes. And, under the category of the place of religion in the college's program, the Court looked at the nature of the religious observances on campus (including the extent

of religious symbolism in the physical surroundings and whether students are required to participate in religious ceremonies), the place of religion in the curriculum . . . and the place of religion in extra-curricular activities.

On the basis of these tests, the Maryland court did indeed find that the two Catholic institutions, St. Joseph's College and the College of Notre Dame, were "legally sectarian." (So also was Western Maryland College, a Methodist school.) When the defendant schools appealed the decision, the U. S. Supreme Court—for technical reasons—declined to review the case.

Naturally enough, the *Horace Mann* decision sent a shudder through the entire Catholic higher-education establishment. The Supreme Court's refusal to review the case did deny force to the decision outside the State of Maryland. But even so, courts in other states could find its rationale persuasive and its tests of "legal sectarianism" handy ones. If this happened, then those states would prohibit their own agencies from distributing federal funds to Catholic institutions, thereby killing millions of dollars' worth of indirect federal aid. Moreover, until *Tilton v. Finch* offered both sides a welcome new chance at Supreme Court adjudication, the *Horace Mann* case was the leading recent case on the issue. As professionals, the lawyers for the Catholic colleges and for religious orders could only counsel their clients to prepare for the worst. This helps to explain the 1967 wave of laicizations in college and university governing boards. Whatever its other overtones, practical and spiritual, laicization was the response to a legal threat that showed no signs of blowing over.

In *Tilton v. Finch*, the legal strategy of the defendant Connecticut colleges is best described in football terms as an end run. Instead of challenging directly the stringent test of sectarianism in *Horace Mann*, the defendants are claiming that another, more realistic test has been developed. In Wilson's words:

> That test requires that, when a statute is challenged on Establishment Clause grounds, there be "a secular legislative purpose and a primary effect that neither advances nor inhibits religion." [The] test was most recently applied by the Supreme Court in 1968—in the case of *Board of Education v. Allen*—when it upheld New York's textbook loan law, and we . . . contend that test is dispositive of the Establishment Clause issue in *Tilton*. . . .
>
> In the *Allen* case, the Supreme Court ruled that church-related schools perform two functions, religious instruction and secular education, [and] that what the Establishment Clause prohibits is involvement by the government with religious instruction . . .

By this logic, a federal grant to a church-related college is constitutional as long as the money is used for facilities or programs which are non-religious in nature.

As a second line of argument, the defendants in *Tilton v. Finch* are urging that the criteria used to test sectarianism in the *Horace Mann* case are "unwieldy and unmanageable . . . and produce a misdirected inquiry." If the courts must ascertain whether a given institution is primarily educational or primarily religious, "the only proper criteria to consider are whether the college is accredited, whether the college is open to persons of all religious faiths, and whether the college fosters an atmosphere of academic freedom comparable to that existing at non-church-related colleges."

So it seems that in due course the Supreme Court will be solemnly asked to decide whether a church-run institution can offer unbiased instruction in secular subjects or whether the ancient urge to proselytize will somehow always prevail. To me, this question is an absurd one to ask about the Catholic Church in America. Given our society (and given also what we've learned about ecclesiastical economics), I frankly disbelieve that the church possesses either the resources or the willingness to try to transform today's college students into a race of converts. Further, while some Americans undoubtedly do believe that only propaganda, never truth, will be taught in a classroom where there's a crucifix on the wall, I'm not of their number. Therefore, to editorialize, in my opinion both sides would do best to abandon their legal charades. Opponents of federal aid should give up the attempt to devise criteria by which "sectarianism" can be objectively measured. The church itself should call a halt to pretended laicizations (though not to genuine divestitures based on internal economic need). And if institutions—whether Catholic or Baptist or Methodist or Lutheran—satisfy government-imposed standards of academic quality and fiscal responsibility, federal funds should be made available to them.

CHAPTER FIFTEEN

The Religious Orders: The Fight for Survival

This long discussion of laicization and the battle for federal aid, although vital, has led us away from our major theme, the economies of the religious orders themselves. It's time, I think, to return to that theme. The laicization of their institutions, however momentous, is only one of the many moves the orders are making in their private struggle for material survival. In the wake of the Second Vatican Council—and under the external economic pressures we've been measuring all along—the religious orders are already doing what the diocesan church has thus far refused to do. They are transforming themselves from within; and the main concern of even conservative leaders is that change is coming too slowly. Yet one of the first things to change has

347

been the concept of leadership. To choose just a few examples from a file brimming over:

- In September, 1968, the Daughters of the Sacred Heart of Jesus and Mary of Wheaton, Illinois, voted to end the pyramidal structure of authority in favor of government by "group consensus." Explained Sister Dolorine, the provincial of the 400-member congregation, "from now on, [we] will be structured as a circle with all members at the same level." The move had the approval of the general directress of the German-based order, Sister M. Aristilde Flake.

- At a general chapter held in Villanova, Pennsylvania, the 600-year-old Order of St. Augustine adopted as an official policy a pledge to "become more active and more aggressive in pursuit of peace and justice." Among other changes in its constitution, the order approved the shortening of the ninety-minute-a-day Divine Office.

- In June, 1970, the Very Reverend John F. Fitzgerald bowed out as superior general of the Paulist Fathers. His post will be abolished, and the Paulists will elect an eleven-man council headed by a president to direct the order. The 260-man order also established a three-man mediation committee to arbitrate disputes between superiors and subordinates.

In sum, the religious orders are striving to switch from authoritarianism to democratic forms of government. The surprising fact, I think, is that so many of them are succeeding.

At the same time, the orders know that they must free themselves from archaic notions of religious economics and set up viable new economic structures. And this aspect of their struggle is proving nightmarishly difficult. To understand why, we should first piece together a complete picture of the old system of monastic economics, the system which still rules the minds of many religious administrators. In point of fact, the system is a composite. Every one of today's religious orders owes its economic structure to a blend of differing economic ideals. None of these ideals is new: the oldest, Benedictinism, is actually sixteen centuries old. But all are still important. Therefore, let's consider the economics of Benedictinism, of Franciscanism and of monastic life after the Council of Trent.

St. Benedict, who was really the founder of monasticism in the West, called for a life of work and of prayer; and by work he meant primarily agricultural labor. From the fifth century until now, Benedictine monasticism has been based on his pastoral economic ideal, that of the monastery as a self-sustaining economic microcosm, a little world based on tillage and on the care of flocks and herds. Indeed, we might define all Benedictine monks as voluntary serfs bound to the land. Even today, their labor is intended only to support them and to supply as well the few exterior requirements of the community. Any surpluses are either bartered for the few implements the monastery workshops cannot produce or else used for expansion.

To say the least, the economics of a St. Francis were— and are—very different. Where the Benedictine was a farmer, the Franciscan was a beggar. Where the Benedictine cultivated the fruits of the earth for the glory of God, the Franciscan accepted from the charitable what little he himself needed. Anything extra he either gave at once to others or turned over to the Franciscan community. Only as the order established itself did this simple mendicancy evolve into something more formal and more sophisticated: fund-raising. In time, this ritualized begging became the Franciscan mainstay. Today's raffles and bazaars, gift-seeking and legacy-hunting may seem light-years distant from Assisi. Nevertheless, the religious orders and the diocesan church owe to the Franciscans the idea that charity—

unbudgetable and unpredictable, yet unfailing—should be the basis of the ecclesiastical economy.

The Counter Reformation of the sixteenth century brought with it a great wave of monastic reform. And with reform came a new concept of religious economics. For the Jesuits, the Vincentians and the other newly founded orders, the Catholic monastic should be a trained specialist. Whether as a teacher, a doctor or nurse or a propagandist for the faith, his skills were of great economic value to society. By offering the skills of their members in return for money enough to survive, the orders reasoned that they would be rendering the maximum possible service to the church, to the laity and to God. This distinctively modern emphasis on the sale of services is part of the philosophy of most religious orders today. Yet, contemporary monastic economics still owes far too much to the older Benedictine and Franciscan theories.

Although life close to the soil may be just as pleasing to God today as it was four centuries after Christ, in economic terms Benedictinism—at least in this country—is obsolete. In an era when the small farm is vanishing, the religious community that ties up its capital in farmland, agricultural equipment and livestock is courting economic disaster. Even with the advantage of its "slave labor," the monastic farm is a drain on the resources of the community. Yet dozens of these farms are still being operated today. In most cases, the monastery farm barely yields produce or fruit or dairy goods enough to supply the community itself, with perhaps a few bushels of apples left over for Father Superior to present to the local bishop. On this scale, the economics of farming are such that the community would do better to buy at the supermarket. Granted, there are some exceptions. With his usual testiness, Martin A. Larson "exposes" in his book a number of the most ambitious agricultural operations of the religious orders. These range from jellymaking (the Trappists) and breads (the Benedictines) to ranching (Benedictine "cowboy monks" run 500 head of cattle on 2,300 monastic acres near Aspen, Colorado). Larson's allegations to the contrary, however, these efforts are more picturesque than they are profitable. Today, most of them, including the Benedictine ranch, do well to break even.

Only in California, where the religious orders have become vintners, do the economics of Benedictinism pay off. From Los Gatos, the Jesuits bottle and market their Novitiate brand of altar wine with fair financial success. The returns make the Jesuit novitiate economically self-sustaining. The Christian Brothers have become even more successful, as the largest producer of brandy in the U. S. Their wineries yield a before-tax income of close to $4 million a year.*

But these *are* exceptions. So unremunerative has monastic agriculture become today that a number of the orders are closing down their farms and selling off the property. For example, the Clerics of St. Viator, a 100-man community, owns 80 acres of prime land in Arlington Heights, Illinois, a Chicago suburb. Until 1965, about half of the property served as a truck-farm for the novitiate. But the manpower shortage took its toll, and in June, 1970, the Viatorians were getting ready to develop the property as a commercial housing project. In an even more striking instance, the five priests and three brothers who make up the entire membership of the Order of Carthusians in this country have reached the same decision. With the enthusiastic endorsement of Père André Poisson, minister-general of the Carthusians, these agrarian monks abandoned farming in 1970. In the spring of that year, they hired a New York realty consultant to help them develop their property in Arlington, Vermont, into a modern ski resort.

* After a hard-fought court battle, the Christian Brothers lost the tax exemption on income from their wineries in 1959, on the ground that they were not a priestly but a lay order.

Like pure Benedictinism, Franciscan mendicancy as a way of life has all but vanished from the church. The few orders which still station their members in public places to beg alms from the passers-by do so more as a gesture to tradition (or as a penance) than as a serious attempt to gather money. But other forms of fund-raising are almost as primitive as begging and are as inefficient economically. And these are still being pursued by many orders. Thus, for a modest fee, Catholic religious install, stock and replenish the racks of pious pamphlets to be found in countless parish churches. The gift shops which cluster around Catholic shrines are very often operated by religious for the benefit of their local institutions. Almost every day, devout Catholics receive in the mail dispirited little brochures offering for sale fruitcake or handmade lace or flowery renderings of prayers. Communities of priests and of nuns are the senders. Catholics in particular are outraged by these commercializations of the faith.

But far worse than commercialization is the waste of manpower on projects so unproductive at a time when manpower is in desperately short supply.

To make the point that even a flourishing monastic economy is in part the prisoner of the economic past of the church, we need an example that can be studied in detail. Let's therefore turn to the Marianist Province of Cincinnati.

The Marianists, or Brothers of Mary (not to be confused with the Marian Fathers or with the Marist Fathers, two entirely separate orders), are one of the larger religious orders. In 1970, a membership of 529 priests and 2,905 lay brothers ranked the Marianists 22nd in size among all Catholic orders. More than one-third of this membership (241 priests, 1,070 brothers) is concentrated in the United States. The order is a young one as orders go; it was founded in France in 1817 by Père William-Joseph

Chaminade, an intense priest caught up in the struggles of the church during the Revolution and the Napoleonic regime. Father Chaminade's ideas of what the Marianists should be were all-encompassing and just a bit obscure. He apparently saw his order as forming the nucleus of a network of lay organizations. These literary, educational and political fraternities, their official Catholic status a secret to outsiders, were to constitute an underground church in the bitterly anticlerical Europe of the day. It does seem as if Chaminade had in mind an idealized, even a romanticized version of the Society of Jesus, minus the Jesuit authoritarianism which he personally detested. But this is hard to demonstrate. In any event, the Continent in the early nineteenth century was a jungle of secret societies, cabals and lodges or social clubs set up to mask revolutionary (and counter-revolutionary) plotting. The heady atmosphere of intrigue would have been inspiration enough for an eager conspirator on the side of the church.

Whatever Chaminade's dreams for the Marianists, the realities turned out to be both prosaic and traditional. Setting aside the visions of their founder (during the last years of his life, Chaminade was forbidden by Rome to play any part in the affairs of the order), the Marianists became missionaries and educators. Like so many other orders, they came to this country to preach and to set up an academy. And like so many other French orders, they migrated to the Ohio Valley region. In 1849, the Cincinnati Province was formally established. A year later, when the first four members of the province founded their academy in Dayton, the provincialate was moved to the smaller community, where it still remains.

The academy is now the University of Dayton, a major institution with a student body of 7,500 and a physical plant officially valued at more than $30 million. Nearly half of the 90 Marianist priests of the province, and about one-quarter of the 345 lay brothers, are involved in teaching and administration at the university. The university itself is a separate corporation. Unlike the Jesuits, and in a fashion even more conservative than that of the Holy Cross Fathers, the Marianists have retained legal ownership of the university property. But the avowed policy of the order is to vest operating control of the university in a mixed board of trustees. On the board, laymen, all of them Catholics, are in the majority.

As well as running their university, the Marianists of the Cincinnati province commit themselves heavily to secondary education. In Dayton, separate Marianist communities operate three of the Catholic high schools. Similar "houses" have been established in Memphis, Tennessee, Covington, Kentucky, Cleveland, Ohio, Pittsburgh, Pennsylvania and Kalamazoo, Michigan, to staff high schools in those cities. Following the pattern we recognize as typical, each of these communities is headed by a superior who reports to the provincial in Dayton. In 1970, the communities ranged in size from thirty members (St. Joseph High School in Cleveland) to ten members (Catholic High School in Memphis). Including the Marianist community at the University of Dayton, the province utilizes about three-quarters of its manpower in education.

But the Marianist fathers and brothers do much else besides. Their missionaries serve in eight foreign countries. So far-flung are the Marianist missions in Kenya, Nigeria and Malawi that the province shares with the three other U. S. Marianist provinces the cost of an air service to supply personnel and equipment. (In 1968–69, this Mission Air operation cost Cincinnati $7,869.34.) At home, the province must feed, house and educate its scholastics and its lay novices, perform the administrative services for its separate communities and handle the finances of an organization with a total net worth of close to $45 million. These operations are complex ones. The two senior executives of the province, the Very Reverend William Ferree, S. M., the provincial, and Brother William A. Bruggeman, S. M., the treasurer, have done their best to instruct me in the mysteries of the internal administration of the province.

From the financial reports Brother Bruggeman made available, I learned that the University of Dayton, evidently the exception among Catholic universities, was operating in the black. For the year ending June 30, 1969, its revenues from current sources totaled $22,240,699. Current expenditures came to $21,667,404, which left the university a surplus of $573,295. Outlays for renovations and unbudgeted expenditures for a new university computer center reduced this surplus to a bookkeeping deficit of $377,702, not enough to be disturbing.

According to the records, the Marianists are equally good at running high schools. In 1968-69, tuitions and fees of $1,294,065 more than covered the school operating expenses of $1,097,864. In the Catholic high school business today, a return of better than 15 per cent looks very good: indeed, almost too good. The figures puzzled me until I realized that out of the nine schools they operate, the Marianists actually own only one, Cathedral Latin High in Cleveland. The other eight belong to the diocesan school systems. This means that the bishops bear all plant expenses, including not only construction and maintenance costs but also the costs of the mortgages on the properties. Free from the burdens of realty ownership, the Marianists simply market their teaching manpower at a profit.

The Marianist educational activities are thus self-sustaining. And as we might expect, these activities bring in a substantial proportion of the income of the province itself. The financial statement of Marianists of Ohio, Inc. (the legal title of the province) reveals that in 1968–69, the Marianist teaching communities turned in to the provincialate $421,144.37, or about two-thirds of the total provincial income of $635,351.37. This sum was derived from assessments which in the high schools average about $800 per man, and which jump to $2,200 per man at the University of Dayton.

The province took in another $214,407 from such sources as fees for clerical services ($72,270.56), current donations ($17,094.09) and interest ($19,721.82) on a scholarship fund of about $400,000. This fund, and the income ($55,857.86) from an item listed on the statement as "Franklin Street," we'll consider a bit later.

Earlier, we saw that the Jesuits of the New York province spend nearly three-quarters of their income on the "upkeep of personnel in training." The Marianists, with a much smaller number of scholastics (75 to the Jesuits' 322 in 1970) must still lay out nearly 60 per cent of their revenues for the education and training of new members. In 1968-69, the operation of Marianist College, the scholasticate, and other houses of study cost the province $347,480, and another $73,866 was paid for the advanced studies of Marianist priests and brothers. Most other provincial expenditures follow on a more modest scale the pattern already familiar from our survey of the expenses of the Jesuits in New York. Administration, health care, aid to the one Marianist school and to other provinces and miscellaneous items all crowd the expense side of the ledger.

Unlike the Jesuits, however, the Marianists have pledged provincial as well as institutional income as security on debt. To build at Marianist College and at the University of Dayton, the province borrowed $712,000 from other Catholic institutions (via B. C. Ziegler & Co.). In addition, the Mount St. John Trust Fund, the Marianists' own endowment fund, was tapped for a loan of $442,946. And mortgages on several Marianist properties total $534,972. The interest on this long-term debt of nearly $1.7

million costs the province about $80,000 a year, or less than 5 per cent. Brother Bruggeman is far from unhappy about the price of the money. But he's not pleased that debt service costs equal about 12 per cent of operating income, or that total indebtedness has now reached a similar one-eighth of the province's assets of $14,126,538.* "We're retiring debt at the rate of about $50,000 a year," he said, "and we just can't seem to go any faster."

Despite their indebtednesses, and despite the rising costs which produced an operating deficit of $103,381 in 1968-69, the Marianists of Cincinnati are in much better health than are most other religious orders. In part, this strength is the product of the Marianist managerial philosophy. "We're not interested in owning property. We're not interested in being in the real estate business. Or in running companies." So Brother Bruggeman says, and I believe him.

Although he would never admit it, Brother Bruggeman has played a key role in modernizing the management of the province. "Things have changed," he says simply. "When I got here in 1958, we still had the old organization. There was an Office of Zeal to look after the missions, an Office of Education for the schools and the university, an Office of Temporalities to take care of business affairs. I became Director of Temporalities. Then there was Mount St. John. It was what we call a motherhouse, and everything was out there—the provincialate, the scholasticate, the novitiate, a retreat house for laymen. As part of the old process of self-sustenance, there was even a truck-farm on the place. But that's gone now."

Mount St. John is still the location of the scholasticate and a center of other Marianist activity. However, the novitiate has been relocated, and the provincialate has been moved to "High Acres," a magnificent mansion in a showcase residential section of Dayton. The luxuriousness

* Exclusive of the assets of the University of Dayton.

of High Acres, indeed, is something of an embarrassment to the Marianists. The house, with its acres of gardens, was a gift to the province from the Rikes family of Dayton industrialists and retail merchants. It possesses all the serenity that Catholic religious could ask for. Its size, moreover, permits High Acres to be used both as a business office and as a residence for the seventeen members of the staff of the provincialate. "Our neighbors have accepted us," I was told during my visit. But some of the younger members of the order are evidently less accepting than the neighbors. They question the appropriateness of so lavish a headquarters for a group sworn to poverty, and the upkeep of the property (which runs to nearly $25,000 a year) seems to them very expensive. "We'll have to make a decision on this issue some day," Brother Bruggeman says, "but we're fortunate to have the use of so fine a place for the time being at least."

As an aside, let me add that if anyone thinks so much luxury has affected the Marianists, he should share a meal with the residents of High Acres. Served cafeteria-fashion, luncheon on the day of my visit consisted of a good, nourishing soup, a helping of Spam, a hot-dog roll (the cook makes a point of economizing by buying day-old baked goods), a piece of fruit and plenty of Kool-Aid. Nobody went hungry, but nobody feasted, either.

When Brother Bruggeman mentioned the Office of Zeal, my curiosity was naturally aroused and I pressed him for more details. The old-fashioned name of this Marianist department has been changed to Marianist Missions, Inc. But the function of the department, mission support, is still the same. Marianist Missions, Inc., is a piece of Franciscanism in action, and, unlike the truck garden at Mount St. John, which represented Benedictinism, this Franciscan economic effort is still prospering. I find the mission organization's blend of ancient ideals and modern techniques both fascinating and revealing. To finance their mission endeavors, the Marianists of Ohio combine religion and direct-mail advertising in a successful fund-raising business. In 1968-69, this enterprise netted the order nearly $400,000.

To the tens of thousands of lay Catholics on their mailing lists, the Marianists address several different types of messages. To one group, they offer "spiritual bouquets," printed leaflets of special prayers much in favor among the devout of a generation or two ago. These are mailed out at Christmas, at Easter and at other times during the religious year. The recipients are asked to make contributions by return envelope to the Marianist Mission Fund. A second and larger group is invited to enter a "spiritual alliance" with the Marianists. Remembrance in the prayers of mission priests is promised and regular contributions are requested. Still another group is invited to send Mass intentions in to the order.* These are forwarded to a Marianist brother at Mount St. John. After recording the amounts received, he in turn forwards a check for the total to the Marianist Procurator General in Rome. The money is then distributed to the various mission areas.

From contributions (including interest on a cash account of nearly $125,000), Marianist Missions, Inc., realized $1,462,402 in 1968-69. In addition, Mass stipends and special gifts, both designated as restricted income, brought in $57,445. So the total receipts of this enterprise equaled $1,519,847.

To operate it, the Marianists have put together their own mail-order house, with a lay staff of fifty-five persons. The total payroll is nearly $200,000. On postage, materials and printing, the mission organization spends another

---

* In Catholic theology, a Mass intention (more accurately, a "special intention") is simply the spiritual purpose to which the celebrating priest dedicates the Mass. Any Catholic may ask a priest to offer the Mass for any good intention. Among priests, the term has taken on the additional meaning of a financial contribution for the furtherance of a religious cause. After deducting his personal stipend, the priest must pass on this contribution to those raising funds for the cause.

$590,000 a year. Total expenditures in 1968-69 were $1,126,738, leaving a net "profit" of $393,108. Except for a sum changing hands as rent (the $55,857.86 "Franklin Street" item mentioned on p. 356), the province itself receives none of this mission money. The funds are pooled with other trust funds of the order—one of Brother Bruggeman's fiscal innovations—and are dispensed at the discretion of the trustees of the mission corporation. Most of the money is spent the year after it is received on budgeted mission activity.

Despite the current success of this venture in Franciscanism, the Marianists are aware of its limitations. "Spiritual bouquets" are no longer a major source of support, and direct appeals for aid to the missions are gradually supplanting the indirect appeal tied to the religious theme. Moreover, operating costs are rising. Increases in postage rates and in the wages of lay employees will cut into the net receipts of the mission corporation. Brother Bruggeman can foresee the day when the direct-mail plea, like the home-grown vegetable, will cost more than it's worth. "At that point," he says, "we'll shut it down. But we still have a long way to go."

The Marianists, then, refuse to be trapped by economic tradition. Their means of escape are the hard-headed insistence on selling services and the willingness to innovate. For instance, consider investment-making. Until the late 1960's, the provincial administration did with the restricted funds of the province much what the Ordinaries of the diocesan church still do with their various trust funds. Each fund was isolated from the others and its principal invested (or banked) independently. To cut down the cost of managing the money, Brother Bruggeman devised the idea of a common investment fund. Called the Mount St. John Trust Fund, this fund now holds about $1 million worth of capital from several sources. The first of these Brother Brugge-man calls simply the "brothers' patrimony."

As we noted earlier, the religious who takes the simple vow of poverty does not relinquish all of his rights to property. He may still legally own or inherit it. And while he must relinquish the usufruct of the property, he may do so in favor of his religious order. Because this happens frequently, the canonists have carefully regulated the transaction: the church wants no lawsuits or claims by outsiders that a religious order has bilked them of property. So if a religious assigns to his order the usufruct of what he owns, the order in turn is canonically obliged: a) to preserve intact the value of the property; and b) to return the property to the individual (or pay him the equivalent in cash) if he ever leaves the order. As a further safeguard of the individual's property rights, most orders forbid members who take simple vows to make absolute gifts of their property to the order. Only after the death of the member will the order accept as a bequest the legal title to the property.

A trust arrangement is the legal answer for the problem of assignments of usufruct. Over the years, lawyers for the church have designed such trusts to conform with the civil laws of the states, and church officials take them for granted. Every religious order has its special trusts for the patrimony of its members, and the Marianists are no exception.

The Mount St. John Trust Fund also holds the money given or bequeathed to the order for the support of Marianist College, the provincial seminary. And mission funds (including restricted gifts to Marianist Missions, Inc.) are part of the pooled capital. Approximately half of the total assets of the fund ($442,946) have been borrowed by the provincialate, presumably to meet construction expenses at Mount St. John itself. About $500,000 more of the fund's money is now in the hands of Frank Cummings, the Dayton manager of Merrill, Lynch, Pierce, Fenner & Smith. For additional investment advice, Brother Bruggeman retains Scudder, Stevens & Clarke.

The Marianists are obviously practical men about their investments. And in budgeting and financial management, the provincialate is now beginning to demand of the separate teaching and mission communities the same unvarnished efficiency that it is achieving at High Acres. In these areas, much of the detail work is done by Brother Bruggeman himself. For instance, the budget manual used by each of the nine school administrators is his own personal production, as are the forms and records that accompany the manual. Similarly, the provincialate began in 1969 to insist on receiving periodic expense account reports from members on individual assignments.

But no matter how devoted to good management a treasurer may be, the endorsement must also come from the top, and Brother Bruggeman is lucky in his superior. Father Ferree, the provincial, is not only an experienced administrator in his own right ("I was a Vatican bureaucrat for years," he told me), but a management theorist of no small proportions. In fact, he is now assembling the materials for a treatise of management ethics, one volume of which, *Administration and Social Ethics*, is being used as a text at the University of Dayton. A comment or two from this work gives a good idea of Father Ferree's attitudes toward his own trade.

For a variety of reasons, Father Ferree writes, the administrators of religious communities have failed to benefit from "the remarkable development of administrative theory in the present century." So old and so stable are the religious orders that their leaders feel they "can afford to be independent of the fashions of the moment." Besides, the real managerial revolution has occurred in business and in military activity, fields remote from the concerns of Catholic religious leaders.

> There are also certain psychological hazards . . . which a large number of religious administrators seem unable to outmaneuver. Some exhibit a curious inability to distinguish between "supernatural motives" and incompetence: the less reasoned, planned, and technically competent a decision is, the more they seem tempted to regard it as "supernaturally" oriented! . . .
>
> Some superiors nourish . . . a kind of detestation for "machinery" in matters which touch the human personality very closely, and profess to be staunch defenders of what they identify as "the liberty of the spirit." Certainly, no one can quarrel with such sentiments, so they must be honorable men. In point of fact, however, no one is bothered about their sentiments: it is their intelligence which is in question. . . .

From the tone of these passages, it's obvious that Father Ferree disapproves of sloppy administration, especially when better techniques are ready at hand. Father Ferree points out that Catholic orders involved in educational and hospital administration possess in their own institutions models to study. However, the superiors of the orders seem unable to apply to provincial or even general administrations the lessons they learn from institutional management. "One often gets the impression," Father Ferree concludes, "that provincial and general administrators are largely reduced to answering their daily mail!"

When an insider delivers a rebuke so stinging, we do well to pay special attention; and I for one suspect that Father Ferree has put his finger on exactly the tenderest issues of Catholic ecclesiastical management. But Father Ferree has in mind something more to the point than a scolding. He believes that, in this century, the mission of the church is broadening and shifting, becoming less institutional and more personal.* Efficient management of the existing system, however desirable it may once have been, is no longer enough of a goal. As well as improving economic administration to suit the needs of a church now pressed for men and money, those who run church organizations today must learn also how to nurture change.

In Father Ferree's own province, the administration feels well able to do in practice what its chief executive officer sees as vitally necessary. And the Marianists, their economy under control, are making radical changes. For example, no longer must all the members of a Marianist community dwell in one residence. Instead, small groups of members may move into separate apartments, coming together only on special occasions. Far more than an outsider can possibly imagine, changes like this one alter the routines of monastic life. But the sense of mission remains. "The high-rise apartments for the aged, and those fancy new singles apartments, are the ghettos of twenty years from now," Brother Bruggeman says. "We're moving into them today to be able to help when we're needed."

At Mount St. John, the Marianists are setting up a series of "experimental apostolates." One of these is an instruction center for Catholic business executives. Another is the Bergamo Conference bureau. Named for the birthplace in northern Italy of Pope John XXIII, the annual Bergamo Conferences bring together Catholic religious, diocesan clergy, Catholic laymen and the members of other faiths. "We frankly don't know what will emerge from Bergamo," Brother Bruggeman told me. "But we do know we must try for this type of dialogue."

Not every religious order is as confident as the Marian-

---

* Father Ferree would state, I'm sure, that these shifts are in fact a return to earlier ideals (for instance, of Father Chaminade's) which the church, imperfect as it always is, then lacked the skills to recognize or to administer.

ists of Ohio that the call for renewal can be answered. Faced with the need to change, some of the orders are calling general and provincial chapter meetings, setting up committees, appointing study groups and attempting to change from within. Others are turning to the outside "professionals," the management consultants. And in the most curious development of all, new types of consulting enterprises are springing up to specialize exclusively in the problems of religious orders. These hybrids are alliances between Catholic ecclesiastical organizations and lay management engineers.

One such mixed partnership involves the Catholic Education Research Center (CERC), an organization formed in 1967 at Boston College, and The Stanwyck Corporation, a Washington, D. C., research and development outfit. CERC itself has a mixed staff of lay and religious consultants. Stanwyck had done $17 million worth of secular consulting work, mostly for the Department of Defense. This odd organizational team is now busily selling its services to an eager but uninformed market, the religious orders of women. The standardized proposal CERC-Stanwyck presents to prospective clients explains management consulting in terms deemed simple enough for nuns to understand.

> In the same manner as the radio repairman examines the subsystems [the tuner, amplifier and speaker of a radio] to determine malfunction and then proceeds to the component level [the tubes, resistors, circuits and chassis], the systems approach to management considers the . . . subsystems described later in the proposal.

If CERC-Stanwyck succeeds in selling a full-scale study, the client is promised information about eight areas: 1) objectives, 2) organization, 3) communications, 4) finances, 5) personnel, 6) efficiency, 7) physical facilities and 8) "internal and external environmental factors." A completed CERC-Stanwyck study is an impressive-looking document.

For instance, the study completed recently, for the Dominican Congregation of St. Catharine of Siena contains nine chapters and eight appendices and weighs nearly four pounds. Unfortunately, the report is written in a language so full of ecclesiastical jargon on the one hand and management gibberish on the other that its recommendations, some of them useful, are lost in a jungle of verbiage. As a matter of interest, the report does note that budgeting and auditing procedures are nonexistent and investment management primitive in the 750-member order, even though the sisters own assets of more than $13 million and bring in nearly $3 million a year.

In another study, independent researchers George F. Madaus and Patricia J. Fontes analyze the Sisters of Providence, a medium-sized order (four provinces, 1,465 members) which specializes in parochial education. Called a self-study, this report is based on a long but expertly prepared questionnaire completed by 89 per cent of the membership. Among its more dramatic findings:

- over one-third of the sisters feel themselves inadequately trained to give religious instruction;
- 25 per cent of the sisters feel that the religious vows, as practiced today, are meaningless in the twentieth century;
- 54 per cent feel that the Catholic parish (in which most sisters are located as teachers) fails to meet the needs of today's church;
- 32 per cent feel that parish priests do not understand Catholic education.

The report recommended modest but important changes in administrative practice, recruiting and internal communications.

Other consultants, of varying abilities and reputations, have also scented the presence of this big new market for their services. Among the smaller firms, Knight, Gladieux

& Smith, Inc. is promoting itself as a specialist in ecclesiastical economics. Heald, Hobson & Associates is acting as consultant to half a dozen orders on the reorganization of their college administrations. Of the nationally known consultants, McKinsey & Co., Inc. has done management analyses for the Jesuits. Cresap, McCormick and Paget, Inc. completed in December, 1969, a massive study of the government and resources of three provinces of the Religious of the Sacred Heart of Mary.

The details the consultants collect vary sharply from order to order. But in each of the dozens of reports I've read, the conclusions are virtually identical. According to the management experts, the Catholic orders badly need: a) more vigorous leadership; b) better communications between the rank and file and the executives; c) better lateral communications between provinces; d) more efficient fiscal procedures; e) professionalized recruiting and personnel policies; and f) better planning for the future. The same could be said, of course, for every other human enterprise. And the religious superiors who commission the consultants are quite aware that the reports finally submitted will be filled with precisely these pious generalities. Of the elaborate study lying on her desk, the provincial of one New York-based order said to me: "We knew everything they were going to tell us. But some of our people had to hear the bad news from an outsider."

Another recurrent comment on the abilities of the consultants is: "They did as well as they could, but no one outside the church can really understand how a religious order works." There's some truth in this statement. For any exponent of rational management, it's often frustrating (and sometimes impossible) to urge reason upon an organization which, responding at any hour to an inner command, may choose instead to do something gloriously irrational. More serious, the consultants are by and large experts in corporate reorganization. But Catholic religious today are not simply seeking counsel on reorganization. They're asking for help with a revolution. Not too many management engineers feel at home on the barricades.

Nevertheless, the religious superior is learning some useful lessons from the paid outsider. First, he's discovering how little he really knows about his own organization. The information famine of which we spoke in our survey of the diocesan church is no less critical among the religious orders. Indeed, because the communities of the orders are so widely diffused, the shortage of information is likely to be much more critical. Inexact as are the methods by which the consultants gather information, at least these methods do yield some data: about finances; about the relationships between the order and the outside world; about the personal feelings of individual religious. For the superior today, imperfect information is infinitely better than none.

Secondly, the consultant is teaching the superior that the problems of running a religious order, even in the midst of a revolution, are not unsolvable. The outsider may not know how a community of hundreds of priests or nuns or brothers *should* be governed. But his insistence that it *can* be governed is a tonic for the hard-pressed provincial or superior-general. More than anything else, I think, this message of cheer is what earns the consultant every penny of his substantial fee.

Given the gravity of the crises afflicting the orders, is this optimism at all justified? As we've seen, most of the orders have abandoned the romantic economics of Benedictinism; and many are too proud to beg shrewdly. If they divest themselves of their institutions and rely entirely on marketing their skills and services, will they be able to survive? My own answer to this key question is a cautious yes. Despite the odds against them, I think the orders will survive. In the complex situation we've been studying, some factors do seem to be working in favor of the orders.

First of all, the orders possess material assets which obviously do serve as a buffer against blows to their economies. And here we can appropriately ask: how much are these assets worth? Neither in magnitude nor in dollar value do the holdings of the 611 religious orders compare with those of the diocesan church in the U. S., which in Chapter Twelve, I estimated as being $26 billion. The sheer bulk of the real estate the bishops hold in their 18,000 parishes assures the diocesan church of supremacy in total church wealth. Nevertheless, the orders are collectively worth a great deal of money. We can best discover how much by dividing their holdings into two sectors, public and private.

In the *public* sector are the public institutions owned or controlled by the orders. In 1971, this list included 206 colleges and universities, 37 junior colleges, 817 high schools, 346 elementary schools, 764 general hospitals, 200 orphanages and 250 homes for the aged. By putting together information from such official sources as the college accrediting agencies, the American Hospital Association and the private schools associations, it's possible to fix fairly exactly the financial standings of these public institutions. According to the most recent figures, colleges and universities controlled by religious orders possess land, plant and equipment worth $1,993,039,675, and endowment funds totaling $296,144,139, for an asset total of almost $2.3 billion.

The voluntary private hospitals of the country control assets worth $15 billion. Hospitals owned by Catholic religious orders account for 30 per cent of this total, or $4.5 billion.

The high schools and the elementary schools I estimate as being worth approximately $520 million. Other institutions (with less elaborate physical plants) can be valued at $80 million. The public institutions of the religious orders are therefore worth about $7.4 billion.

As *private* holdings of the religious orders, we can list first the institutional properties the orders maintain for their own use. These include the provincialates, novitiates and community houses of every one of the 484 orders of women, 103 orders of priests and 24 orders of brothers in the U. S. The total number of such residential and administrative properties is at least 3,000. (Note, however, that of the 161,000 nuns in this country, 85,000 are teaching nuns. Most of these sisters live in convents owned by the parishes in which they teach.)

Also included are the training centers of the religious orders, the seminaries and scholasticates. In 1971, these numbered 383. And we should add to the list as well the commercial properties owned by some of the order: the wineries, dairies, bakeries, farms, gift shops and other businesses.

The private holdings of the orders also include cash and investments. As we've seen, a provincialate is a financial headquarters. There, the provincial and his treasurer control those funds used for training, for missionary work and for other internal activities. On a typical provincial statement of finances, such capital funds are classified as "current" or operating funds; as "agency" funds held for the colleges, hospitals or communities to which they actually belong; and as "special" funds for retirement, insurance, patrimony and education. Any stocks or bonds owned by a religious order are purchased from these funds. And investments made by the province are kept strictly separate from the invested endowment funds of the institutions controlled by the province. This means, for example, that the $5.9 million endowment of Fordham University is invested entirely independently of the $16 million fund controlled by the New York Province of the Jesuits, with which Fordham is affiliated. As in the Catholic diocese, financial administration in the religious order is totally decentralized.

In this private sector, comprehensive information about the holdings of the religious orders is almost impossible to assemble. So numerous are the orders, and so decentralized is each one, that generalization from even a fair-sized sample of data becomes risky. But from the financial reports of thirty-four of the religious orders, I found one point in particular both logical and enlightening: the assets of provincial institutions are always far greater than the assets held by the provinces themselves. This certainly is true of the Marianists. And it's true also of the New York Province of the Jesuits. There, in fact, the total asset values of the four colleges and the nine high schools affiliated with the province come to $125.5 million, a figure which is nearly eight times as great as the value of the assets controlled directly by the provincialate.

In sum, I think it's safe to assume that the private holdings of the orders account for not much more than 10 per cent of the total holdings of the orders. If we could somehow add together the values of all the houses, seminaries, farms and stocks and bonds of the orders across the country, these might be worth as much as $750 million. Perhaps $150 million of this total is held in cash and securities. The final total of the assets of the orders, according to my reckoning, is thus 8.2 billion.

Better deployment of the private-sector assets just mentioned would obviously aid the orders in weathering their current crises. Indeed, the management consultants are urging on religious orders such drastic measures as the liquidation of under-utilized real estate assets and the formation of pooled investment funds. But even without making optimum use of their capital, the religious superiors can be certain that bankruptcy is no threat.

On the question of survival, another economic truth may prove more important than this backlog of cash. Ironically, the shortage of manpower which poses the gravest threat to the old monastic system is in some measure an actual benefit to the new. Because nuns, religious priests and brothers are so scarce, the orders can demand—for the first time in monastic history—realistic prices for the services of their members. In the Catholic colleges, universities, hospitals and private schools, there's a good chance today that such demands will be met. In the parochial schools, as we'll see in the next chapter, this issue is very much more in doubt. If the pastors and the bishops are forced to pay the same wages to teaching sisters that they pay their lay teachers, then the economic crisis in parochial education will turn into an economic collapse. Yet the salaries of the teaching nuns in the parochial school systems have been inching upward. And if state aid to parochial education ever does become a reality, then wage parity between lay and religious teachers will almost certainly be the end result.

Another factor working in favor of economic survival is that the existing manpower of the orders possesses skills of a very special kind. Nowhere else in our national labor force is there another group so large, so well trained and so eager to do work with the poor, the disadvantaged, the handicapped and the ill.

Our society has committed itself to the costly struggle against these social ills. The Catholic Church is already a leading ally of government in the welfare effort now being undertaken on a national scale. In some urban areas, for example, 50 per cent or more of all federal antipoverty programs are being run by church organizations. Over the next decade, I expect to see this alliance between the religious orders and the secular welfare establishment grow stronger still. Many of the orders now in teaching or in hospital work may well derive their future economic support from the sale of their services to secular welfare agencies.

Internal shifts in labor-pricing and the growth of new markets for the labor of religious do give the religious orders considerable hope for survival. But economic safety for the present membership of the orders obviously does not insure the long-term survival of monasticism itself. Economically, the best the orders can do today is to buy time: time enough to learn how monastic life can be made meaningful to newer generations. This will be the real test. For hundreds of years, Catholic monasticism has been a life lived in secret. By definition, the monastery—and the convent in particular—has been a *hortus conclusus*, a private garden. And private institutions today are not in favor with the young. Yet paradoxically, the positive values of lives lived in close community are openness, generosity and love. These virtues are highly prized by young men and young women today, and youngsters hunger for the sense of community so clearly gone from American culture. If the Catholic religious orders do open themselves outward and reject the old inhumane narrownesses, there could be another great resurgence of monasticism in the church. But whether or not this will happen, no one can say for sure.

A few pages ago, I mentioned the Religious of the Sacred Heart of Mary as being one of the many religious orders which have turned to the management consultants for aid. As an epilogue to everything we've seen of the orders and their problems, a brief look at this one order seems to me highly appropriate. For one thing, the order has gained the reputation of possessing great wealth. For another, its apostolic mission sets it apart. Founded in France in 1848, the Sisters of the Sacred Heart of the Immaculate Virgin Mary now numbers nearly 2,000 members. Its nine provinces and 95 communities are located in France, England, Ireland, Portugal, Brazil and Mozambique as well as in the United States. According to the official financial report, in 1969 the net worth of the order was $67,307,555.76 and its annual receipts totaled $20,525,407.79. About 55 per cent of the net worth and nearly 75 per cent of the income comes from the activities of the sisters in the U. S.

As we should expect by now, most of the assets are in the form of the land, buildings and equipment of the institutions owned by the order. But in exploring the details of the sisters' finances, I was intrigued to discover that the French Province lists among its other properties the Domaine of Bayssan-le-Hault, a producing vineyard. In 1969, its yield in grapes was "slightly deficient, because of a dryness which persisted from the spring right up to harvest time." Still, the order took in nearly $12,000 from the sale of its fine French wine.*

From the beginning, the apostolate of the RSHM sisters has been education of a special kind. In the delicate phrases of a report prepared by Cresap, Paget and McCormick:

> Programs and educational facilities [are] operated at the elementary, secondary and college levels. The persons to whom such education has been directed have had varied backgrounds, but there has been particular emphasis given to the education of those who might logically be expected to be future leaders and opinion-setters.

When I asked one of the RSHM sisters to interpret this mandarinese, she smiled and said, "It's just their way of telling us politely that we run schools for rich Catholic kids." This, certainly, is one of the things the sisters do. In New York, their Marymount School at 84th Street and Fifth Avenue is one of the two schools to which wealthy

---

* It may seem almost too symbolic of the passing of Benedictinism, but the manager of Bayssan-le-Hault reported to the generalate that he was counting on the money the government would pay for the land it needed to build the Béziers-Narbonne highway past the vineyard.

or socially aspiring Catholic families prefer to send their daughters. At Marymount (as at the even more exclusive Convent of the Sacred Heart, which is run by another order), parents can still be certain that young ladies are not only well taught but—only the French phrase will serve—*bien élevées*. From Marymount each year comes a cluster of the young "leaders and opinion-setters," the Dalys, Donahues, Ryans and Lenihans who make their debuts at the Gotham Ball and thereafter sparkle in Catholic society. (Of the Gotham Ball, a harmless enough Thanksgiving dance held for the benefit of the New York Foundling Hospital, one past participant still speaks with a shudder. "It was horrible. They dyed thousands of carnations a special red to match Cardinal Spellman's robes, and at midnight he popped through a screen of them to have us all kiss his ring.")

Some graduates of Marymount in New York will go on either to Marymount Manhattan College or to Marymount College in suburban Tarrytown. Similarly, well-to-do Catholic girls can attend Marymount schools and colleges in such other gilt-edged communities as Arlington, Virginia, Boca Raton, Florida and Palos Verdes Estates, California. In this country, the Religious of the Sacred Heart of Mary run five colleges and twenty-five private academies. The sisters also teach in twenty-two parochial schools. In addition, American members of the order conduct Marymount International Schools in Surrey (England), Neuilly (France) and Rome.

These nuns clearly pursue one of the most sophisticated apostolates Catholic religious life has to offer. But the RSHM sisters are anything but complacent about their proximity to wealth and status. And they're by no means rich themselves. According to the Cresap, Paget and McCormick report, which is thoroughly documented, "the financial situation [of the three American provinces studied] indicates a financial crisis of the most serious magnitude." While the consultants seem to have missed the fact, one big reason for the crisis is that the sisters are straining their resources to finance special works of charity. For instance, since 1966 the RSHM sisters on the staff of Marymount College in Boca Raton have given their summers to the service of "1,500 adult migrant workers and their families, making the complete facilities of the college available for these summer pilgrims who were not wanted in the 'Gold Coast' towns in Florida's vacationland." (I'm quoting the account of Sister Mary Hester Valentine in *The Post-Conciliar Nun.*) Other American members of the order are conducting a school for Italian children as an offshoot of the Marymount International School in Rome. Such special projects cost money. Given their manpower problems and the economic difficulties of operating their regular schools,* the RSHM nuns are foolish even to attempt these extra ventures. (Cresap, Paget and McCormick, in fact, want the sisters to close down their Boca Raton college and discontinue the Italian school.) But the nuns aren't in business to make money or to be prudent. "We have a witness," I was told, "and at whatever cost, we must live out our mission."

Their courage on major economic issues is matched by their hardheadedness on smaller matters of money. Almost by definition, nuns are good housekeepers. Thus, from Sister Michael, the treasurer of the Eastern American Province, I learned that there were economic reasons behind the modification (or the abandonment) of the traditional apparel of religious. "A nun's habit doesn't cost very much money," Sister Michael told me, "only $35 or $40 for the material.

---

* The Cresap, Paget and McCormick report reveals that new entrants in the New York Province and the Virginia and International vice-provinces had declined from seventy in 1960 to one in 1968. Three of the five colleges and four of the eleven schools of these areas suffered operating deficits in 1968.

In the days when you had to use wool from a black sheep, a habit cost even less. And of course, we do our own sewing and tailoring. But what you don't realize is that in every convent, two or three of the sisters had to spend hours of their time each week in washing, bleaching and ironing the linen, with every fold just so. We can't afford to do that kind of labor any more. If it weren't for wash-and-wear fabrics, almost no nuns would be wearing habits today. [Today, in fact, even the ruffs of the Swiss Guards at the Vatican are made of drip-dry Dacron.] And here we just decided to give up on the habit entirely."

Because this is an epilogue, we must foreshorten our view of the Religious of the Sacred Heart. We can barely take the time to meet Sister Jogues Egan, who was until July, 1970, the provincial of the Eastern American Province and whose governance of the sisters has (as one sister phrased it) "brought us into the twentieth century." Sister Jogues, a great crusader for educational reform among religious, made available to me the details of what she called "our sad story." But I'm unconvinced that the story will end sadly, because things do change in the church. As evidence, let me quote from the original constitution of this order.

> [Religious] will contract no intimate friendships with any person. Particular friendships are the bane of Communities. They give rise to divisions, parties, jealousies and rivalries, which quickly ruin the interior spirit and lead to the violation of all the vows.

And from the draft of what will eventually be the new constitution:

> We have gratefully accepted [chastity] of God, with full and mature consciousness of the dignity and sanctity of marriage. . . . However, this gift cannot be understood primarily in terms of personal sanctification. . . . Love for

Christ is reflected in personal relationships that give life to the community and are also a source of support and inspiration for each religious.

As I see it, the monastic revolution has only barely begun.

CHAPTER SIXTEEN

Who Should Support the Parochial Schools?

On December 7, 1884, the Third Plenary Council of the Roman Catholic hierarchy of the United States, meeting in Baltimore, ended its session. Headed by Archbishop (later Cardinal) James Gibbons of Baltimore, the council had been authorized by Pope Leo XIII to enact legislation suitable for the church in this country. All conciliar decrees had the force of law. One in particular was to shape the entire future of the Catholic Church in America. Its key clauses:

I. That near every church a parish school, where one does not yet exist, is to be built and maintained *in perpetuum* within two years of the promulgation of this council, unless the bishop should decide that because of serious difficulties a delay may be granted.

IV. That all Catholic parents are bound to send their children to the parish school, unless it is evident that a sufficient training in religion is given either in their own homes or in other Catholic schools . . .

This pronouncement placed the seal of orthodoxy on an educational effort already nearly a century old and already steeped in controversy. As far back as 1789, John Carroll, the first American Catholic bishop, had exhorted the 30,000 Catholics of the country to build schools for their children. In New York, the lay trustees of St. Peter's Church set up a parochial school in 1800. By 1806, 220 pupils were enrolled. Ironically, under the 1795 Act for the Encouragement of Schools, St. Peter's received from the New York City treasury a subsidy of $1,565.78.

But long before the Baltimore decree of 1884, Catholic parochial schools had ceased to benefit from public funds. Throughout the first half of the nineteenth century, as the idea of the public school gained support, elementary education became increasingly secularized. When religion was taught at all, it seemed to Catholics strongly Protestant in bias. And when no readings from the Bible or lessons in Christian doctrine were conducted, Catholics found the schools alarmingly godless. The bishops, the priests and the parents therefore wanted something different. Despite the internal struggles of the American hierarchy with lay trusteeism, despite a desperate shortage of qualified teachers and despite the withdrawal of local or state financial aid, dozens of parish schools had been built by 1840. But not until the brilliant, arrogant and demagogic Bishop John Hughes of New York entered the arena did the whole question of parochial education (and its cost) become a pressing public issue.

To the growing numbers of Irish Catholics in his see,

Bishop Hughes was the absolute embodiment of the ideal prelate: stern, austere and strict. And in the defense of his faith against insult and injury—whether real or imagined—Hughes was truly fanatical. Reasoning coldly that "whether we succeed or not in getting our portion of the public money, in all events the effort will cause an entire separation of our children from (the public) schools and excite greater zeal on the part of the people for Catholic education," in 1840 Hughes launched a venomous attack on the public schools of New York. These, he asserted, were hotbeds of anti-Catholicism. Before the Common Council of New York City, Hughes argued that because the public schools were filled with "influences prejudicial to our religion . . . to whose action it would be criminal in us to expose our children at such an age," Catholics needed their own schools. Catholic schools, moreover, were fully entitled to public financial support. Unmoved by this perverse plea, the Council turned down by a vote of 15 to 1 His Excellency's request for funds. So Hughes did what New Yorkers have done for generations. He took his case to the New York State Assembly. The charges and counter-charges exchanged between the bishop and his opponents in Albany contain more invective than they do good sense. But by the time Hughes had finished, he had his dearest wish. Catholics were indeed convinced that public schools —and public officials—were instruments of persecution. At whatever cost, parishioners would willingly establish their own schools.

But Hughes and the Catholic Church paid a bitter price for this victory. Hughes himself was thunderously articulate and a fearsome adversary in debate. On the basis of this one bishop's inflammatory utterances, non-Catholics found it easy to believe the very worst of their Catholic neighbors. In whipping up "greater zeal for Catholic education," Hughes had fanned as well the flames of Know-

Nothingism and bigotry. The resulting conflagration convinced him that his defensiveness was well-justified. As the anti-Catholic riots of the 1850's were to prove, Hughes had united his flock, but only by alienating it from the surrounding political and social community. On the issue which occasioned this separation, the education of children, the wounds have never really healed.

In education itself, the consequences were at once immediate and long-lasting. Into the Maclay education bill of 1842, the lawmakers of New York State wrote a bleak proviso. "No school . . . in which any religious sectarian doctrine or tenet shall be taught, inculcated or practiced" could receive financial aid from the state. In one form or another, such a provision found its way into subsequent school legislation in New York and into the education laws of most of the other states. All the while, Rome was watching. In 1875, the Sacred Congregation for the Propagation of the Faith, the Vatican body which then held sway over American church affairs, issued an instruction on Catholic education in this country. The wording reveals an almost frantic hostility to secular schooling. "It only remains, then, for the prelates to use every means in their power to keep the flocks committed to their care from the public schools." Across the United States, the response of politicians and voters was to enact constitutional amendments outlawing any state aid whatever to parochial schools.

And so, by the time the Third Plenary Council made canonically mandatory the establishment of parochial schools, paranoia had supplanted reason on both sides. The attitudes of Catholic Americans and of those who opposed their stand had congealed into forms which are all too recognizable today. On the Catholic side, there was contempt for the irreligion of the public schools, fear that such schools would cost Catholic children their faith, mistrust of the techniques used by public educators and resentment at being made to pay twice, as taxpayers and as Catholics, for the education of the young. On the non-Catholic side, there was healthy anger at the self-righteousness of prelates who spoke—or who could claim to speak—for all Catholics. But there was also neurotic suspiciousness of a "foreign" religion, morbid fear of a Catholic takeover of the public schools and dread of subsidizing religious indoctrination in the schoolroom.

In this already tainted atmosphere, the Baltimore decree of 1884 officially committed the church in America to a private struggle for educational betterment. The story of this struggle, for all that it contains unsavory episodes and inglorious chapters, is the story of a brave adventure against long odds. Indeed, though most Americans are unaware of the fact, the history of Catholic education in America is a singularly American success story, one that deserves a more detailed telling than we can give it here. But the Baltimore decree did much more than inspire this success. With its promulgation, an even greater educational opportunity disappeared. The decree muffled and eventually silenced those moderates within the church who spoke up for the reconciliation of Catholic and secular education in America. For instance, few Americans today have ever even heard of John Ireland, Archbishop of St. Paul, who in 1890 called the public schools "the pride and glory of America," and who set up successful experiments in co-operation between Catholic parishes and local boards of education. Instead of heeding Ireland, American Catholics, and non-Catholics as well, heard only the voice of Cardinal John Farley, Archbishop of New York, who declared in 1916:

> If the authorities of the city came to me and offered to maintain all my schools with city money on the conditions they would place on them, I would say: "I will have none

of your money"; I would say what was said to Judas when he came to give back the money he had received for betraying the Saviour: "Go to perdition with your money!"

The rhetoric of paranoia is strong rhetoric. Scores of speeches like Farley's have spurred on millions of Catholics to spend, to build and to sacrifice for an ideal of good schools which would also be Catholic schools. Since the days of the Baltimore pronouncement the urgings of the hierarchy have brought forth an educational system which, despite its backwardness and inwardness, still challenges the impersonality and rigidity of most public education today. Beyond any doubt, this system has strengthened in their faith the generations of Catholics who have grown up in our officially nonsectarian land. More than one pope has rightly labeled the parochial schools the crowning achievement of the church in America.

And yet, in terms of what could have been, the parochial education movement in this country has fallen tragically short of success. Because its exponents have been —and are still—as shortsighted as its most bigoted opponents, the system has long polarized the American community. Because its resources are in the final analysis limited, it has denied Catholic children the facilities, the equipment and the teachers all children need to learn about today's world. And as we're about to see, the staggering cost of maintaining this heroic but quixotic apostolate has now nearly crippled the Catholic ecclesiastical economy.

Today, not even the most complacent Catholic prelate dares to deny that parochial education is in deep trouble. On the contrary, the bishops are loudly proclaiming their difficulties to everyone who will listen; and their difficulties are grave. Because the Catholic Church is changing and opening outward, we all can hope that the voices of the Hugheses and the Farleys will be stilled forever. But the great questions still remain. What should Catholic Americans do about the educational system their fathers and grandfathers fought so hard to create? And how should those who are non-Catholics react to the crisis in Catholic education? By the end of this chapter, my own responses to the issues will be made quite clear; and so, perhaps, will some possible answers to the crisis itself. But first we must do here what we have so often done before, survey the scene to learn exactly what's happening in this particular economic sector.

Seen as a whole, the Catholic parochial school system is a formidable educational enterprise. According to *The Official Catholic Directory*, in 1970 the total number of parochial elementary schools in the 160 U. S. sees was 9,271. Parochial, interparochial and diocesan high schools totaled 1,189. In the elementary schools, the student population was 3,348,421; in the high schools, 658,122; for a total enrollment of 4,006,543.* All told, the parochial elementary schools hold almost exactly 10 per cent of the 36,542,000 schoolchildren under fifteen in he United States. About 5 per cent of this country's high school students attend Catholic diocesan high schools.

A few comparisons will illustrate the scope of this establishment. On the elementary level, the Roman Catholic parishes of the U. S. operate more than twice as many schools as there are public schools in all six New England states. Only in one state, New York, are there more public high schools than there are in the U. S. diocesan church. And in the Catholic parochial schools of America, student enrollment exceeds by nearly 10 per cent the total combined public-school population of Minnesota, Iowa, Missouri, Nebraska, Kansas and North and South Dakota.

Until 1970, no one could even guess how much money

---

* Independent of the diocesan church, the religious orders own and operate another 335 elementary schools and 765 high schools, with enrollments of 65,189 and 357,591, respectively. These figures are not included in the totals given for parochial-diocesan education.

it cost to operate these 10,460 Catholic schools. In his 1966 treatise *Costs and Benefits of Catholic Elementary and Secondary Schools*, Rev. Ernest Bartell, C.S.C., the Notre Dame priest-economist who comments frequently on church finance, complained that

> virtually no attempt has yet been made to gather the data and to provide the comprehensive and systematic analysis of costs and benefits of the Catholic schools that should be a prerequisite for reasonable and consistent educational policy decisions.

Elsewhere in his treatise, and also in the speeches he gives regularly, Father Bartell talks about "the three billion dollars spent annually on education by the American Church." But this is at best a guess, and one which apparently covers all Catholic education, parochial and non-parochial, from the school through the university. In a story headlined "Catholic Schools May Drop 2 Million Pupils," *The New York Times* (April 6, 1969) quotes "church officials" as saying that the parochial school establishment is a "$1.7-billion-a-year operation." The "officials" in question were probably one man, Msgr. James C. Donoghue, director of the Division of Elementary and Secondary Education of the United States Catholic Conference. But other USCC officials tell me that the figure reported by *The Times* was "just a ballpark estimate."

In December, 1970, however, an official estimate of the total outlays for Catholic elementary and secondary education in this country was made public for the first time. A report prepared by the National Catholic Education Association and financed by the Carnegie Corporation gave the 1969-70 total operating expenses for all Catholic schools as $1.4 billion. About $800 million of this total was spent on the elementary schools, the balance on the secondary schools. The figures come from the NCEA "data bank," a

computerized processing center set up in 1969 with Carnegie funds to gather and store information about all of the
country's Catholic schools. Of the total, nearly 10 per cent
($123 million) was spent on the physical plant of the
schools: i.e., on "land, buildings, furniture and equipment."
As recently as 1967-68, the bishops and the religious superiors were spending money on physical plant at the rate of
$171 million per year. By any standards, these are huge
sums of money. The total parochial and diocesan budget,
for instance, equals $1.2 billion, or about 55 per cent of the
total ordinary income of all Catholic parishes, which I estimated in Chapter Eleven as being $2 billion a year.

Significantly, these operating costs are nowhere near
evenly distributed among the parishes and sees of the
church in the United States. Nor, or course, are the schools
themselves. A rapid survey of a few more official statistics
will shed light on the true pattern of school operations and
school finance. Such a survey will also reveal the inherent
limitations of the system of schooling the church has built
in this country.

In 1970, *The Official Catholic Directory* reports,
slightly more than one-half of the 18,244 U. S. Catholic parishes operated parochial elementary schools. This
one-out-of-two ratio did not mean, however, that the
schools were neatly spread checkerboard-fashion across the
country. Rather, they were clustered thickest in the major
centers of Catholic population. Of the 9,271 parochial
schools, 3,898 were concentrated among the 5,381 parishes
of the twenty largest Catholic sees. On average, seven out
of every ten parishes in these sees ran elementary schools.

In contrast, consider the twenty sees which rank from
100th to 120th in population size on my list of all 160 Catholic sees. In 1970, these sees contained 1,509 parishes, but
only 563 parochial schools. Instead of being 70 per cent,
the ratio of schools to parishes was about 38 per cent.

These figures point out the obvious truth that the schools are where the people are, not where the ecclesiastical geographers have mapped out parishes. But the figures also suggest other truths. Thus, in no see have the Ordinaries ever achieved the goal of a school for every parish. And the smaller the local Catholic population, the more remote this goal.

Next, let's ask another statistical question: out of all Catholic elementary and high school students, what proportion receives its education in these parochial and diocesan schools? According to *The Official Catholic Directory*, nearly 4.1 million pupils attended these schools in 1970. But the same source also indicated that 5,484,498 Catholic elementary-school and high-school students were enrolled in public schools.* Again, as a general rule, the smaller the diocese, the higher the percentage of its students in the public schools. But even in the very largest sees, the parochial and diocesan school systems lack the capacity to handle local Catholic student populations. For instance, in Chicago, where 444 of the 451 parishes operated schools in 1970, and where 210,530 pupils were enrolled in the parochial schools, 124,822 Catholic youngsters nevertheless attended public elementary schools. In New York, 139,788 students went to the 316 parochial schools, but another 95,000 were enrolled in the public schools. In Boston, the 203 parochial schools had a total enrollment of only 93,390 while 240,650 Catholic children were at public school.

In citing these figures, I'm in no sense indicting the church for its failure to live up to the promise it once made in Baltimore. That promise was the promise of a different era, and the promise was given to a very different constituency. But if we're to reach rational conclusions about today's American Catholic schools, we need to know the

* These figures and those which follow represent the numbers of public-school students given "released time" during the school day for Catholic religious instruction and who are therefore identifiable as Catholics.

limiting realities. At their peak enrollments of several years ago (1964-67), these schools served considerably less than 50 per cent of the Catholic school-age population. Today, only about 41 per cent of that population is being educated in Catholic schools.

So in fact the church is overstraining its entire economy to support a school establishment which excludes nearly 60 per cent of those it intends to reach.

How serious is this economic strain? The following examples supply eloquent testimony.

- In Buffalo, a diocesan spokesman announced a $400,000 deficit in school operations for fiscal 1968-69. Bishop James A. McNulty has since closed twenty of his 192 schools.
- In the Archdiocese of Los Angeles, the 1970 deficit in school operations was $9.3 million.
- In Boston, a six-volume study of parochial and diocesan schools recommended a drastic cut in school services and a slash in enrollments from 143,000 in 1970 to 80,000 in 1975.
- In New York, the chancery reported a deficit of $2,160,000 in the finances of the twelve diocesan high schools in 1968. And the study of the schools commissioned by Cardinal Cooke predicted deficits of $31 million or more *per year* in parochial school operations by 1972.

In April, 1969, Bishop William E. McManus, Director of Education of the Archdiocese of Chicago, shared with his fellow prelates some gloomy truths about the country's Catholic schools. Addressing a general meeting of the National Conference of Catholic Bishops, Bishop McManus said:

> Indeed, Catholic schools presently are having some dark days—enormous debts contracted during the boom period, mounting expenses mainly because of a larger number of

better paid lay teachers, and inflated costs for virtually all purchases. Worst of all, we find that . . . weekly contributions are diminishing in many parishes.

Later, the bishop asserted that, "serious as are the schools' financial problems, they are not the main crisis." Perhaps not. But the crisis in finance alone is enough of a disaster for the church in this country.

As for the causes of this crisis, we've been cataloguing them steadily all along. Some of them we know to be internal causes linked to weaknesses in the management of the church itself. The pastor who can't balance a checkbook, the bishop who builds like an ecclesiastical beaver, the school board monsignor who never sets foot in a school, the lay yes-man who makes his living selling real estate to the chancery—all of these stock figures of the postwar boom in the church have contributed to the school crisis. For these ambitious men, who have spent the dollars of Catholic Americans so freely for so long, I suggest that the present condition of the schools is a bleak reckoning.

Other internal causes are more impersonal. Surely no one man or group of men or women is to blame for the sudden slackening of the flow of vocations to Catholic religious life. A whole conflux of factors adding up to a social revolution is responsible for that. Nor could any one man —not even Pope John XXIII—claim the credit for the tremendous outburst of renewal which, as it transforms religious life itself, also means irrevocable change in the aims of teaching religious. Long before the Second Vatican Council, in fact, the 256 orders of teaching nuns in America had begun reform in their special apostolate. Above all, the sisters saw that to educate others, they must educate themselves. The story of the Sister Formation movement, by which the training of nuns in this country has been revolutionized, is truly one of the great stories of education in America. Here, unfortunately, there's no room to tell this story. But the inspired women who initiated Sister Formation showed others how to plan, administer and finance advanced training for thousands of teaching religious. According to Sister Mary Emil, I.H.M., a founder of the movement, in 1952 "only sixteen religious communities in the U. S. required a Bachelor's degree of [their] elementary teachers before entrance to the classroom." By 1966, "the standard acceptable program for the training of sisters [was] a five-year program [including] four academic years, leading to a Bachelor's degree." Despite incredible difficulties, the movement produced remarkable results. Between 1955 and 1970, the percentage of sisters holding a college degree before beginning to teach has jumped from 7.1 per cent to 51 per cent.

In the church as elsewhere, knowledge is power. And the women who have so painfully educated themselves in the service of the church are no longer willing to give themselves blindly to "the works of the parish and the diocese" as teachers. Whether or not the Catholic orders survive their crisis, one thing is certain. Never again will they consent to contribute the subsistence labor on which the pastors and bishops, without due concern for practical economic realities, could base parochial education in America.

Finally, of course, there are the external causes. Although the men who run the church have been anything but alert to the threat of inflation, for inflation itself the church is obviously not responsible. As Bishop John Wright of Pittsburgh said to me before he became Cardinal John Wright of Rome, "It's not the Pope's fault that the dollar is going to hell." Nor is it the fault of the Pope that in our society all services, including education, command higher and higher prices. Or that the demand for *better* education should have forced on Catholic schools as well as on public schools the burden of newer, broader and costlier programs. Nevertheless, these things have happened, and they too have sharpened the crisis in the Catholic schools.

In an earlier chapter, we noted the dual strategy being developed by the Catholic religious orders to meet the similar financial crisis in their own institutions of higher education. Still in the formative stage, this strategy involves laicization on the one hand and the aggressive pursuit of private and government aid on the other. In the diocesan church, no such clear-cut strategy has as yet emerged. In place of the systematized planning and deliberate movement the situation calls for, the bishops have so far attempted only localized, impromptu action. As we'll soon learn, they are becoming increasingly vocal about what they might do. But their major response to date has simply been to begin closing down, at the rate of about 400 per year, some of the hardest-pressed Catholic schools.

The lack of planning behind these closings is confirmed by the findings of a study group investigating recent trends in Catholic education. Dr. Richard H. Metzcus, an assistant professor of education at Notre Dame, headed this project, which was dubbed "Operation Schoolhouse." In November, 1969, the group published a report based on information supplied by 147 diocesan school superintendents and 346 school administrators. The key conclusions were: a) that school closings and the eliminations of whole grades from schools were largely the "result of emergency measures"; b) that these cutbacks "did not proceed from any consensus of the Catholic people" concerned; c) that the bishops and their chancery aides, not the diocesan school boards, made most of the decisions; d) that "an insufficient supply of religious as teachers, poor financial support and dwindling enrollment" were the ranking causes of shutdowns; and e) that closings were usually brought about without firm plans for utilization of abandoned properties."

Such arbitrary school closings, indeed, disturb Catholic educators as deeply as they do the laity served by the schools. Thomas O. Jones, a New York business executive who processed the financial data for Cardinal Cooke's school study, explained to me why sensitive Catholics are so troubled. "Almost everywhere, the schools least able to support themselves are the inner-city schools. Their rich parishioners have left for the suburbs. The kids are poor, and many of them are black and Puerto Rican. But these are just the kids the sisters want to teach. If we close these schools," he finished a bit angrily, "what kind of a church are we?"

In New York, the prospect that the chancery might close down inner-city schools has spurred the supposedly conservative clergymen of the archdiocese to quick action. In October, 1969, Cardinal Cooke appointed a special commission of pastors to investigate the problem. Acting on the commission's recommendations, Cooke then set up a system under which affluent parishes are committed to share their funds with impoverished inner-city congregations. Unrelated to other central financing arrangements, this system assesses well-off parishes 5 per cent of their annual ordinary income if they themselves are operating schools, more if they are not saddled with their own school expenses. A committee of priests (some appointed by the Cardinal, others elected by the priests themselves) determines which parishes should receive grants. The New York chancery announced the plan in April, 1970. Within sixty days, initial contributions from the parishes of the suburbs and other wealthy areas had reached the million-dollar mark.

Another reaction to this same situation comes to me from Msgr. Charles O. Rice, pastor of Holy Rosary parish in Pittsburgh. As a matter of fact, we have already met Msgr. Rice. He was my host at the Press Club luncheon described in Chapter Two. Among priests, Msgr. Rice is something of a celebrity. His monthly columns have been nationally syndicated in the Catholic press. But although he's a wit and a *bon vivant*, there's nothing of the rectory dilettante about Msgr. Rice. On the contrary, he's a committed radical. Best known as Pittsburgh's "labor priest," he marched with the steelworkers during the great strikes of the 1930's and 1940's. To the embarrassment of the whole hierarchy, he said of Cardinal Spellman's efforts to break a gravediggers' strike in New York, "A scab is a scab regardless of whether he wears cardinal red or denim blue." And in January, 1970, Msgr. Rice preached at the funeral of his friend Joseph A. Yablonski, the United Mine Workers executive who was murdered after daring to challenge the top leadership of the UMW.

At his own request, Msgr. Rice was transferred in 1965 from a well-to-do suburban parish to Holy Rosary, which is in the black ghetto Homewood area of Pittsburgh. There, one of his first moves was to hire a black Protestant layman as principal of the parochial school. Despite the alarm this caused in the chancery, the Holy Rosary school is thriving. In the silky voice of an Irishman contemplating battle, Msgr. Rice told me, "If they ever try to close this place down, they'll have a bit of a fight on their hands." Before tangling with a pastor as tough as this one over inner-city education, any bishop would undoubtedly think twice.

Such efforts to save distressed Catholic schools certainly testify to the gallantry of their sponsors. But neither the hasty abandonments now taking place in many sees, nor the last-second rescues of a few marginal schools, represent true answers to the nationwide crisis in parochial education. Answers, if any exist, must be sought elsewhere.

For a small but highly articulate Catholic minority, the answers lie in the most drastic action of all: disestablishment. The members of innumerable small discussion groups and of one growing organization, the National Association of Laymen, favor nothing short of a halt to parochial education. The role of spokesman for these concerned Catholics has for nearly a decade been played by a quiet-voiced, shrewd lady from New Hampshire, Mary Perkins Ryan.

In 1964, Mrs. Ryan published a book called *Are Parochial Schools the Answer?* and discovered that she had articulated what many other Catholics were also wondering. Significantly, Mrs. Ryan had long been involved in the movement to reform the Catholic liturgy and to refocus worship on the great central mystery of the Eucharist. In its appreciation of the economic problems of parochial education, her critique is thoroughly practical. But Mrs. Ryan's major concern is that of the liturgist who sees education as not the chief mission of a "people of God."

> To be in the work of education at all today means providing a specialized professional service. It cannot be done on the side. If the Church itself, through its basic diocesan and parochial structure . . . remains in the field of education . . . that work cannot help claiming a great part of the Church's total effort. . . . But mass education in the United States cannot help being "big business." Can the Church in our country with or without public support—continue to provide this auxiliary service and, at the same time, effectively pursue her first and true objective?

Mrs. Ryan feels that her church, whatever the circumstances in the past, can no longer bear the burden of its schools. The schools, indeed, are "an obstacle to the pursuit of today's aims," which are those of "putting ourselves . . . in as close contact as possible with the Christ who speaks to us and on us in His Word."

Instead of attempting to use church-run schools to "form good Catholics," Mrs. Ryan would devote the personnel, energy and money of the church to other forms of religious instruction. In the long run, she feels, the education of adult Catholics to a real understanding of the church is of infinitely greater importance than that nuns should be made to teach geography or arithmetic. And with the help of trained specialists in religious teaching, Catholic parents are better able to educate their children in religion than are the harassed sisters (or the inexpert lay teachers) who preside over the classrooms of the parochial schools.

How many American Catholics agree with Mary Perkins Ryan that these schools, their usefulness at an end, must go? Nobody knows for sure what lay opinion is. The bishops naturally tend to take for granted that Catholics do want their schools. But one recent attempt to sample opinion on this issue has yielded some provocative evidence to the contrary. In 1968, the late Cardinal Richard Cushing of Boston commissioned from the nationally known firm of Louis Harris Associates a poll of public attitudes toward the Catholic schools of his archdiocese. Those polled included 1,721 Catholic and 1,060 non-Catholic laymen, and the Boston College researchers who actually conducted the poll questioned in addition 144 diocesan priests, 197 teaching sisters, 60 lay teachers, 63 members of public school boards and 23 public school superintendents. As part of another larger study, the results of the poll were supposed to have been kept confidential. But in early April, 1970, copies on microfilm were given to the Boston newspapers by someone in the chancery.

According to the survey, 84 per cent of the Catholics polled preferred formal church-run programs of religious education for children to parent-supervised religious training in the home. But as the *Boston Herald Traveler* (April 13, 1970) reported,

> When asked to choose between Confraternity of Christian Doctrine (after-school classes) and full-time parochial schools, 50 per cent of the respondents chose religious education groups for young children and 47 per cent preferred CCD for teenagers. . . . Only 26 per cent chose elementary schools as preferable and 12 per cent would prefer Catholic high schools.

"Even among those with children in Catholic schools, the CCD programs are felt to be deserving of more support from the church than full time schools," the survey states.

Plainly, what was true of 1,721 Catholics in Boston may well not be true of the 48 million Catholics who are the laity in America. Yet this Boston survey is suggestive. Today's Catholics, the survey strongly hints, are much less impassioned than were their parents about the need to preserve the faith by building up the schools. Furthermore, lay Catholics worry less than does the present generation of Catholic bishops about the fate of the schools.

The bishops themselves, beset by problems as they are, are nevertheless far from willing to give up on parochial education. Bishop Ernest J. Primeau of Manchester could and did write a fair-minded foreword to Mary Perkins Ryan's challenging book. Bishop Charles A. Buswell of Pueblo, Colorado, could call the book "a valuable contribution." But prelates like these are rare, and most of the bishops and archbishops of the land are horrified at the mere thought that the parochial schools might die. For instance, in May, 1969, Cardinal Cooke said in a special report to the priests of his archdiocese (presented, appropriately enough, over the chancery's closed-circuit educational TV system), "We're in parochial education to stay." I did note that the Cardinal immediately went on to announce increased allocations for the archdiocesan CCD program. But I'm certain that he meant exactly what he said about the schools. For that matter, Cardinal Cushing himself said of the Boston survey just cited that "It is merely the raw data from which we will make our decisions concerning the future of our Catholic schools. . . . Let me assure you that we are continuing our long-standing commitment to the religious school and quality education for all of our children." And at a special meeting held late in December, 1970, forty one of the U. S. bishops reaffirmed the determination of the whole hierarchy to keep the parochial schools open. "Closing the schools is not the solution," Cardinal John Dearden of Detroit said at the close of the private conference. Dearden and the others who attended are senior members of the hierarchy. They pronounce, if they do not actually make, the official educational policy of the church.

What the bishops desperately want, of course, is state aid for parochial education. By a variety of means, the American hierarchy is pressing hard for such aid. For the most part, their methods today are in strong contrast to the arrogant you-owe-us separatism of earlier decades. Even these milder methods often do arouse public resentment, and the occasional heavy-handed or clumsy bid for aid stirs up plenty of local protest. Nevertheless, the church has already gained some support in its new-style campaign, and other, larger victories are within reach.

In focusing on this key issue, the first thing we should do is summarize the current (summer, 1971) status of state aid to Catholic schools. Next, we should examine the tactics the church is using to sell aid-to-education measures to lawmakers, and note the legal basis on which the legislators in their turn justify allocations of public funds to private schools. Once this groundwork is in place, we can deal intelligently with the crucial questions. Is the case for state aid a valid one? On what basis, if any, should American secular society lend support to these religious schools?

At this writing, twenty-three of the fifty states give no aid whatever either to Catholic schools or to other church schools. These are Alabama, Alaska, Arkansas, California, Colorado, Florida, Georgia, Idaho, Iowa, Minnesota, Missouri, Nebraska, Nevada, North Carolina, Oklahoma, South Carolina, Tennessee, Texas, Utah, Virginia, Washington, West Virginia and Wyoming. A glance at the map of the United States indicates the pattern. Except for Mississippi and Louisiana, none of the Southern states grant aid to parochial schools. Nor do the "Bible belt" states of the Midwest and Southwest or the prairie states of the Far West.

Six other states give limited amounts of aid in one area only, that of transportation. Thus, Maryland provides bus transportation for handicapped parochial school children. Montana allows students at private schools to ride public-school buses if they pay a fare. Arizona and North Dakota permit parochial-school pupils to ride free on public-school buses if there's enough room and if the buses travel only to the public schools. South Dakota allows similar transportation if the students receive part of their instruction in public schools. In Maine, local voters may approve bus transportation for Catholic-school students but the state provides no subsidies for such service.

Another seven-state group provides bus transportation but no other form of aid. This group includes New Jersey and Delaware in the East; Illinois, Indiana, Kentucky and Kansas in the Midwest and Oregon in the Northwest.

Fourteen of the states provide broader aid to parochial-school students. These states are Massachusetts, New Hampshire, Rhode Island, Vermont and Connecticut in New England; New York, Pennsylvania, Ohio, Michigan and Wisconsin in the Northeast and north central regions; Louisiana and Mississippi in the South; and New Mexico and Hawaii. Apart from bus service (provided by six of the thirteen states and permitted on a local-option basis by another six), the nature of the aid varies. Aid can include school-nurse and other health services (Connecticut, New York, Michigan, Wisconsin), school lunch subsidies (Massachusetts, New Hampshire, Mississippi), textbooks (New York, Pennsylvania, Rhode Island, Louisiana, Mississippi, New Mexico, Hawaii) and free use of public-school gymnasiums (New Hampshire). The most extensive aid

program in this country (according to a 1969 survey by
the *Lutheran Witness Reporter*) is operated by Pennsylvania under a so-called "purchase of services" arrangement. Under this arrangement, the state uses racetrack
tax revenues to pay for the services of lay parochial-
school teachers and for textbooks and other materials in
science, mathematics, foreign languages and physical education. In 1969, Pennsylvania allocated $4.3 million for this
program.

In Michigan, an even more ambitious program (nick-
named "parochaid" by the press) was approved by the state
legislature in July, 1970. This program was to provide
about $7 million worth of aid per year to non-public
schools. As many as 900 schools would receive direct
grants from the state to cover 50 per cent of the payroll
costs for lay teachers of secular subjects in the schools. But
the program, strongly supported by Michigan's Republican
governor, William G. Milliken, has become a scorching
political issue. In September, 1970, the Michigan Supreme
Court declared the program constitutional. But another
court ruling guaranteeed a public referendum on a constitutional amendment which would outlaw the entire program. In November, 1970, Michigan voters approved the
"Proposition C" amendment by a substantial margin. As
a result, not only the "parochaid" program but all other
state aid to private schools was cut off at the end of the
1970-71 school year. Even advocates of the no-aid amendment felt that its provisions were too harsh. Catholic educators and others in favor of state aid asked the Michigan Supreme Court to rule on the constitutionality of the
amendment itself. But the ban on aid was upheld, and
Cardinal John Dearden, Archbishop of Detroit, indicated
that at least half of the 328 Detroit parochial schools would
be forced to close for lack of funds by June, 1971. The

closings could add at least 80,000 students to the population of Detroit's already crowded public scsool system.

As this situation illustrates, even in states which have already extended some aid to church-related schools, the whole question of aid can be reheated for voters at election time. And at any time, groups opposed to the idea of state aid can test in the courts the validity of legislation providing for aid. Such court tests are currently being made in Hawaii, Wisconsin and Pennsylvania as well as in Michigan. And the United States Supreme Court has agreed to review the Pennsylvania test case.

Opposition to state-aid bills comes from many sources. In Michigan, for example, the chief opponents of the "parochaid" bill were the 75,000 member Michigan Education Association, the strongest teacher union in the state, and State Senator Sander M. Levin, who just happened to have been running for governor that year against Governor Milliken. (Levin lost.) In Pennsylvania, a taxpayer group has forced the issue into the courts on grounds of constitutionality. In Maryland, opposition to state aid is being rallied by the strangest organizers of all, the members of the Catholic National Association of Laymen. In November, 1969, Donald Nicodemus, executive vice president of this group, told a special state commission studying the question that the NAL stands "unequivocally opposed" to aid for parochial schools. Calling these schools an "antiquated educational system," Nicodemus and his group favor an end to parochial education and its "waste of the resources of the Church."

Defeat of pending state-aid legislation will undo the patient tactical maneuverings of many archbishops and bishops. According to *The New York Times*, November 25, 1970, thirty-three states are considering such legislation. Following the advice of such professional lobbying organizations as the National Conference of Catholic Bishops Washington secretariat and the National Catholic Education Association, the bishops have kept their campaigns for aid low-key and matter-of-fact. As we've seen, the bishops have commissioned special studies of their schools to muster evidence of their need for aid. They have appeared at behind-the-scenes meetings of legislative committees to testify to the economic difficulties of the schools. They have encouraged influential laymen to form groups able to tell the Catholic side of the story. One such lobbying group, the Committee for Educational Freedom, has slowly built up a following in the Deep South, the Midwest and New England over the past five years.

Catholic bishops have also formed alliances with other sectarian educators, to make the issue one of aid to all church-related schools, not just Catholic schools. Above all, the bishops have learned to accept moderate gains. They now know that state aid, if it comes at all, may have to take the form of limited, indirect aid. Because students and parents are safer beneficiaries legally and politically than are the schools themselves, the bishops have muted their demands for the direct cash support they most want.

Only occasionally have either the bishops or their aides been guilty of immoderation. The most glaring instance I've noticed is several years old. This was the behavior of some members of the local hierarchy during the 1967 election campaign in New York State. One feature of that campaign was a public referendum on a new constitution to replace the patchwork document that had served the state for more than a century. The proposed new state constitution contained no clause forbidding state aid to church-related schools. The 1894 Blaine Amendment, which made such a restriction part of the old constitution, was thus up for repeal. For this reason, the church in New York State campaigned very hard indeed for the adoption of the new document. In the Diocese of Brooklyn, pastors were reportedly assessed $120,000 by the chancery to cover the cost of leaflets and other materials. And shortly before his death, Cardinal Spellman publicly exhorted Catholics to vote for the new constitution as "a document worthy of support by the people." Apparently, the publicity given the Cardinal's statement convinced a good many New Yorkers that the church was "meddling in politics." State Republicans, who had good reasons of their own not to want the constitution accepted, spread the word gleefully in the rural districts upstate. The newspapers and the radio and television newscasters also saw in "repeal of the Blaine amendment" a colorful issue in an otherwise dull election year. Some of the media treated the story as if the new constitution were about to destroy the public schools and establish Catholicism as the official state religion of New York.

At a meeting of the National Catholic Education Association in Washington the day after the election, Msgr. Edgar P. McCarren of the New York chancery gave his version of the result. "The constitution was overwhelmingly defeated. We were clobbered! It was something like two-and-a-half to one." Msgr. McCarren naturally made no reference either to Cardinal Spellman's intervention or to the lobbying from the pulpit that went on during the campaign. But others at the meeting told me privately that these exercises of ecclesiastical muscle did the cause of the constitution much more harm than good.

The 1967 disaster in New York seems to have convinced the bishops that overt political action on the school-aid issue is self-defeating. But the hierarchy has yet to abandon entirely another tactic dear to its membership, reiteration of the threat that shutdowns of parochial schools will mean dire economic consequences to public schools in the affected communities. Catholic bishops, school administrators and pastors love to argue that if the Catholic schools are closed, in a see of good size, tens of thousands of children will descend on the public schools. This influx of new pupils will so overload the public school systems that school taxes will necessarily soar upward. Furthermore, the argument continues, the use of professional religious as teachers has kept parochial-school costs low by comparison with those of public schools. It's therefore cheaper for the community to finance the Catholic schools than it would be to educate all Catholic children in the public schools.

In my own opinion, there's more than a little truth in this argument. One reason why the crisis in parochial education should disturb all Americans is simply that this crisis will hit every one of us, Catholic or non-Catholic, squarely in the pocketbook. Furthermore, the implications of wholesale closings of Catholic schools are much more complex than most advocates of parochial-school aid seem to think. Thus, given the grim mood of the American taxpayer, I'd venture that sudden shifts of parochial-school students into public schools would lead not to increased school budgets and taxes but rather to bigger classes, slashes in some school programs and further declines in the quality of public education.

Even if I'm wrong, however, the tactic of threatening to close parochial schools strikes me as a singularly poor approach to the goal of keeping them open. The major reason is one of credibility. For 150 years, the church has done battle for its schools in the open arena of American public opinion. After so many decades of witnessing this struggle, most Americans simply refuse to believe that the bishops will ever give up and close the schools. First, because Americans believe the myth of church wealth—a myth which the church itself has taken pains to foster—the notion that the Catholic schools might have to be closed for lack of funds seems incredible to most hearers. Secondly, the church has never substantiated its claims of the cash value of its schools to the taxpayer. So when a spokesman like Winifred R. Long, research director for the NCEA in Washington, claims that parochial school closings during 1968 and 1969 are *already* costing American taxpayers "well over a third of a billion dollars per year," her audience is skeptical.

Interestingly enough, one of the strongest responses to the use of this it-will-cost-the-taxpayers argument comes from within the hierarchy. Msgr. James C. Donoghue of the United States Catholic Conference told a *New York Times* reporter in April, 1969, that threats to close down parochial school systems were "bordering on blackmail." To quote the account in *The Times*:

> The total closing threat, [Msgr. Donoghue] said, is political and tactical. It may have some value in showing how parochial schools save money for public schools but I have my doubts about its use.

Instead of scattered closings of schools, woeful forecasts, inept politicking and veiled threats, the bishops and their spokesmen could be doing things far more useful to their cause. In a moment, we'll consider the positive (and essential) alternatives. But it's now time to answer the first of the great questions which must be answered if such alternatives are ever to have meaning: is the case for state aid to parochial schools a valid one?

In purely economic terms, the schools do need the help. This entire book, in fact, is a demonstration that the church can no longer support its schools. Propagandizing by the church and mythmaking by its enemies may obscure the truth. But the truth that emerges from our study is that the Catholic Church in America lacks the resources to continue what it began so proudly 170 years ago. As we've seen, poor management has much to do with this economic failure. But poor management alone is not to blame. The root causes of the distress are economic and social forces over which the church has had no control. These forces affect not only the church, moreover, but every other major institution in our society. And no secret assets or hidden treasuries exist on which the bishops could, if they pleased, levy to keep their schools alive.

So the bishops are once again doing as they did at the very beginning of their struggle for their schools. They are petitioning the whole American community for the money they need. In blunt terms, the past arrogance and intransigence of the church on education give these prelates much to answer for. Having once heard the Farleys and the Spellmans proclaim the godlessness and the worthlessness of American public education, the non-Catholic American who does listen to the Primeaus and the Cookes today does so, I feel, in a forgiving spirit.

Nevertheless, as one member of this community, I think we should listen. For one thing, I think a measure of state support can be justified on the basis of economics. Whatever their drawbacks—and no schools, private or public, are free of drawbacks—the Catholic schools do take in nearly 4.5 million of our 50 million elementary and high school students, or not quite one out of every ten. Largely because of the subsistence-level pay of Catholic teaching religious, these schools have been less costly to operate than have been public schools of comparable size. This situation may well change. For one thing, the per-pupil costs of Catholic schools (which, in the handful of dioceses where the figures have been computed, vary remarkably from parish to parish) are by no means as low as the bishops and their education directors would have us believe. Typically, the Catholic parish accounting system either ignores or else charges off to some other part of the physical plant many operating expenses which should actually be charged to the school. And as increasing numbers of nuns and brothers leave the schools, the higher salaries of their lay replacements will force parochial-school payrolls closer and closer to the levels found in the local public schools.

Yet it's still true today that Catholic schools are less expensive than public schools. To the extent that a given state can count on parochial schools to educate some of its sons and daughters, its taxpayers are getting a bargain. To put the same thought another way, tax dollars spent to subsidize Catholic schools will go farther than would the same dollars spent on public schools.

But the economic argument carries us only so far. Granted, if a state does come to the aid of its Catholic schools, its communities may be able to keep their tax rates low and realize other short-term economic benefits. But what of the less tangible long-range benefits? In particular, is the *quality* of Catholic parochial education today high enough to justify an investment by all of the citizens of a state in all of its Catholic schools?

As every concerned parent of a school-age child knows, the quality of an education is unnervingly difficult to measure. The educators themselves are stymied by the problem of assessing whatever mysterious thing an education is supposed to be and to do (whether in the third grade or in graduate school). After years of placing our trust in the letters or numbers on report cards, and after accepting as powerfully significant the results of the I.Q. tests, the achievement tests and the batteries of other tests given in our schools, we're gradually realizing that numbers on score sheets can tell us few positive truths about the development of our children. The numbers do, however, have negative value. Even critics of testing concede that test results can help parents and teachers identify youngsters who have learning problems and who are lagging in intellectual development. When it comes to rating whole schools, test scores properly interpreted give educators and accrediting agencies a fairly accurate yardstick by which to measure *comparative* quality.

Parochial-school students do take many of the same tests which are given to students in the public schools. From the statistical results which have been made public,* we can learn almost nothing about what might make parochial schools good and valuable institutions of learning. But the results certainly indicate that the parochial schools in general rate on a par with the public schools. In terms of pupil achievement on standardized tests—i.e., in terms which we have so far been willing to accept for all schools —the Catholic schools are *no worse* than the public schools. If we as taxpayers were to back these schools, we would not be sentencing the children who attend them to an education markedly inferior to that of their counterparts in the public schools.

The question of quality in education, however, is no longer being considered on the basis of numbers alone; and I for one thank God that it's not. Catholic parochial education may be as good as public education today. From what I've seen of the Catholic schools in action, I'm prepared to accept that it is. But how good is American public education? What standards and what goals have we as citizens been willing to accept for the 44 million children attending public schools? A growing body of hard evidence makes unmistakably clear something that millions of Americans know in their bones to be true. Namely, that public education in this country is itself in desperate straits. In the fall of 1970, one commentator said of our public schools:

* For instance, in the 1966 Notre Dame Study of Catholic Elementary and Secondary Education, a major research project funded by the Carnegie Corporation and published as *Catholic Schools in Action*; and in *The Education of Catholic Americans*, by Catholic sociologists Rev. Andrew M. Greeley and Peter H. Rossi, also published in 1966.

It is not possible to spend any prolonged period visiting public school classrooms without being appalled by the mutilation visible everywhere—mutilation of spontaneity, of joy in learning, of pleasure in creating, of sense of self. The public schools . . . are the kind of institution one cannot really dislike until one gets to know them well. Because adults take the schools so much for granted, they fail to appreciate what grim, joyless places most American schools are, how oppressive and petty are the rules by which they are governed, how intellectually sterile and esthetically barren the atmosphere, what an appalling lack of civility obtains on the part of teachers and principals, what contempt they unconsciously display for children as children.

This bitter indictment is not the work of an antiestablishment revolutionary. On the contrary, its author, Charles E. Silberman, presented it in the introduction to a four-year study of public education sponsored and financed by the Carnegie Corporation and published as *Crisis in the Classroom*. Needless to say, professional educators are unhappy enough about Silberman's attack to question sharply his credentials and his qualifications. But for those of us who witness or who remember what we do to children in our schools, the truth speaks for itself.

And so, irony lies heavy on the notion that the Catholic schools must somehow prove themselves to be as good as the public schools if non-Catholic taxpayers are ever to consent to support them.

Surely, given the state of public education and the desperate need for its reform, we as taxpayers should be viewing the question of aid to parochial schools in a radically different perspective. Perhaps we should be asking ourselves whether the Catholic schools (and the Lutheran schools and the yeshivas of some Jewish congregations) might not have something to teach public educators about the art of education. Perhaps we should be wondering whether or not such private schools, just because they are

private, are doing things and trying things that public
schools cannot do and dare not try to do. To investigate
these matters will take time, but the time will be well spent.
And if our investigators discover that parochial education
possesses an intimacy, a vitality and a humanity of its own,
we would do well to help the church keep it alive.

To conduct a search for the special qualities of the parochial schools is beyond my own capabilities and far beyond the scope of this book. Nor do I wish to sentimental-
ize on behalf of schools with which I'm not familiar, or
indeed on behalf of the Catholic Church.* I suspect that
bad Catholic schools display a rigidity and a lack of concern for children as children that make so-so public schools
seem paradises by comparison. But I also suspect that good
Catholic schools provide a far more humane environment
for children than most public schools provide. If this is so,
then the rhetoric of the men in Catholic chanceries, however trying, should neither discourage us nor enrage us.
Among other things, this book has suggested that the bishops are not always the church. With this in mind, we
should offer our support to the Catholic schools. They, not
the bishops, are the part of the church non-Catholics need.

How best could state and local agencies put money into
parochial schools? In seeking an answer to this question, the
lawyers, the legislators and the public administrators who
will ultimately take charge of the problem must, I feel,
avoid two pitfalls. On the one hand, they must avoid transfers of money directly to the official church. The reason is
simply that the ecclesiastical economy is too primitive to
handle such funds in acceptable fashion. The accounting
and record-keeping systems necessary for quick, exact
transfers of money from chancery to parish and from par-

---

* For those who want an interesting but somewhat rosy view of a
parochial school as a going institution, I suggest *Parochial School: A
Sociological Study*, by Joseph H. Fichter, S.J. Written about a southern
school in the mid-1950's, this classic is not yet too dated to be revealing.

ish to school (and for accurate reports on what happens to the money) do not exist in most sees. The administrative skills needed to finance a school out of two kinds of funds, private and public, are rare among pastors. And to be candid, the implications of full accountability and fiscal responsibility are not yet very well understood by the men who run the official church.

On the other hand, the conditions under which financial aid is granted must not be so restrictive that the schools, to qualify, are forced to become thoroughly secularized. Although the notion may be unpalatable to many non-Catholics, it's likely that the very qualities which may make parochial schools worth preserving—the warmth, the sense of community, the modest scale—are interwoven with the religious character of the schools. To be effective, aid must support the secular activities of these schools without violating their Catholic character. Otherwise, the parochial schools will become nothing more than pallid imitations of the public schools.

Already, some techniques are being worked out which apparently do avoid these problems. In Michigan and Pennsylvania, lawmakers have developed a concept of state aid as a package of diversified forms of financial support. As we saw earlier, these forms range from cash allowances for school bus and textbook services all the way to direct payment to pastors of part of the school payroll for lay teachers. Many other possibilities are being proposed, including tax-deductibility of the tuition charges for parochial schools, cash vouchers with which parents could purchase the educational services of their preference and even total takeover of existing parochial school systems.

Because so little can be known in advance about such possibilities, it seems to me that in states where voters do consent to put money into parochial education, pilot programs should be set up to test the different alternatives.

Pilot projects, too, should be initiated in other areas where church schools and public schools could profitably share their resources. For instance, the time is ripe to devise new experiments similar to the so-called Poughkeepsie Plan, which nearly a century ago offered promise of cooperation between church and state. According to a historical review of Catholic education prepared for Cardinal Cooke's committee on parochial schools in New York:

> Dr. Patrick McSweeney, newly appointed pastor of St. Peter's in Poughkeepsie, N. Y., sought to solve the pressing financial problems of his two parish schools by arranging to lease the parochial school buildings to the Poughkeepsie Board of Education. The Board would operate them as public schools and pay for the secular education they offered. . . . [Footnote:] The agreement had the following features: the public school board agreed to rent the present school building for one dollar per year; the school board would have control of the building during school hours; at other times, [the parish] would have control; all teachers would be under the control of the Board; a thirty-day notice was all that would be required to terminate the agreement.

Despite attacks by both Catholics and non-Catholics, the Poughkeepsie Plan actually flourished in that city from 1875 to 1898. Only when the State Superintendent of Public Instruction declared the arrangement unconstitutional were the agreements cancelled.

Variants of the Poughkeepsie Plan are feasible today. Take for example an inner-city parish which operates a school. To keep the school alive, the pastor could be allowed to make a double arrangement. First, he could either sell or lease the school plant to the state (which would then become responsible for maintenance). He could then have the individual lay teachers sign contracts with the city's school board. This transfers these teachers from the payroll of the parish to that of the public school system. The salaries of teaching sisters would still be carried by the parish. The secular curriculum would be controlled by the local board of education (which would have to work closely with the diocesan school authorities) in conformity with state laws. Religious instruction would be given in the classrooms on a released-time basis. The school would in fact operate in much the same way as before. But the double burden of plant upkeep and lay teachers' salaries would be shifted from the parish and the diocese to the public agencies of education.

I've sketched in this one method of giving aid to parochial schools only to illustrate that the mechanics of aid can work without either subsidizing religion or doing violence to it. Other methods should prove at least as workable; and administrators more expert than I should find these easy to devise. No one technique, of course, could be universally applicable. The school in the affluent suburban parish might seek a type of aid very different from the type granted to the ghetto school. (The rich school might ask for money so that it could grant scholarships to needy students.) The rural diocesan high school system, with its few units spread over great distances, might be able to handle state funds directly through the chancery. Urban systems, with their dozens of schools, might be better off if aid were channeled to the individual schools.

How much money would it cost to subsidize Catholic schools? Earlier, I estimated the cost of running the country's parochial and diocesan schools as $1.2 billion a year. This total includes the cost of plant construction and maintenance as well as the operating expenses of the schools themselves. It is no part of my argument to suggest that the taxpaying public should finance this entire budget. But its largest and fastest-rising component, the outlay of the schools for the services of lay teachers, does seem to me a legitimate, logical choice for public support.

At present (1971), the Catholic schools employ about 65,000 lay teachers. Almost all of them teach the secular curriculum of the schools. From the salary averages for teachers in non-public schools given in the 1970 *Statistical Abstract of the United States*, we can approximate the base payroll for these teachers as being $390 million a year. To this base we must add a certain amount to cover Social Security and other payroll taxes and the cost of such fringe benefits as medical insurance and pension plans. In private industry, these extras can cost an employer as much as 35 per cent of his payroll. In the church, where fringe benefits for lay employees are held to a minimum, the percentage is closer to 10 per cent. Even so, the total wage outlay for this 65,000-man labor force will approach $430 million a year.

If we as taxpayers assumed this entire expense, we'd be spending less than one-sixth of what we spend every year on the Federal highway program. For that matter, we'd be spending only about one-quarter of what we spend on toys and sporting goods each year. To make the point in still another way, every year we spend on our public schools a total of nearly $30 billion. An increase in this budget of 1.5 per cent a year would be enough to cover the wages of all lay teachers in the Catholic schools. I think we can afford this price. I think we should pay it.

But before any such sums of money are contributed to the schools of the church, the church itself must change its ways. To qualify for state aid, or federal or local aid, every diocese must make public its financial condition. Its balance sheets must be complete, its properties—in particular, its school properties—must be independently appraised and its financial statements must be both detailed and comprehensible. As we've seen repeatedly, the church has long suffered from a self-induced scarcity of information. For the sake of the schools, this famine must be ended.

Then, at the national level, an official church organization (either the National Conference of Catholic Bishops or the National Catholic Education Association working under NCCB sanction) must conduct a diocese-by-diocese survey of the schools. Every Ordinary would be required to cooperate and every pastor instructed to make available the financial and other data required. Those running the survey should in their turn be required to make the results public. As was the case in the study of the parochial schools of New York, the raw data taken from the parish books and financial reports should be put through a new mill: i.e., processed to separate the true costs of running the schools (especially the physical plant costs) from the general expenses of the parishes themselves. In sum, the mandatory first step toward school aid must be that "comprehensive and systematic analysis of costs and benefits of the Catholic schools" for which Rev. Ernest Bartell of Notre Dame pleaded in 1966.

Only if the bishops voluntarily produce such a complete study, and if the study does make evident the inability of the church to continue its schools, should state and federal officials begin to plan legislation. Because federal funds will undoubtedly be needed to augment state funds, the Department of Health, Education and Welfare is the logical creator of a model bill for Congress to consider. And because the type of aid we're considering does call into question the constitutional issues discussed in Chapter Fourteen, an early court test of any approved legislation is essential. After decades of sidestepping the problem, the church, its adversaries and the American public should decide conclusively whether or not direct aid to Catholic schools (and to those of other denominations) is synonymous with the establishment of a state religion. As I hope I've made clear, my personal view is that the two are poles apart. Instead of defending ourselves against that mythical day when, on orders from the Pope, the Catholics take over the country, we should be helping Catholics to renew their educational philosophies and contribute these to a country which sorely needs diversity and variety of purpose in education.

By relieving the church of its most pressing economic burden, won't state and federal aid to Catholic schools indirectly subsidize the church as a religious institution? I think it probably will. Furthermore, there are certain to be elements within the church which will regard an aid-to-education program as a "triumph" for Catholicism over the forces of godless secularism, not as an opportunity for the church to make good on the great promises of the Second Vatican Council. But every kind of giving involves the risk of ingratitude on the part of the recipient. My own belief is that the church has changed profoundly over the past decade; enough so that today's bishops would accept school aid responsibly rather than complacently. In any case, the advantages of financially healthy parochial school systems outweigh any harm the far-right wing of the church could possibly do.

To be sure, school subsidization would alter the entire economy of the church in this country. Would Catholics stop giving money to the church? Or, if they continued to give, would the parishes and the dioceses suddenly find themselves piling up surplus revenues? Here again, pilot projects in school aid might give churchmen, economists and the public an idea of what to expect. Easing of the pressure to support the schools might lead some Catholics to cut back on their weekly donations. But others, especially the younger parishioners, might actually be inclined to give more generously if they felt the money would be spent on works of religion and charity, not on education. No doubt a few pastors and bishops would revel in their sudden surpluses. But we're more likely instead to see an end to such unappetizing forms of fund-raising as the bingo night and the charge for admission to the parish-school basketball game.

My own guess is that giving to the church would not decrease. And it's obvious that the bishops would find new uses for funds no longer needed for the schools. Many chapters earlier, we noted the increasing interest of the diocesan church in welfare projects bearing little direct relation to religion. Efforts to finance the projects through diocesan development funds are already being made in many sees. Money released from the parochial-school sector of the diocesan economy would most likely be put into such novel ventures as low-income housing corporations, clinics, credit unions and even "MESBICS," or minority-enterprise small business investment corporations. All of these ventures, of course, are aimed at helping the poor, and especially the black poor. The church already has a foothold in the ghettos of our cities. Its own inflexibility has in fact won it this position. For while white Catholic parishioners have been free to abandon their city parishes for the suburbs, the churches have necessarily remained behind. Some are bastions of white society in the ghetto areas, serving small remnants of their original parishioners and living off of the savings of past years. But more have attempted to serve the people of the ghettos. In many an urban neighborhood, the only representative of white society trusted by black Americans is the church. Given the economic opportunity, the bishops wish nothing better than to increase their commitment in this one area where the need is so evident.

With this account of the problems and the possibilities of the schools, we take our last leave of the domestic economy of the church. We know now how the church in America operates. We have visited its rectories to audit the parish books. We have conferred with the money-men of its dioceses and with the executives of many of the religious orders. We have come a very long way. Throughout, I have stressed the economic decentralization which is so crucial to church finance and the canonical limitations on the power of even the most powerful churchmen. These factors, in defiance of legend, make the church in this country economically independent of Rome. Indeed, despite its difficulties, the American church is one of the very few divisions of the entire church which serves as a mainstay of the Vatican's own economic efforts.

Nevertheless, although the economy of the Vatican is a thing unto itself, to the Vatican we must go. One reason is that the myth of Vatican wealth and power reinforces the myths we have encountered about church wealth in this country. Until we gain some sense of the papacy as a functioning economy, we shall not have laid these American myths to rest. Another reason is that the economic links between the Vatican and the financial community in the U. S. are of critical importance to the papacy today. But the best reason of all is simply that the Vatican, seen from any angle, is a fascinating place. And the truth about its economy is far more intriguing than any legend could be.

CHAPTER SEVENTEEN

The Vatican: The Oldest Economy

There are many ways to enter the Vatican. If you're a tourist—or a pilgrim—you'll certainly want to use the front door. So from the Ponte Sant' Angelo across the Tiber, you'll follow the Via della Conciliazione (a monument only to the lack of taste of its creator, Mussolini) until you stand at the edge of the Piazza di San Pietro, St. Peter's Square. Directly ahead of you is the huge Egyptian obelisk brought to Rome by the Emperor Caligula in A.D. 37 and moved to its place of pride in 1586 by the equally imperious Pope Sixtus V. Far beyond is the broad flight of steps leading up to the cathedral. On either side, Bernini's magnificent colonnades sweep outward to enclose the immense oval of the piazza. At your feet, inset in the cobbled pavement, is a line of white travertine marble. When you cross that line, you're officially in the territory of the popes.

By entering St. Peter's or by visiting the Vatican Museum and the Sistine Chapel, sightseers and worshipers can easily penetrate even deeper into papal territory. But unless you're a dignitary on your way to an audience with the pope, or someone on official business or one of those who lives or works in the Vatican, you won't be permitted to use any of the other gateways to this small realm. The Swiss Guards, whose blue and gold ceremonial uniforms were supposedly designed by Michelangelo, will bar your way. They'll be polite but firm, and if necessary they can back up their firmness by using some very modern police methods. And you'll miss even a glimpse of the beautiful gardens of the Vatican and of the winding streets, the courtyards and the ancient structures of the tiny but impressive papal domain.

The dignitary (a term which in the Vatican can include everyone from Sophia Loren to Richard M. Nixon) customarily makes his entrance through the Bronze Doors at the right of St. Peter's itself. Beyond these doors, the Scala Regia (the "royal stairway") leads upward into the richly furnished halls and chambers of the Apostolic Palace. In one or another of these rooms or passageways, the pope will receive his guest. The exact location will depend upon the pope's schedule for the morning, the status of the visitor and the nature of the audience arranged.* Even the private audiences granted to heads of state are held in the formal surroundings of the big library on the third floor of the palace. The study on the fourth floor, right off the

* Papal audiences today are of five kinds: 1) general, usually held in St. Peter's basilica for thousands of visitors; 2) semi-private or *baciamano*, brief meetings with small groups in the antechambers to the library; 3) official, for those making a state visit to the Holy See, held in the third-floor library; 4) private, granted only to individuals of rank within or outside the church; and 5) special, which are unscheduled and kept secret.

pope's bedroom, is accessible only to the pope himself, to his secretaries and to a very few insiders.

A lesser guest, one visiting the Vatican not to see the pope but on official business of some sort, enters the Vatican through the Arch of the Bells. To reach this gate, you must walk (or drive—the arch is just wide enough to admit a car) across St. Peter's Square and pass to the left of the steps leading to the cathedral. You'll then find yourself in a narrow lane between St. Peter's on your right and an administration building on your left. At the end of this lane is the Arch of the Bells. There, the guardsman on duty will check your credentials. For strangers, a pass is required. This will be issued in a small antechamber around the corner from the arch itself. With your pass in hand, you're free to proceed. In theory, you may only follow the most direct route to wherever your errand takes you. But in the Vatican, surveillance is casual. As long as you look reasonably purposeful, you can tour the grounds and admire the gardens, which are often considered the loveliest in the world.

Finally, if you're a citizen of Vatican City or a "regular" who works there, you can come and go through St. Anne's Gate. This you reach by walking to the right of the cathedral and the Apostolic Palace, through an arch in the colonnade and down the street which runs parallel to the old wall of the Vatican. St. Anne's Gate is the service entrance to the papal domain. Through it pass the trucks, cars and motor-scooters of those who maintain the Vatican's physical plant and meet the daily needs of its citizens. (As a memento of my own visit to the Vatican, I treasure a snapshot of a Coca-Cola truck parked just outside the doorway which leads to the secret archives section of the main Vatican library.) By day, the atmosphere of St. Anne's Gate and of the crooked streets inside is as noisy and bustling as that of any other busy intersection in Rome. At night, however, things quiet down. In fact, any Vatican-dweller who stays outside later than 11:30 will find himself locked out. He has to call the Swiss Guard to be let in.

If these are the ways into the Vatican, what lies inside? The best physical description of today's Vatican that I've ever read is the one given by Curtis G. Pepper in *The Pope's Back Yard*. Pepper, one of the few contemporary journalists (and perhaps the only American) to have won the trust of the Vatican's crusty officialdom, makes the realm of the popes sound enchanting. Here are a few excerpts.

There are treasure rooms filled with jewels and crowns worn by emperors and kings. There are declarations of war and love letters written to a queen. There are tunnels and trap doors leading to secret rooms where lonely Popes have prayed, confessed their sins, and died. . . .

The Pope's private apartment has a marble bathroom, two television sets, a cinema hall, private elevator and a penthouse terrace. [Pepper tells me that in 1967, the weight of the earth hoisted up to make a garden for Pope Paul VI nearly broke down the roof of the Apostolic Palace.]

There is a little railway station made of white, yellow, pink, and green marble. A garage shelters carriages with red velvet thrones used by Popes long ago, standing next to elegant old automobiles with gold door handles.

There is also a jailhouse, a sports field, and a fire station with a fire pole. Finally, tucked into one corner, there is a little village which has everything from a butcher shop to a shoemaker. . . .

Vatican City takes up an area the size of a farm in Kansas or of a medium-sized golf course—107.8 acres. One can walk across it in fifteen minutes. It is that small. Indeed, it is the smallest sovereign state in the world.

Besides the Pope, there are other citizens living in the Vatican. At last count there were 881 men and women, plus 24 boys and girls—as well as five dogs, about twelve canaries and nobody knows how many cats.

To this collection, Pepper adds still other fascinating statistics. In Vatican City, he tells us, there are 30 streets and
squares, 42 palaces, 10,000 rooms and 208 staircases with
3,813 steps. There are about 50 elevators, including the one
which runs between the pope's apartment and the lower
floors of the Apostolic Palace. (This one has a silver St.
Christopher's medal on the wall of the cage.)

To maintain the 50 acres of lawns and gardens requires
a staff of 20 gardeners. The carpenters, masons, electri-
cians, plumbers and others who take care of the churches
and palaces number in the hundreds. The select 70 or 80
craftsmen who belong to the maintenance crew of St.
Peter's itself are all members of a special guild, the San Pie-
trini, founded in the sixteenth century. These acrobatic
workmen, trained from childhood, swarm over every inch
of the enormous cathedral. They keep it clean inside and
out, and they install the lights, the wiring and the other
equipment needed for the ceremonies and services conducted in the world's largest church. (The workmen's
compensation insurance on the *sanpietrini* is reportedly the
most expensive in Italy. St. Peter's is a hazardous place to
work.)

Who pays these insurance premiums? Who pays the salaries of the *sanpietrini?* Of the Swiss Guards, the firemen,
the postal employees, the printers, the gardeners and the
other lay workers of the Vatican? Of the several thousand
priests and nuns who also work within its walls? When a
pope decides (as Pope Paul VI has done) to double the
transmission strength of the Vatican radio station and to invest in such costly conveniences as a helicopter and an IBM
360 computer system, where does the money come from?
For that matter, how much money does a pope make each
year?

To answer questions like these, we need to know far

more about the Vatican than the guidebooks ever tell us. First of all, we need to understand the complexities of Vatican government, for the Vatican is the seat not of one government but of three. Secondly, we must dip into the economic history of the papacy, because the economy of the Vatican today is very much the product of the past. Finally, we must study the ideas and the motives of the present Pope, because Paul VI is an administrative reformer who is bringing momentous change into the financial and managerial structures of the Vatican.

In Chapter Five, I made the point that the Pope, whose full official title takes up eight lines of type in the *Annuario Pontificio*,* is always given first his title as *vescovo di Roma*, bishop of Rome. By definition, then, the Vatican is a diocesan chancery; and of the three governments mentioned above, one is the government of a Catholic diocese. The Diocese of Rome is no minor responsibility. Its Catholic population in 1969 (the most recent year for which figures are available) was 2,490,978. This makes Rome slightly larger than Chicago, the most populous of all U. S. sees. The 223 Roman parishes are served by 400 secular priests and 412 priests who belong to religious orders. (Nearly half of Rome's parishes are run by the orders.) The Diocese of Rome contains 284 parochial and diocesan schools and, because its bishop is naturally expansion-minded, new parish churches are being added at the rate of about ten per year.

Although the popes do make ceremonial appearances at diocesan functions, they play little part in the actual management of the Diocese of Rome. Since 1198, in fact, administrative control of the pope's own see has been dele-

* For the record, the full papal title is: "Bishop of Rome, Vicar of Jesus Christ, Successor to the first of the Apostles, Highest Pontiff of the Universal Church, Patriarch of the West, Primate of Italy, Archbishop and Metropolitan of the Province of Rome, Sovereign of the Vatican City State, Servant of the Servants of God."

gated to vicars general. The Vicar General of Rome is always a titular bishop, and for the past 400 years the post has gone only to a cardinal. The present incumbent is Cardinal Angelo Dell'Acqua, sixty-seven, a veteran of the Vatican state department who is a moderate in matters of Catholic doctrine and a trusted adviser of Pope Paul's.

The diocesan chancery is located in the Lateran Palace, which is legally papal territory but which is across Rome from the Vatican itself. The economy of the diocese, like that of all Catholic sees, is an independent entity. Diocesan revenues are canonically reserved to the diocese itself. Except for the Peter's Pence collection, called in Italian dioceses *l'obolo di Pietro*, and except for other normal yearly assessments and collections, none of the $25-million diocesan annual income goes to the papacy.

Of central economic importance to the popes are the two other governments which make their headquarters on Vatican soil. Few laymen make the distinction between these two ruling organizations; and, indeed, especially in money matters the lines separating them are often hard to draw. Nevertheless, we must keep in mind that a contemporary pope is not only the head of a worldwide ecclesiastical government but also the ruler of a civil state, the sovereign state of Vatican City. The government of the church is 2,000 years old. That of the state, strictly speaking, dates only from 1929. Together, they are the basis of the papal economy.

If we go far enough back in time, we reach the point at which no distinction between civil and ecclesiastical papal government was necessary or even possible. In the very earliest centuries of the papacy, the bishops of Rome derived their revenues from the land, just as did the emperors of the decaying Roman Empire.

The enthusiast who wades through the church historians can trace in the growing complexity of papal finance the whole history of Western economics from the end of the Roman Empire to the end of the feudal era 900 years later. After the centuries-long depression which followed the barbarian invasions of Rome, the papal economy revived under Charlemagne. But the rise of secular feudalism during the 'eleventh century, though it made feudal landlords of many bishops, deprived the popes of control over their estates. Under Hildebrand (who reigned from 1073 to 1085), the papacy emerged from near-bankruptcy and freed itself from political dependence on the Roman nobility. Hildebrand, an administrative genius, launched the first of many economic reforms. Loans to the papacy were repaid, debts collected and expenses brought under control. The old association between state finance and the personal wardrobe and jewel-box of the pope was supplanted by more professional money management. A single financial department, the *camera*, consolidated the books and the assets of the pope and his court.

During the twelfth century, the beginnings of an international financial structure are detectible. The *census*, a tax based on population, was the main source of support. But because the papacy was expanding its political and ecclesiastical interests, this flat tax yielded too little money to justify the expenses of collection. By the year 1199, the *camera* was ready to turn to a more modern form of levy, a tax on the income of the clergy. The first such tax called for a one-time payment of 2.5 per cent of income. But in 1228, when Pope Gregory IX needed money for his war against Frederick II, he ordered the clergy of England, France and Italy to pay him 10 per cent of their ordinary income for the year.

This clerical income tax sufficed for nearly a century. Not only did it cover the costs of the political and military ventures of the papacy in Europe but it also financed the crusades. By 1300, however, the popes were once again spending more money than the existing tax return was bringing in. The problem was not one of the form of the tax, but rather one of a conflict of interest between the ecclesiastical and the secular powers. A medieval pope could call on the secular authorities to enforce the payment of papal taxes by local Ordinaries, abbots and priests. But he did so at some risk. In return for their collection services, the kings and nobles of Europe demanded a share of the revenue. At best, this cut into the pope's own share. And because princes as well as popes needed money, a secular ruler who collected revenues on behalf of his nominal overlord in Rome might well defy the threat of excommunication and appropriate the funds for himself.

During the Middle Ages and later, the popes did derive revenue from the Papal States of Italy. But these were intended only to support the papal household. In much the same way, the Kings of England (by consent of the nobility) were awarded the revenues of the Duchy of Lancaster for their private support. But no more than most English kings could the popes "live of their own" and still meet the expenses of a government. For the period of the so-called Babylonian Captivity (1305-77), moreover, the popes who dwelt in Avignon received almost no income at all from their properties in Italy.

Like a modern bishop with an expensive school system, a pope in the Middle Ages was always short of money. He could borrow funds, first writing himself a rescript of exemption from the canons prohibiting usury. But the cost of servicing the debt was heavy. Besides, politically as well as economically, pledging the credit of the papacy to a secular lender was very dangerous. It meant jeopardizing the independence, and thus the authority, of the one institution in Europe which claimed always to be supreme above all others. As an analogy, consider what happens whenever the United Nations, unable to collect its dues from the Iron

Curtain countries, must turn to the United States for support.

It's not surprising, then, that the medieval popes tested many methods of raising revenue. In the index to one study, twenty-two separate fiscal techniques are listed. Among the more picturesque were annates, fruits during vacancies, services, quindennia, spoils, procurations, indulgences, compositions, oblations and tribute. Singly and in combination, these assessments kept the papacy alive as an international, or rather a supernational, organism. With significant exceptions (e.g., Peter's Pence, then a direct annual gift from a king to a pope, and indulgences, sold directly to laymen by licensees of the popes), all of these various taxes were levied on the clergy. The local hierarchies were made to bear the ultimate burden of raising money from the laity.

Nor is it surprising that the papal *camera* rapidly became the most sophisticated financial and administrative center in the Western world. Because funds flowed in from dozens of different countries, the papal chamberlains were faced with the physical and arithmetical problems of currency exchange. They had to learn how to speculate in the various currencies and how to bank them for safekeeping and future use. Because the amount of money in circulation was limited, the treasurers of the popes became dealers in valuables other than money: in precious stones, in spices and oils, in wines and in other commodities. Because the inflow of funds was continuous, accurate records had to be kept. So the cameral priests borrowed bookkeeping skills (via Venetian monks) from the merchants of the Middle East and became the finest accountants in Europe. By the end of the fourteenth century, the *camera* was a highly specialized Treasury Department. Its experts could do almost anything with money that a modern government exchequer can do today.

Even though the papacy itself was rich, the popes

spent their money as fast as it came in. They spent it on wars, on subsidies to princes who might then favor papal policy, on diplomacy and on the costliest preoccupation of all, the liberation of the Holy Land. Only rarely did a medieval pope die leaving a full treasury to his successor. True, the wealth of the entire church was enormous. For instance, it's estimated that in 1250 the church owned three-fifths of all the arable land in England. Yet the papacy is not the church; only a fraction of the yield of this wealth ever found its way to Rome. And instead of accumulating income, the popes used it.

In terms of economic history, the papacy functioned in medieval Europe as a kind of primitive venture capital firm. Thus, the bribes popes paid to secular rulers, especially in Italy, became the foundations of many private fortunes. The banking and mercantile activity generated by the *camera* made capitalists not out of churchmen but out of goldsmiths and traders. The huge sums turned over to feudal kings and nobles to pay for the crusades were seed money, too. The crusades opened up commerce with the Middle East, and made great fortunes for the impoverished nobles who took the cross. Indeed, some secular warlords won kingdoms and dukedoms in Palestine, in Cyprus and in Malta. But these were secular kingdoms, and their wealth was vested in secular princes. If the crusading popes are seen as making "overseas investments" by means of their holy wars, the profits from these investments were finally realized by lay Europe. The one thing the papal economy did purchase for the papacy was survival.

All that gives rise to the legend of Vatican wealth, in fact, came much later, during the Renaissance and the Counter Reformation.

From the beginning of the fifteenth century through the end of the seventeenth, two great trends mark the economic history of the papacy. The first is the increasing material splendor with which the popes saw fit to surround themselves. The second, in ironic counterpoint to the first, is the decline of their real economic power.

Any general historian of this period can trace for us the decay of papal supremacy. From crusades, the wars of the popes degenerated into squabbles with the princelings of the minor Italian states. From an exercise of divine prerogative, papal diplomacy diminished into a perpetual bargaining for military support. Although the material resources of the papacy were still great, the ambitions of the men who controlled the resources turned strangely inward. Deprived of the substance of power, the popes used their official revenues and their personal wealth (rich men were likelier to win election than poor men) to create an illusion of power. When Pope Martin V entered Rome at the end of the Great Schism in 1421, he found sheep grazing in the deserted streets and churchyards. His first official act was to begin the reconstruction of the papal palace on Vatican Hill. For the next 200 years, the popes were to concentrate lovingly on the same few acres of land in their capital city. The major function of the papal economy became that of financing the demolition of the old Basilica of St. Peter's, erected 322-337, by the Emperor Constantine, and the building of the new. Before this task was done, the popes had hired ten chief architects, including Leon Battista Alberti, Bramante, Michelangelo and Bernini. The total amount of money spent is incalculable (in part because the early records, except for drawings, have been lost; in part because much of the work of one pope often consisted of undoing the work of his immediate predecessor).

Under the most notable of the rebuilding popes, Pius II (r. 1458-64), the extravagant Sixtus IV (1471-84) and especially Julius II (1503-13), the proceeds from the market in indulgences went not to the *camera* but directly into the privy purses of the popes themselves. These same popes also reserved for their own use such other revenues as spoils (the personal property of all archbishops, bishops and abbots who died within two days' journey of Rome) and the fruits of vacant sees. In addition, the popes profited directly and hugely from the Renaissance practice of selling for lump sums the offices at their courts. Because these transactions were so dubious, the archivists of the Vatican have never released the documents which reveal the privy incomes and expenditures of the Renaissance popes. Much of what they took in certainly went to their avid relatives. But much also was poured into the great basilica and the complex of palaces surrounding this central place of Catholic worship. Despite all vicissitudes (including the Sack of Rome in 1527), the work on St. Peter's and the Vatican continued. Though nobody knows how many millions of florins were spent, the intensity of the effort suggests that St. Peter's absorbed, over the two centuries of its building, more than half of the total papal revenues.

During the sixteenth and seventeenth centuries, after the reforms of the Council of Trent, the facts of papal finance become less and less clear—but the myths of papal wealth begin to grow. Earlier, when the popes reserved for themselves increasing proportions of the ecclesiastical revenues, the *camera* devoted itself almost exclusively to just one task, the finances and government of the Papal States. These were the domains controlled by the popes since the days of the Roman Empire, with boundaries unchanged since the year 1200. From the Mediterranean coast of Italy near Naples, the Papal States stretched northward across the entire Italian peninsula to within fifty miles of Venice on the Adriatic Sea. Metaphorically, the Papal States formed a tourniquet 100 miles wide on the calf of Italy. In addition to Rome, this band of territory included the major cities of Urbino, Bologna and Ferrara.

In 1968, Pope Paul VI finally opened to scholars the archives of the Vatican for the period from 1500 to 1846. I myself have not visited the Vatican archives or interviewed the archivists. But as far as I know, no studies have yet been published of the tangled finances of the papacy between the Council of Trent and the mid-nineteenth century. During the early decades of this 300-year period, the Protestant Reformation, the Thirty Years' War and the rise of Protestantism in England must have disrupted the flow of ecclesiastical taxes into the papal coffers. But as we have seen, the popes continued to draw income from the clergy and from their own domains. Later, the Holy See became almost a client state of the Hapsburg dynasty. But the extent to which the popes were beneficiaries of the Spanish kings (and of the wealth of the New World, which these kings controlled) is purely a matter of conjecture. After the Council, the sudden rise of the Jesuits to prominence and secular power strongly suggests that they played a key role as economic servants of the papacy. Their communities and institutions must have proved fertile sources of ecclesiastical revenues. Their skill at raising funds may also have aided the popes, although the more romantic legends of their contributions* were pieces of anticlerical propaganda.

Still later, during the eighteenth century and well into the nineteenth century, the papal economy was crippled by revolution and by the Napoleonic Wars. In 1797, the French armies of the Directory, under Napoleon, invaded the Papal States. The ensuing Treaty of Tolentino cost Pope Pius VI his cities of Bologna and Ferrara, the entire Romagna and the town of Avignon, plus 36 million lire (about $6 million). Nine years later, Napoleon, then Emperor, ordered the annexation of all papal territories by the French Empire, kidnapped Pius VII and pressed him to re-

---

* In the eighteenth century, for example, the Jesuits were said to have discovered gold mines in Uruguay, the profits from which supported the Holy See.

nounce his claims to temporal sovereignty. The Pope refused, and persisted in his refusal so successfully that Napoleon gave up his effort to destroy the papacy. Pius VII was released and returned to Rome in 1814.

"The very moment when the world was in motion was the moment that they chose to stand still." Christopher Dawson's astringent comment on the Jesuits of the nineteenth century could readily serve for the papacy and, indeed, for the entire church at this time. After the downfall of Napoleon, when the Congress of Vienna (1815) convened to shape the future of Europe, the Holy See allied itself firmly with the forces of the *ancien regime*. Cardinal Consalvi, the Secretary of State of Pope Pius VII, was called by Lord Castlereagh "the ablest man at the Congress." Consalvi argued convincingly at Vienna for the restoration to the Pope of the Papal States and for the perpetuation of Vatican control over those territories. In return, he was prepared to throw the moral authority of the papacy behind the supporters of monarchy (which is to say reaction) everywhere in Europe. Morally, Consalvi's bargain was degrading. It allied the popes with all the ruling opponents of human freedom and betterment on the continent, and this "alliance between throne and altar" made the Catholic Church part of the official machinery of repression. Politically, Consalvi's shrewdness proved disastrous. In 1830 and again in 1848, the reactionary regimes supported by the Holy See were torn by revolution. The Papal States themselves, denied any measure of representative government and ruled from the Vatican, became a center of revolution in Italy. Only by using force could the popes keep order in their dominions. Routinely, the force was applied by papal gendarmes (Dawson terms them "virtually Papal brigands") called *Sanfedisti*. Under their police-state rule, Dawson continues, "the Papal States obtained the name—not without reason—of being the worst governed territories in Europe." Worse still, when in 1860 the 7,000-man papal army proved inadequate to prevent invasion by the liberating forces of Count Cavour, Pius IX, the vicar on earth of the Prince of Peace, unhesitatingly called in the French army to defend Ancona.

In making his bargain at Vienna, Consalvi was defending above all the right of the papacy to hold temporal property of its own. Shorn of such possessions, he reasoned, the Holy See would be at the mercy of every power in Europe; and no pope would ever be allowed to remain aloof from secular political struggles. In addition, Consalvi foresaw a dark future for the entire church, a day when the dioceses and religious communities of Europe would no longer be able to contribute toward the economic support of the Holy See. Without domains of its own, the papacy would collapse and the long rule of the church be ended.

In actual fact, the temporal rule of the Catholic Church did end on September 8, 1870. On that day (not quite a week after the Prussian victory at Sedan crushed the French and their power to intervene in Italy), Victor Emmanuel II massed 50,000 troops on the borders of the Papal States. He then politely begged Pope Pius IX (in a formula which has since become depressingly familiar), "to permit the royal troops [to] preserve public order." In reply, the Pope issued a *pro forma* denial of access to papal territory, the denial which contained the memorable phrase: "I bless God that he permits Your Majesty to crown with bitterness the last days of my life." Pius IX in fact lived for another eleven years, refusing either to accept the generous terms of the Law of Guarantees promulgated by the Italian government or even to leave the Apostolic Palace.

The Law of Guarantees acknowledged the popes as heads of the Catholic Church. As temporal sovereigns, moreover, they could continue to engage in diplomatic activity. The government guaranteed the papacy an annual income of 3,225,000 lire and the tax-free use of the Vatican, the Lateran Palace and Castel Gandolfo (the papal summer residence about fourteen miles from Rome). But the law did not clearly define the papal right to even a small amount of territory or concede in so many words the political independence of the papacy.

On this issue the temporal destiny of the papacy was to be in dispute for the next fifty-eight years. Sustained by their ecclesiastical revenues, which despite Consalvi's pessimism did not disappear, the reigning popes who followed Pius IX (Leo XIII, Pius X, Benedict XV) each year went through the ritual of returning the government's 3,225,000 lire. Not until the reign of Pius XI (1922-1939) was this so-called "Roman Question" finally settled. In 1929, after years of semi-official negotiations, a treaty was concluded between Italy and the Holy See. Its signatories were Benito Mussolini and Cardinal Pietro Gasparri, the papal Secretary of State. Although Mussolini's treatment of the church shortly afterward turned brutal, the Lateran Treaty marked the beginning of a new political and economic era in Vatican history.

Economically, this new day dawned only barely in time to brighten a murky scene. To understand the worsening financial problems of the papacy during the fifty-eight years of papal "exile within the Vatican," we must briefly revisit the mid-nineteenth century. In 1860, the loss to Cavour's Piedmontese forces of two-thirds of the papal domains reduced the annual ordinary income of the papacy from $10.8 million to $5.2 million. Extraordinary income, mostly from Peter's Pence collections, added $1.5 million worth of revenue each year. To meet the normal expenditures of the papacy, including the expenses of administering the remainder of the Papal States, this $6.7 million total was entirely adequate. To pay for his war against Piedmont, however, Pope Pius IX had borrowed $24 million from a French banking syndicate. The principal plus interest at 5 per cent was repayable over ten years, which made the annual cost of servicing this debt $3.6 million per year. This left the papacy with only $3.1 million worth of income to cover the rest of its expenses.

By 1868, two years before the last bits of papal territory were lost, the ordinary income of the papacy had dropped even further, to less than $300,000 per year. Private gifts and the Peter's Pence collections made up most of the difference. But expenditures for the year came to nearly $8 million. Had the French government not assumed part of the unpaid papal debt, the Holy See would have been insolvent.*

After 1870, the income of the papacy (now derived entirely from ecclesiastical taxes, Peter's Pence and offerings by individuals) leveled off at about $2.5 million per year. Most of this income was spent on maintaining the Vatican and on meeting its payrolls. Periodic short-term loans were also negotiated and repaid. It's quite likely, for example, that the Vicariate of Rome (which as we've seen is responsible for Rome's diocesan administration) advanced funds to the papacy, at least until the Italian anticlerical legislation of the late 1870's tightened the budgets of the diocesan church in Italy.

On this narrow economic base, the operations of the papacy continued well into the twentieth century. It must have been difficult for the state secretaries of the popes after Pius IX to refuse the $645,000 proffered yearly by the Italian government under the Law of Guarantees. On many occasions, it seems, the Administration of the Goods

---

* The figures given in this account are from a report made in 1868 to the American bishops by Cardinal Herbert Vaughn, the Nuncio of Pope Pius IX to the Second Plenary Council of Baltimore. (Totals are converted into dollar values of the period.)

of the Holy See* lacked the funds to finance even such essential Vatican services as the Sacred Roman Rota and the various congregations of the curia. Nor were the individual popes helpful. In particular, the generosity of Benedict XV (1914-22) endangered the entire Vatican economy. According to the account of Carlo Falconi (in his book *The Popes in the Twentieth Century*), Benedict was charitable in the syle of a Renaissance prince. His private chamberlain, Msgr. Arborio di Sant'Elia, recalled many instances when the pope, grieved by the woe of some poor soul, stuffed several thousand dollars into an envelope and mailed it off forthwith. Such was his liberality, in fact, that at his death the safe in his apartment was discovered to be empty. Benedict had completely exhausted the privy purse, which since the Council of Trent had been filled from two sources: gifts brought to the pope by archbishops, bishops and abbots when these prelates made their periodic visits; and private offerings made by wealthy laymen. Not only had Benedict spent these donations, but he had also given away substantial sums taken from the coffers of the Administration of the Goods of the Holy See. "The Lord will provide," said this Pope, "that is His task." Nevertheless, his survivors were so hard-pressed for cash that the Administration had to borrow $100,000 from a Rome bank to cover the expenses of Benedict's funeral and of the conclave of cardinals which elected his successor, Pius XI.

The Lateran Treaty, concluded seven years later, put an end to the economic insecurity of the Holy See, at least for the half-century that followed. The treaty was in fact a tripartite agreement, consisting of a diplomatic pact, a

---

* In 1878, Pope Leo XIII named Cardinal Nina, his Secretary of State, as the official administrator of the apostolic properties and funds. In 1880, a committee of cardinals was given a "consultative vote" on financial matters. In 1883, the administration of Peter's Pence collections was added to the duties of this body, and again in 1891 and in 1926 its scope was widened.

financial convention and a concordat dictating the future relations between the Vatican and Mussolini's Italy. The key financial agreements closely followed those of the Law of Guarantees, which the Italian governments had observed unilaterally ever since 1871. Under the diplomatic pact, the land and buildings of Vatican City, of the Lateran Palace, of three Roman basilicas (St. John Lateran, Santa Maria Maggiore and St. Paul) and of Castel Gandolfo were considered papal territory. These are the components of the present independent Vatican City State, of which the popes are sovereigns. In compensation for the loss of the Papal States, the financial convention provided for a payment to the Holy See of 1.75 billion lire (at 1929 rates, about $92.1 million). Under the Concordat, the Italian government agreed to make Catholicism the state religion of Italy, to accord tax exemption to the church and its organizations and to pay the salaries of the diocesan priests of Italy. (The $600 per year being paid to each of Italy's 30,000 diocesan priests makes the total amount of this state subsidy $18 million per year.)

The political consequences of the Lateran Treaty were both far-reaching and disturbing. In retrospect, there's little room for doubt that this agreement committed the papacy to the political support of Fascism in Italy and led directly to the Concordat of 1933 with Hitler's Third Reich. This is not the place to discuss in detail the Byzantine diplomacy of Pope Pius XI during the 1930's. (Carlo Falconi, himself a passionate antifascist, points out that if the Pope did sanction the vile dictatorships of Italy and Germany—and of Spain, Portugal and Hungary besides—he also forbade the hierarchy of France to associate the church with the anti-republican right wing of that country.) Suffice it to say here that in attempting to appease Mussolini, Hitler and their fellow dictators, Pius XI was not alone. Like the Daladiers and the Chamberlains, moreover, Pius XI and his successor, Pius XII, were to suffer for their realism and their silence.

Our concern is with money.

On June 9, 1929, a few months after the signing of the Lateran Treaty, Mussolini's treasury turned over to Cardinal Gasparri approximately $39.7 million in cash and another $52.4 million in the form of 5 per cent government bonds. The total represented the indemnity for the loss of the Papal States. On the same day, Pius XI issued a *motu proprio* (executive decree) forming the *Amministrazione Speciale*, the Special Administration which would handle these funds. From what we know of the canon laws governing church finance, we should be able to deduce the Pope's purpose. By creating this new juridical personality, he meant to keep the indemnity proceeds entirely separate from all other Vatican funds. (Since 1926, the Administration of the Goods of the Holy See had been charged with the responsibility for these other funds.)

To supervise the new Special Administration, the Pope named a committee of three curial cardinals. Gasparri, the Secretary of State, was its head. As the executive responsible for the fund itself, however, Pius XI appointed a layman, Bernardino Nogara, a fifty-nine-year-old former vice president of the Banca Commerciale Italiana. For the next thirty years, Nogara's ideas and methods were to dominate Vatican finance. And Nogara himself will therefore be a central figure in our narrative.

About this investment specialist, journalists have woven the legends they always do weave about financiers who shun personal publicity. In Nogara's case, of course, the legends also contain a spicy dash of ecclesiastical secrecy. Thus, Nogara became a "Vatican mystery man," a "financial wizard" whose stealthy maneuverings in international finance made the Vatican into a worldwide economic power. For instance, one amateur Vatican-watcher told me in Rome that Nogara's craving for anonymity stemmed from the fact that he was Jewish and therefore afraid of embarrassing the Vatican. Then, in his gossipy but wildly inaccurate book, *The Vatican Empire*, the American reporter Nino Lo Bello accords to Nogara's supposed genius the most fervent tribute of all.

> [N]o other single individual, pope or cardinal, gave as much impetus and muscle to Vatican finance as did Bernardino Nogara, the invisible man who started out to be an architect and succeeded in building a financial empire.

To give Lo Bello his due, he does a fair job of gathering the undramatic facts of Nogara's life. But in fitting the facts together, Lo Bello suffers from his own innocence of economic knowledge. And in interpreting what he finds, he's dominated by his belief that the Vatican is stupendously rich. Unfortunately, as we'll see, Lo Bello's own information seldom substantiates his conclusions.

Certainly Bernardino Nogara was a capable financier. But he was far from being an "invisible man." On the contrary, Nogara was a well-known figure in Italian banking and economic circles. In 1919, he represented Italy on the Economic Council of the Versailles Conference; and he later served for five years in Berlin as a member of the Inter-Allied Reparations Commission. Nogara was in fact known for his specialized work in international banking and currency transactions long before Pius XI named him to run the Special Administration.

According to Lo Bello, Nogara "had come to the attention of Vatican officialdom through Pope Benedict XV, who had made personal investments in Turkish Empire securities with [Nogara's] help and advice." But I find very unlikely that a pope would care to invest money in the bonds of a Muslim state. Equally unlikely is the notion that any banker would have recommended as a prudent investment the bonds of the country known before World War I as "the Sick Man of Europe." And as dubious, given Benedict's spendthrift habits of charity, is the assumption that this Pope ever had personal funds available to invest.

Stripped of romance, the facts of Nogara's appointment were these. With a fund of $92.1 million in hand, Pope Pius XI and his Secretary of State chose as their chief investment officer an Italian banker thoroughly versed in international finance and of outstanding professional reputation. Their candidate, moreover, was known to have no previous Vatican connections and therefore owed no favors to curial officialdom. Nogara himself was as cautious about accepting the job as the Pope had been in selecting him. He is said to have secured from Pius XI himself approval of two special conditions: 1) that he not be restricted by religious or doctrinal considerations in his investment-making; and 2) that he be free to invest Vatican funds anywhere in the world. The Pope assented. During the years that followed, the Pope did one more vital thing. He himself left Nogara alone, and he saw to it that no one interfered with Nogara's operations.

Despite his freedom, Nogara faced certain problems and encountered some obvious restrictions. The first of his difficulties arose from the very nature of his assignment. He was expected to safeguard the new funds in his care and to make them grow. At the same time, however, he was expected to supply a substantial part of the annual income of the Holy See, perhaps as much as 70 per cent. As any mutual-fund manager will tell you, these objectives are not altogether compatible with one another. The speculation which the professional uses to force capital growth is too risky for the investor who must provide an immediate yield for his client.

In addition, Nogara had to contend with political difficulties. More than $50 million of his $92.1 million was in the form of Italian government bonds. While these bonds did pay 5 per cent interest and thus afforded the Vatican an income of $2.3 million a year, Nogara must have been uneasy about having so much of his capital tied up in fixed-yield securities. These, however, he knew he could neither trade nor sell. For better or for worse, his client had been forced to make a loan to Mussolini's corporate state. Although Nogara was eager to diversify—and to inter-nationalize—the Vatican's indemnity holdings, he had to accept a long-term involvement in the domestic economy of Italy.

As I reconstruct the situation, Nogara did what any other shrewd banker would have done. He formulated a dual investment strategy. First, he gradually moved out of Italy as much of the Vatican's cash fund as possible. This he did by the classic methods of *arbitrage* and of longer-term speculation in foreign exchange. These techniques require some explanation, but in the hands of a professional like Nogara, their purpose is simple: to transfer funds from one currency into others and to acquire a profit on the way.

Briefly, *arbitrage* is the delicate art of squeezing such a profit out of the daily fluctuations in the relative values of world currencies. For example, suppose you've got a certain sum of money in, say, lire. If you know or suspect that twenty-four or forty-eight hours from now the value of the franc will rise in relation to the lire (e.g., that instead of being worth 120 lire the franc will be worth 121), you'd be wise to sell lire and buy francs *today*. Do this often enough, successfully enough and with large enough sums and you'll make lots of money even on very small shifts in currency values. Iron nerves, a mathematical mind and a crystal ball also help. *Arbitrage* is not for amateurs.

As the name implies, speculation in foreign exchange involves the purchase of one currency on the bet that its future value will be higher in relation to another. (Or it might mean the sale of one currency on expectation of a drop in its relative value.) This game becomes more interesting when it's played with perhaps two dozen currencies for periods ranging from one week to six months ahead; and more interesting still when the objective is to come out with all holdings converted at a substantial profit into one favored currency.

Today, *arbitrageurs* and speculators in foreign exchange are called all sorts of unpleasant names, especially by the officials of those governments (including our own) which are most hurt economically by speculation. The Swiss, whose own currency is the only one in the world to be backed 120 per cent by gold, have long been exceptionally gifted at trading for gain in other peoples' currencies. Hence the term "the gnomes of Zurich," which implies that Swiss bankers and financiers are constantly toiling in silence and secrecy to undermine the economies of other nations.

During the 1920's, however, playing the world money market was considered perfectly respectable. The unsettled economic conditions which followed World War I made the decade a paradise for successful gnomes, whether of Zurich, London, Rome or New York. Nogara's entry into this arena on behalf of the Holy See came late in the decade. But even though the early 1930's were depression years, they were no less fruitful than the 1920's for a well-financed trader in foreign exchange. It's highly probable that within a few months of the day he first took control, Nogara had transferred into other currencies (and securities) those millions of lire he was free to move. How much of a profit he netted for the Special Administration on these initial transactions has never been revealed and (for reasons to be covered shortly) may not even be known.

Another maneuver completed his strategy. With his

inescapable investment in the bonds of Italy barring more investment abroad, Nogara set about improving the Vatican's domestic financial position. Here again, the facts are unobtainable and the results, slightly more visible, are clouded by myth.

To understand what Nogara apparently did do with the Italian investments of the Vatican, we must understand also what Benito Mussolini was attempting to do with the entire Italian economy. In theory, Mussolini was a socialist. He professed to believe in state ownership and control of agricultural and mineral resources, of factories, of transportation facilities and of all other means of production. In practice, however, Mussolini was an *Italian* socialist. He knew well that in his country, no one who owned anything —whether a hectare of farmland, a small shop or a factory —would ever willingly part with it, even if a government offered to pay generously in return. So for the first years of his rule, Mussolini concentrated on winning material gains for those who owned nothing, the industrial workers of northern Italy. Indeed, as we've noted, one major reason for his conclusion of the Lateran Treaty was to increase his popularity among the Catholics of the north.

But when the economic crisis of the 1930's struck Italy, Mussolini possessed the legal powers to act. His response owed something to socialist theory, something more to his shrewd sense of public relations and a great deal to his desire for power. He saw that by taking advantage of the depression, he could do peacefully what no Italian leader could have done by violence. He could turn Italy into a quasi-socialist "corporate" state. His method would involve, first of all, the modern state's ability to borrow, and, secondly, direct government intervention in the economy.

Nogara himself was one of those who gave Mussolini his opportunity.

In 1929, the three Italian "banks of national interest," the Banco di Roma, the Credito Italiano and the Banca Commerciale Italiana had all been caught in the disaster which followed the collapse of the Creditanstalt of Vienna.* All three banks were crucial to the economy of Italy. When their directors sought aid, they asked Nogara to serve as a consultant in the negotiations with the Duce. The result of the dictator's deliberation with the financiers was a government agency through which Mussolini could put the Italian state into business for itself. Mussolini named this new bureau the Istituto per la Ricostruzione Industriale, or I. R. I. What made I. R. I. so powerful was simply that it could issue bonds—that is, borrow money in the name of the people of Italy. The lenders would be the banks (and the insurance companies, mortgage-loan companies and other financial institutions) which were in so much trouble.

The proceeds from the sale of these bonds I. R. I. would use to acquire ownership of key companies in industries crucial to the Italian economy. So in effect, I. R. I. was Mussolini's tool for forcing holders of capital to put up the money for the nationalization of Italy's basic industries. Among its acquisitions were the Italian Air Line (later Alitalia), the three major communications and transportation companies and the very same banks which had come to Mussolini for assistance.

In many cases, I. R. I. was able to negotiate directly with the owners of the organizations it wished to acquire, a relatively easy thing to do in a country where even very large companies were privately or closely held; and easier still in a dictatorship. In some instances, I.R.I. bought con-

* Predictably, writers who like to mythologize Vatican finance claim that the Vatican is closely tied to all three banks. In fact, none of the three is linked to the Vatican, though all do some banking business for the church. The Banca Commerciale Italiana, Italy's largest bank, was formed in 1894 by a group of five German banks, to help finance the industrialization of northern Italy.

trolling blocks of stock on the open market, paying the rock-bottom prices of the depression years and permitting minor shareholders to retain their interests. To Americans, so arbitrary a piece of state capitalism seems repellent. We prefer subtler methods of involving government in the private sector of our economy. But in Italy, I. R. I. worked. It pleased the financiers because their capital was earning more in government-backed I. R. I. bonds than it could have earned anywhere else. It pleased the industrialists because I. R. I. paid higher prices for their stockholdings than any other investor was willing to pay and still kept the owners in office as management. It pleased labor because plants stayed open. Most of all, I. R. I. pleased Mussolini himself, because through it he could exercise iron control over the biggest companies in the economy.

In the formation of this state-owned holding company and in the accompanying reform of the entire banking system, Nogara played the part of a professional adviser to Mussolini's free-wheeling regime. Because the Vatican obviously did have a stake in the survival of the Italian economy, Nogara felt free to help plan the measures that would allow survival and encourage recovery. (For similar reasons, financiers like Bernard Baruch and Joseph Kennedy were eager to help President Roosevelt rescue the U. S. financial community.) Then, once the banking crisis was over, Nogara saw in I. R. I. an intriguing opportunity to invest Vatican money in Italy's economy. It's possible that Mussolini put pressure on Nogara to persuade him to take his next step. But it's more probable that Nogara, as one of the architects of I. R. I., had faith in its future. In any case, Nogara arranged to exchange some of the Special Administration's original 5 per cent government bonds for the new bonds I. R. I. was issuing to raise funds for its activities.

Under this new dispensation, Nogara's Special Administration was still a bondholder. But his I. R. I. trans-

action had added a second issue of securities to his eggs-in-
one-basket portfolio. As long as the government could
spur on the corporations it now owned to greater economic
effort, the Vatican, like its counterparts in private finance,
would draw its interest income. At the same time, Nogara
could demonstrate to the Fascist regime that the Holy See
was contributing to Italy's economic recovery. Given the
delicate situation he had to face, Nogara could congratulate himself on the immediate results. Longer-term planning
of domestic investment strategy would necessarily depend
on Mussolini's next moves.

What Mussolini did do next belongs to history. Nothing keeps an underdeveloped industrial economy humming
better than does a nice war. In 1936, Mussolini began his
small-scale war against Abyssinia, and Pope Pius XI himself blessed the departing Italian troops. Then, following
the example of Hitler in Germany, the Duce also started
preparations for a major conflict in Europe. What Nogara
thought of so evil an economic medicine, nobody knows.
Like the rest of Italy, he swallowed it.

Preoccupied as he was with the Administration's domestic holdings, Nogara could not have been neglecting
foreign investment. If my earlier conjecture is correct, then
by 1930 he had shifted into the currencies and securities of
countries outside Italy roughly $40 million of the funds in
his care. No one I have interviewed, either within the Vatican or in banking, knows what Nogara did with this money.
One possibility is that he turned his lire into U. S. dollars and
used the money to build up a portfolio of stocks in major
American corporations. But to say the least, the years
1930-34 were not ideal years for stock-market activity.
Later, Nogara did turn his attention to stocks, and he may
have made a few cautious purchases (not only in New York
but also in London and in Zurich) at this time. But with
most of the Special Administration's foreign currencies,

I think Nogara did something entirely different. I think
he used them to buy gold.

Although the glitter of gold fascinates all of us, the
professional understands that dealings in gold are really
only another form of currency speculation. The reason is
simple. Unless you're a jeweler, own a dental laboratory,
are a specialized manufacturer or are simply a miser, the only
thing you can do with a large quantity of gold is to sell it.
That is, exchange it for one or more of the world's many
currencies. Which currencies you choose will naturally
depend on your appraisal of the international money
market. So although you're ostensibly trading in a heavy
yellow metal, you're actually trading in money. With this
key thought in mind, it's easy to see why governments are
jealous of the right to determine exactly how much an
ounce of gold (or a ton of gold) is worth in their own currencies. And why in order to do so, governments limit
private transactions and try to monopolize large-scale purchases and sales of gold. They covet not the gold itself
but the power to control the money-market values of their
currencies. If they lose this control (as they periodically
do), then speculation gets out of hand and leads to economic
crisis, especially in international trade.

Until April 19, 1933, the United States Treasury Department would buy gold from any seller. The official
price was $20.67 per ounce. More significant, the Treasury
would also sell gold to any buyer, domestic or foreign,
private or governmental, who could meet the price. On
April 19, however, things changed. The treasury was still
willing to buy gold, at the much higher price of $34.45 per
ounce. But it would thenceforth sell gold only to licensed
buyers (jewelers and other users) and—on a large scale—
to other governments. The United States thus repudiated the
gold standard. To quote economist Robert Lekachman
on the domestic effect of this move, "the thinking within

the [Roosevelt] administration was that the resulting flow of gold into the country would have the effect of raising the domestic price level," and thus of easing the depression. If you happened to have owned gold at the old $20.67 price, however, the monetary shift meant that your gold was now worth many more U. S. dollars. And if you had faith enough in the U. S. economy to want to hold its dollars, you might well sell back some of your gold.

Nogara, I'm certain, had gold to sell.

To see when and where he got his gold, let's make the next step a step backward in time, to 1931. In his superb book *Once in Golconda*, financial chronicler John Brooks describes what was happening:

> Over the summer of 1931 a series of banking panics and failures swept over Europe. Hoover's one-year moratorium on intergovernmental payments, proposed in June and accepted in July, eased the situation only temporarily, and in September the once-imperial British pound, kingpin of world currencies for a century, was forced off the gold standard. . . . As the United States continued to cling precariously to the gold standard—that is, to sell gold in exchange for dollars to all comers on demand—a drain from its Treasury to foreign countries began that within six months would cut the nation's gold reserve in half.

The Vatican, I'm certain, was one of those "foreign countries." Through European banks, Nogara bought from the U. S. Treasury $26.8 million worth of gold at the then-standard price of $20.67 per ounce, paying a handling charge of $51,665 in the process.

For a state financier, the logic of such an arrangement was obvious. It made sense for the Vatican to sink some of its assets into this most saleable of commodities, if only for use as collateral against future loans. Then, too, with Italian politics unsettled and Europe in economic chaos, nearly 800 pounds of gold ingots in the basement of the Federal

Reserve Bank in New York looked comfortingly solid and secure. Finally, Nogara must have known that sooner or later the dollar, too, would be forced off of the gold standard. If that happened, then simply by reselling gold to the Treasury at the new, higher price, Nogara could realize a substantial profit, in dollars if not necessarily in purchasing power. (As things turned out, the resale could have netted the Special Administration a dollar profit of nearly $15 million.)

To gain the safety and the liquidity of gold, Nogara did have to give up something. Namely, the use of the $26.8 million and the interest the money might have earned elsewhere. But in 1931, interest rates were low and conventional investment activity almost at a standstill. The 5 per cent Italian government bonds in the safe of the Special Administration were yielding a regular income of more than $2 million a year, enough of a return to please Pope Pius XI. So it seems that Nogara had little to lose and a great deal to gain by sinking money into gold.

Did he then complete the cycle in 1933 and sell gold back to the Treasury for U. S. dollars? He may have done so, because the Pope, in the style of his Renaissance predecessors, had embarked on a large-scale building and renovation program, in Vatican City itself and elsewhere in Rome. Much of the money to construct the new buildings came from sources other than the Special Administration. The Vatican's green, pink and yellow marble railroad station, for example, was a gift from Mussolini's government. Guglielmo Marconi himself gave the Vatican its first radio station. But the Pope's need for funds to finance the rebuilding were still pressing. To meet these needs, Nogara may have had to sell some gold. But most of what he had purchased he retained. Gold was too good an investment.

At this point, we should pause to gain perspective on this

remarkable Vatican investment program. The first point to note is its scope. The $92 million placed in Nogara's hands in 1929 obviously was a lot of money. Yet even though dollars then were worth more than they are today, we're still not considering sums of billion-dollar magnitude. I underscore this fact for a good reason. A realistic appraisal of today's Vatican wealth must be based on our awareness of the situation at the start of the papacy's "new economic era." Unless we draw the lines in the right places and add up the figures correctly now, we'll allow the old myths of limitless Vatican wealth to obscure the truth entirely.

Also worth noting is the technical sophistication of Nogara's program. This made Nogara unique among Vatican officials. As we've seen, dealings in currencies, in government financing and in gold are not staggeringly difficult to grasp in theory. In practice, however, the day-to-day activities of any one investment specialist are hard even for other experts to follow. In the Vatican, the only real experts were Nogara himself and the small staff of lay accountants he assembled. His immediate superiors were churchmen, none of whom understood finance. Pope Pius XI himself possessed no financial training. Nogara therefore had no one with whom to discuss his activities or his investment tactics. To the church leaders who employed him, his maneuverings were as mysterious as they were to the world outside.

Furthermore, what Nogara did was technically illegal. To see why, let's once again quote Msgr. Harry J. Byrne, co-chancellor of the Archdiocese of New York, on his specialty, the investment of church funds.

The Holy See itself has indicated that speculation is a form of business activity prohibited in clerical and religious affairs, and in ruling speculative practices out it used the Italian equivalent of the phrase "playing the market." "Playing the market" is a reference to the purchase of securities with the purpose of deriving a[n] . . . increase in capital value and the consequent profit upon resale.

In support of his point, Msgr. Byrne cites the canon laws themselves and a judicial decision of the Sacred Congregation for the Propagation of the Faith.

Although Nogara's investment strategy undoubtedly was conservative (after all, what more conservative investment is there than gold?), his tactics were necessarily speculative. With the Pope himself as client, Nogara faced no canonical entanglements. As long as Pope Pius XI was alive, no Vatican tribunal questioned Nogara's activities, no legalistic-minded cardinal or monsignor spoke out openly against him. Still, although the Vatican is a society of obedient men, it never has been a monolith. In the pope's backyard as in any other small community, moreover, ignorance breeds suspicion. So there were mutterings and rumors about Nogara, his privileged position and his "unlawful" transactions. Indeed, some important churchmen felt uneasy about this layman in their midst.

For me, the fact dispels forever the image of the Vatican as a kind of ecclesiastical super-bank filled with brilliant moneymen in clerical attire. As much for protection against Vatican troublemakers as for reasons of finance, Nogara made the Special Administration a very private enclave within the already private world of the Holy See. His working methods clearly show that he neither needed nor wanted help from priestly amateurs. In his small office on the third floor of the Apostolic Palace, Nogara at first employed only two people, a male secretary and a bookkeeper. Both were laymen. Only very slowly did this staff expand. During the twenty-nine years of Nogara's activity, the payroll of the Special Administration was never to number more than a dozen employees. The actual investment decisions (and the placing of the orders to sell or buy) were Nogara's alone.

One incident illustrates perfectly the place of Nogara's Special Administration in the power structure of the Vatican. On February 10, 1939, Pope Pius XI died. His successor, of course, was Pius XII, who as Cardinal Eugenio Pacelli had replaced Cardinal Gasparri as Secretary of State in 1932. As head of the three-man commission of cardinals in nominal charge of the Special Administration, Pacelli had learned early of Nogara's insistence on doing things his own way. Worse still, he had heard rumors that Nogara's extra-canonical practices had cost the Special Administration dearly. One account placed its losses at nearly half of the total entrusted to it in 1929. Furthermore, the new Pope came from a family which had long rendered legal and fiscal aid to the Vatican. (For instance, Ernesto Pacelli, his uncle, had been head of the Banco di Roma during the lowest ebb of the papal fortunes, and had advanced sums regularly when revenue was slow to come in.) For a job so vital, his own relatives might therefore be better-qualified than a sixty-nine-year-old holdover from an earlier regime.*

As one of his own first administrative moves after being elected, Pius XII appointed a special commission to investigate the Special Administration. Presumably, auditors from other Vatican financial offices (to be discussed later) were called in to check the records. Nogara himself was closely questioned. But the scrutiny proved the suspicions of the pope to be entirely unfounded. The supposedly missing money was that percentage of the original total which Nogara had transferred out of Italy and invested in gold and other overseas holdings. The Italian bond port-

---

* I've heard that Carlo Pacelli, the Pope's nephew and then as now an able lawyer, strongly advised against replacing Nogara.

folio had been broadened. As the original bonds had matured, Nogara had either purchased new government issues (as he did with I.R.I.) or else shifted the capital into investments in private companies. As for the net result, Nogara had increased the initial capital of $92 million by about 50 per cent. Much of this increase took the form of what accountants call "unrealized appreciation": i.e., gains in the values of assets which are still being held and which are not yet sold. Gains of this size are typically the product of a solid but not a spectacular ten-year investment record. In addition, however, during the decade of Nogara's operations the Special Administration had turned over to the papacy nearly $20 million worth of cash income. To a knowledgeable investment officer, Nogara's double feat of raising portfolio values and at the same time providing income—both accomplished during a severe depression—would connote first-rate money management. To Pope Pius XII, it seemed like a miracle. He never again doubted Nogara.

CHAPTER EIGHTEEN

Vatican Finance: Myth, Reality and Performance

In 1939, the new Pope had need of talented investment advisers, for the war which seemed inescapable would seriously disrupt Vatican finances. The Vatican itself would of course be officially neutral. Presumably, other governments would continue to respect the diplomatic immunity of the papal nunciatures (embassies) and delegates' residences (in countries like the U. S. where no formal embassy existed). Accordingly, in any country the Ordinaries could safely forward to their nuncio or apostolic delegate domestic funds normally sent on to the Holy See. In turn, the Vatican Secretary of State or the Pope himself could instruct the individual diplomats of the church to hold the funds, to invest them, to bank them or to spend them on needed local projects. The diplomatic pouches of the Vatican could be used to transmit such instructions. If papal diplomatic couriers were unable to make their journeys, Radio Vatican could beam short-wave code messages abroad.*

But a means of controlling overseas funds was only a partial answer to the wartime economic problems of the papacy. Although the Lateran Treaty guaranteed the Vatican its independent diplomatic status, the domestic currency of the tiny state remained the Italian lira. To meet its payrolls, to pay its bills for food and other supplies and to cover additional operating expenses, the Vatican obviously needed a plentiful supply of lire. Ordinarily, its Italian revenues more than filled this need, and even during a war these would not cease. But if a war did come, Pope Pius XII was determined to do as his predecessor, Benedict XV, had done during and after World War I. That is, make the papacy into a great center of charity. This would cost money, more money than the Vatican gained from its domestic holdings. However, a war in which Italy was one of the belligerents would certainly mean strict controls over the lira as over all currencies. This in turn would make difficult (in Italy, nothing is impossible) the conversion of the Vatican's foreign currencies into Italian money. If a war were to cripple the Italian economy, the Holy See might be able to survive. But neither its diplomatic services in the cause of peace nor its charitable efforts could be carried out.

During the early years of World War II, the economic problem was not too serious. With the U. S. a neutral, the

---

* By this time, the Vatican State Secretariat knew that its centuries-old diplomatic cipher had been broken. In 1927, Herbert Yardley, a brilliant, eccentric cryptologist who worked for the U.S. Department of State, cracked the cipher. William Hurley, U.S. Ambassador to Italy, was a devout Catholic. He apparently leaked to a Vatican representative the news that the code was compromised. But the papal cryptographers must have been assured that Yardley would keep their secrets, because they continued to use the code.

flow of income from this most prosperous sector of the church remained uninterrupted. At the time, this income might have been worth $3 million a year. The dollars could be freely converted to lire if necessary. The currencies of other nonbelligerents could also be handled in the same fashion.

But when the United States entered the war in 1941, the situation changed. To be sure, direct communication with the Vatican was still theoretically possible. In punctilious observance of the Lateran Treaty, Mussolini's government continued to deliver to the Vatican mail and cables from all warring countries, including the U. S. (Even during 1944, when German troops were in control of Rome, this service was maintained.) Under the conventions of neutrality, the Apostolic Delegate in Washington, Msgr. Amleto Cicognani (later a cardinal and Secretary of State under Pope Paul VI), could lawfully have mailed a package of money to the Holy See. In practice, however, the German U-boat fleet and the Luftwaffe were effective barriers against any such attempt.

There remained Switzerland. Throughout the war, papal diplomatic couriers traveled freely between the Vatican and its neutral neighbor to the north. The sealed pouches that accompanied them contained some curious items. Among the strangest were the coded dispatches of the various diplomatic representatives to the Holy See who (thanks to the fortunes of war) were "immured in Vatican City" * At different times, the diplomats of both sides found it necessary to abandon their residences in Rome proper and to seek refuge inside the Vatican. To both sides, Pope Pius XII extended the courtesy of the Vatican communications service. Dispatches to the governments

---

* The phrase is that of Rev. Robert A. Graham, S.J. His book, *Vatican Diplomacy*, is a good source of detailed information about Vatican policy during World War II.

concerned could be sent via courier from the Vatican through Italy to the Apostolic Nunciature in Berne, Switzerland. There, the papal nuncio would forward unopened to the appropriate capitals the messages of their isolated ambassadors, delegates and *chargés d'affaires*. Each side seems to have accepted the Pope's rule that the Vatican's pouches were not to be used to transmit military information.

Along with this singular correspondence, the Vatican's messengers carried the official diplomatic mail of the Holy See. And this almost certainly included instructions on matters of economic policy. For years, the Special Administration had done business with various Swiss banks, including in particular the Crédit Suisse of Basle. With the war in sight, Nogara had undoubtedly done for the Vatican what other European investment experts had done for their rich private clients: built up substantial reserves of Swiss francs and of other currencies. These the willing Swiss could be ordered to convert to lire for use in Italy. The money itself could travel safely by diplomatic pouch to the Vatican. It's also conceivable that overseas funds belonging to the Vatican were pledged as collateral for loans to be repaid after the war. But I have no way of knowing for certain whether or not such pledges were made and honored. Nor would I hazard a guess about how much money Nogara had made available in the Swiss bank accounts and deposit vaults of the Holy See.

In Rome, another aspect of wartime economics disturbed the Vatican. As we've seen, the generalates of most of the major Catholic religious orders are located in Rome, though not in Vatican City itself. Most of the assets of a religious order, of course, are dispersed among its communities and institutions. As a rule, a generalate keeps on hand only enough cash to meet current operating expenses. Its fixed assets will be the building in which it is housed, perhaps a plot of land and not much more. But the superior general of an order may also hold title to certain restricted funds (e.g., funds destined for missionary work). At any given time, his cash deposits may therefore be sizable. During the war as always, scores of orders had their headquarters in the Eternal City. Most of their money was on deposit in the ordinary banks of Rome.

As long as the U. S. was still neutral, the situation of the religious orders posed no problem. But the moment this country entered the war, the flow of funds to and from the generalates slowed to a trickle. Some of the lesser orders found themselves in financial difficulties and applied to the Vatican for help. Others had ample funds at their disposal in Rome but no way of transmitting money to provinces, communities and missions outside Italy.

For his part, Pius XII was concerned about the vulnerability of the generalates. If the war went badly, the Fascist regime might confiscate—or simply plunder—the properties and the funds it had so far left strictly alone. Or the regime might even collapse, to be replaced by an openly anticlerical socialist or communist government or by no government at all. At the same time, the Vatican needed lire to cover its rising expenses. And the Pope wanted to build up cash reserves to finance the great outpouring of papal charity which he felt would sooner or later be necessary in a Europe torn by war.

He turned over the problem to a forty-five-year-old *sostituto* (under-secretary) in the Secretariat of State. Msgr. Giovanni Battista Montini, who is now Pope Paul VI, consulted Nogara of the Special Administration and other lay professionals (we'll encounter them later) involved in Vatican finance. He then proposed to Pius XII a solution very much in line with the Pope's own avowed interest in managerial efficiency. Namely, a Vatican bank.

Initially, the bank would serve the immediate needs of

the religious orders and of the papacy. It would safeguard money. It would accept deposits, record internal loan transactions and channel funds into the Pope's own accounts. In some ways, the proposed new financial agency would resemble the diocesan central financing arrangements which had recently gained a foothold in the United States and with which we're already familiar. In the Vatican, however, a central fund could be more than a private internal lending agency. If the Pope wished, it could be an actual state bank, one that not only held funds on deposit but also offered checking, investment and other banking services. If you're conducting affairs on an international scale, a private bank can be a very useful institution.

Pope Pius XII had in mind no such wide-ranging institution. But the immediate usefulness of a quasi-bank was evident. So on June 27, 1942, he issued an edict creating the *Istituto per le Opere di Religione*, the Institute for the Works of Religion. Like the Special Administration, the Institute was under the nominal charge of a commission of cardinals. During the war years, its operations were managed by Msgr. (now Cardinal) Alberto di Jorio, a Vatican civil servant who reported through Msgr. Montini to Pope Pius. A small staff of lay bookkeepers and cashiers was assembled and given an office in the Apostolic Palace. (It was located in the Cortile Sant' Uffizio, the Holy Office Courtyard, just downstairs from the papal apartment.) Once the books were set up, messages were sent to the superiors general of the religious orders. They quietly withdrew funds from the commercial banks and savings institutions of Rome and redeposited the money in the Institute. Di Jorio promptly began to arrange emergency loans for needy religious orders. He also borrowed funds in the name of the Pope to finance Vatican war charities.

Needless to say, the Institute released no official financial reports. Although its offices have always been one of the sights which Vatican insiders take their friends to see, the Institute has kept silent about itself. Even today, the only official reference to the Institute in the *Annuario Pontificio* is the statement that "its function is to provide for the custody and administration of capital destined for works of religion."

In 1942, the initial deposits in the Institute couldn't have been worth more than a few million dollars. By the end of the war, however, deposits and actual disbursements were running at the rate of about $25 million a year. This growth was the result of the large-scale fund-raising done (mostly in the U. S. and Canada) to pay for the Pope's charitable projects. To see how this financial aid was arranged, we must look back at a curious excursion undertaken in February, 1943, at the height of the war. The traveler who made that excursion was the Most Reverend Francis J. Spellman, then Archbishop of New York but not yet a cardinal. In his capacity as Military Vicar (roughly equivalent to chief Catholic chaplain of the U. S. armed forces), Spellman had secured official government permission to tour American overseas bases in Africa and Great Britain. During a stopover in neutral Lisbon, he also secured permission to fly to Rome for a ten-day visit to the Vatican. Astonishingly enough, the Fascist government of Italy agreed to let him make the trip. The press speculated that Spellman, as President Roosevelt's personal representative, was being sent to ask Pius XII to initiate peace talks between Italy and the Allies. No such plan existed. But while Spellman never did reveal all that happened during his stay in Vatican City, his authorized biography does state that he and Pope Pius "certainly discussed war prisoners and war relief." (The Pope was especially concerned about the treatment of the thousands of Italian P.O.W.'s in North Africa.)

I'm certain that the Pope wanted Spellman to set up a national fund-raising organization in the U. S. for purposes of war relief; and that Spellman, forthrightly and patriotically American, agreed only with reservations. He may have made the point that American Catholics would be reluctant to give money directly to the Pope for presumable use in Italy, an enemy country. He may have insisted that any money raised in the U. S. should also be spent in the U. S. for the food, clothing, medical supplies and other needed material, which could then be shipped to Europe. The Pope could not have been pleased by these truths. But as a former Vatican diplomat and as a friend and admirer of his American archbishop, Pius would have accepted them. The result, I think, was an intelligent compromise. At least, subsequent history suggests as much. Later in 1943, the National Catholic Welfare Conference launched Catholic War Relief Services. In 1943 and 1944 alone, the church channeled through this charitable corporation almost $40 million worth of donations and special parish collections for overseas relief. Most of this money actually was spent in the United States for food and materials to be shipped overseas. But Spellman, too, knew how to compromise. Furthermore, his devotion to the Pope was utterly sincere. So it's more than probable that some of the money CWRS raised was transferred directly to the Vatican. Some, indeed, may have reached the Pope as early as the fall of 1943, while the war in Italy was still to be decided.

In September of that year, Enrico Galeazzi, a lay Vatican official and a close friend of Archbishop Spellman's,* made a hurried trip from Rome to New York and Washington, D. C. His purpose was to protest on behalf

---

* Galeazzi and Spellman had met during the latter's stay in Rome during the 1920's. Both had worked on the playgrounds the Vatican was constructing for the children of Rome. Galeazzi later became the chief architect of Pius XI on the Pope's rebuilding program in Vatican City, a post he retained under Pius XII.

of the Pope the American bombings of Rome. The city had been bombed twice, on July 19 and on August 13, 1943. In the July raid, an attack on a freightyard had severely damaged the papal basilica of San Lorenzo. The Pope, horrified, had immediately withdrawn from his account in the Institute for the Works of Religion his last 2 million lire. With this cash (worth about $100,000) in a satchel, he had driven with Msgr. Montini to the scene of the bombing. While the Pope comforted the demoralized and the dying, Montini had handed out the money in a dramatic gesture of papal charity.

On his mission of protest, Galeazzi spent five days in the United States. Accompanied by Spellman and by Archbishops Stritch of Chicago and Mooney of Detroit, he pleaded with President Roosevelt to guarantee the safety of Rome. (The President made no promises.) During Galeazzi's stay, Spellman could have presented to him a substantial sum of CWRS money for the Pope; and I'm fairly certain that Spellman did so. At the time, a check drawn on an American bank would have been useless. But in Lisbon on his return trip, Galeazzi could have exchanged U. S. dollars for Italian lire. In due course, the money would have replenished the Pope's account in the Institute. Of the total, which I estimate as being $10 million, part might have been credited to the accounts of the religious orders from which the Pope had borrowed money. Or the repayment of these internal loans might have been delayed and the whole of the American money spent (in Switzerland or Spain) for relief supplies. Whatever the case, the money would have been used for charity, though in ways very different from those CWRS made public at the time.

On June 4, 1944, Rome fell to the Allied forces. Pope Pius and his aides were no less relieved than were millions of other Italians that, for them, the war was over. In his adulatory biography of the present Pope, Paul VI, writer

Alden Hatch gives a neat summary of the background of postwar developments.

> The Pope's native land had suffered even more in World War II than in World War I. Then only the extreme north had been invaded, but in World War II battles had been fought throughout the length of the peninsula. Furthermore, Italy had been on the winning side in 1918, but in spite of Marshal Badoglio's attempt to switch sides in 1943, Italy was a defeated nation in 1945, and her political situation was once again chaotic.
>
> In 1946, by a narrow margin, the people of Italy renounced the monarchy and approved a new republican constitution. But the election of 1948 was the critical one. The Italians' postwar misery made them seem ripe for a communist takeover.

Hatch and many others have described the decision of Pius XII to play an active role in the election campaign of 1948. The politics of that decision, from the role of the Vatican in the formation of the Christian Democrat party to the Pope's pre-election speech ("The great hour of Christian conscience has come") in Rome, are documented elsewhere. Here, we should concentrate on the economic policies which grew out of the defense of Italy against communism.

At the end of the war, the Vatican was not only solvent but (at least by comparison with 1919) materially rich. Nogara's prewar purchases of gold and his adroit handling of other indemnity funds invested abroad * had nearly doubled the foreign investment holdings of the Special Administration, to about $80 million. The Vatican's domestic investments had yielded some income even during the war. More important, the Christian Democratic govern-

---

* With a balance of about $13 million left after the purchase of U.S. gold, Nogara probably went cautiously into the U.S. securities market during the mid-1930's. Whether or not the war interrupted his trading is impossible to say.

ment had agreed to assume the fiscal obligations of its
Fascist predecessor. Meanwhile, in Canada, the U. S., Mexico and other countries, funds unavailable because of
the war were now accessible to the Holy See. The Pope's
charitable program, its caravans of trucks pushing northward in the wake of the Allied advance, had cost millions
of dollars. But the money to pay for the program had
been separately donated, and neither ecclesiastical revenues
nor Lateran Treaty funds had been tapped for that purpose. In an Italy where almost anything could be had in
return for a pack of American cigarettes, the papacy was
almost the only private economic power.

During the prewar decade, moreover, Pope Pius XI had
put together a whole group of lay professionals to handle
legal and financial affairs for the papacy. Within this group,
Nogara himself was the key man. But others, working
independently of Nogara, also played important roles.
Among these others, Enrico Galeazzi, mentioned above as
a friend of Archbishop Spellman's, was one of the leaders.

Another important name on this list of laymen was that
of Carlo Pacelli. Years before his uncle became Pope, this
member of the family acted as legal counsel to the papacy.
A specialist in international law and in what in the U. S. is
known as administrative law, Pacelli handled the legal side
of Vatican domestic investment negotiations.

Pope Pius XII inherited this triumvirate of lay specialists from his predecessor, and he knew and trusted all three
men as few popes have trusted their lay advisers. During
the late 1930's and even during the war years, he added
other laymen to this small group. To run the Institute for
the Works of Religion, a lawyer named Massimo Spada
was brought in as administrative secretary. One of his aides
was a former professional banker, Luigi Mennini. Shortly
after the war began, a Swiss banker, Henri de Maillardoz,
agreed to serve as a consultant to Nogara and the Special

Administration. These laymen and a very few others actually ran the major economic bureaus of the Holy See. Associated with them were two or three priests of the Secretariat of State, including in particular Msgrs. Battista Montini and Alberto di Jorio.

With their master, Pius XII, these men had shared the long difficult years of establishing Vatican strength and autonomy. They had learned the art of tailoring papal financial needs to the demands of Mussolini's regime. All were therefore versed in the legal and administrative niceties of an economy in which the government both aids and competes with private enterprise. Their skills had made the papacy financially independent, not only of the various national Catholic hierarchies but also of any secular state. As Catholics, as patriots and as capitalists, all saw in communism only a hateful enemy. As political realists, the Pope and his lay aides knew well that an Italy in economic ruin would be an Italy ripe indeed for a communist takeover. Conversely, a recovered and prosperous Italy could be secured against such a threat. And the economic recovery of Italy would also be of great material benefit to the Vatican itself.

So for reasons at once religious, moral, political and economic, the Pope and his economic advisers made a vital decision. As before the war, the Vatican would involve itself in the economy of Italy. But in contrast to the previous domestic investment policy, the passive policy of a moneylender to the state, the Vatican would now pursue an active program of ownership and development in certain critical industries. In addition to being a bondholder, the Holy See would become a stockholder. The first and most significant instance of this change in investment direction was the acquisition in 1949 of a 15 per cent interest in an established (1870) Italian realty and construction company, the Società Generale Immobiliare.

In a rebuilding Italy, construction would obviously be a basic industry. A capital investment in a construction company would therefore be a vote of confidence in the country itself and a declaration of the investor's determination to be part of its revival. For the Special Administration, moreover, the gesture was relatively inexpensive and the possibilities excellent. For only about $1.5 million, Nogara secured actual operating control of the company. He himself declined to serve on the board of directors. But the appointment of Enrico Galeazzi as a vice president and director served notice that the Vatican meant to play an active managerial role. As an architect and civil engineer who was also a seasoned construction executive, Galeazzi was thoroughly qualified to be an officer. Not only could he promote S.G.I. as a commercial builder, he could also lead the company to ecclesiastical building and rebuilding contracts and—eventually—to the development of properties owned by the church.

At about this same time, Nogara also began buying into other construction or construction-oriented companies. Of these, the most important was Italcimenti, a Bergamo-based organization which (as the name implies) was a major prewar supplier of cement and other construction materials. Reasoning that roads and roadbuilding, public utilities and other large-scale projects would be urgently needed, Nogara once again bought a minority but controlling interest for a reasonable price. Massimo Spada was duly installed as a director. For the moment, previous management was retained in office.

From this base, Nogara very gradually expanded the Special Administration's ownership interests. His customary strategy was to acquire minority stockholdings, to secure directorships for his own nominees and to play no role whatever in management. Contrary to myth, the Vatican no more "runs" the companies in which it invests than it dominates the entire Italian economy. Nor have its Italian investments always proved successful, as we'll see shortly.

In addition to making direct investments on behalf of the Special Administration, Nogara continued the prewar policy of lending funds to the state-owned industrial cartels. The biggest direct investor has always been the Italian government. The Vatican may conceivably be the largest I.R.I. bondholder. But in Italian finance as in that of every other country, there's a considerable difference between owning the shares of an enterprise and being a bondholder. Only to a very minor extent has the Special Administration ever bought stock in I.R.I. companies. Its managerial control over these companies is nil.

In 1956, Bernardino Nogara retired at the age of eighty-six. As his successor in charge of the Special Administration, he chose Henri de Maillardoz, the Swiss banker and former director of the Crédit Suisse who was already serving as a consultant to the Vatican. By the time he retired, Nogara had seen the economic policy of which he had been a chief planner begin to show results. Under Galeazzi, the Società Generale Immobiliare had prospered. It had become the largest construction company in postwar Italy, with assets of nearly $50 million. In a notoriously fragmented industry, S.G.I. had integrated its operations so that planning, contracting, construction and management could be conducted under one roof. Following the lead of major U. S. construction firms, moreover, S.G.I. was acquiring ownership interests in the properties it developed.

Italcimenti had similarly assumed the leadership in its industry, accounting for almost 25 per cent of all domestic cement production. Investments in the bonds of I.R.I. and E.N.I. (Ente Nazionale Idrocarburi, the state-owned oil and gas corporation) were yielding an annual income of perhaps $3 million, more than the total prewar income from all domestic investments. Italy's industrial recovery was assured. As a private operator and as a key institutional investor, the Vatican was solidly part of the growing economy. I think it's safe to guess that by the time Nogara retired, he had doubled the value of the Vatican's domestic securities portfolio, to $100 million.

As for foreign investment, I've already suggested that since the mid-1930's Nogara had been purchasing blue-chip American stocks. During the war, when stock prices rose sharply, these holdings had begun to make money. But because of wartime restrictions, the Special Administration's American brokers would not have received detailed instructions for active trading. Only during the postwar boom could Nogara have begun to reap solid profits. Although I do know that the usual stories about the Vatican's Wall Street operations are untrue, I know nothing of the actual process by which Nogara made his U. S. investments.* Nor would I care to guess at the contents of the Special Administration's U. S. portfolio. But with good information, a cautious professional investor could have done very well between 1946 and 1956. At Nogara's retirement, the stocks and bonds he had bought here were probably worth about $50 million. Added to the value of the gold reserves already discussed, this amount would have brought Administration holdings in the U. S. (where the bulk of overseas investment was concentrated) to a total of nearly $80 million. Once again, Nogara would have doubled the stake with which he had begun in 1929.

Even so, Nogara's successors rather than Nogara himself were to steer the Special Administration and the entire

---

* More than one reporter has assumed that the late Cardinal Spellman was the official U.S. representative of the Special Administration. Supposedly, Spellman handled Wall Street for the Pope. In fact, Spellman had nothing whatever to do with Vatican investment in the United States. Much of the actual investment routine took place in Washington, D.C., where a small group (including lawyers, one well-known corporate executive and the representative of a big New York bank) met regularly to supply information and to execute Nogara's orders.

Vatican economy into the real period of postwar prosperity. To indicate the scope of their achievement—and to come to terms with the limiting realities—let's remind ourselves of what has happened in Italy since the end of Nogara's rule. In 1958, the year not only of Nogara's death but of that of Pius XII, the gross national product of Italy was approximately $31 billion. Its per-capita annual income was about $675. Its exports totaled $3.3 billion. Imports came to $4 billion, which meant an adverse trade balance of nearly three-quarters of a billion dollars. The economic status of the country, improved as things were, could be summed up in one sentence: the major ambition of every Italian worker was to own a noisy but efficient Vespa.

Ten years later, in 1968, Italy's GNP had climbed to $88.5 billion. Its annual per-capita income was nearly $1,400. Its exports had nearly quadrupled, reaching $12.3 billion. Imports had risen to keep pace, to a total of $12.5 billion, while the adverse trade balance had been cut by two-thirds. Italians by the thousands were buying cars to use on their $7 billion *autostrada* system. The economy did have its problems (including inflation and that eternal Italian stumbling-block, a shortage of capital). Nevertheless, Italy had achieved a spectacular economic recovery. In this recovery, the Vatican, like every other supplier of investment capital, had played a part. But were its financiers the chief agents of the boom?

To argue that the Vatican was the dominant force in the country's resurgence is to argue that the mouse on the elephant's back is taller than the elephant itself. A dash of recent economic history is the best answer to this argument. Thus, during the late 1940's and the early 1950's, most of the capital for the initial postwar reconstruction of Italian industry (in fact, nearly $3 billion) came not from the Vatican but—via the Marshall Plan—from the United States Government. Similarly, the treaties and trade agreements of the 1950's which created the European Economic Community did more than ten Vaticans could have done to revitalize Italian light industry, marketing, employment and consumption. And during the 1960's, far more investment capital flowed into Italy from Switzerland, Germany and the U. S. than from Italian domestic financial institutions, the Vatican included. In terms of its own relatively modest economic needs, the Vatican has thrived during the boom. But in terms of the entire Italian economy, the Vatican is the beneficiary, not the prime mover, of the country's prosperity.

Furthermore, the Vatican's participation in the largest components of the Italian economy is confined either to a minority shareholding or to a secured creditorship. To be sure, minority stockholders and bondholders are very often given seats on corporate boards. The individuals who serve may be distinguished specialists in law or finance or economics. Their expertise may make them most useful to management. But by definition, the individual board member (unless he owns the necessary stock) exercises no managerial control whatever. And for every "Vatican" director of these big companies, there are five directors who represent other, secular interests.

In 1968, Nino Lo Bello claimed that the Vatican "owns outright, controls, or influences by its substantial though minority stockholdings," a total of twenty-four Italian companies. In fact, most of these are small even by Italian standards. Seven are worth less than $1 million apiece. Only three, Cartiere Burgo (paper), A.I.C.I. (cellulose) and Pantanella (pasta) have assets of more than $15 million. None is worth more than $25 million. And over the past six years, fourteen of the twenty-four have lost money. In 1968, the total assets of all these companies equaled $105.7 million. (Their shares, of course, may sell for either more than or less than the per-share book value of their assets.) With its minority holdings in S.G.I. (worth $25 million), in Italcimenti ($19 million), in Fiat and in other major companies, its interests in the twenty-four smallish corporations Lo Bello lists gave the Special Administration a stock portfolio which in 1968 was worth about $200 million. To this figure must be added a total for the Administration's bondholdings, which I estimate at roughly $100 million. If I'm correct, then the Vatican's stake in the Italian industrial economy was worth approximately $300 million in 1968. Interestingly enough, Swiss, German and American investments in Italian industry were worth more than five times as much.

Such figures reduce to absurdity the argument that the Vatican rules supreme over the Italian economy. Yet while these estimates do deflate the legend of Vatican wealth, they also testify to the skills of the professionals who have inherited Nogara's money-management post. From the end of the reign of Pope Pius XII (1958), through that of his successor, Pope John XXIII and into the reign of the present pope, these men have tripled the worth of the papacy's domestic portfolio. If they have done as well with the Vatican's foreign investments, then the Holy See's total holdings are now well over the $500 million mark. By the standards of the professionals, this is an excellent record for a well-managed, medium-sized private investment operation.

On Vatican economics, the too-brief reign of Pope John XXIII made almost no direct impact. The sudden decision to call a Council into being, the preliminary maneuverings of "liberal" and "conservative" churchmen to control the official agenda, the explosive effect of Pope John's personal desire for *aggiornamento*—none of these was allowed to affect the mechanisms of income-gathering, of investment or of expenditure. John, in addition to being perhaps the greatest of all popes, was a realist. He left the daily business of his realm in the hands of his business servants.

Only in the reign of Pope John's successor did the economic system of the papacy begin to change. The initial instrument of change was a written document, a papal constitution entitled *Regimini Ecclesiae Universae*, or "Government of the Universal Church." First made public on August 18, 1967, this 10,000-word report on Vatican government called for what *The New York Times* correctly styled a "sweeping reform" of the Roman Curia. Among the major changes ordered by Pope Paul VI were:

- the elimination or absorption by other bureaus of three of the curial Congregations;
- new guidelines governing the tenure of curial personnel, including terms of office limited to five years and renewable at the Pope's discretion and mandatory retirement at age seventy-five;
- the reorganization of the Secretariat of State as the organ of papal control over all Vatican offices.

Until now, I've said very little about the actual governance of the Holy See. Now, however, an explanation is essential. In brief, the separate but related parts of the Holy See are governed by committee. Through committees accountable to the Secretariat of State, the Pope himself rules more or less directly over the "pontifical family," the civil, diplomatic and ecclesiastical establishment of the papacy. The financial organizations we've been discussing are parts of this larger establishment. So also are such varied organizations as the Vatican Library, the papal household (including the nuns who do the cooking) and the sixteen permanent commissions which look into matters of special concern to the popes.

Vatican City, the physical headquarters of the Holy See, is likewise governed by committee. The Pope appoints a commission of cardinals to supervise the Vatican City State. The commission, too, is a subsidiary of the Secretariat of State. The public services of Vatican City—its electricity, sewage disposal, road repair, postal system, police department, courts and jail—are managed by laymen who report to the governing commission.

This much of the story is fairly straightforward. However, more important, more complex and far more difficult for any pope to manage is the Roman Curia, the system of committees which regulates the worldwide activities of the church. Canonically, the popes reign supreme over the Curia as they do over all other ecclesiastical organizations. But by its very nature, the Curia defies papal governance. Although many popes have tried, reorganizing so powerful a bureaucracy is a staggering task. Indeed, until Pope Paul's reforms of 1967, this web of committees had remained virtually undisturbed since the Council of Trent.

When Pope Paul first announced his reforms, the Roman Curia consisted of twelve Sacred Congregations. The members of these permanent committees were all cardinals appointed by the popes. Perhaps the best way to explain the Curia as it was before reform (and as in large measure it still is) is to name its various committees, or Sacred Congregations, and to summarize their functions:

The fourteen-member Sacred Congregation for the Doctrine of the Faith, also called the Holy Office, rules on all questions of faith and morals within the church. It can, if it sees fit, override the decision of any other curial congregation.

The Sacred Consistorial Congregation, or Congregation for the Bishops (twenty-eight members), creates new dioceses, appoints new bishops and has the power to discipline the bishops.

The Sacred Congregation for the Oriental Church has jurisdiction over the dioceses, bishops, clergy and laity who observe the Oriental rites of the church. (These 9 million Catholics, most of them dwelling in the Middle East, are the descendants of those Eastern Christians who remained loyal to Rome after the split with the Byzantine church in 1054.)

The Sacred Congregation for the Discipline of the Sacraments (twenty-eight members) deals with questions about the seven Catholic sacraments. For example, this congregation determines when and where Masses may be celebrated. It also grants dispensations from impediments to marriage.

The Sacred Congregation of the Council (thirty-seven members) has jurisdiction over priestly discipline. It also supervises programs of religious instruction and rules on financial transactions within the church.

The Sacred Congregation for Religious (thirty members) has authority over all Catholic religious orders and communities.

The Sacred Congregation for the Propagation of the Faith (forty members) controls the missionary efforts of the church, including the raising and allocation of funds and the appointment of bishops and secular clergy in mission areas.

The Sacred Congregation for Rites (thirty-eight members) approves changes in the liturgies (the ceremonial acts) of the sacraments. It also hears the causes of candidates for beatification and canonization.

The Sacred Congregation for Ceremonies (thirteen members) designs and regulates papal ceremonies and other religious ceremonies involving the College of Cardinals.

The Sacred Congregation for the Extraordinary Affairs of the Church (fifteen members) is merely the curial name for the special section of the papal Secretariat of State which deals with diplomatic affairs and with concordats between the Holy See and civil governments.

The Sacred Congregation for Seminaries and Universities (thirty-seven members) has jurisdiction over all Catholic schools and institutions of higher learning. In addition, it is responsible for increasing the numbers of the priesthood.

The Sacred Congregation for the Reverend Fabric of Saint Peter (twenty-two members) is in effect the Building Commission for Saint Peter's Cathedral. It supervises the operation and maintenance of the cathedral itself and of the mosaic factory in Vatican City.

Merely to list these committees is to give you an idea of the complexity of curial bureaucracy. And the list itself is only the tip of a much bigger iceberg. Each of the Sacred Congregations, in fact, is a sizable bureaucracy in its own right. In addition to its roster of cardinals (given above), a typical congregation possesses a large staff of religious and lay personnel. It may also possess a large board of consultants recruited from other congregations or from anywhere in the church. Most congregations, moreover, are divided into four or five sections and subdivided into dozens of bureaus, which makes room at the bottom for still more clerks, *minutanti*, accountants and other minor functionaries.

At the top, every congregation is headed by a cardinal-prefect.* As the personal delegate of the pope, a prefect is canonically required to review every situation and to approve every act of the congregation. His fellow cardinals are present only to advise him; formal voting is never undertaken. However, no one cardinal can possibly keep up with the flow of work of a major congregation. Like the pope himself, the prefects must delegate much of their authority. In practice, the executive responsibility in an important congregation is shared by a small minority of the

---

* Sometimes the pope himself is the official prefect. For routine matters, a cardinal takes the pope's place and the title of sub-prefect.

cardinals—and by the titular archbishops and bishops who are the aides of this working minority. What's true for the individual curial congregation is equally true for the Curia as a whole. In the Roman Curia, as in the United States Senate, power ultimately rests with a small group of men who, because they gain posts on many key committees, form a single interlocking directorate. Given the unwieldy size of the curial congregations and the advanced age and uncertain health of so many of the cardinals who serve on them, such an inner circle must exist. Otherwise, very little church business would get done at all.

Historically, the Curia has always been dominated by such small groups of executives. Since Trent, the qualifications for membership in the inner curial circle have remained constant. First and foremost, members must be Italians, who speak the language and understand the folkways of a predominantly Italian bureaucracy. Secondly, all must manage to be full-time residents of Rome. The cardinal who serves as a residential archbishop in Holland, Canada or the Philippines cannot also supervise a Vatican congregation and contend with the daily politics of the Roman Curia. Thirdly, those who would be members of the curial inner circle must possess patience—and longevity. In the Vatican as in the U. S. Senate, seniority opens many doors.

It would serve no purpose here to name the members of the inner circle in 1967 when Pope Paul initiated his program of curial reform. Many of the Vatican conservatives who belonged to this group have since retired; some have died. And other writers have chronicled how desperately these curialists struggled against the ideas and the enactments of a church which sought renewal. The important point is that Pope Paul saw the Roman Curia as too strong and too obstructive to be left alone. Its inefficiencies challenged his sense of proper administration. Its independence threatened the papacy itself. He therefore had every reason to undertake the task of reorganization and reform. Most important for our purposes, the Pope ordered the centralization of all Vatican financial affairs. This was to be accomplished by means of two more changes: a) the establishment of a Prefecture for the Economic Affairs of the Holy See; and b) the merger of the Administration of the Goods of the Holy See (the bureau in charge of ecclesiastical revenues) with the Special Administration, in a single office called the Administration of the Patrimony of the Holy See. Both the new Prefecture and the combined Administration office were to be part of the Secretariat of State.

In my opening chapter, I quoted the official description of the Prefecture and its function. Basically, it's a central budgeting and accounting office for the Sacred Congregations and the other Vatican prefectures, the first of its kind in the history of the church. Through this office, Pope Paul will be able to know the revenues (and to check the expenditures) of the separate and powerful ruling bureaucracies of the church. For instance, without making a special inquiry he can find out the total received to date of the $32 million which flows in each year from mission collections, fund drives and donations to the Sacred Congregation for the Propagation of the Faith (now known by the less militant title of the Sacred Congregation for the Evangelization of Peoples). He can determine what it costs the papacy to maintain the basilica of St. Peter's. As important, the Pope can now do what no other pope has ever been able to do—he can assign budgets to his civil servants and determine how expertly—or how poorly—they handle money. For a man with a $20-million-a-year overhead (including salaries, maintenance and other ordinary expenses), a budget is a vital tool.

In a move symbolic of the independent status of the

Prefecture, the Pope has housed it in modern offices outside Vatican City (but overlooking St. Peter's Square).

As for the Administration of the Patrimony of the Holy See, its functions have remained much what they were before the merger. The former Administration of the Goods is now the Ordinary Section. Its job is still to collect the church taxes and Peter's Pence sums due the papacy and to make available to the Pope (who draws no salary) the cash he needs. The Special Administration has now become the Extraordinary Section, but its task is still that of managing the investment portfolios derived from the original Lateran settlement funds. Together, the two sections provide the income the Pope needs to run his realm. In the late 1960's, this income was averaging approximately $25 million per year.

Why these changes in the Vatican's smoothly operating economic machinery? Obviously, Pope Paul sees what some American bishops also see, the need for more centralized, more efficient church finance. The man who in 1942 saw the virtues of a Vatican bank for the religious orders can be expected to look for better ways of handling all Vatican money. But the good administrator's search for efficiency seems to me to be only part of the answer. Behind the official press releases and the descriptions in the *Annuario Pontificio*, I find evidence of a momentous shift in Vatican economic policy, the first such shift in forty years. To view this newest development—which as I write is still unfolding—we must first note certain other by-products of Pope Paul's curial reforms.

One of these has been a gradual transfer of economic authority from the Vatican laity to the Vatican priesthood. As in the past, the economic agencies of the Holy See are mixed agencies. In the new Administration for the Patrimony of the Holy See, in the Prefecture for Economic Affairs and in the Institute for the Works of Religion (which has long since added ordinary banking services to its deposit and loan functions), laymen still handle the investment-making and the accounting; while commissions of high-ranking churchmen are in official control. Until 1968, as we've seen, the lay experts were free to operate much as they wished. But since that pivotal year of reform, lay autonomy in Vatican financial affairs has waned. One reason is the toll taken by time. Of those accomplished laymen who began their financial labors under Pope Pius XI, only one, Carlo Pacelli, remains active today. Henri de Maillardoz, Enrico Galeazzi, Massimo Spada and the others have all either retired or become semi-retired "consultants." Theirs was Nogara's tradition of independent operation, but the Pope has seen to it that the tradition was not handed down to their successors. As these men have withdrawn, their lay replacements have been given less power. And active churchmen (some of them trained by the lay experts who are gone) have been moved into key economic posts.

For example, as Director General of the Prefecture for Economic Affairs, Pope Paul picked Dr. Giorgio Stoppa, a lay accountant and economist. But Stoppa's tenure in this office is not permanent. Rather, he's on leave from his regular post in the Administration for the Patrimony of the Holy See. At the Prefecture, his superior is the sixty-four-year-old Cardinal Egidio Vagnozzi, who until 1968 was the Apostolic Delegate to the United States. Similarly, when Enrico Galeazzi resigned from Vatican service in 1968, he gave up no fewer than four posts. The first, that of Architect of the Apostolic Palace, was left vacant. All of the others had to do with the finances of the Vatican City State. Each has gone to a single lay specialist.

Meanwhile, as the lay Old Guard gives up its power, the names of certain ecclesiastics appear and reappear on the governing commissions of the various economic agencies. Thus, Cardinals Sergio Guerri, Alberto di Jorio and Egidio Vagnozzi each serve on at least one of these commissions. (Di Jorio actually runs the Administration for the Patrimony of the Holy See. He also serves on the Commission for the Institute. Guerri heads the Commission for the Vatican City State.) Then, too, Msgr. Giuseppe Caprio, a titular archbishop, is one of Pope Paul's new breed of Vatican financiers. Caprio, fifty-seven, is secretary of the Administration and "consultor" to the Institute.

Perhaps the most remarkable member of this small group is an American, Msgr. Paul C. Marcinkus, titular bishop of Orta. About this youngish (forty-nine) prelate, the Italian press is beginning to tell sensational stories. According to an article in *Vita* (a weekly newsmagazine):

> When President Nixon visited the Pope [in 1969], the interpreter was Marcinkus. During the delicate political preliminaries to the Pope's trip to Uganda, the man in charge has been Marcinkus.

Vita might have added also that during Pope Paul's 1966 pilgrimage to Jerusalem, it was the brawny arm of Marcinkus that protected the Pope from the jubilant crowds which threatened to crush him. According to one Vatican-watcher, "Marcinkus is on his way to becoming Montini's Spellman." And while curial gossip is usually wrong, the Pope obviously does like and trust his American protégé. The best indication is the speed with which Marcinkus has ascended the Vatican's career ladder. In 1966, he was holding down a modest post in the Secretariat of State. By the end of 1969, Pope Paul had made him administrative secretary of the Institute for the Works of Religion.

Merely to name the members of this new small group of Vatican financial officials is to underscore that there's been a change. All of these men are at ease with the lay experts who staff the agencies. But beyond any question the laymen are now subordinates in fact as well as in name. Apart from being priests, moreover, the members of the Pope's economic "cabinet" have much else in common. Without exception, these men are career diplomats, trained like Pope Paul himself in the Secretariat of State. Except for di Jorio, who at this writing (1971) is eighty-five, all are relatively young men. All are fiercely loyal to their embattled Pope. And all of them share the economic philosophies of Pope Paul himself.

In marked contrast to Popes Pius XI and Pius XII, this pope is not by instinct a capitalist. In a well-known passage from his 1967 encyclical *Populorum Progressio* (*The Development of Peoples*), Paul VI makes very clear his distaste for laissez-faire economics.

> It is unfortunate that in [industrial] society a system has been constructed which considers profit as the key motive for economic progress, competition as the supreme law of economics, and private ownership of the means of production as an absolute right that has no limits and carries no outstanding social obligations.

While the Pope has said nothing with which an enlightened American businessman would disagree, he has staked out new economic ground for the papacy to occupy. In fact, Pope Paul is an advocate of centralized economic planning and of strong government control over private enterprise. His positive theories are a blend of faiths: in the mixed private and state economies of Europe's Christian Democratic countries; in benign but authoritarian government; in the applicability of Catholic social ethics to industrial and post-industrial technocracies; in the urgent need to develop the nations of the Third World.

Whatever Pope Paul VI personally advocates, moreover, he does his fearless best to carry out. (As evidence, we need only note his despairing but unflinching stances on the crucial doctrinal issues of his reign, contraception and the question of priestly celibacy.) This compulsion to act upon what he feels is right helps explain why the Pope has striven successfully to transfer Vatican economic power from laymen to his own fellow-priests and trusted aides. For Pope Paul the advocate of economic control, lay autonomy in the financial affairs of his own realm is as unthinkable as a birth-control clinic housed in the Apostolic Palace. The Nogara philosophy that investment-making must be unrestricted by considerations of doctrine is today incompatible with economic morality. What the popes needed to do forty years ago, or even ten years ago, they should do no longer. Having secured its financial independence, the Holy See must end its efforts at financial aggrandizement. The Vatican must not become too rich. And the only way to assure this goal is to concentrate in the hands of the priests the final authority over Vatican finances.

Indeed, no one is more horrified than Pope Paul himself at the rumors of Vatican wealth. It was at his personal insistence that the *Osservatore Romano*, the official Vatican newspaper (which loses $2 million a year), printed in early 1969 a formal denial of Nino Lo Bello's exaggerations of Vatican wealth. Furthermore, this Pope has journeyed into the Third World. In lands where (to quote Gandhi) "the only acceptable form in which God should dare to appear to man is the form of bread," the image of the church as rich is disastrous. Above all else, Pope Paul wants to erase this image forever.

His determination to do so accounts for some radical reversals in Vatican economic policy. The first of these involves the incredibly convoluted dispute between the Italian government and the Holy See over a question of taxes. In December, 1962, the parliament passed a law requiring all foreign investors to pay a *cedolare*, a 15 per cent tax, on the dividend income they received from their Italian investment holdings. The government then in power contended that the Vatican, as a "foreign investor," had to pay the tax. The lawyers for the Holy See stoutly denied any tax liability, basing their case on the exempt status guaranteed by the Lateran Treaty of 1929. In session after session of the ensuing Italian parliaments, this issue has provoked fiery debate. Whenever a Christian Democratic government has attempted to favor the Vatican, the Socialist and Communist deputies have unleashed storms of protest. Apparently, some taxes have been collected on Vatican holdings. But when and how much these have been, nobody knows for sure. In 1967, the rate of the *cedolare* was doubled, to 30 per cent. This the Vatican absolutely refused to pay. One spokesman even insinuated that, to avoid the tax, the Holy See would liquidate its entire Italian securities portfolio.

According to writer Peter Hamill, who was on the scene:

> [T]here was a sizeable amount of criticism within the Vatican about the handling of the affair. The younger, more progressive men [felt] the Vatican should own up and pay the tax. But they possess[ed] no real power. The power remains in the hands of the older, conservative men known as "the Pacelli group" after Pope Pius XII.

A year later, however, Pope Paul's curial reforms had begun to take effect. The younger men acquired the power. And in October, 1968, the Vatican publicly offered to settle the tax issue by paying in installments a total of $7 million. Long embarrassed by the dispute and by its attendant publicity, Pope Paul and his new advisers did their best to end both.*

An even more astonishing break with tradition came only a few months later, during the spring of 1969. In a series of secret meetings involving Cardinals di Jorio and

* At this writing (1971), they have not yet succeeded. The government has been unable to resolve its internal differences on the issue.

Guerri and Msgr. Marcinkus, the Special Administration negotiated the sale to a French syndicate of its holdings in the Società Generale Immobiliare. For the Vatican's 15 per cent of the company, the price was slightly less than $30 million. The go-between in the transaction was a shrewd Sicilian lawyer, Michele Sindona, who for nearly a decade has specialized in international business mergers, acquisitions and transfers of ownership. Furthermore, according to *Time* magazine (November 28, 1969), Sindona's opposite number in the final bargaining session was none other than Pope Paul himself.

The minute the news of the sale leaked out, the press began to speculate that the Holy See, angered by the government's hard line on taxes, was carrying out its threat to clear entirely out of the Italian investment market. In fact, the Vatican intended no such drastic move. But Pope Paul had made the decision to avoid such highly visible involvements in finance. Patrick Riley, writing for the National Catholic News Service in June, 1969, interviewed one Vatican official who said of S.G.I.: "It seems to own the whole of Monte Mario [one of Rome's fastest-growing residential areas]. This gives the impression that the Vatican is a rich landlord. That's the last sort of image Pope Paul wants the Church to have." Another "very high official of the Holy See" (probably Cardinal John J. Wright) told Riley: "Pope Paul's whole orientation, his whole temper of mind, is to divest the Holy See of its properties."

"Of course," Riley's first subject added, "he could not sell everything. He would have to keep a certain reserve, a line of defense."

For obvious reasons, this official must be right. Pope Paul, after all, is deeply devoted to the papacy; and for there to be a papacy at all, there must be money enough to support it. So the Pope is hardly likely to give away the temporal assets so dearly won by earlier pontiffs. Nor, despite his love of an occasional dramatic gesture, is Paul a real-life Hadrian VII (the fictional pope in Frederick Rolfe's novel who liquidated all the wealth of the Holy See and gave the money to the poor). Instead, I think Pope Paul has in mind other, cooler strategies. His ideas are those of the American college students and professors (and some administrators) who urge their trustees to invest endowment funds only in companies which make "good"—i.e., socially beneficial—products. Like the socialist son of a capitalist father, the Pope wants to do good with his money.

One of his latest economic moves is perhaps his most revealing. During his return flight from Uganda on August 2, 1969, the Pope had pondered deeply the plight of the Third World. In Rome, he swiftly involved Msgr. Marcinkus and another key aide, Msgr. Giovanni Benelli (Vatican Under-secretary of State) in an ambitious project. This was the formation of a private international syndicate which would invest money in Africa. The Pope wanted Marcinkus to explore the possibilities of the syndicate with other prospective participants. The initial capitalization was to be $50 million. Banks, industrial corporations and other individual investors in the "have" countries could join the Administration of the Patrimony of the Holy See as shareholders in this charitable mutual fund. The return might be low, but the moral dividends and the political advantages would be very high.

For more than a year, Marcinkus and Benelli have been lining up support for this incredible idea. They have been to Washington to discuss the Pope's scheme with David Kennedy, at the time President Nixon's Secretary of the Treasury and now head of Chicago's venturesome Continental Bank. They have reportedly also been meeting with representatives of the Ford Foundation and with Robert McNamara, head of the International Bank for Reconstruction and Development. According to *Vita*, by February, 1970, both the Ford Foundation and McNamara's World Bank had agreed to participate. So also had thirteen U. S. commercial banks and four major American corporations. But as I conclude my book (in November, 1970), Pope Paul's Third World investment program has yet to begin operating.

Whether or not the program itself succeeds, it does illustrate perfectly the economic theory now dominating the Vatican. Like many another government, that of the Holy See is shifting away from private enterprise and into what might be called charitable economics. Throughout this en tire study of the Roman Catholic ecclesiastical economy, we've seen many instances of the tension between the need for gain and the need to do good. In the parish, in the diocese, in the provincialate and in the Vatican, we've watched as priests struggle to be efficient businessmen and yet not merely men of business. This story, I'm sure, is not about to end. But from the example of the church, we ourselves can learn much. At its best and at its worst, the ecclesiastical economy is a model in miniature of what man has done —and of what he can do— with his worldly goods.

CHAPTER NINETEEN

Epilogue: Manage
What Thou Hast

When all is said, the Catholic ecclesiastical economy remains unique. Other kinds of organizations can tell us something about church economic structure and about the way the structure works. If you can follow the intricate patterns of finance that take shape on the pages of a business conglomerate's annual report, you can sense the ebb and flow and seepage of finance in the church. If you've ever raised funds for your college, worked for a foundation or served on the board of a charity, you know a good deal—more, perhaps, than you think you know—about the financial side of the church.

Yet resemblances are not identities. In the final analysis, the church beggars all comparison. It uses money in special ways. Attitudes and ideals which have little to do with finance govern the men who make its economic decisions. Even when churchmen talk and look like Rotarians, they think and feel like churchmen. And so, the economy of the Catholic Church must be understood and judged as a thing apart.

We know enough now to understand the finances of the church in the United States. From the parish to the archdiocese, we've witnessed how $2.3 billion a year is raised and spent by the church. We've looked into the religious orders and made the essential connections between their economies and those of the dioceses, schools, colleges and hospitals of the church. We've come to realize that the economic health of the American church matters not only to Catholics but to non-Catholics also; in fact, to every taxpayer and every citizen who wonders how best to reconcile a troubled church with a troubled state.

Given enough time, we could learn to understand church finance in other countries. We'd find that in Europe and South America, church wealth and church power manifest themselves in ways sharply different from what we know of the church in the United States. In the Catholic countries of Western Europe, for example, the state subsidizes church institutions directly. In West Germany the government taxes its citizens for the support of the particular churches to which they indicate they belong. Even in Protestant Great Britain, state aid to Catholic schools is taken for granted. These and other economic differences exist between the church in the U. S. and the church in Central and South America. South of the Rio Grande, the diocesan church is poor by comparison with the religious orders. The reverse, of course, is true here. The orders, which originally brought Catholicism into South America, still do dominate in terms of prestige and of wealth, which they hold mostly in the form of land.

Because church finance is so different abroad, we'd have

to struggle to estimate the total wealth of the church in each of the major countries and then of the church world-wide. To cite the most obvious problem of valuation, a parish church in the U. S. does figure on the diocesan balance sheet as a real estate asset with a definite, if arbitrary, value. But what about a parish church in Rouen or Linz, one which is not only a contemporary center of worship but also a centuries-old architectural masterpiece? If it's insured at all, its insurance value bears no relation to its true worth. For that matter, what value could we assign to St. Peter's in Rome?

Another problem is that of determining which of its property rights the church in Europe and South America is free to exercise. In countries where cathedrals, churches, shrines, monasteries, hospitals and schools are regarded as national treasures, and often maintained out of public funds, the church may not dispose of such properties without the permission of the state. Does the church really "own" these properties at all? Disentangling church wealth from national wealth is sometimes impossible. Church officials, indeed, make no effort to do so. If we ourselves wanted to put a price on the property owned but not freely owned by the church abroad, we'd need to invent a whole new system of accounting.

For the sake of an estimate, however, we could assume that church wealth is roughly proportionate to national wealth. If this is so, then most of the wealth of the church is concentrated in the richest of the world's nations, the United States. Because I'm quite sure that ecclesiastical and secular wealth are closely correlated, I'm willing to go even further. I believe that the church in the U. S., with its $34.2 billion worth of assets, holds between 50 and 60 per cent of all the assets of the Catholic Church worldwide. This assumption would make total church assets worth approximately $70 billion; a huge sum, though by no means uniquely huge. For instance, the total wealth of all U. S. corporations, $549 billion, is nearly eight times as great. But such conjecture, although it's diverting, is as much a side issue here as it has been throughout this book. Adding up the total wealth of the church is a game. The essential thing is to understand how the wealth is managed. If we did study church finance around the globe, we'd uncover a fascinating array of fiscal and administrative arrangements. But we'd also confirm that, everywhere, church wealth is diffused among many separate institutions and authority over church wealth is decentralized.

Repeatedly I've stressed the paradox that the Catholic Church, supposedly an organizational monolith, is in fact managerially decentralized. Now we must weigh the meaning of decentralization in the church—and judge its effectiveness. In essence, financial power in the church is divided and subdivided for two reasons. The first is simply that a decentralized organization is much less vulnerable than a centralized one to destruction from without. Always the church has felt that it must be able to lose parishes, dioceses, provinces and even whole national properties to its enemies, without suffering total destruction as a result.

The second reason for decentralization is to protect the church against the rapacity—or, conversely, the compulsive generosity—of its own officialdom. In the church, only a pope can command more than a limited amount of economic power. In practice, not even a pope could exercise unlimited power. The rights of the thousands of bishops and religious superiors to the control over their own temporalities are by definition curbs on papal power. In effect, decentralization in the church starts at the very top of the monolith. Further down in the hierarchy, decentralization guarantees that no one man can either accumulate or dissipate the wealth that's needed to sustain the church. Economic skirmishing can take place, a given official can amass wealth, another can give away money and goods haphazardly. But neither hoarding nor extravagance can go far enough to threaten the entire church.

Indestructibility from without and stability within are the obvious goals of decentralization. In turn, decentralization is the method of operation of an organization which is determined simply to survive. Survival may be the least glorious of the accomplishments of the church, but it has survived. And on the basis of its 2,000 years of successful survival, it's rash to quarrel with the church over its management formula. Nevertheless, the world is changing. What we've seen of the church today almost compels us to ask whether or not decentralization is still workable. In an age when human survival is in doubt, can a principle of management as old as the Caesars assure survival for the church?

In the post-industrial United States, we know that decentralization has produced two vast flaws in church management. Administratively, the American church is suffering from a famine of useful, usable information about itself and about the society in which it is rooted. Between parish and parish, diocese and diocese, province and province, few channels are open through which timely information can flow and good ideas be interchanged. Decentralization, moreover, has led to great unevenness of managerial performance. As a result, some parts of the church are solvent or even wealthy, other parts are poor, and the system offers no remedy.

The other major flaw is financial inflexibility. To shift funds from a trust or an institution with a surplus to a program or institution in need of money, an individual bishop or religious superior must stretch his canonical authority to the limit. Only by means of the creakiest economic machinery can one bishop or superior borrow money from others, or lend money to others. Meanwhile, most church wealth is either non-liquid or underutilized or both. Today, the church in the United States must grapple with economic problems which are national in scope, not local or regional. In particular, the problem of financing Catholic education requires action by the whole church. Decentralization makes concerted action almost impossible. Far from assuring survival, this threatens survival.

If the church is in economic trouble where it's richest, how well can it be faring elsewhere in the world? The Vatican periodically makes gloomy announcements about the lack of growth of the Catholic population and about the drastic world shortages of priests and nuns. But the Vatican always is gloomy about the perils threatening the church in a decaying world. I suspect that while the church in other countries is smaller and poorer than it is here, so also are its problems more localized and therefore under better control. In Europe, at least, decentralization is probably still working. But nobody knows for sure. Absurdly, the church itself is now so decentralized that nobody in power can know how well decentralization *does* work. Yet, year by year, the need to know grows greater.

As I've said earlier, I think the American church can still remedy its administrative problems. Implicit in almost every chapter of this book are blueprints for improvement. Formal management training for priests and nuns, better short-term planning, the acceptance by church leaders of their accountability to the lay public—these are the immediate answers. None of them does violence to the great tradition of decentralized control. On the contrary, they free local administrators to strengthen the local institutions which are the economic base of the church. From these first moves, others should follow. At the national level, the church urgently needs an office of economic research, where financial data can be collected, processed and studied and where continuing financial records can be kept. As urgently, the bishops and the religious orders need national central financing arrangements to ease the movement of money between dioceses and provinces nationwide. Development banking for poverty areas and investment management services for pooled endowment capital should be part of the central financing operation. And non-Catholic laymen as well as Catholics should be invited to play a professional part in the management of money for the church. These proposals undoubtedly are less orthodox than those mentioned above, but only the very last one is a radical departure from tradition. Indeed, if the Vatican itself can run both a banking service and an investment office, so presumably can the bishops of the American church.

These are methods of improving the management of an affluent church in a post-industrial nation. Would they be applicable elsewhere? I can't say for sure. Nor can anyone be certain that in the church of today, better management will be enough to assure long-range survival.

In the introduction to this book, I noted the reason why it may not be. Enormous changes—in the way Catholics worship God, in the way they view man—are sweeping over the church. To most of us, these changes in Catholic doctrine and theology, even when they make headlines, might seem primarily personal matters, affecting the way each individual Catholic feels about and practices his religion. But in the church, every shift in doctrine, every theological development, large or small, has its effect on the institutional economy. For instance, a simplification of the garb worn by an order of nuns has theological implications; the change would be symbolic of the fuller life nuns now enjoy in the church. But because the modified clothing would be cheaper to sew and less costly to launder or dry-clean, the change would also mean a saving (possibly a substantial one) of time, labor and money.

For an example on a much broader scale, take one of the

most crucial issues confronting the papacy, the Roman Curia, the national hierarchies and, indeed, the whole church today, the issue of priestly celibacy.

Whether or not a Catholic priest can be a married man is a basic theological question, one involving the relation between the two charisms, or special graces given directly by God, of chastity and of the priestly vocation itself. So far, of course, the church does not admit married men to the priesthood, and it forbids priests who marry to continue in their duties. But if the church were to reverse this stand, one notable result among all the others would be a drastic change in parish and diocesan economics.* The married priest would have to be paid enough of a cash salary to support his family. Who would decide this amount? The priests themselves? The bishops? In many parishes, the assistant pastors would marry while the pastor remained unmarried. Should the superior receive less money than his subordinates? In the aggregate, a priesthood which included married men would cost the church millions of dollars more a year than the present priesthood of the unmarried. What effect would this increase have on the current Catholic ecclesiastical economy?

Problems like these are serious enough to terrify some church administrators. Yet there's another way entirely of looking at the matter. If married men could become priests, the church might be able to attract to its service thousands of laymen who had previously been outstanding executives or professionals. Such recruits could bring into the church not only dedication but skill and experience as well. They might not cost the church money at all. By improving the financial performance of the parishes and other institutions

---

* As I write (Spring, 1971), the issue is on the agenda of the fall meeting of the Synod of Bishops in Rome. It's remotely possible that Paul VI will be the Pope who shifts the position of the church on the issue and makes possible a priesthood of the married.

they serve, they might do much to create a more vital church.

Precisely because events in the spiritual life of the church always do have economic repercussions, nobody can predict today what will be the material status of the church of tomorrow. The historians will tell you that in the past the very movements and events which churchmen themselves believed would be most disastrous economically turned out to be successful. For this reason, I refuse to be what Pope John XXIII actually called some of his bishops and cardinals—a "prophet of doom." Furthermore, I think we should wish the church well in its struggle for spiritual renewal and economic survival. Catholic or not, Christian or not, we gain by the work the church does in education, in charity and in mercy. We also owe a debt to the church as the curator of so much of our cultural heritage, and as the exemplar of the remarkable idea—remarkable at least in our time and our land—that money isn't everything.

About the Author

JAMES GOLLIN knows from the inside the games great institutions play with money. To his report on the finances of the Catholic Church, he brings fifteen years of experience in insurance, corporate financing, fund-raising and business journalism. His first book, *Pay Now, Die Later*, published by Random House in 1966, was a provocative study of the American life insurance industry. Even before it appeared, Mr. Gollin had embarked on the five years of travel, interviewing and research which gave him the background for *Worldly Goods*.

A native of St. Louis, Missouri, Mr. Gollin grew up in Scarsdale, New York, and has an A.B. and M.A. in English from Yale University. The author, his wife and their two sons live in Manhattan.